Printed in memory of Dr. Gary Farley and in honor of his service to the Lord and to the Pickens Baptist Association.

Organized and compiled by Bonnie Gates Windle

Spring Hill Baptist Church

Carrollton, AL 35447

TABLE OF CONTENTS

MISSION HERITAGE

CHURH HISTORIES

HISTORY OF THE 5 FOUNDING CHURCHES

Gary Farley

(May 24, 1936 - Feb. 14, 2020)

Dr. Gary Farley, the former Director of Missions for the Pickens Baptist Association, died in Tuscaloosa, Alabama, on February 14, 2020, due to complications following a series of strokes.

A memorial service will be held at a later date.

Dr. Farley was a specialist in the sociology of rural and small churches, and wrote hundreds of magazine articles, journal articles, and book chapters addressing diverse topics, ranging from Baptist theology, to sociological studies of church fellowships, to a number of practical helps for bi-vocational pastors serving smaller congregations. While recovering from his initial stroke, he continued writing from his bed a meditation on what were to be his final days, titled "Farther Along…"

Dr. Farley first came to west Alabama following a reshuffling of personnel at the former Home Mission Board of the Southern Baptist Convention in 1997. During the first decade of his tenure at the Pickens Baptist Association, he helped nurture greater cooperation between the white congregations that he coordinated and African-American congregations meeting in the same area.

A rash of church fires in 2006 saw these relationships deepen, as Dr. Farley called upon friends in the African-American and white church fellowships to join together in the rebuilding efforts and to minister to one another in a time of need.

In 2008 Dr. Farley turned his attention to the arrival of the Federal Correctional Institution in Aliceville, Alabama. Again, looking to ministry partners in the Pickens County area that he had developed relationships with, he helped assemble a team that would be able to work with inmates immediately upon their arrival. Worship, Bible study, and support groups were prepared to meet the unique needs of Latina, African-American, and white women—both in English and Spanish. Dr. Farley himself delighted in the Bible study classes that he facilitated, deeming the women there "...some of the brightest and best students I have ever had."

During conversations with family in his final weeks, Dr. Farley wondered at his weakened state, but repeatedly pointed to the journey of faith that he had navigated over the past decades, musing that God had again and again found ways of situating him in the right place at the right time to do significant good for the Kingdom. Even as hospital caregivers attended to him he would play hymns for them on his harmonica, often playing: "Farther along we'll know all about it / Farther along we'll understand why / Cheer up my brothers, live in the sunshine / We'll understand it all by and by."

Dr. Farley is survived by his wife of fifty-eight years, Jacque, their four children, five grandchildren, and one great-grandchild.

In lieu of flowers, the family ask for donations be made to Spring Hill Baptist Church, or Pickens Baptist Association for the prison ministry.

A PERSONAL WORD FROM MRS. JACQUE FARLEY

Gary was involved with small churches and rural communities from his early years accompanying his parents as they helped start a church plant in the rural area outside Kansas City, Missouri—going on to pastor and preach at other small churches near the city. He always showed interest in the history of each church and its community. If that was not available, he carried out his own research to satisfy his inquisitive mind.

After completing seminary he was hired to teach sociology at Carson-Newman College in Jefferson City, Tennessee, and continued to preach and do interim pastorates in small-membership rural churches in the area. There he continued to compile community histories in order to understand these towns and their people better. After thirteen years in east Tennessee, he moved to Oklahoma Baptist University in Shawnee, Oklahoma, filling the WMU Professor of Sociology position. While teaching he also became more involved with the work of the Southern Baptist Convention with small churches and home missions, writing extensively on the American farm crisis of the early 1980s. By the mid 80's he was offered the opportunity to serve with Quinton Lockwood in the Rural/Urban Missions Department of the Home Mission Board of the SBC in its Atlanta headquarters.

In 1996 during the restructuring of the HMB into the to the new North American Mission Board, SBC leadership decided to move the convention's focus away from rural churches, shifting instead to mega-churches and suburban-urban evangelism. Gary did not feel the Lord had released him from his calling to serve small churches in small towns, however. He struggled for the better part of a year with how to reconcile his longstanding dedication to rural churches with a denomination that had re-prioritized the focuses of its ministry. After a period involving a great deal of waiting and prayer, he was contacted by the Pickens Baptist Association (PBA) in west Alabama regarding the position of Director of Missions. Ultimately, we determined that the Lord's will for us was to serve Him in Pickens County.

Our work and life in Pickens County were a joy and a rewarding experience the majority of the time. Gary loved the rural surroundings and enjoyed getting acquainted with the church communities and the other folk in the area. He studied and wrote about those activities at length.

The compilation of writings in this book are from a notebook Gary had in his library entitled ***PBA History.*** Thanks to Bonnie Windle for preparing these texts where they can be shared with those interested. Much of Gary's writing is available online for free (www.ruralchurch.us) and in periodicals where he was published (www.ethicsdaily.com). Gary loved to study, think, and write and wanted to freely share and discuss thoughts of others with them. We think he would be happy to finally share these writings with you, and we believe he's waiting for us all to discuss them with him later.

Jacque Farley
July 25, 2021
Broken Arrow, Oklahoma

Dr. Gary Farley was a faithful follower of Christ, who set an example for all of us in how to love, serve, and share the Gospel with others. He was a friend, and encourager, and a person who valued all people, no matter their condition or situation in life. He was an excellent historian, who spent many hours collecting, recording, preserving, and sharing the story of God's work, particularly in and through Pickens Baptist Association and her churches. His research was thorough, his analysis insightful, and his writing clear and informative. Dr. Farley served as a commissioner on the Alabama Baptist Historical Commission from 2004 through 2011. During his tenure, Dr. Farley served four years as Chair of the Oral History Committee, two years as Vice Chair of the Commission, and lead the ABHC as Chair in 2011. Alabama Baptists are blessed to have had such a dedicated servant leader, who worked so diligently to record and preserve Alabama Baptist and Pickens Baptist Association history for current and future generations. Gary fulfilled the instruction found in Psalm 102:18, "Let this be written for a future generation, that a people not yet created may praise the Lord." Dr. Farley's work informs us, encourages us, and inspires us to record and preserve our own stories and those of our families of faith.

Dr. Lonette L. Berg
Executive Director
Alabama Baptist Historical Commission

Dr. Gary Farley receives a special recognition for service on the Alabama Baptist Historical Commission

Tribute

When I became director of the Samford Extension Division in 2014, one of the first calls I received was from Gary Farley. He wanted me to know of the work that had been started at the Aliceville Federal Corrections Institution through Samford University and the churches of Pickens County. His love for the ladies incarcerated in that women's prison was obvious and his concern from their standing with Christ and their faith growth was always close to his heart. Through Gary's urging, former Samford Extension director, Jim Pounds, worked with Gary and the prison chaplains to begin offering Bible courses to the prisoners. In the fall of 2014 I went with Gary to the facility to sit in on the course he was teaching. I left that day impressed with the obvious love that Gary had for those girls, the compassion for which he expressed his love for them, and the depth of biblical knowledge he possessed. Over the next few years we continued to enlist area pastors, along with Gary, to teach our Biblical Studies Diploma courses to the prisoners both in the medium security prison, and the light security camp located on the same property. In any given academic year, we would have well over 100 ladies take one of the courses offered.

Each year in May, Gary and I would go into both the prison and camp to award diplomas to the ladies who had completed the required courses for graduation. The ladies would come into the room in full regalia with smiles as big as the world, so proud as we handed them their diploma. The last time I saw Gary was in May 2019 at the graduation ceremony. There he sat, smiling and clapping as each of the ladies received their diplomas. For him it was more than an academic achievement that the ladies accomplished, it was a spiritual milestone. Gary's legacy and love for those girls lives on as we continue to offer our courses to the ladies of the Aliceville Federal Correctional Institution and camp.

Kevin D. Blackwell, D.Min, M.Div
Assistant to the President for Church Relations
Ministry Training Institute, Director

If anyone ever asked me some of the favorite people I've met in my 70 years, the name Dr. Gary Farley would be at the top of the list.

We became great friends through our love of Alabama's churches, communities, and people. We both served on the Alabama Baptist Historical Commission and were passionate about visiting West Alabama Churches celebrating historic milestones and presenting them plaques commemorating that occasion.

I was obsessed with WMU (Women's Missionary Union) and Bro. Gary fanned the flames. He always invited me to attend his 2-day Annual Meetings. Several times he asked if I would speak on Lottie Moon, Annie Armstrong, and Kathleen Mallory Missions to boost the giving from his Association.

He was a Mission Minded Man! The Farleys invited me to go on a mission trip up top of Sand Mountain to minister to Hispanics (another love of his).

Whether it was the Homeless, Hispanics, Black History, or Prisons, Bro. Gary fought for their rights. One of his greatest challenges was enlisting and training volunteers for the women's prison in Aliceville, Alabama. He called on former colleagues and professionals in many areas to help prepare the Pickens Baptist Association for the great mission field that was being offered.

His greatest cheerleader was his wife, Jacque. They were my dearest friends. I could hardly wait to cross the county line from my native Tuscaloosa County to join those two in whatever endeavor they were spearheading in Pickens County. Whether visiting in his home, the Association Office, or a rural church, I could learn of his latest radio broadcast, writings, histories, or his beloved harmonic music.

So when, Dr. Gary Farley arrived in heaven on February 14, 2020, he was welcomed by a great cloud of witnesses and faces that he recognized as colleagues, pastors, converts, friends, and family. I hope that he'll be there to welcome me at Heaven's Gate.

Angie Mills Cooper

Baptist Friend and

Alabama Baptist Historical Commission

Having served as a pastor in the Pickens Baptist Association for over 46 years, I am honored to have spent many of those years serving alongside of Gary Farley as my Director of Missions. I was able to witness first hand his passion for the history of this Association and of the Churches and Associations in the surrounding area. Dr. Farley dedicated countless hours to the preservation of this history and was absolutely meticulous for its accuracy. It is my honor to highly recommend this compilation to all of those who care about our foundation of faith. I am also thankful to our Lord for endowing Dr. Farley with the knowledge and ability that led him to creating this historical masterpiece.

Mike Hall, Pastor
New Salem Baptist Church
Moderator of Pickens Baptist Association

Dr. Gary Farley's Research

Dr. Farley arrived in Pickens County inquiring about the history of each church in the county association. From there he went on to research the early history of church planting in Central West Alabama.

One of the early ministers that attracted his attention was Rev. Daniel Perrin Bestor, Baptist minister and teacher, was born February,1797, in Suffield, Conn., and died April 9, 1869, in Mobile. Rev. Bestor came to Athens, Alabama in 1817. He went on to pastor churches in Greensboro, Gainesville, Sumterville and Columbus, Mississippi. Rev. Bestor was committed to education, especially female education. He served as a University of Alabama trustee as well as being a founding trustees of Judson College and Howard College/Samford University.

Dr. Farley conducted considerable research into the life of Lincoln Clark. Born in 1802 in Conway, Massachusetts. He was graduated from Amherst College in 1825. After studying law, he moved to Alabama in 1831 and commenced practice in Pickensville, Alabama. He served as member of the Alabama House of Representatives in 1834, 1835, and 1845. He moved to Tuscaloosa in 1836.In 1848 not wanting his children to be exposed to slavery, he moved his family to Dubuque, Iowa. He served several terms in the U S Congress before moving to Chicago to practice law.

Gary searched for years attempting to locate the Underground Railroad through Pickens County. Oral tradition has it that there were caves along the Tombigbee River which gave shelter to the runways. Dr. Farley identified a published memoir of a runaway slave in Pickensville, Alabama. The slave hid in an attic where he could watch his former owner's mercantile store in Pickensville.

Mary Bess Paluzzi
Associate Dean for Special Collection Emerita
UA Libraries, Tuscaloosa, Alabama

The Lord had given Dr. Gary Farley, "Bro. Gary", a great zeal and desire to unite and inform the believers, especially in the rural communities. He tried to bring awareness, respect, resources, and information to the body of Christ, knowing we all have different gifts but are all part of the same body of Christ. Bro. Gary was a joy and enjoyed being in service and fellowship at the Galilee Baptist Church, in Panola, Alabama. Prayerfully this information he collected and penned can bring us to a closeness in Christ, Bro. Gary, and practice some of my Ideals, of being Vocal, Visible, and Vital.
Truly missed!
My friend and my brother!

Bob Little
Pastor, Galilee Baptist Church, Panola, Alabama
1 of the 9 Churches burned by Arson (2006)
1st dually Alliance Church in West Alabama
Partner in Church plant at FCI-Aliceville, Alabama

Dr. Gary Farley was a lifestyle missionary. His heart and head were always looking for ways to proclaim Jesus to the world.

In 2003 I had a talk with him at his office about PBA churches getting together to sponsor missions not only in our county but also in other states and countries. Immediately, he began to make plans for this to happen. His view was to involve churches together for this type of mission work.

This became a revitalization of PBA churches taking part in missions and Gospel outreach. His vision was to get churches, small and large, to participate in global missions. It was like a rebirth of church organized missions that PBA people had been doing for years.

The specific areas were Brazil. Eastern Europe and Central America and it was a little like the birth of the church sponsored missions that happened at Antioch with Paul and others.

Dr. Farley also was a fun person. On mission trips traveling to the northeast, we needed directions and he said, "No worry, I can direct you by looking at the sky." On another trip he took along a huge box of Snickers candy bars. Dr. Farley also liked to wear tennis shoes and bright red socks. Many other events I could tell.

W. O. (Buddy) Kirk
Evangelism Director and
Mission Coordinator

Known to me warmly as Brother Gary, Dr. Gary Farley had a significant impact on many, myself included. While he was a recognized historian and teacher, I think of him as a storyteller – one of the finest. He had the uncanny ability to completely captivate anyone regardless of age, education, background, or station. Brother Gary was a voracious reader, and I have enjoyed many of his recommended books and reading materials, often shared with me along with thoughtfully placed highlights as a guide to particularly salient points. As a lifelong learner, he was ever in pursuit of more and more information, but it wasn't enough for him to simple gain knowledge – he wanted, perhaps even needed, to share what he knew with others. I will always cherish the years spent as his neighbor and friend, and am pleased and proud to see this publication, as he continues to tell us stories even now.

Joe Irwin
Friend and Neighbor
Fellow Church Member

Tribute to Rev. Dr. Gary Farley

Men build institutions so that four hundred years later their descendants can say, “that’s what he left”. Rev. Dr. Gary Farley built his institution by collecting history. His gifts in the Ministry stretched far and near in the communities of Pickens County. Wherever there was history to be found, you could find Dr. Farley.

I was blessed to spend time with him sharing about the history in the Pickensville Community, specifically The Historic Pickensville Rosenwald School, an old African American schoolhouse located on Jim Lock Road and also the Stagecoach Inn located on Highway 14, both in Pickensville, AL.

See the pictures capturing some special moments spent with him reminiscing and sharing the making of history in our community.

Paulette Locke-Newberns
Project Director of the Historic
Pickensville Rosenwald Museum and
Community Center and
Neighbor and Friend

Tribute

I had the privilege of knowing Dr. Gary Farley after they moved to Rivermont. I found him to be a kind and considerate person who was a delight to visit with. He was an avid reader and was extremely well versed in a variety of subjects, especially the Bible. He attended Springhill Baptist Church where he was highly respected by all. He was always willing and eager to fill in the pulpit or as teacher. He shined because of his knowledge of the Bible and is great missed by the church.

He and I usually had lunch together after church and I thoroughly enjoyed those visits. His recall was amazing, especially for his age. He had a huge library and it was as if he knew the authors of most of the books.

He was a champion for the less fortunate, and it showed in his conversation and actions. Much of his study and research was of the slave era. He spent a lot of time looking for documents about the subject.

Although, it hurts to lose him, it is a tremendous comfort to know that he lived his life for Christ and is reaping his rewards.

Mitchell Roberts
Friend and Neighbor
Retired Superintendent
RAFES Research Centers
Mississippi State University

Upon my completion of seminary in 2004, I had the great privilege of coming to work with Dr. Gary Farley at the Pickens Baptist Association in Alabama. I soon learned he was a dedicated student of history. He always had fascinating stories and historical facts to share about our local area, local churches, and various areas around the state of Alabama and the United States. He was an avid reader and lifelong learner. He was a gifted writer as well using his many skills and abilities humbly in service to the Lord.

Dr. Farley was often sharing his writings and doing seminars focused on rural church ministry. Many phone calls, emails, or other inquiries tapped into his vast expertise in this field.

He encouraged our Associational churches to have their church records archived for future generations. Often, he was the courier to Samford University for this to be processed. He made available a microfilm reader at his office for those doing research.

In addition, he did some video recordings interviewing missionaries who had gone out through the years from our Association to serve with the Southern Baptist Foreign Mission Board (Now International Mission Board). He encouraged the churches to check these videos out from the office so they could learn about these missionaries.

Each year at the annual meeting, he presented written histories on the host churches. He began compiling these histories, along with histories of our local Association and neighboring associations, which are included in this book.

Praise the Lord for Dr. Farley's love of history and his desire to preserve it for future generations. I dearly loved him as a friend and colleague. It was a joy, honor, and privilege to serve alongside him in ministry. I will forever be indebted to him for the investment he made in my life and ministry.

Janet Estis
Association WMU Director, PBA

Left Top: Jacque and Gary, Christmas 2018

Left: Gary and Jacque on 50th Anniversary with Sons,

Matthew and Daniel, and daughters,

Amelia and Clarissa

Right: Gary playing his harmonica with Daisy, their dog

Left Top: Gary and Hunter Davidson at VBS
Left: Gary on Holy Land Trip with Amelia and Mobile Group
Right: Gary with James Spann, friend and local tv weatherman, at Baptist Center Volunteer Luncheon

Left - Rev. Dr. Gary Farley and Paulette Lock-Newberns exploring Historical Stagecoach Inn located in Pickensville, AL. *Right* – Dr. Farley and Paulette Stinson-Lavender sharing about the Underground Story. *Bottom* – Grand Opening of the Pickensville Rosenwald Museum and the Pickens County 200 Alabama Bicentennial Celebration. Dr. Garley and guests saying pledge of allegiance to the United States Flag.

Left Top: Bro. Gary preaching at Springhill
Left Middle: Gary keeping style with daughter, Amelia
Left Bottom: Gary's red tennis shoes and socks
Right Middle: Gary congratulating Pastor Bob Little for Prison Award along with Pastor Tommy Winders and prison official
Right Bottom: Gary with neighbor Mitch Roberts resting in Atlanta after drive from home

Studies in the History of The Pickens Baptist Association of West Alabama

with attention to its neighboring associations, the history of its affiliated congregations, its missionary heritage, and its historical documents.

Gary Farley
Director of Missions

Celebrating 300 Years of Baptist Associations in America

Philadelphia 1707

Reflections
Cahaba 1818
Buttehatcha 1828
Tuscaloosa 1834
Union (Pickens) 1835
Pilgrims' Rest 1837
Columbus (Golden Triangle) 1838
Bigbee 1852
Sipsey 1890
African American Associations Here

Reflections on the 300th Anniversary of Baptist Associations in America
Gary Farley
DOM/Pickens Baptist Association

During 2007 we are celebrating the 300th anniversary of the first association of Baptist churches formed in what has become the United States of America. This was the Philadelphia Baptist Association. Initially, it was comprised of fewer than 10 congregations. It took the London Confession of Faith as its doctrinal statement. (Today Southern Baptists alone have about 1,200 associations and 43,000 congregations. Other Baptist groups would about double these figures.)

Paul Stripling, former director of missions for the Waco, Texas area, has written a book, *Turning Points,* to provide a background for the celebration. Stripling identified 10 events/developments which have shaped associational life over these three centuries.
I laid his list over against my study of our 172 years as a rural association in Alabama. The resultant list of *turning points* in our life is a little different and a little longer, 15, not 10, than that of Stripling. The differences relate primarily to setting and size of our associations, Waco and Pickens. Since the Pickens is more similar to most Baptist Associations, old and rural, our list reflects the life of most of the Baptist Associations, I feel that it needs to be shared. For anyone reading this list and serving elsewhere, consider reflecting on the history of turning points in your association. When I shared it with Paul Stripling, a long-time friend, he was very complimentary.

1 The Great Awakenings of Religion in America, ca. 1750 and 1800, multiplied the Baptists and thrust them, and the Methodists, into a rush to evangelize the western frontier. The first churches in our area appeared ca 1823, and in 1835 an association was formed by these churches, 19 initially. (Prior to 1835 the churches in our area were affiliated with either Buttehatcha or Cahaba associations. Both were Calvinistic.

2. There was great diversity among Baptists in the 1800's which resulted in the splintering off of some portions of the Baptist movement–primitives, anti-mission boards, free will, Reformers/restorers (i.e., Disciples of Church or Christian churches), and freedmen—all formed separate denominations during the 19th Century. Like most, our association experienced some of these splinterings.

3. Conventions, usually seeking to organize the Baptist movement within a state or a portion thereof, were birthed, beginning in 1821 as the nation settled the frontiers, and in 1845 the Baptist in the South formed a regional convention, the SBC. Our association elected to join both the Alabama and the Southern Conventions in the 1840s. This is an important fact. Many churches and associations predate the conventions. (It is for this reason that the concept of the autonomy of the local church is a precious one.

4. The annual meetings of the rural associations throughout much of the 19th Century were like a camp-meeting. They were three or four day affairs. Typically, they met in the fall at a host church. While the messengers dealt with business issues and heard reports, a revival like meeting with lots of preaching was held for the non-messengers in a nearby grove, arbor, or meetinghouse of another denomination..

5. The association was concerned about planting new churches in the new communities forming in its area, the revitalization of churches that had fallen on hard times, the doctrinal purity of congregations, and the harmonious life of congregations. As the Baptist movement grew, new programs such as Sunday School and Woman's Missionary Union were added to the work of the conventions. And as the conventions and their institutions grew, their representatives visited the annual meetings to seek support for the programs, boards, and agencies.

   Apparently, feeling the need to be more than just an annual reunion of the Baptist family in an area, associations formed an executive committee to transact the work of the association between the annual meetings. This was a major shift in the life of an association. It was a shift from an event to an organization or institution.

6. About 1900 associations began to allow women to serve as messengers. This predated the Federal Government and the SBC in granting voting and speaking rights to women. In recent years the women have been the majority of messengers at the annual meetings of our association.

7. About 1920 the state and national convention leaders encouraged the associations to redraw their boundaries to coincide with county lines. Many did so. Our association lost several churches and changed its name from Union to Pickens in 1924. What had been created as a "centered affinity" group was recast as a " bounded geographic" group. (Recently, some associations have moved toward the affinity model and away from the geographic one For example the association in Memphis changed its name and its focus from Shelby County to Mid-South.)

8. In 1925 the Cooperative Program was adopted by the state and national conventions. It did not include the associations in the sharing of the funding. In time, this resulted in the domination of associations by conventions. One consequence has been that most associations have not been adequately funded.

9. The number of rural Baptist churches declined from about 1890 to the end of World War II. The conventions launched, following that war, a program to strengthen rural churches, moving thousands of them from being quarter or half-time, to worshiping every Sunday and having a full complement of programs and activities. To make this happen conventions and the Home Mission Board assisted associations financially in hiring a missionary and in providing training for them. This made it possible for Baptists to grow in rural areas while many of the mainline Protestant denominations were closing rural and village churches. Adding regularly employed staff greatly impacted associations in rural areas. The turning point was that leadership tended to shift from the moderator to the missionary.

10. Urbanization following World War II brought far greater diversity among associations. In cities like Atlanta, Memphis, and Louisville there was a great challenge to plant new congregations and provide social ministries. Suburbanization since the 1970s has left some of these city associations diminished. They have lost congregations and members.

The former rural associations ringing the cities have grown dramatically. Here we find that increasing numbers of the residents of the communities served by our churches work in Columbus or Tuscaloosa and commute daily to work.

11. The growing diversity among associations in Baptist life (note in 1900 the Pickens association, the Tuscaloosa and the Columbus Associations were of similar size and economic strength) has, or should have, resulted in customizing of relationships between and among conventions and associations. The tasks and challenges of Pickens are not the same as Golden Triangle and Tuscaloosa, or Atlanta, or Shelby, or Bigbee, or Cullman

12. Many of the larger, urban associations developed "programs" and institutions of their own. Often this resulted in a push for the churches to serve the work of the associations. This was a radical change from the traditional idea that the association existed to serve the needs of the local churches, helping them and their members to be missional. Often there is a very fine line here, one that an association like ours has to watch carefully. For example, we need to be very careful that a ministry like the Baptist Center does not become a ministry of the PBA, but rather is a ministry of the churches coordinated by the PBA. This is a very real difference.

13. The push after World War II to move the Southern convention from a regional to a national body was facilitated by the deployment of associational missionaries to start and develop new congregations in the North and the West. Often, their culture is more that of an "administrative structure" imposed from the outside than a natural development from the "grassroots". For example, the state of Iowa was divided into associations in a way that looked more like a tic-tac-toe board than like a strategic plan to group churches into "natural areas".

14. Because of the relative homogeneity of the rural associations, the denominational conflict of the past, almost three decades, has not had much of an impact there. So, it has not been the turning point that it has been in an association like Atlanta or as in Waco as noted by Stripling. But it has changed the conventions to which our association relates and the services which they provide to us.

15. But there does seem to be a consensus that the entities of the Southern Baptist Convention do not understand and do not serve well the needs and concerns of rural churches and associations. Our state convention does much better.

16. Many rural associations are challenged by the need to refocus from being the jobber for convention programs" to being focused on mission work. This means finding people groups and places to form congregations and ministries. It means supporting mission efforts in places beyond its bounds where needs are great and the resources are limited. It means designing mission efforts that anyone within a church in an association can become a Great Commission Christian. Being in a smaller church with limited resources is not handicap.

For an organization to survive, it needs to continue to make adjustments to its changing environment. Many churches and associations that have failed to do so have gone out of existence across the past three centuries. Most rural associations have not had to deal with as serious and challenging a set of adjustments as have the metropolitan ones. But most have made the appropriate changes.

The Baptist movement has been very effective in rural America across these three centuries. I believe that having the connections and the support which comes from associations has contributed greatly to this effectiveness.

Our rural association is doing many good things. There is much more that needs to be done. It has changed and will continue to change. It is 172 years old. It will continue as far into the future as anyone can see.

In the articles which follow I will trace the direct genealogy of our association. It begins with Cahaba which was the first association the central part of Alabama. It continues through Buttehatcha which covered the northwestern part of the state and lapped into Mississippi. Next is Tuscaloosa, then ourselves, then Pilgrim's Rest which was formed by the 'anti-board" churches in our midst, then Golden Triangle which like us came out of Buttehatcha, then Bigbee which was formed to our south and finally Sipsey to our east. Mention is made of our two neighbors to the north, Lamar and Fayette, but I do not yet have enough information to write an adequate sketch of their history.

I hope that you find these articles of interest. I plan to do a set on the pioneer preachers and churches of our association for the annual next year. Our association will celebrate its 175th anniversary in 2010. These articles are intended to prepare for this event. As always, I welcome comments and corrections. I plan to have all of these articles placed on our associational webpage http://pickensbaptist.com

Reinventing Rural Old Convention Baptist Associations
Gary Farley

For the past 12 years I have served our rural association of Baptist churches as the Director of Missions. We now have 37 congregations, most of which are in a single county, Pickens, which lies between Columbus, MS and Tuscaloosa, AL. The county has about 20,000 residents of which about 11,000 are anglo. The county bridges the plains of the Black Belt and the foothills of Appalachia. The churches report almost 4,500 resident members. They contribute nearly 4% of their undesignated offerings to the association, or about $115,000. The total income of the association is nearly $150,000. Most of the churches are bivocational and have less than 100 in worship. Since we have no dominant town, we do not have any dominant churches. We are blessed with good pastors, godly laypersons, good ministries and a strong missionary spirit.

The association has reinvented itself four times across these years. Let me describe and date each of these forms taken by the association. As we celebrate our 175th anniversary, we need to think about our history. Thank God. Plan for the future.

1. Frontier Stabilizer and Extender. 1835-1870

All 19 of the churches which formed our association back in 1835 were open country churches. Even as towns were formed along the Tombigbee River and in Carrollton as a county seat, Baptists were very slow in forming churches within them. But our early preachers were active in seeking to form new congregations in the rural communities as they developed. Early conflicts over support of mission boards and over high Calvinism brought losses which were addressed by the formation of more new congregations and evangelism. Brush Arbor revivals were common. Annual meetings dealt with inspiration, encouragement, doctrinal questions and related business. Often one or more of the pastors would be hired to do mission work within the bounds of the association for a part of the year. Typically, while the messengers were meeting in a church house, a brush arbor revival meeting would be in progress nearby.

Our churches were "covenanted communities" which expected and promoted life transformation in its members. Church discipline held each member accountable to all. There was a strong emphasis on living according to the teachings of Jesus. The church order played a major role in promoting peace and stability in the emerging frontier communities which they served.

The association joined the Alabama and Southern Baptist Convention in the 1840s. Soon one of its daughters, Martha Foster Crawford, was sent by the Foreign Mission Board to China. Since then 20 more have been appointed as foreign missionaries. And many other sons and daughters moved west in this period carrying the Gospel to the new frontiers in our land.

2. A New Cause Replaces the "Lost Cause", 1870-1890

With the exodus of the freedmen from the churches, membership was cut by about one-third across the association. While from the beginning some of the churches had Sunday Schools, they became a passion during this era. Both long time associational moderators of this period and beyond, one a pastor and one a layman, were strong Sunday School men. Apparently, in order to keep Sunday School before the people the association added quarterly district Sunday School conventions and formed an Executive Committee. This was a major reinvention. The association moved from being a three or four day annual reunion of the missionary Baptists in our area to being an ongoing, year around, organization.

The programs of the annual meetings came to be increasingly filled with representatives from state and national Baptist organizations promoting their work and collecting funds. Denominational identity was a second purpose of the life of the association. Elsewhere, this was driven by conflicts with other denominations such as the Disciples of Christ, the Methodists, and within ours the Landmark movement.

3. Industrialization and Resettlement of the South, 1890-1940

During this era four railroad lines were built across our association. This killed most of the rough river towns where we had been slow about starting new congregations. The railroad caused the formation of six new towns in the territory served by the association during this era. With some help from the state convention, congregations were formed in four of these towns. And rural churches moved to the other two towns. Further, new churches were formed in at least four short-lived sawmill villages. However, they did not last longer than the towns. And later two mill town churches were formed as second churches in two of the new railroad towns. Our stock of congregations became more diverse. Interestingly, the Primitive and the Free Will Baptists continued to be almost totally rural.

Several of the old open country churches closed during this period, apparently as the result of their members moving to the villages and towns. Others were severely weakened. Another lasting result of this period was greater diversity among the churches of the association. Probably because of competition with other denominations, the town churches sought pastors with some formal education. These churches seemed to be more responsive to the several new programs -Brotherhood, WMU and BYPU- that were being introduced by the denomination. Weekly worship was a goal for them.

And the association, like many others, responded to the encouragement of the denomination to reformulate itself from being essentially a "centered affinity group" to being an association of the cooperating Baptist churches in a particular county, a "bounded organization". In 1924 the name was changed from Union to Pickens and soon the several affiliated churches in surrounding counties moved to the dominant associations in their counties.

In 1925 the state and national conventions adopted a new financial plan, the Cooperative Program, which served them well. While associations were not included, the conventions have encouraged the churches to support their associations.

4. Transformation of the Open Country Churches. 1940-1990

My position, like several hundred others, was created in 1947 with help from the state convention to implement the Long Range Rural Church Program. This was a program of the Home Mission Board. Its purpose was to help the many rural churches in the old convention have worship every Sunday, the basic programs of the denomination active, a pastor on the field, support missions, and become more closely tied to the Baptist denomination. This happened in the first decade of the effort, for the most part. The primary job of the Director of Missions in this period of time was to change the rural churches in the Old Convention. His annual reports focused on the "promotion" of the national and state denominational programs.

In 1951 only six of our churches had weekly worship services. Eleven of the thirty-one congregations had worship only one Sunday a month. Today thirty-six of our thirty-seven congregations have weekly worship services. The focus of rural associations like ours was to help each congregation have the full set of denominational programs and to do them well. We imported the language and practice of the factory into the life of our churches with superintendents of this and that, standards of excellence, and many, many reports.

To the north and west Southern Baptists were actively becoming a national denomination with significant gains particularly in the west. Directors of Missions were deployed to coordinate and direct these efforts. These DoAMs were to plant new churches, maintain the current churches and create an association. Often with success, these associations divided and repeated the process. Our success, particularly in the west, is a great missions story.

The reinvention of Old Convention rural churches was a wonderful thing. And much of the success of Southern Baptists was in small town places in the North and the West. [illegible] made it possible for us to stay and to expand in country places while the mainline denominations had to close and combine congregations. And while the leadership of the denomination really wanted to replace bivocationalism, they were pragmatic enough to soon realize that this just could and would not happen. About 1975 they began to affirm and support bivocationalism to a great extent. (I had just done a graduate thesis on bivocationalism and this brought me to the attention of the old Home Mission Board. The direction of my life was changed. I went to serve at HMB's rural program in 1984.)

5. Expediting Great Commission Work. 1990---

About 1990 while I was working with the rural church program at the Old Home Mission Board, I began to hear questions being raised first about the cost-benefit ratio of having a Director of Missions and later about having associations at all. Since the purpose for which the position of DoAM had been created had been accomplished, other than to have a place for a broken-down old preacher to slip into retirement, why continue it? Further, some began to suggest that with the communications revolution, the conventions could now go directly to the churches, so the association was not needed. And, increasingly in response, DoAMs demanded that the associations be "full partners in the mission enterprise, not simply funnels for and promoters of state and national programs.

When I came to Pickens Association, January of 1998, I felt that it needed a fourth reinvention. I took my clues from Rick Lance our state convention leader who soon set as his focus helping every Alabama Baptist be a Great Commission Christian. I could see that most people in our small churches could not address many of the tasks set forth in the Great Commission as we then operated. Their church lacked the resources to do many ministries. They lacked the resources, and perhaps the vision, to try innovative approaches to evangelism. And they did not have within their congregations enough persons and skills to put together a team to do mission work in some other venue.

Elsewhere in the Book of Reports you will find a list of the cooperative ministries we are currently working on. My driving value is that with 4,500 resident members we can do most anything that a mega church can do for the Kingdom.

The Baptists of our area are proud of their association and its efforts. I am aware, however, of at least three potential dangers:

- Continuing Industrial Age Thinking – These new initiatives become the property of the association, not of the churches and their members.
- Overload – Trying to do too much and expecting everyone to help and participate in all that we do.
- Resistance by me to a church taking something that the association got started and "doing their own thing." We must always remember that the association is in place to serve the churches, not the churches to serve the association.

Further, let me identify four other concepts which have informed my efforts in Pickens Association:

- Be a mission strategist. Commuters, Prison, Hispanics, Retirees are our growing "people groups".
- Be a centered, not a bounded association. State and county lines do not constrict our work.
- Be proactive in training newly called to ministry. Grow our bivocational pastors/staff.
- Realize that money follows ministry/missions.

Underlying and informing the analysis that I am sharing with you is one of the most important contributions of the social sciences. It is that any social organization – a business, an army, a government, a family, a church, a football team, or an association must successfully address four issue areas:

1. ***Adapt to a changing social environment.*** The four reinventions of our association, as well as its origins, have been prompted by change in the socio-economic environment. Missionary Baptists did so well and have prospered. Primitives and Free Wills did not and have declined.

2. ***Goals and their achievement have driven the association in each era.*** While we honor ou traditions we were not limited by them. We focused on goals that addressed the challenges of a changing social environment.

a. Evangelize and plant new churches on the frontier. Provide some social orde through keeping the covenant.

b. Use Bible Study in many settings as a way to reach, teach and keep the children anc their families.

c. Planted churches in the new towns and among new people groups.

d. Helped weak congregations become full-program congregations.

e. Making the Great Commission something that every Baptist can do personally. We are facing new opportunities and challenges. Baptist Center, Mission Trips, 100 Godly Womer ministries at the Prison, Bible Study in nursing homes and jails, new racial and ethnic congregations.

3. ***Organize an appropriate structure to deal with each version of the area association.*** The Associational organizations that the conventions helped associations develop in the 1950's and 1960's served us well to meet the challenges of that era. But we need to restructure for our current times. This will call for true creativity because no longer can we expect "one size to fit all." In Old Conventior States, like Mississippi and Alabama, there are at least half a dozen different kinds of associations, eacl needing a somewhat different structure.

a. Mega
b. Meg fringe
c. Metro
d. Metro fringe (rural with growth)
e. Rural, stable, or in decline
f. Old time way maintained

I see our association as a "d" with a "c" to the east and to the west and "f" to the north east anc to the south and two "d's" to the north

Our "d" association has identified four opportunities, perhaps five, to address in our refocusing and restructuring:

a. Hands on mission opportunities.
b. Responding to the settlement of commuters from Columbus and Tuscaloosa.
c. Ministries in the new prison
d. Retirees on the Tenn-Tom.
e. Partnering with our Missionary Baptist Brothers.

Elsewhere, variable such as market share, total membership, resources, and territory will need to be factored in.

4. ***Maintain Your Borders/Market.*** Competition and conflict are reality, even in church life.

a. Attacks by the enemies – Satan, Secularism, and Wolves in Sheep's clothing.
b. Invasion by other "Christian" denominations, and cults.
c. Expansionist colleagues.

Cooperation and mutual submission should be the Christian, Baptist way. Seek it.

I hope that you will spend some time reflecting upon what I am sharing here with you. I invite you to look at other resources on our web-pages www.ruralchurch.us. Www.pickensbaptist.com. will be glad to discuss any of this in greater detail. I would welcome suggestions for improvement.

This article was prepared for and presented to the Directors of Associational Missions at their meeting in August 2008 at the State Convention building in Jackson. They agreed that it is important fo associations to reinvent themselves.

Cahaba Association of Baptists in Alabama
And its relationship to Pickens Baptist Association
Gary Farley

When the first two Baptist churches in Pickens County were formed, Enon in 1823 and South Carolina in 1824 (now Aliceville and Ethelsville) they affiliated with the closest association of Baptist churches for fellowship, good counsel, and cooperative efforts. The association was named Cahaba, after the river that runs through central Alabama. Cahaba Association had been formed a few year prior in 1818. The driving force for the formation of the association was Elder Moses Crowson. He served as moderator. The charter congregations were:

Mulberry, Montgomery
Enon, Blount
Ebenezer, Tuscaloosa (now First)
Cahaba Valley, Cahaba
Union, Dallas
Salem, Marengo (probably, old First of Greensboro)
Canaan, Blount

The association adopted a Calvinistic Articles of Faith as its stackpole of orthodoxy. It covers the same points that appear in the 1835 Articles of Faith adopted by the Union (now Pickens) Association, but the order and some of the wording is a little different. The Rules of Decorum which governed the annual meeting is also very similar to the Union one.

In 1819 Cahaba corresponded with the Flint River Association in northeast Alabama and with the Tombeckbee (now Bethel) in southwest Alabama. New churches that year included Bethel, Cahaba; Bethel, Tuscaloosa; Alabama, Dallas; Ruhamah, Blount; Hebron, Shelby; Rehobeth, Cahaba; Ebenezer, Cahaba; New Hope, Marion; and Enon, Cahaba. Hosea Holcombe who will play a major role in early Alabama Baptist life, was pastor at Rehobeth and Thomas Willingham, who will play a key role in the controversy over missions in the Union Association in 1837, was at New Hope. (At this early point in Alabama history county boundaries were fluid, so some of these locations later changed in name, but not in actual location.)

By 1823 there were 54 churches affiliated with the association. One now found churches in Bibb, Jefferson, St. Clair, Perry, Pickens and Green–mostly in the territory that the association began serving in 1818. (The loss of Marengo from the list is the result of Green county being formed and the Salem church, which soon would host the forming of the Alabama Baptist State Convention, is now listed as being in Green.) Charles Stewart, a stalwart in Pickens County church and political life until 1857, along with Charles U. Nall were the messengers from Enon Baptist Church in Pickens at the 1823 meeting. All 54 of the churches were still small. None had as many as 100 members. Several of the Jefferson County churches were dismissed to form the Mt. Zion association in 1823. (Later, it would become an anti-mission board association, the mother of the Primitive Baptist movement in the state.) In the years to come it would become the mother and grandmother of several more associations. (Note: the spelling of Greene is not consistent in the records.)

In 1824 a second Pickens County church, South Carolina, served by Elder Jacob Crocker, affiliated with Cahaba. It had 22 members and Enon 21. The following year it and Enon left to become part of a new association, Buttehatcha. (See my other piece on that association.)

Also in 1825 the association calls for the churches to begin having regular monthly prayer meetings on the first Monday. The churches in England, it was reported, have been doing this for 31 years with significant success.

In 1828 Grant's Creek and Gilgal churches in Tuscaloosa County join the association. Fourteen years later Grant's Creek will join Union Association which much later will change its name to Pickens Association. And in 1832 Friendship which was in Greene County, joins. In 1835 this church becomes a member of the Union Association. It is two letters from that church which triggered the 1837 conflict and division of the Union Association between those who opposed mission and other boards and those who felt that a church might support such a board. In this year, 1828, the 23 churches of Cahaba reported 217 baptisms and 1101 members. Interestingly one messenger to the association from what is now Tuscaloosa First was W. Martin a licensed African American preacher. Thirty-five of the baptisms were at Grant's Creek, swelling the membership to 52.

In 1833 the association hears from a new Canaan Association in Jefferson County. This seemed to have been formed from some of the churches in Mt. Zion Association. In this same year many of the Tuscaloosa churches leave to form an association of that name. However, First, Mt. Pleasant, and Grant's Creek churches in Tuscaloosa County remain in Cahaba. Some 597 baptisms were reported that year and the membership swelled to 1818.

In 1835 Cahaba begins correspondence with the newly formed Union and the Choctaw associations on the west. The latter lay just south of Union with churches in both Alabama and Mississippi. Like Union it too was soon torn by the missionary board controversy. At this time Daniel Bestor who will play a key role for the next several decades in Baptist life, appears as the pastor of Salem in Greensboro.

In 1837 the Cahaba Association meets with the Grant's Creek Church. Mention is made of the people camped at the church. In those days the annual meeting of an association included elements of the popular camp meeting format. Among the ministers serving the Grant's Creek church was George Washington Baines, the grandfather of President Lyndon Baines Johnson. Baines soon left to do church planting in Arkansas and Texas. From Tuscaloosa First came President Woods of the university, John Dagg, a professor and later the first writing Baptist theologian in the South, and J.H. Devotie, an important pastor in the Black Belt for years to come. The associational annual letter for that year was authored by Dagg. In it he supports mission efforts and Sunday Schools. (Grant's Creek had had a Sunday School from its beginning which was one of the first in Alabama.) To further show their support of mission and evangelistic efforts the association hired Bro. John Dennis as their missionary. He was to start and strengthen churches in the area served by the association.

Membership reports in 1838 show Siloam at Marion with 269, Grant's Creek with 212, and First in Tuscaloosa with 167.

In 1839 a resolution was introduced and passed in support of the newly founded Judson Female Institute in Marion. The association was meeting at the Siloam church in Marion that year. On Sunday the preachers of the association conducted worship at Siloam and at the Methodist and the Presbyterian churches in the town. This was a common practice in that day. At this meeting First Tuscaloosa leaves Cahaba and moved to the Tuscaloosa Association.

The following year the association meets at Grant's Creek again. J. C. Foster, pastor there is serving as associational clerk. And at the end of the meeting Grant's Creek asked to be allowed to leave and join the Union, now Pickens Association.

I wonder if the hand of Basil Manly, senior, cannot be seen behind this. He had come from the First Baptist Church of Charleston, South Carolina in 1837 to be president of the University of

Alabama. He had been a leader in the formation of the national and regional denominational bodies. He soon became a dominant force in Tuscaloosa First Baptist. He was a close friend of the Foster families. It seems that he might well have reasoned the by moving First Tuscaloosa to the Tuscaloosa Association and Grant's Creek to Union, there would be a strong force in favor of missions and benevolent enterprises in each of them. Certainly, J. C. Foster becomes an important leader in Union. He was a champion of missions, of Sunday Schools, and of education. He served as moderator for more than a quarter of a century.

When Cahaba Association met the following year Union was represented by William Stansel and by William Manning, both strong supporters of missions and education. And President Manly was among those who preached to the assembled congregation.

In 1844 most of the 27 churches in the association were located in Perry, Dallas, Greene and Bibb counties. A total of 350 were baptized that year swelling the total membership to well over 2,000. The following year the association passed a resolution celebrating the formation of the Southern Baptist Convention. There was great excitement that the Domestic Mission Board of the new convention had located in Marion. Note was taken of the death of Charles Crow who had been a great leader of the association. He had served many years as its moderator.

In 1846 the association accepts into its membership the Second Baptist Church, a predominantly African American congregation, of Mobile. For the next several decades the minutes of the association have a good bit to say about the Domestic Mission Board which it hosted in Marion.

In 1861 shortly after the start of the Civil War Cahaba had 34 churches and more than 3,000 members. Most of them were in Perry County. The African church in Mobile had more than 300 members. In 1867 there are 40 churches. Five of these are know to be African American. Since several did not report that year, I will not include a figure for total membership. It seems that by 1871 the African American churches had moved to other connections. Salem of Greensboro is no longer a member. In 1878 the total membership was 2257 in 29 churches, mostly in Perry, Hale and Dallas Counties.

In the next few years the association lost Howard College to Birmingham and the Domestic (Home) Mission Board to Atlanta. And Selma association was formed in Dallas with the loss of many congregations.

In 1920 the association reported 27 churches in Perry and Hale counties with about 2,000 members. Today it has 15 churches and about 2,000 members. Bill Wallace, who once pastored Reform First, is the associational missionary, serving on a part-time basis.

Buttehatcha Baptist Association
1825 to 1840
Gary Farley

South Carolina Baptist Church, now Ethelsville, hosted the annual meeting of the Buttehatcha Baptist Association in early October of 1831. This association was formed five years earlier. The roster of affiliated churches at the 1831 meeting included five from Pickens County–South Carolina, Big Creek, Antioch, Enon, and Unity. Enon is now Aliceville First Baptist. The other three are long closed. Unity was near the current New Salem Missionary Baptist Church and Big Creek was near Pine Grove Missionary Baptist Church. By 1833 Antioch had disappeared. Since some of the early members of Fellowship Baptist Church transferred from Antioch, my guess is that it was located in the Reform area, too. In 1831 Antioch reported 25 members; Big Creek, 41; South Carolina, 45; Enon, 58; and Unity 28. (There is an Antioch Presbyterian Church today serving the area northwest of Reform. This may be the area where the Antioch Baptist Church was in the 1830s.)

Enon had been constituted in 1823 and South Carolina in 1824. They had both been affiliated with the Cahaba Association before Buttehatcha was formed. Big Creek and Unity were formed in 1829.

In 1826 when Buttehatcha was formed, it included eight congregations as follows: New Hope, Zion and Elbethel in Mississippi; Macedonia, Enon, South Carolina, Friendship and Sarepta in Alabama. The following year it added Friendship (Tuscaloosa), Bethlehem (Greene), and Union (Marion). And in 1827 it met at Union in Pickens County and added Antioch, Spring Hill, Canaan, Bethel, Hopewell and Salem. All of these churches were in Alabama. (I have not been able to determine anything about Union's location.

The founding pastors of the association included Lemuel Pruitt, Wm. H. Cook, H. Petty, R. Portwood, P. May, Jacob Crocker and Charles Stewart. P. May along with Nathan Roberts and Richard Holly were excluded from fellowship in 1831 for becoming "Campbellites."

In 1833 Buttehatcha Association met at Union Meetinghouse in Marion County. It welcomed several new churches, including Fellowship, Pilgrim's Rest, and Ebenezer from Pickens County. Bulah was also welcomed as being from Pickens. But today that part of the old county is in Greene County. Providence and Bethany, both of Pickens, had affiliated the previous year. Fellowship and Ebenezer continue to be active churches. Pilgrim's Rest was then near Pickensville. Its old building now stands in the Sapps community. Providence closed in 1881. It was formed as an "arm" of the South Carolina Church. It was located, I assume, in the area where the present day Providence Missionary Baptist Church is in northwest Pickens. Bethany was located near the village of Vienna. It is long since closed and has been replaced by an African American Primitive Baptist Church. Providence reported 82 members and Enon had 79 in 1833.

At that meeting several churches were dismissed to join the new association to be formed in Tuscaloosa. Counting them there were 33 affiliated churches with a total membership of 1720. So, the average membership had grown to about 50.

In 1834 Liberty joined the association. It continues to be a church down to the present in the Pickens Association. And Serepta which had been listed as being in Greene was now listed as being in Pickens. The total was then 11 churches in Pickens, although three of them were across the Sipsey river in the area that is now in Greene County.

That year the association was comprised of churches from Marion, Fayette, Walker, Pickens, Tuscaloosa and Greene Counties, Alabama and Lowndes and Monroe Counties, Mississippi. The association had a total of 35 churches with 1820 members.

The association decided to divide again with all of the churches south of the "Coldfire" creek being formed the next year into a new association named Union Baptist Association. This involved 15 of the churches that were currently affiliated with the association, churches in Pickens and Greene counties. This meeting was scheduled for September of 1835 at Bethany Meeting House. (Since South Carolina and Providence were north of Coldfire, they stayed in the Buttehatcha Association. In 1835 they were joined by Bethlehem, which is still an active church.

Note was made in the 1834 minutes of a conflict between E. Nash and Henry Petty in the Zion Baptist Church of Lowndes County, Mississippi. In 1835 Petty was pastoring Pilgrim's Rest. He became a leader of the new association and was to play the major role in the division of the Union Association at its 1837 meeting.

Union Association had 19 churches affiliate with it when it formed. The 15 churches from Buttahatcha were joined by Forest of Pickens, Antioch of Perry, Buck Creek of Tuscaloosa, and Five Mile of Greene. The total membership was 1,087. Big Creek reported 111 and Rehoboth of Greene, reported 183.

When Buttehatcha met about a month after the Union Association was formed, Charles Stewart and Richard Wilkins attended as messengers from Union. They brought a query, "Did the Churches below Coldfire act in accordance with the resolve of our last Association? The answer from the association was that they did. Stewart and Wilkins had been active leaders in Buttahatcha. Apparently, Petty and Cook were raising a question about the legitimacy of the Union Association. The Buttehatcha Association reported 23 affiliated churches with a total membership of 896.

At the 1836 session a resolution was adopted by Buttehatcha condemning benevolence (mission) organizations. This was related to a reaction to the Canaan Association letter which was rejected by the association. The letter from Canaan was supportive of mission societies, Sunday Schools, temperance societies and various benevolences. This action also called for the ending of a fraternal relationship with the Canaan association.

This decision to condemn these activities and agencies seemed to have been challenged at the next annual meeting. A resolution was adopted noting that the association should not "lord it over" the local churches, but the association continued to refuse to have anything to do with the mission boards and other agencies at their annual meetings. Richard Wilkins represented Union at this meeting. No mention was made of the division of Union Association over the support of mission boards a few weeks earlier at its 1837 annual meeting. Buttahatcha had 26 churches with 980 members at this time. It must have been this issue which caused several churches to withdraw and form the Columbus association during the coming year.

Nor was any mention made of the formation of a Primitive Baptist Association, Pilgrim's Rest, in the territory being served by the Union (Pickens) Association. This occurred the following month, November 1837. This new association would become one with which the Buttehatcha would correspond and be in fellowship with for decades to come. The new association had about 588 members in 12 congregations. The leaders where Elders Henry Petty, Wm. H. Cook, Jeremiah Pearsell, and S. C. Johnson. The churches included Bethlehem, Rehoboth, Bethel, Canaan, Serepta and Five Mile Creek in Greene County and Bethany, Salem, and Pilgrim's Rest in Pickens. In several instances there were missionary minded members in these churches who formed other congregations. Examples would be Springhill out of Pilgrims' Rest, Mt. Zion out of Bethany, and Clinton out of Rehoboth.

The next minutes for Buttahatcha that were available at the Alabama Baptist Historical Library were for 1839. It has now added the word Primitive to its name. Among the associations with which it was in correspondence was Pilgrim's Rest. Among the resolutions adopted was one that called for the rejection of baptisms performed by missionary Baptist preachers. The die was cast.

From the minutes of the Columbus, Mississippi Association one learns that many of the churches there had withdrawn in 1838 to form a new association. This included the Pickens County churches South Carolina, Bethlehem and Providence. However, in 1839 Buttahatcha reported a small church in Pickens with the name Providence. I imagine that this was a split out of Providence. The relationship between the Columbus Association and the Union, like that with the Tuscaloosa, continued to be strong and useful across the years.

The name of the association in 1840 is listed as the Regular United Primitive Baptist Buttahacha Association. The total membership was 807 in 27 congregations. It corresponded with Mt. Zion Association over near Birmingham and Pilgrim's Rest in Pickens and surrounding counties. In 1882 the number of churches affiliated with Buttahatcha stood at 20 with 574 members. In 1886 the association divided with 11 of the churches becoming the Hopewell Association. It was located in Lamar, Fayette and Tuscaloosa Counties. This association lay between Buttahatcha and Pilgrims' Rest. Across the years the Primitive associations and churches have slowly died.

The articles of faith or doctrinal statements of the Buttahatcha and Union were the same. Both were very similar to those of Columbus, Tuscaloosa, Cahaba, and Canaan. All were Calvinist. The differences between these associations had to do with mission boards, financial support for pastors, Sunday Schools and Temperance societies.

It seems that there was a strong interest in missions in most of the churches in this region. So, as the data suggests, the Primitive movement was greatly reduced in following and the missionary portion grew. A continuing issue for Christians ever since the early churches to which the Apostle Paul wrote has been how to relate to the culture. Does one accommodate? If so, what are the guidelines. It seems that to refuse to accommodate results in decline. But too much accommodation can result in the movement losing its focus; i.e., it gives up too much.

History of Tuscaloosa County Baptist Association
and its Relationship to Pickens Baptist Association
Gary Farley

This association dates from March 23, 1834 when 13 churches met at Hopewell Meeting House to form an association. Thomas Baines was elected Moderator and John Thomas served as clerk. The previous fall several of these churches had been dismissed from Cahaba Association for this purpose. Notably absent from this meeting was Ebenezer which would become Tuscaloosa First and Grant's Creek which had hosted the state convention of Baptists the previous year. Tuscaloosa First affiliated with the association in 1840 and became a major force.

The Articles of Faith adopted were Calvinistic and in harmony with Cahaba and Buttehatcha Associations. October of 1834 the new association met again. This time is was at the Spring Hill Meeting House in northwest Tuscaloosa County. Baines and Thomas were re-elected. A church was added and the total membership stood at 963. At this time the state capitol was in Tuscaloosa and the state university was there as well. Consequently, it was a very strategic and important place.

The charter congregations were *Big Creek* (now Coker), Friendship, Philadelphia, Spring Hill, Mt. Tabor, *Bethany,* Bethel, *Gilgal*, Sardis, Salem, *Hopewell*, Haysop, Dunn's Creek, and Mt. Moriah. (The italicized churches continue in the Tuscaloosa County Association.) Spring Hill, Dunn's Creek Mt. Moriah, and Hysop continue in other associations.

The association does not have a full set of minutes. Of great significance is the missing of the 1837 and 1838 minutes. (But most of the others can be found at the Alabama Baptist Historical Commission Library at Samford. And an excellent centennial history, *History of Tuscaloosa Baptist Association*, was prepared in 1938 by Judge Henry B. Foster who served as Moderator for many years.) This was a time when serious controversy was raging between those who would not support mission societies and those who would. However, in 1844 all of the 1834 churches were still present in the association. So, this issue may have been much less severe in Tuscaloosa than it was in Pickens County to the west.

In 1837 Dr. Basil Manly, Sr. came from the pastorate of the First Baptist Church of Charleston, South Carolina to be president of the University of Alabama. He was a strong advocate of mission boards. And he became a major influence among Baptists in West Alabama. After its first decade, the association counted 33 congregations and 2,072 members. Of these congregations, perhaps five were in northern Pickens, two in Bibb, one in Walker, and the rest in Tuscaloosa County. Since many of the new churches were formed in 1838-1840 and the membership doubled, it appears that the missions controversy resulted in revival. This was the case in Pickens also.

There were two significant other issues in the churches during the first decade. One had to do with charges of "Arminianism" being brought against David Andrews, by some in the Salem church. Apparently, Andrews was an effective missionary and formed several new congregations which then constituted as the North River Association. Beginning in 1841 the Choctaw Association sought to resolve the animosity between the two associations, taking the role of mediator. Fellowship between them was achieved in 1849 when the two associations began corresponding. Mt. Zion church in Pickens county withdrew from the association in protest. (This church became Primitive.) Also during the first decade some of the early pastors became "reformers," or followers of Alexander Campbell and moved to that denominational family.

Several of the early ministers, including Joab Pratt, Thomas Baines, and Holland Middleton followed the westward settlement and continued to plant churches on in Mississippi, Arkansas and Texas. Beginning in the mid-1840s and continuing to the War Between the States much attention was given to the evangelization of the slaves. In 1864, while the membership figures remained flat, the number of congregations increased to 35. At the outset of the war the churches in the association counted 403 "colored" members. Following the war most of the freedmen formed congregations of their own..

In the latter part of the Nineteenth Century two new associations were formed, primarily, from Tuscalcosa association congregations. Sipsey was birthed on the west and Pleasant Grove on the east. Sunday School work was a focus beginning at that time. The women began organizing mission groups. The association provided support for Alabama Central Female College which was housed in the old building of State Capitol.

Moving into the Twentieth Century the Tuscaloosa Baptist Association had 30 congregations with 2,372 members. Tuscaloosa First was by far the largest with 683 members. Following the emerging pattern of the denomination, efforts were made to encourage all of the churches in the county which were cooperating with the state convention to become affiliated with the association. As industry came to the county and the University grew, so did the Baptist family. In 1933 there were 52 churches in the association with 9,667 members. A major ministry of the association became the Chair of Bible at the University. The association was also very active in the Temperance Movement.

With further industrialization during and after World War II, population grew and so did the Baptist membership. A total of 59 churches with 16,531 were reported in 1955. The association lost several churches during the turbulent 1960s to independency. But the association continued to grow with 63 congregations and 28,134 members reported in 1973. With this base the association developed a camp and provide good services for children and other groups. The camp was later sold and the funds invested to provide money for planting new churches and doing ministry. Wisely, new churches have been planted on the growing edges of the city. This expansion includes work in Hale and in the traditional territory of the Sipsey and the Pleasant Grove Associations. This has been done in a cooperative fashion.

Today there are 85 congregations with 30,000 resident members in this association. The population of the area served by the association is about 150,000. So, the Baptist work is very effective. For more than 20 years the association has been led by Bro. Jerry Wilkins. He has associates who focus on education work and on small church work. So, while there is great diversity among the churches of the association, it continues to be solid and effective.

History of Union (Pickens Baptist) Association
Gary Farley

Bethany Meeting house near Vienna in Pickens County hosted the constituting sessions of the Union Baptist Association, the first week of September, 1835. The previous Fall the Buttehatchie Association had decided to divide, with the churches south of Coldfire Creek being dismissed to form the new association. Of the 19 churches attending and affiliating with Union, 14 had been members of Buttehatchie. The others were either coming from Cahaba Association, or were newly constituted.

Pickens County churches were Bethany, Beulah, Big Creek, *Ebenezer*, *Enon* (now Aliceville), *Fellowship, Forest, Liberty*, Pilgrim's Rest, Sarepta, and Unity. Greene County churches included Bethel, Bethlehem, Canaan, Five Mile, Rehobeth, and Springfield. Buck Creek was in Tuscaloosa county and Antioch was in Perry County. (The italicized churches continue to be affiliated with the association which is now known as Pickens Baptist Association.)

The first moderator was Rev. Richard Wilkins. The first clerk was Rev. W. R. Stansel. Fortunately, all of the minutes of the Union/Pickens Association have been preserved. They are available on microfilm at the Alabama Baptist Historical Library at Samford University and in the PBA office in Carrollton. Many of the churches have had their minutes microfilmed, a free service, and these are also available in the associational office. Wilkins and Stansel, like their colleagues in ministry, were "planters" and served several congregations each year, bivocationally.

A conflict over cooperating with mission boards erupted at the 1837 meeting. This mirrored a wide-spread controversy in the Baptist movement. The anti-board churches withdrew to form the Pilgrim's Rest Primitive Baptist Association. This included nearly half of the churches and more than one-half of the members of the churches in the Union Association. However, the next few years were times of revival and church planting in the area served by the association's affiliates. Many of the new converts were slaves. In 1844 the association reported 1,493 members in 23 congregations. This was more churches and members than before the split.

Beginning in 1838 and continuing for nearly 50 years the association, annually, had one of its own prepare a Circular Letter which dealt with some theological topic. These were adopted and printed in the annual minutes with a request that each of the churches read and discuss the letter. A reading of these letters today reveals a scholarly bent for very well-informed pastors and laymen, although few of them had any formal theological education.

In the mid-1840s several of the Greene County churches asked to be dismissed in order to form what is now the Bigbee Association. In 1850 two of the churches found the association's Articles of Faith to be too Calvinistic for their liking. They withdrew and became the founding members of the Mt. Moriah Free Will Baptist Association. This group continues today.

The following year a daughter of the Grant's Creek Church in Tuscaloosa County, Martha Foster Crawford, was appointed as a missionary to China by the Southern Baptist Foreign Mission Board. Since then 19 others from the associations have served that board and its successor.

At the end of the War Between the States, Union Association counted 28 churches with 2,586 members. About one-third of the members were Freedmen. Over the next five years most of the Freedmen withdrew to form congregations of their own. About 1872 the new African American churches formed the Lebanon Missionary Baptist Association.

The Sunday School movement was the center of attention in the association for the next two decades. In addition to the three or four day annual meeting of Union, there were also quarterly Sunday School Conventions. A merchant layman, W. G. Robertson of Carrollton, was the champion of this movement. Robertson's wife, Sarah, was the leader of the Woman's Missionary Union. Since 1905 women have served regularly as messengers to the annual meetings of the association. In recent years, they have been in the majority.

At the dawning of the Twentieth Century, the churches were all open country and village churches. Carrollton, the county seat, claimed only 400 residents then. In the mid 1890s a rail line built across south Lamar County and new churches were added in Millport and in Kennedy. A few years later a railroad line was laid across Pickens County from Columbus, Ms. to Tuscaloosa, Al. New churches were planted in the emerging rail towns of Reform and Gordo. The old South Carolina church was moved to the new town of Ethelsville. And when another line was built from Reform toward Mobile, the Enon church moved to the new town of Aliceville. While the population of the territory served by the Union Association (most of Pickens, south Lamar, west Greene, and southeastern Tuscaloosa Counties) remained at about 30,000, it shifted from farmsteads and villages into the new towns. Consequently, several open country churches closed in the last decade of the Nineteenth Century.

In 1924 the association changed its name to Pickens Baptist Association. At the time there were 31 churches in the association with 2,928 members. Two of the churches were in Tuscaloosa County and two were in Greene County.

When the association celebrated its centennial in 1935, long-time moderator, M. B. Curry, a layman and attorney, prepared a history of the association. It was printed in the annual for that year. It listed the pastors who served the churches through the years, the dates that churches joined the association, the location of annual meetings, and other important data. At that time the association had 29 congregations with a total of 3,206 members. Only one church was not in Pickens County.

As a rural county, the economy of the area had been based on cotton farming and timber harvesting from the beginning. Industrialization came with the importation of cotton mills, and sewing factories. An electronics plant and an industrial felt plant brought the total number of industrial jobs in the area to about 3,000 by 1980. Since then, these have been lost. Today much of the work force commutes to Tuscaloosa or Columbus daily. Agriculture has added ranching, aquiculture, and poultry to its mix of activities. The timber industry remains strong.

With the assistance of the State Board of Missions, Pickens Association hired its first full-time associational missionary in 1848, Ms. Emma Burgin, who had grown up in the Hebron Church. She was a recent graduate of Southwestern Baptist Theological Seminary. She resigned in 1950 and was replaced by Rev. James Caldwell. He served on a part-time basis until 1956. Mr. Joseph Dean, a layman, served the Pickens Association as missionary from 1957 until his death in 1972. These early missionaries assisted the churches in developing their educational and mission programs and in moving to having worship services every Sunday. They were a part of a cadre of missionaries who helped transform rural Baptist work in the 1950s and 1960s.

Rev. Oel Hendrix was called as missionary in 1972 and served until his retirement in 1989. He built a strong commitment in the churches to the work of the association. He led in the building of a small office building on the property of the missionary home. It is now the Lydia guest house. Later he acquired the land on which the current office building stands. Rev. Ernie Carroll served from 1989 to 1997. He initiated the strong social ministry program at the Baptist Center in Stansel. He also led in the construction of a fine office complex for the association in Carrollton. He moved to the Friendship Association. in Blount County. He was followed by Dr. Gary Farley in 1998. Farley had spent the previous 13 years directing rural church work for the Southern Baptist Convention with the Home Mission Board. He has served bivocationally.

Currently, the association has 34 affiliated churches, one under watchcare, and an Hispanic mission. The resident membership stands at 4,100. In addition to the five continuing founding congregations noted above these are Arbor Springs, Bethlehem, Calvary, Carrollton, Coal Fire, Cross Roads, Double Branches, Ethelsville, Emmanuel, Flatwoods, Friendship, Garden, Gordo, Hebron , Hickory Grove, Highland, Mineral Springs, Mount Pleasant, Mount Tabor, New Salem, Neueva Vida, Pickensville, Pine Grove, Pleasant Grove, Pleasant Hill, Reform, Spring Hill, Stansel, Union Chapel and West End. Galilee has applied for membership.

The association looks toward the future with hope. The four-laning of US highway 82 across the association should help draw new residents to the area and help retain old ones. Efforts ae being made to encourage people to retire to Pickens. Http://ruralretirement.us Industry is expanding both in Tuscaloosa and Columbus, Ms. A branch campus for Bevell State College has opened in Carrollton. And a Federal Prison will soon be built and opened in Aliceville. These developments will provide new opportunities and challenges for the churches of the Pickens Baptist Association.

Pilgrim's Rest Primitive Baptist Association
and its Relationship with the Pickens Association
Gary Farley

At some point between 1932 and 1940 the old Pilgrims' Rest Primitive Baptist Association dissolved. It would have celebrated its centennial anniversary in 1937. The last record that I have found thus far is the printed minutes of the annual meeting of the associational meeting of 1932. It was held at Salem Primitive Baptist Church, south of Gordo. The 1933 meeting was scheduled to be held at Pilgrim's Rest near Carrollton. At this time there were only three congregations–Salem, Pilgrim's Rest, and Bethlehem in the association. The total membership stood at 41. The association had four active ministers–J. R. Thornton, J. A. Hollingsworth, C. M. Springer, and J. C. Burkhalter.

An interesting resolution was adopted at the meeting. It reads, "We, the Pilgrim's Rest Association, have set resolution to not allow any extreme doctrines either on predestination, arminianism or any other doctrine in which the old King James Bible will not sustain and do not hold church fellowship with any one who indulges in such things." I take this to mean that they were not hyper-calvinists as are many Primitive Baptists, then and now.

Back in 1837 a division arose among the Baptists in Pickens County, as elsewhere, around the topic of supporting mission societies. Those who saw these and other benevolence agencies as non-biblical withdrew from the Union Baptist Association which had been formed two years earlier. They took as their name Pilgrim's Rest, from a church in the emerging association.

Hosea Holcombe, a preacher who favored support of mission boards, published a history of Alabama Baptists in 1840. He dates the formation of this association as November, 1837, at the Rehoboth Church in the Clinton community of Greene County. The leaders were Henry Petty, William Cook, Jeremiah Pearsell and S. C. Johnson, all elders. Initially the association had 12 churches with about 600 members. It appears that it was about the same size as the continuing Union Association which had 12 congregations also and about 500 members after the split. (Note Holcombe, I understand, has been identified by some as the preacher who gave Reform its name, rather than Lorenzo Dow. Since Reform got its post office in 1842 and since Holcombe visited Pickens County several times in the 1830s, this claim has more historical support than the Dow claim in that his travels in the area predated the establishment of Reform by at least 20 years.)

The earliest listing of the churches in the Pilgrim's Rest Association which I have found comes from the 1853 associational minutes. Then there were 10 congregations with 311 members. In that year Union (now Pickens) reported 26 churches with 1,612 members. Further, the Greene County churches in the old Union Association had helped form a new association which served Greene and Sumter Counties a few years earlier and were no longer a part of the Union Association. So, the missionary churches had grown both in number and membership while the Primitives had declined in membership.

Pilgrim's Rest, Bethany, Liberty, Salem and Sarepta were the Pilgrim's Rest Primitive Baptist Churches in Pickens County, all in the Sipsey valley. Rehobeth, Bethlehem, Bethel, and Five Mile were in Greene County and Hepseby had the Choctaw Agency as its mailing address. In 1857 the minutes of the association find Sarepta is not listed. But Zion is added. This may be Zion in the community north of Gordo. One finds both a Primitive and a mission board friendly congregation going by the name of Zion there for many years. The Zion that was in the Pickens Baptist Association closed about 1940.

In 1907 minutes of the Pilgrim's Rest Association there are only 7 churches listed. Liberty, south and east of Gordo was the strongest with 66 members. The others are Sarepta, Salem,

Pilgrim's Rest, Mt. Pleasant, Five Miles, and Bethany. Note that the Primitive churches continued to be rural and did not start new churches in the towns of Pickens County.

Also of interest is their Articles of Faith. The 1907 Articles of Faith for the Pilgrim's Rest is almost identical to those of the Pickens Baptist Association. There is some small difference in the order of the appearance of articles, but the language is almost identical.

Small changes crept in by the 1932 meeting. Then, the articles of Pilgrim's Rest included the washing of feet as one on the ordinances of the church, and called for the exclusion of any member who is a member of some secret society. But it's basic doctrines continued to parallel those of the Pickens Association.

By 1940 it appears that the surviving churches from the old Pilgrim's Rest Association had moved to the Hopewell Primitive Baptist Association. Hopewell had hived off of the Buttehatcha Association at the end of the Civil War, ca. 1866. It's Articles of Faith are also very similar to those of Pilgrim's Rest and Union. Its territory included North Pickens, Lamar, Fayette, and parts of Tuscaloosa Counties. Most of the churches through its history have been in the Sipsey Valley.

The 1940 minutes lists 10 churches with 138 total members in Hopewell. The Pickens County churches included Zion, Mt. Zion, Liberty, and Salem. Among the others is Little Hope, a very interesting name for a church. This annual meeting was conducted at Salem.

Today Salem, Liberty, and Pilgrim Rest survive as historic buildings. The others are small, but faithful congregations. One cannot but ask the question as to why, when the two associations began with similar strength, the one shrank and died and the other has grown and prospered. From a human perspective, the answer may be that the one was focused on maintaining "the old way" and was satisfied to continue the tradition of its annual meeting, while the other focused on planting new churches in the communities of Pickens and Greene County that did not have a missionary Baptist Church.

As I have become acquainted with people in the churches affiliated with the Pickens Baptist Association, I have noted that many of them have roots in the old Primitive churches. But, for a variety of personal and theological reasons they have become missionary Baptists.

I would be interested in finding additional copies of the old minutes of the Pilgrim's Rest Primitive Baptist Association. I would like to read the minutes of the churches affiliated with it. The Alabama Baptist Historical Commission would like to copy these records and add them to its collection.

At the other end of the Baptist family spectrum is the Free Will Baptist. The association which serves Pickens, Mt. Moriah, is also tied to our association. In 1850 Bro. Ellis Gore led this church and a Salem church into the Free Will faith. He planted a number of churches in Pickens and Tuscaloosa Counties. Today the Mt. Moriah Free Will Baptist Association has 13 congregations. I will attempt to gather more information on this association for future publications.

The Golden Triangle Baptist Association
Columbus, Mississippi
and its Relationship with the Pickens Baptist Association

This association was formed in 1837-38 by churches that had been affiliated with the old Buttehatcha Association. It was comprised of churches that supported mission causes and boards which were located north of the Cold Fire Creek in Alabama and on in Mississippi. Its formation was more controversial than that of Union (Pickens) Association, but it did not experience the internal conflict which impacted Union in 1837.

The association officially organized in November of 1838 and took the name of Columbus. The founding congregations included South Carolina (now Ethelsville), Providence (near our Hickory Grove), Oak Grove, Mount Zion, Columbus and Lebanon. (Note: the first two of these churches soon became attached to the Union (Pickens) Association.

As with Union, this new association retained the Calvinistic Articles of Faith that had informed the old Buttehatcha Association. Mission support was the issue. Two decades later efforts were made to reunite the associations, but this failed.

Through the years Union and Columbus and their successors have maintained good relationships. Pastors have moved back and forth between these associations and they have worked cooperatively on several projects.

By 1841 there were 15 churches in the Columbus Association with a total of 1,122 members. Mount Moriah in Pickens County was among the new congregations. (A decade later it became the mother church of the Free Will Baptist movement in this area)

In 1861 the association reported 28 congregations with 2,856 members, about half of whom were African Americans. In the years following the Civil War most of the freedmen moved to new African American congregations. So, the Columbus Association reported in 1881 a total of 24 congregations with 1,658 members.

The minutes of the association contain the names of many men who played important roles in the life of Mississippi and Southern Baptists. Among these were W. Carey Crane and JR. C. Burleson, J. B. Gambrell who moved on the Texas and became great leaders. S.S. Latimore who began his ministry here moved on to provide important leadership for Baptists in Mississippi. The same was true of Lee Compere who was a pioneer missionary among the Creek Indians. Three presidents of the Home Mission Board, Daniel Bestor and I. T. Technor, and J. B. Lawrence served as pastor at Columbus First across the years. It was Technor who moved the board to Atlanta. It was Lawrence who steered the board through the Great Depression. And the current DOM for New Orleans, Joe McKeever, also pastored First.

The association today has two major state universities within its bounds and a Baptist Hospital. It also has a major Air Force base. And after years of stagnation, new industry is coming and the future looks bright. This is a major responsibility. About 124 thousand persons live in the three counties–Loundes, Clay, and Oktibbeha–served by the association. The current Golden Triangle association was formed in 1976 when Columbus merged with its neighbors.

Today the association has 64 congregations. The resident membership is 18,619. Remember our good neighbors to the west.

Bigbee Baptist Association
and its Connection to the Pickens Baptist Association
Gary Farley

Many of the Baptist Churches of Greene and Sumter Counties are members of the Bigbee Baptist Association which dates itself from 1852. Today it has churches at Sumterville, West Greene, Clinton, Eutaw, Friendship, Gainesville, Boligee (Friendship), York, Livingston, Cuba, and Epes, and open country churches named Zion, Bellamy, Beulah, Shorts, Christian Valley, Siloam, and Ward. Most of these churches are in the southern part of Sumter County.

This area was Choctaw Indian territory until 1830. As settlers moved in, they formed Baptist Churches. These, in turn formed an association which, like the others in Alabama, was torn in the 1830s by conflict over the use of mission boards to plant churches on the frontier and overseas. (In northern Greene, several churches affiliated early with the Union Association.)

This early association of Baptist Churches was named, appropriately, the Choctaw association. It included churches in Sumter, Choctaw, and Greene Counties in Alabama and Noxubee, Kemper, Winston and Leake Counties in Mississippi. The initial effort to have an association was in 1834. After the mission board conflict it was restarted in 1839. In 1849 several of the Union Baptist Association Churches moved their affiliation to the Little Bigbee, another short lived organization. Then in 1852 this group and some Choctaw Association churches formed the Bigbee Association.

The charter churches were Hopewell in Belmont, Christian Valley in Brewersville, Providence at Warsaw, Gainesville, Friendship in Choctaw, Sumterville, Jones Creek (Epes), Clinton, Siloam, Eutaw, Black's Bluff, Gaston, New Prospect, Friendship in Forkland, Rehoboth in Choctaw County, and Pleasant Ridge in Greene. The moderator chosen in the first meeting was William Woodward. The first clerk was Jeremiah Brown.

Anti-mission board sentiment continued to be strong, particularly in Greene County. The Free Will issue did not seem to reach into Bigbee, however.

Some of these early churches, specifically those in the river towns of Warsaw and Gainesville, grew to be very large prior to the Civil War. Providence at Warsaw had over 400 members; Gainesville, nearly 400; and Friendship at Forkland, nearly 300. Most of the members were slaves. These and other churches were able to attract well prepared pastors who played important roles in Baptist life both in Alabama and nationally. Basil Manly, Jr., the son of the president of the University of Alabama, upon graduating from Princeton, became pastor at Providence in Warsaw and at Sumterville. Later he was pastor of the First Baptist Church of Richmond, Va., and a founding faculty member of The Southern Baptist Theological Seminary. Daniel Bestor pastored the Gainesville churches and others in the association. He later served at the head of the Domestic Mission Board of the new Southern Baptist Convention. He was pastor of the First Baptist Church in Columbus, and he served an African American church in Mobile during his ministry. And like many others of his contemporaries, he served also as an educator. E. B. Teague was also an educator and a pastor. He served the Clinton, Eutaw and Selma churches.

The Bigbee Association adopted Articles of Faith that, like the New Hampshire Confession of Faith, were Calvinistic in orientation, but allowed for human response to the grace of God. The first extant copy of annual minutes is from the second meeting held in 1853 at Clinton, Alabama. The second extant copy is from 1856. The remainder are available on microfilm at the Alabama Baptist Historical Library.

In the early days the association supported a Native American pastor, Peter Folsom, to work among the Choctaws. The churches also were very active in evangelizing the slaves. Numerically, 1861 was a high water mark for the association. It counted 23 churches and 2,861 members. After the war the freedmen began to form their own churches and withdrew from the Bigbee churches. This severely weakened many of the churches because at the time about two-thirds of the membership of the churches were freedmen. The combined membership reported in 1860 was 2,721. In 1869 it was but 657.

The Providence Baptist Church provides an example. Following the war it relocated from Warsaw to a new town, Sherman. The church, ironically, took a new name, Stonewall. Its membership was less than 50, down from over 400. It passes from the pages of history in the early 1880s. However, it may live on as the source of First Baptist Church, Dancy, a Missionary Baptist Church, and several other African American congregations in the Panola area..

In 1882 the Bigbee Baptist Association reported 25 churches with 1,234 members. Most of the churches were very small. Demopolis reported only 17; Eutaw, 18; Gainsville, 64; Livingston, 33; and York, 26. In 1900 it had 23 churches and 1,160 members.

For many decades the area served by Bigbee Association has experienced declining population. Greene now has about 9,900 citizens, and Sumter has 14,798. More than three-fourths of the citizens are African American. Due to the demographics of the area, the work has been hard and slow for Alabama Baptists. But God has blessed. Our work is strongest in the southern part of Sumter County. Leon Ballard while serving as bi-vocational pastor at York served two years as President of the Alabama Baptist Convention in the late 1990s.

Two important arteries of commerce run through this association. One is the Tennessee-Tombigbee Water Way. The other is Interstate 59 highway.

The University of West Alabama (formerly the Livingston Women's College) is located at Livingston in Sumter County. Since 1968 the associational missionary has also served as the director of Baptist Student Ministries on the campus. Jake Duke holds this position. His predecessor, Dr. Bruce Gentry, served in this role as did Robert Ford, Charles W. Barnes . . . Across the years professors and other employees of the University have served as pastors in the churches of the Bigbee Association.

Across the years 51 churches have been affiliated with the association. Some in Marengo and Choctaw Counties have joined other associations. Several others have disbanded because of declining population.

Bigbee from its beginning has been very progressive. It has been a strong supporter of missions. The WMU there was among the first in the state. Guiding spirits were Miss Charlie Stewart and Miss Annie Grace Tartt. The foundation for this was built upon earlier organizations for Aid and Bible distribution. It, along with Pickens and Tuscaloosa Associations, claim Mrs. Martha Foster Crawford, pioneer Southern Baptist missionary to China. Also the presence of a women's college in Livingston must have contributed to leadership by women there. Bigbee also contributed Mrs. Ida Mitchell Stallworth who during much of the 1920s and 1930s led WMU work in Alabama. Women first appeared as messengers to the association in 1889.

Perhaps from the same source, Sunday School work was advocated early. The churches have supported missions and the work of Alabama Baptists faithfully through the years.

Like other Black Belt counties and the associations that serve them (.e.g, Cahaba) the changing economy has resulted in dramatic loss of population. Today the two counties, Sumter and Greene, have only about 25,000 persons down 2/3rd from 1860. Bigbee has only 17 congregations with 1,295 resident members. For several years the Baptist Student Ministries director at West Alabama also served as director of missions. This has recently changed. Now the association is seeking either a bi-vocational DOM or will connect with an adjoining association for leadership.

Sipsey Baptist Association
and its Relationship with the Pickens Baptist Association
with some notes about Lamar and Fayette Associations
Gary Farley

In the fall of 1890 14 churches formed the Sipsey Association. All were rural churches. All had previously been connected to the Tuscaloosa Association. They adopted the same Articles of Faith as Tuscaloosa. The primary reason for the creation of this new association was the convenience of not having to travel such a long distance for meetings. This organization had been several years in the making

Seven of the churches were located in Tuscaloosa County's northwest quarter. Three were in southeast Fayette County and four were in northeast Pickens County. The Tuscaloosa churches were Bethabara, Corinth, Dunn's Creek, Moore's Bridge, Oak Ridge, Spring Hill, and Chapel Hill. The Pickens churches were Pleasant Grove, Mt. Tabor, Flat Woods, and Double Branches. (Interestingly, all of these congregations are now in the Pickens Association.) The Fayette churches were New Hope, Friendship and Mt. Hebron.

J. M. Chism was the first moderator and James White was the clerk. Since most of the churches are in the basin of the Sipsey River this name was taken. Across the years there have been 27 congregations affiliated with the association. Several have moved to other associations. Only two have closed.

Across the years nearly 250 men have pastored churches in Sipsey Association. Some of them have come from adjoining associations and many move back and forth between the associations. Consequently, there are good relationships among the associations. In most instances the pastors have served bivocationally.

The area served by Sipsey Association continues to be rural and sparsely settled, for the most part. There are no towns, no industry, and presently no schools. In the past most of the residents were farmers. Today, many commute daily to jobs in Tuscaloosa. However, the area around Lake Tuscaloosa is rapidly suburbanizing. Some Tuscaloosa association churches are now serving that part of Sipsey's traditional territory. Apparently, Sipsey's may become more of an association that is an "affinity" group than a geographical one as time passes.

While Sipsey did not experience conflicts related to anti-mission board sentiment, controversy related to Arminianism, or the loss of African American members due to having been formed in 1890, there is a strong anti-mission and Calvinistic sentiment in the area which sometimes spills over into the churches. Conversely, dwelling in a somewhat hostile environment, the Sipsey churches appear to be unusually loyal to the state convention and to the national convention.

Currently there are 14 congregations in the association with a total of 1,432 resident members. The names of the churches are Arbor Springs, Bethabara, Bevans Chapel, Big Hill, Crossroads, Dunns Creek, Hopewell, Macedonia, Mores Bridge, Mt. Hebron, New Hope, Rock Solid, Spring Hill, and Zion Community.

As a relatively small association it has very few associational-based cooperative ministries. Most activities beyond the annual meeting are training events related to the basic programs of Southern Baptist Churches. My experiences in the association remind me of those I had in the 1950s in a rural Baptist Association. This past summer it hosted a "Horse Whisperer" event with more than 1,200 in attendance.

Like many Alabama Associations the position of fieldworker or missionary was added about 1950 with the assistance of the State Board of Missions. Those who have served in this position include Foster Mills, G. L. Pearson, Thomas Findley, J. L. Mouchette, J. L. Noland, Lenwood Hocutt, J. S. Pate, J. W. Dubose, Neil Nichols. Thomas Vaughn, Bill Stokes, and Henry Trull. Hocutt served for 24 years. Recently, Max Stripling assumed the position, part-time, of associational missionary. Stripling is the former Superintendent of Schools in Pickens County. He is a strong supporter of Alabama and Southern Baptist work. Pickens Baptist folk will recognize many of the men listed above because they severed churches in this association across the years.

Moderators have often served for many terms. Among these are J. B. Ferguson, S. W. Clements, L. R. Spencer, T. W. Shelton, J. J. Crowe, Erskine Stripling, John Stamps, and John Pate

WMU work was not begun in the association until 1950. Mrs. R. H. Richardson was the first director. Women in the association continue to have a secondary role in associational life and in the annual meetings.

From its beginnings Sipsey has strongly supported Sunday School work. It adopted the practice of that era of holding quarterly Sunday School Conventions. This broadened and expanded the work. In the late 1930s the churches began to add Vacation Bible Schools to the program of work of the churches. The also added what is now called Discipleship Training.

The association does not have an office building. And with no town within its bounds, there does not seem to be a central gathering place. Yet the people of the association have a deep attachment to it. An office is maintained at Arbor Springs Baptist Church, north of Northport.

(The other two associations which join us to the north are Lamar and Fayette. Both are less than 100 years old. It seems that each one appeared as an effort by the more progressive churches to modernize early in the 20th Century. But I do not have enough information to do a history at this point.)

Briefly, the Lamar County churches formed an association about 1860 called the Yellow Creek Baptist Association. Apparently, responding to the encouragement of the denomination to form county based associations, most of the Lamar churches in Yellow Creek in 1911 formed the Lamar Baptist Association. Joining them were churches then in the Union or Pickens Association–Spring Hill, Millport, Kennedy and Pleasant Grove, all in South Lamar.

(Fayette Association dates from 1918 when it changed its name from New River.)

THE RULES OF DECORUM

1. The Association shall be opened and closed by prayer.
2. But one person shall speak at a time and he shall rise and address the Moderator.
3. No member shall be interrupted while speaking unless he depart from the subject in hand or use words of personal reflection.
4. Every motion made and seconded, shall come under the consideration of the Association, except withdrawn by him that made it; and if there are two or more motions before the Association on the same subject at one time, the first motion shall be the first in order.
5. Every case taken up by the Association, shall first be decided on, or withdrawn before another is offered.
6. When any thing is taken up by the Association after allowing time for debate, the Moderator shall take the question, and those in favor of the thing proposed, shall rise on their feet, and those against it shall keep their seats; the decision thus made shall be announced by the Moderator immediately.
7. No person shall depart from the service of the Association without leave.
8. No person shall speak more than twice on the same subject, without leave obtained, nor shall any proposition be made to close the subject until the debates are gone through.
9. The appellation of brother shall be used in our addresses to one another.
10. The Moderator shall be entitled to the same privilege of speech as any other member, provided he appoint some other member to fill the chair while speaking, but shall not vote unless the Association be equally divided.
11. Any person breaking the rules of decorum, shall be reproved as the Association may think proper.

(Taken from Minutes dated 1835)

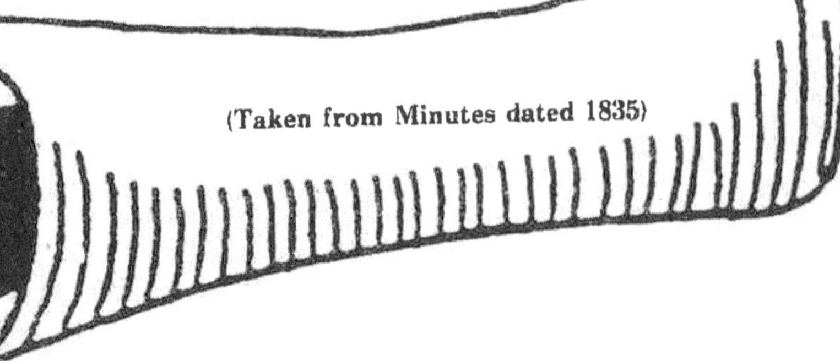

Articles of Faith

Article 1. We believe in only one true and living God, the Father, the Word and the Holy Ghost.- Deut. IV-39; 1 Cor. VIII-6; and 1 John V-7

2. We believe that the Scriptures, comprising the Old and New Testaments, are the one word of God, and the only rule of faith and practice. 2Tim. III-16; Rom. XV-4 and III-2.
3. We believe that Adam, by sin, fell from the state of purity in which he was created, that all his posterity are degenerate, and that all human nature is corrupt and depraved. Rom III-12; Gen. I-26-28; III-6-8.
4. We believe that man is utterly unable, by his own free will and ability, to recover himself from the fallen state in which he is by nature. Heb IX 22-23; I Peter II-24; III-18.
5. We believe in the doctrine of election, and that God chose his people in Christ, before the world began, Eph. I-2-5; Titus I-1 and 2.
6. We believe in the covenant of redemption, and salvation by grace, entered into by the Sacred Three, in behalf of the elect, on whom grace and glory were settled forever, in Christ, their covenant head. Psalm IXXXXIX-2 and 4; and XXVII-37; Eph. I-3-5; 2Tim. I-9.
7. We believe that sinners are justified in the sight of God, by the imputed righteousness of Christ only, and that they receive pardon and reconciliation through Him. Rom III-22-26.
8. We believe that God's elect shall be called, regenerated and sanctified by the influence and operation of the Holy Spirit. 1 Peter 1-2; Mal. III-17.
9. We believe that saints shall be preserved in grace, and that none of them shall be lost. John X-27-29; Romans VIII-31-39; 2 Tim I-9.
10. We believe in the resurrection of the dead, and the general judgment, and that the joys of the righteous, and the punishment of the wicked will be eternal. Job XIX 25-27; John V-28-29; Matt. XXV-31; 34, 41-46.
11. We believe that baptism and the Lord's Supper are ordinances of Jesus Christ; that true believers are the only fit subjects of baptism; that immersion in water is the Apostolic mode; and that none but regularly baptized members have a right to commune at the Lords table. Matt. III-6-16; Mark I-9; XVI-16; John IV-1-2; Acts II-38-41; VIII-12 XVIII-8; Luke XXXII-17-20; John XIII-2-41

From 1948 PBA Annual. These articles date from the founding of the association. 1835

Pickens Baptist Churches the Early Years
Gary Farley

Friday, September 22, 1837 was unseasonably warm. A large crowd had gathered at the Big Creek Meetinghouse about 4 miles west of Carrollton, Alabama. The crowd was a buzz with rumors concerning a threatened division in the Baptist association. Inside the house about sixty men also visited with one another some in little knotes of serious conversation, others trying hard to be jovial.

Two topics seemed to consume the serious ones. One was an action of the association on the last day of its 1836 annual meeting, an action that was taken after some of the delegates had set out for their homes. In it a resolution was made that "the association protest against any missionary coming into said body." For some years the issue of whether or not to support mission agencies like foreign and home mission boards and other benevolent organizations had been hotly debated among Baptists. In 1835 when 19 Baptist churches "below Coldfire Creek" in Pickens, Greene and Tuscaloosa counties met at Bethany meeting house about 6 miles southeast of modern Aliceville, they had formed an association and took the name Union for it. Apparently, they had hoped that those who differed on the issue of support of mission agencies desired that they could walk in harmony. So, when the this anti-mission board resolution was passed in such a devious way, some felt betrayed. The second topic of discussion was the division in the Friendship church at Forkland in Greene County.

At the appointed time, Elder J. H. Taylor, pastor at Unity and at Forest Baptist Churches, came to the pulpit to preach the anniversary or introductory sermon. He chose as his text Mark 16:15. This passage quotes Jesus telling his disciples to preach the Gospel to all of the nations. He was a proponent of support of mission boards. The next item of business was the election of officers. Henry Petty, pastor at Pilgrim's Rest near Pickensville and Rehoboth near Clinton, two of the larger churches, was elected moderator. He had been an outspoken opponent of mission boards. And Taylor was elected clerk. (Note among the visiting brothers was G. W. Baines, grandfather of President Lyndon Baines Johnson. He would soon move west.)

(The first map shows the location of the churches that formed the association in 1835. In 1837 an additional church was accepted, Salem, which I think is what became the Primitive Baptist Church that was located south of Gordo.)

The following day the association took up the controversy in the Friendship church. (Incidentally, this church continues to the present, but moved to Boligee.) After having the issue present, the body was asked to decide whether the pro-missions or and anti-board segment of the Friendship church was the one that was truly a member of the association. When the vote was taken, Moderator Petty declared that it was a tie vote at 26 for each congregation. His ruling was challenged and as an effort to compromise the association agreed to seat both sets of delegates from the Friendship church. Charles Stewart the host pastor, who during the decade of the 1830s had served as tax collection and a representative to the state legislature, brokered this compromise.

At this point, the hour being late, the association adjourned until Monday. Sunday was devoted to preaching. Usually there was worship in the meetinghouse and in an arbor or two on the church grounds.

On Monday morning Petty, as Moderator, was asked to have the association reconsider the action concerning Friendship. He refused. A motion was made to replace him. At this point Petty and others left the meetinghouse. In November they formed the Pilgrim's Rest Primitive

Baptist Association. It's strength was in Greene County.

When the Union Baptist Association met in 1838 it had lost, from Pickens County, the Bethany church. And it was reported that part of that church had been formed into the Mt.Zion Church a few miles away. This church united first with the Tuscaloosa Association. Also the Pilgrim's Rest church had split. The pro-missions portion in 1842 became the Springhill church which continues to be a part of the association.

Apparently, this decision to support missions coupled with an influx of persons moving to the association triggered a time of revival with more than 300 persons being baptized in the following church year. By 1845 the association had 16 churches, with an addition churches belonging to other associations but located in the county. During the 1840s the churches had begun to add weekly Sunday Schools to there activities and actively evangelize the slave population.

Pioneer Preachers of the Pickens Baptist Association.
Gary Farley

Among the early settlers of were Baptist ministers from the Carolinas and Virginia. Most were farmers and planters. Soon they gathered congregations of Baptists into churches. Apparently, the first of these was Enon (now Aliceville First) in the Garden community. This was is 1823. The next was South Carolina (now Ethelsville) in Yorkville. done by ministers who Among the pioneer preachers were Charles Stewart, Richard Wilkins, William Manning, W. R. Stansel, J. H. Taylor, M. P. Smith, M. C. Curry, J. C. Foster, Jacob Coker, T. S. Thomas, T. Willingham, E. B. Teague, W. W. Nash, Henry Petty, J. P. Taylor, and Ellis Gore. Each of these men did significant work within the first 30 years of life in Pickens County.

I have been able to find information about the origin, family and work of some of these men which I will share in the article. I hope that some of the readers will respond with additional information about those, and fresh information about the others, for whom I have not been able to find any information.

Charles Stewart–was the first pastor of Enon. He was also the founding pastor of Big Creek (1829). He lived in the Big Creek Community. He was born in Chatham county, North Carolina, August 27th, 1794, according to Nelson Smith who wrote a History of Pickens County in 1856. This was also the year of Elder Stewart's death as noted in minutes of the Union Baptist Association. Therein he was eulogized in these words. "Brother Stewart, as a Christian, ever adorned the Gospel of that blessed Saviour, whom he faithfully preached to others. As a Minster ever devoted to that cause our Heavenly Father had committed to his hands. As a Pastor, watchful over his flock, and universally beloved by the people of his charge. And as a Moderator and member of our Association, he was ever kind and courteous toward his brethren; and always acted with that dignity and spirit, which should ever characterize the true and faithful Minister of Jesus Christ. But that strong voice which so often cheered the hearts of his brethren is now hushed in death; and we are persuaded that no minister in the bound of our Association did more to promote the cause of our beloved that our departed brother."

Elder Stewart hosted the critical annual meeting in 1837 at Big Creek when the association divided over the mission question. On four occasions he served as moderator of the Union Association.

Stewart arrived in Pickens County in 1821 after a short stay the Tuscaloosa. He settled in the Big Creek community about half way between Carrollton and Pickensville. In addition to being a pastor and a planter, he was also active in politics. He served as tax collector for Pickens County in 1830 to 1834. This was followed by a term in the state House of Representatives.

Richard Wilkins–was closely tied to the Ebenezer, Fellowship, and Hebron churches as a founder. He was the first moderator of the association, and when the anti-board group walked out of the 1837 meeting, the association turned again to him to be moderator. He was elected in the following year to that post. Wilkins was buried at Hebron in 1848. His wife Nancy who died in 1858 is buried beside him. In the latter years of her life the association raised money to assist her with living expenses. And when she died the association paid for a stone to mark her grave.

The minutes of Ebenezer Baptist Church note his death. He is called the "pastor" of the church from its beginning in 1833, although the records show that other men preached there some of the years before his death. Of course, in that era it was not uncommon for a man to preach and have change of as many as four churches, serving them one weekend per month. He still has kins people in the Hebron Church.

William R. Stansel–was born in the Barnswell District of South Carolina, in 1792, the son of a minister. He lived in Georgia for a time and then settled in the Garden community of Pickens County in 1831. He was a friend of Col. Robert Jemison of Tuscaloosa. Stansel was a wealthy planter. In 1835 he became a preacher as well. In that same year, he served as clerk of the association. Soon he was pastoring Enon church. It prospered under his leadership. He was associational moderator in 1843 and 1844. Based on the circular letters that he wrote for the association, I have concluded that he was a well educated person. He died in 1860 and is buried in the Garden cemetery. The oldest of his 10 children, Martin Luther Stansel, became a lawyer and practiced for many years in the county.

William Manning–first appeared east of the Sipsey in the churches in Greene County. He later pastored the church at Pilgrim's Rest and continued as its pastor when it moved to the Spring Hill community in 1842. From the evidence of his writing in circular letters of the association, he was a well educated person. He moved west in 1845, as did others across the years. I know nothing of his family, his place of birth, or his place of death.

Jacob Coker–was the founding pastor of the South Carolina church. I assume that he was from that state. He passes from the scene early, and I have not been able to find out more about him.

J. H. Taylor–died in 1852. He pastored several of the churches in the 1830s and the 1840s. He passed through the period of controversy in the late1830s and seemed to an effective pastor. He was moderator of the association 1845-1848.

T. S. Thomas–was another early pastor. He also was a judge in Pickens County for a time shortly before his death in 1854. He, like Wilkins, was connected with Ebenezer. He and his wife sold land for the earlier location of the church. He pastored several other of the churches in Pickens and in Tuscaloosa Counties.

M. P. Smith–was born in Virginia. He helped constitute the Beulah church in Greene County in 1833. Later he pastored that church for 44 years. He also served as pastor of Bethel, Forest, and New Hope, all in the association. His memorial in the 1883 minutes of the association notes that he baptize 1,500 persons during his long ministry. He served the association as moderator on one occasion. He was 78 when he died.

J. C. Foster–came to the association when Grant's Creek Baptist Church joined in 1842. He died in 1892. Along the way he was a champion of missions, of evangelism of the slaves, and of Sunday Schools. He served 24 years as the moderator of the association. He pastored the Grant's Creek church for more than 40 years. His cousin, Martha Foster Crawford, was appointed by the SBC as a missionary to China in 1851. The Foster family also provided pastors and professors and leaders among Baptists in Tuscaloosa and Columbus.

W. W. Nash–lived in "Nashville, Alabama" along the Tombigbee near where it flowed out of Mississippi. The town is long gone. He pastored in our association and in the Columbus Association.

Henry Petty–pastored in the area in the 1820s and 1830s. He seems to have been controversial. He was a key actor in the division of the association in 1837. After that time he pastored Primitive churches, mostly in Greene County, it appears.

Ellis Gore–pastored at South Carolina and Mt. Moriah in the association in the 1830s and

1840s. Then he coverted to the Free Will Baptist tradition. He went to North Carolina to be reordained. Most of the Mt. Moriah church followed him out of the association. Some of the membership of South Carolina also followed him. He became the leader of the Free Will movement in Pickens and Tuscaloosa Counties. The Free Will association which serves these counties took the name of Mt. Moriah.

As you can see, to this point I have been able to find only scant material about most of these pioneer pastors. Others, I know nothing about at all. I hope that those who read this article will help me by sharing more information about them.

The Great Revival of 1838-39
G. Farley

In the fall of 1838 when the Union Association of United Baptists met for only its fourth annual meeting at the Unity Meeting House in the Olney community of Pickens County, Alabama, the churches reported only 585 members, a dramatic loss to just more than half of the total reported the previous year. Of these, 146 were newly baptized and transfers from other churches. Another 63 were members in the three new congregations which were joining the association. Altogether, the Union association had only 15 member churches, down from 21 at the previous meeting.

This loss of churches and members was the consequence of a controversy regarding the formation, activity, and financial support of mission boards and benevolence institutions. Its theological basis was the Calvinistic doctrines of predestination and sovereign grace. This controversy was spreading across the Baptist movement in America. In the1836 meeting of the association the issue was raised as to whether or not support of mission boards would be a "test" of fellowship; i.e., if a church contributed to a mission board, it could not be a member of the association. In 1837 a scant majority rejected this proposal.

Subsequently, the "anti-mission board" member churches withdrew from the association. They took the name Primitive Baptists. By this they were indicating their belief that they were maintaining the historic position of Baptists. Within this movement there seems to have been two primary streams--those who opposed any missionary, revival, or evangelistic effort (commonly referred to as "hardshell," "absolutists," or hyper-Calvinist); and those whose opposition was to forming extra-church agencies to hire and pay missionaries for their work (commonly referred to as "anti-board".)

There were some other issues as well--opposition to Sunday Schools, to financial support for pastors, to formal schooling of pastors, to innovations in music, and to abstinence from alcohol. From a present-day perspective it appears that the Primitive Baptists focused on "defending the traditional ways and doctrines" and the Missionary Baptists focused on carrying out the mandate of the Great Commission, Matthew 28:19-20. This is to say that the one tended to be reactive and the other proactive.

To further set the stage for learning about the great revival of 1838-1839, it is necessary to look at the statistics which indicate just what an impact this split in the Baptist movement had in this part of West Alabama. In 1837 the Union association had had19 churches in the central and southern portions of Pickens County and northern Greene, with an additional church in southwestern Tuscaloosa County and one more in Perry, for a total of 21. The aggregate membership stood at 1048. Only 12 of these 21 congregations sent messengers (or delegates) to the 1838 annual meeting. Not only was the association weakened in its count of churches, many of the churches that continued to be affiliated were greatly reduced in their membership. A total 154 persons had been dismissed or excluded from their membership. In sum, it appears that of the more than 1,000 members in the churches that comprised the association in 1837, only about 400 continued.

Perhaps the most hopeful sign for those remaining in the Union Association when they gathered in 1838 was that three new churches had come forward to join with them. One was Oak Ridge in Pickens County, apparently comprised of some of the former members of the Pilgrims

Rest church whose pastor, Henry Petty, had been a leader of the anti-board forces. (There may be some irony here in that Petty was among those who formed the Alabama State Baptist Convention in 1823; ironic in the sense that the convention was formed to support mission and benevolent causes.) A portion of the Pilgrims Rest church continued with that name in the Union Association. And a third portion, the anti-board group, also retained the name of Pilgrims Rest. It was led by Henry Petty, and it became the mother church of a Primitive Baptist association which took the name Pilgrims Rest.) The other two new congregations were Pleasant Ridge which probably came out of Serepta and Concord which probably came out of Rehobeth and subsequently became the Clinton Church. Both of these churches were in Greene County.

When the association met again in the fall of 1839, there was surely a season of great rejoicing and thanksgiving. The 15 churches had baptized 361 persons, the most every baptized in a single year in the Union or in its successor the Pickens Association. And 161 persons had transferred their membership to the churches in the association. The membership was swelled to 956. A new church was added, New Hope in Tuscaloosa County.

We wish that we had fuller records of what happened that year. What were the elements that went into this great revival in the churches? (Only one church did not baptize anyone. This was Friendship in Greene County. But in 1840 it reported 29 baptisms.)

* Prayer?

*Influx of new settlers? In the 1830s the population of Pickens County grew from 6,000 to 17,000 persons.

*Ten or more new churches were formed in the county during this decade to serve the new communities.

*Pastors and people who had committed themselves to missions and evangelism and lived out their commitment by being faithful witness? They took the Great Commission seriously.

* A blessing from God?

*All of these? Probably.

Imagine what it was like at the old Unity church which baptized 68, received another 11 by letter and ended the year with 105 total members. This figures out to be about four new members for every continuing one. Ebenezer received 38 new members for a total of only 48, or about the same ratio. Big Creek was the largest church then with 138 members, adding 38 of them that year. Liberty added 25 and grew to 38. Fellowship added 19 and grew to 57. Enon, now Aliceville, added 40 and grew to 90. Pilgrim's Rest which would become Springhill in 1842, added 17 to swell its membership to 42. And Oak Ridge, north of Pickensville near where route 14 now crosses into Mississippi, gained 21 for a total of 37 members. In sum, the aggregate gain was 80 percent in membership. One must conclude that the old ministers like Charles Stewart, Richard Wilkins, J. H. Taylor, W. R. Stansel, T. Willingham, M. P. Smith, T. S. Thomas (who lost his pastorate at Salem and at Bethany as a result of the missions conflict), W. Manning, and W. W. Nash must have rejoiced and felt vindicated by this great revival.

God continued to bless the Union Association and its churches. In 1840 new churches Mt. Zion and Hopewell joined the association. Mt. Zion seems to have been the missionary element from the Bethany church. It closed in 1898, but an African American Baptist church, Union Valley, continues to worship in its old building. The other was named Hopewell. It listed King's Store as its post office. So, it must have been in the Benevola community. The total membership in the churches of the association had grown to 1,090, more than had been members before the split.

The following year the South Carolina church, now Ethelsville, and the Hebron church joined the association. Hebron was a new church north of Carrollton. South Carolina was an older church, formed in 1824. It joined from the Columbus Association. Prudently, given the fact that some members of the churches were not strongly in favor of missions, the association decided rather than to support mission efforts in West Alabama directly it would set up a society to support mission work that would be an auxiliary to the association.

In 1842 the Grants Creek Church from Tuscaloosa County joined the Union Association. It came from the old Cahaba Association which had tilted toward the anti-missions side. This church was one of the oldest churches in West Alabama. It had operated a Sunday School since 1828 when it was founded. It had ordained Thomas Banes, the great-grandfather of President Lyndon Banes Johnson. It was also the home church of the Foster family. John Collier Foster came to the association with a missions agenda. He promoted Sunday Schools. He lead the association into affiliation with the state convention and later with the Southern Baptist Convention when it formed in 1845. He promoted the planting of new churches within the bounds of the association. And he promoted evangelism and Bible study among the slave population. Across the next 40 years he served 24 as the moderator of the Union Association. And in 1851 his kinsperson, Martha Foster Crawford was appointed by the Southern Baptist Foreign Mission Board as a missionary to China. She served there until 1909. In 1845, when the Union Association, (today Pickens), celebrated its tenth anniversary, it had 24 congregations in the fellowship with a total membership of 1,472 persons. Four of the churches were in Greene, four in Tuscaloosa, and 16 in Pickens County. There were several other missionary Baptist churches in northern Pickens county at this time--Providence, Mt. Tabor, Zion, and, perhaps Salem, just north of today's New Salem. But most of these churches were members of the Tuscaloosa association.

At the end of the decade of the 1840s it would hive off most of the Greene County churches to a new association being formed over there, and issues related to the freedom of one's will and the involvement of a person in the process of salvation would become an issue in some of the churches. Long time pastor Ellis Gore and the Mt. Moriah church would be the well-spring of the Free Will Baptist movement in West Alabama.

The anti-mission board Baptist churches here formed an association of their own in 1837. It seems to have begun with ten churches and nearly 600 members. Across the years these numbers declined. The last records that I have been able to find date from the 1930s. Then there were but four Primitive Baptist churches in the association, including one in Tuscaloosa County, and but a handful a members.

In the history of the Union/Pickens Association there have been other blessed seasons of revival and harvesting of the saved. Some have impacted one or just a few churches at a time. Others, like the revival of 1838-1839 spread across the association. Many of us pray for such a time today. I want to look at other seasons of revival in subsequent articles. If you have information about the early churches and/or their pastors, please share it with us. And I mention several pioneer pastors. Where did they come from? Where did they live? Where are they buried?

Historical Sketches of 8 Pickens County Baptist Churches from 1840.
Gary Farley

Hosea Holcombe asked the Baptist associations and churches of Alabama to provide him with historical sketches. This was in 1839 and the following year, they published the material under the title, *The Rise and Progress of the Baptists in Alabama.* In previous articles I have drawn upon this book to write about the founding of the Buttehatcha, Cahawba, Union and Pilgrim's Rest Baptist Association. In this article I want to quote what Holcombe wrote about eight of the early churches of Pickens county. I will record what he wrote and then in parentheses add explanations from data that was not available to him. Some of the language you will find to be quaint. And the reader must remember that Holcombe was active in the conflicts that divided the Baptist movement at this time. Here goes.

"*Enon,* is amongst the oldest churches in Pickens county--was constituted in August 1823, by Lemuel Prewit and Henry Petty. (This was in the Garden community north of Aliceville. This congregation is now Aliceville First Baptist.) Elder Charles Stewart, was a constituent member, and on the Saturday following, was unanimously called to the pastorship, and served them about ten years. In January 1828, Silas Dobbs was ordained to the ministry; and in 1833, Elder H. Petty was chosen pastor. The church was involved in contention and difficulties for some time, occasioned by several ministers who sought superiority and pre-eminence. Mr. Petty served them about a year and a-half; then Mr. W. R. Stansel was called to take charge of them; and in 1836, John H. Taylor was chosen pastor. The next year, they had W. H. Cook, who divided the church. Then they called again their first pastor, C. Stewart; but before the yeare ended, they recalled Mr. Taylor, who still serves them. (Given the cast of characters, I suspect that the issue concerning supporting mission societies and other benevolence societies was a major factor. Petty and Cook opposed the mission societies and Steward, Stansel and Taylor were supportive.) There were, as the reader will believe, some restless members in his church, who caused disputing and wrangling; but they are now doing well under the vigilant care of Mr. Taylor/ the last two years have been gracious seasons, nearly 50 have been baptized. Their present number is 90; it has been the mother of several other churches."

"*Big Creek,* is in Pickens county, and was organized January 1829; Elder C. Stewart who was instrumental in raising it up, was chosen pastor, and has served them acceptably ever since. This is the largest church in the Association. They have had many precious seasons. In 1832, '5 '6 '8 and '9 they experience revivals and between 200 and 300 were added. They licensed two young men to preach, visit: Coker Lisenbee, and Samuel Adair. This church has had no wrangling, nor perverse disputings about Gospel missions; it has remained firm, and has, we believe, been the mother of four or more churches." (This church no longer exists. It was located on Big Creek, just north of state route 86. I am told that it was weakened when a church was planted at Carrollton. Then when Pleasant Hill was formed most of the remaining members moved there. It closed during the 1930s. The association placed a monument at its old location.)

"*Forest,* was constituted in 1835, with 22 members, by J. P. Taylor, W. R. Stansel, and R. Wilkins; Mr. Taylor was called to their pastoral care--the next year John H. Taylor was called who serves them at present. (Forest is in the Benevola community. The first Taylor was part of the anti-mission board, or Primitive, movement. The latter was for missions. I do not know if they were related.) In 1837, about a dozen members were excluded, who went off from the church on account of the mission subject. They have prospered considerably for the last two years. Mr. D. D. Patterson is a licentate among them; their present number is 63."

"*Liberty,* was constituted in May 1834, by R. Wilkins and S. Dobbs; the former took charge of the church and served them about two years; then S. McGowen ministered to them for a short period; nd in 1838, Mr. C. Stewart was called to the care of them–they have since enjoyed a precious season. (Liberty is west of Reform out the old road, pre-US 82, from Tuscaloosa to Columbus.)"

"*Fellowship,* was raised principally by the labours of Elder R. Wilkins, and was established in church order, in Aug. 1833, Mr. W. was chose pastor; in 1839, Elder T. S. Thomas took charge of them. They have had pleasant times, and made considerable progress." (This church was initially in the Hargrove community. It continues on old US 82 east of Reform.)"

"*Ebenezer,* is about four miles south of Carrolton, organized in Sept. 1833; Mr. W. (Wilkins) serves them as pastor. Recently they have been prosperous; and the Lord has added many precious souls to their number. (This church continues to worship and serve to the present.)"

'*Pilgrim's Rest,*–There are now two churches bearing this name. The original was gathered by the labours of Mr. Petty, perhaps, in 1834.(Actually it was 1828.) The church divided on the mission subject, through the influence of the pastor, Mr. Petty, who has continually waged war against the cause....The other (church) is a member of this body (Union Association). It is now under the care of Wm. Manning; it is increasing in numbers, and we hope thriving in graces. Here are some members of real worth–thoroughgoing in the good cause of God. It may in truth, be said of them, "*thou holdest fast my name, and hast not denied my faith.*" (In 1842 the pro-missions church moved from the Pickensville area to Springhill Academy and became the Springhill Baptist Church. Holcombe continues by memorializing a slave preacher Job who died in 1835 while a member of the Pilgrim's Rest Church. Job began preaching in 1818 and moved with his owner, Mr. Davis, to Pickens County in 1833.) Few better preachers were found in Ala., in those days, than Job. He was generally loved and respected by all who knew him. He lived the christian, and died the Saint.'

"*Unity,* is about ten miles south of Carollton–it is an amiable church, and has prospered greatly. The brethren here, sit in heavenly places under the droppings of the sanctuary. The last year they received 68 by baptism; 105 is their present number. Here are some valuage members who are engaged to promote the cause of Christ, and advance his kingdom i the world. They have Mr. J. H. Taylor for their minister."(It was constituted in 1829. It continued down into the 1830s. The old cemetery can be found northeast of Aliceville near the New Salem Missionary Baptist Church. The sign at the cemetery has an image of the old church building which stood nearby.)

There were other missionary Baptist churches in Pickens County at that time which were not included in the association or in the sketches. Mt Tabor is still in the Palmetto community north of Reform. It was constituted in 1839, but joined the Tuscaloosa Association.

North of the Coalfire Creek were South Carolina, Bethlehem, Mt. Moriah, and Providence. South Carolina continues as Ethelsville, Bethlehem continues south of Millport , but Providence closed in 1890. That part of the county is now served by Hickory Grove. A Black Baptist Church continues at Providence. In 1850 the Mt. Moriah Church decided to become Free Will Baptist led by its pastor, Ellis Gore. Mt. Moriah became the "mother" church of the Free

Will movement in West Alabama. The Zion Church north of Gordo was constituted at this time also. It may have been comprised of the missionary supporting members of what is now the Primitive Baptist Mt. Zion in the northeast corner of Pickens County.

According to the records there were three additional missionary Baptist churches in Pickens County in 1839, Oak Ridge, Hopewell, and Mt. Zion . Oak Ridge was just inside the state line off of state route 14. It closed in the 1890s. Pine Grove now serves that area. Hopewell was an "arm" , or mission, of Ebenezer. It was in the Speed's Mill community. It never prospered. A cemetery by that name is listed on the county map. Mt. Zion was in the Bethany community. It was comprised of persons from the old Bethany church that went with the Primitives. It closed in the 1890s. For many years its building housed the Valley Union Missionary Baptist Church. We know of a church with the name of Antioch being in existence cira 1833 somewhere close to the current Fellowship Baptist Church. At that time Antioch sent out some members to form Fellowship as an arm. My best guess is that it was in the area where there is now an Antioch Cumberland Presbyterian Church, north of Cold Fire. My guess is that it closed just before 1939.

Further, Holcombe did not list several other congregations which had left the Union Association and become Primitive Baptist Congregation. In addition to Pilgrims Rest, which he does mention, there were another Providence, Bethany, Serepta,

In sum there were 17 missionary supporting Baptist Churches in Pickens County in 1840. Only eight continue, in some form, to the present. In 1840 the churches were located in the places where people had settled, other than in the town of Pickensville.

Catalogue of the Circular Letters
of the Union Baptist Association, 1838–
Gary Farley, compiler

Following the division between the Missionary and the Anti-mission Board Baptists at the annual meeting of the Union association of West Alabama in 1837, the association adopted a practice common among Baptist associations of publishing a circular letter every year. It dealt with some topic of theology. Its purpose was to inform the membership of the affiliated churches. Normally, it was authored by one of the pastors in the association. This task was assigned in each annual meeting, with the product to be read and approved the following year. It was then printed in the annual minutes and distributed to the churches in the hope that it would be widely read. The Union association followed this practice for more than 50 years. This desire to educate the members concerning Baptist theology was supplemented for many years by district meetings, and later by quarterly Sunday School Conferences where theological topics were discussed, sometimes debated.

While the language of these letters is dated, one must be impressed with the level of wisdom and the quality of written expression that are found in them. Apparently, many of the pastors of the churches in the Union Association were well read and well schooled in the arts of logic and in written communication.

It is my thinking that a catalogue of the topics dealt with in the circular letters should yield insight into what issues where of great significance to the Baptists in this area in those days. Certainly, the first letter, one that dealt with the Great Commission, supports this thesis. A key element in the division among the Baptists at that time had to do with the mission enterprise. The letter supports missionary efforts.

1838. Great Commission, Matt. 28:19-20. Notes that Baptists have been engaged in missionary efforts from our beginnings. W. Manning
1840. Christian Communion. Meaning, Practice, and Purpose of the Lord's Supper.
1841. Duties of Church Members. 1. Our social Circle. Care for one another. 2. Discipline. Church members 3. The world. Be missionary. W. Manning
1842. On Baptist View concerning Baptism–Meaning, Mode, and Subject. J. D. Knowles (Knowles was not a local pastor. The one assigned the task did not attend. So, this was substituted.)
1843. Prayer. T. S. Thomas
1844. Financial Support of Mission Agencies. J. H. Taylor
1845. Christian Piety. Affection of the heart toward God.
1846. Sanctification. Growth of the Christian in righteousness and holiness.
1847. The Obligation of Masters to Give Religious Instruction to their Slaves.
1848. Obligation of Read and Study the Bible. J. H. Taylor
1849. Obligation of Ministers to Give Full-time service to the ministry and of the churches to provide for their support. M. P. Smith
1850. Powers and Discipline of Churches and of the Association. Charles Stewart. (The issues in the Mt. Moriah church related to the adoption of the Free Will position by Pastor Ellis Gore probably motivated this very interesting letter.)

1851. The Duties and Office of Deacons. M. C. Curry. This is the first letter with the author's name at the beginning of the letter.
1852. Perseverance of the saints. C. B. Sanders.
(This letter was surely called for because of the controversy with the Free Will position in some of the churches.)
1853. Evil of Alcohol as a beverage. John A. Hodge
1854. No letter printed.
1855. The duty of the churches to seek out and encourage youth with the gifts for ministry. J. C. Foster. Includes a strong plea for persons to serve as foreign missionaries.
1856. "One Faith, One Lord, One Baptism." A. M. Hanks. He finds a mid path between the Sovereign Grace position of the Primitive Baptists and the human effort position of the Free Wills. Jesus provides for salvation of persons. But persons must respond.
1857. Doctrine of the Church and of Pastoral Authority. J. C. Foster.
Strong local church position. Rejects institutional authority over the local church. But has a place for the church universal. Mission emphasis..Church is involved in calling out the called. Finally, authority resides in the church under Christ.
1858. Slavery in the South. A. M. Hanks. Given the principles of biblical interpretation and logic of the day, this is a well written piece. Most today would find its justification of slavery to be wrong and in violation of the spirit of Christ. For some this has meant that traditional principles of interpretation and logic need to be re-thought.
1859. Sabbath School. John A. Hodges. Stresses its usefulness.
1860. No letter.
1861. Prayer.
1862. No letter.
1863. No letter
1864. The Importance of Ministerial Education. J. C. Foster. Strong support.
1865. The Doctrine of Election. J. W. Taylor. A strongly Calvinistic statement. Those who are holy are so because God chose them to be so.
1866. The Duty and Importance of Family Prayer. L. M. Stone.
1867. The Evils of Dancing. W. Ashcraft.
1868. The Duty of the Churches to Support their Pastors. J. H. Cason.
1869. The Duty of the Ministers to their Churches. J. W. Taylor
Full-time. Focus on Preaching. Enforce Discipline. Promote the Spiritual Good of the People of his church. Live a holy life. Pray for his people. Exercise care in leaving a church for another.
1870 No Letter.
1871. Importance of Uniformity among Baptist in Faith and Practice. W. Ashcraft.
1872. Theological Schools. J. C. Foster. In favor of.
1873. Scriptural Qualifications for Partaking of the Lord's Supper. W. G. Robertson
1874. Brotherly Love. R. T. Hanks.
1875. Temperance. S. Hildreth.
1876. Articles of Faith. #1 Trinity. J. C. Foster. For the next several years the circular letter discuss one of the 12 articles of faith under which the association was operating. It might be described as an evangelical Calvinist statement. It is similar to Primitives and many

points. But there is not cutting of responsibility of persons to respond to the message of the Gospel. The key is the role of the Holy Spirit in the salvation experience.

1877. Resurrection. J. H. Curry
1878. The Scriptures. R. A. Massey.
1879. The Fall of Man. L. M. Stone.
1880. Inability of Men to Save Themselves. W. G. Robertson
(Robertson was a layman in the Carrollton church and a leader in the Sunday School work of the association.)
1881. Covenant of Redemption and Salvation. J. H. Stinson.
(Stinson was a layman at Springhill.)
1882. Imputed Righteousness of Jesus for salvation. M. G. Lofton
(Lofton was a layman from Unity. He later becomes a preacher.)
1883. Role of the Holy Spirit in Salvation. J. C. Foster.
1884. Perseverance of the Saints. W. G. Robertson.
1885. Ordinances of Baptism and the Lord's Supper. J. H. Curry
1886. Ordinances are to be administered by regularly ordained ministers. H. B. Chapppelle.
1887. Should non-attendance at public worship be a test of fellowship? L. M. Stone
1888. No Letter
1889. Financial Support of Missions. J.H. Curry
1890. No letter
1891. Christian Benevolence. J. T. Smith

At this point this practice seems to have been concluded. The association's leadership of the past 50 years has moved off the scene with the passing of Foster and Hildreth. Curry is now pastoring in Tuscaloosa.

African American Associations with Congregations in Pickens County, Alabama.
Gary Farley

Across the northern part of Pickens County there are several congregations which cooperate with the Canaan Pickensville District Association. It celebrated its centennial is 1976 with a book detailing some of its history. Bro. Bobbie Lee Ellis of Gordo shared a copy with me. The following churches were listed as being among the founding congregations: New Hope, Shady Grove, New Grove, Infant, Pole Bridge, Christian Hope, Pleasant Hill and New Bethel.

In 1895 Dr. C. O. Boothe wrote that the association had grown by then to include 18 to 20 congregations. He noted that the association was centered in Fayette County.

In 2004 the following congregations are listed as being affiliated with the association:

Baptist Home, Reform
Christian Hope, Reform*
Ebenezer, Northport
First Missionary, Fayette
First Missionary, Gordo
Holly Grove, Millport
Infant, Carrollton*
Mt. Galilee, Northport
Mt. Nebo, Elrod
Mt. Olive, Millport
New Grove, Millport
New Home, Gordo
New Zion, Millport
Old Canaan, Fayette
Pole Bridge, Northport*
Providence, Ethelsville
Rocky Ridge, Reform
St. James, Sulligent
Zion Grove, Northport

(Note: I put a star by those churches which are on both lists.)

In the Centennial history one finds that Holly Grove and New Grove both came out of the Pleasant Grove church which is now in the Lamar Association. Providence probably came out of the Providence church in northwest Pickens following the Civil War.

Dr. O. L. Morgan of Millport has long been the moderator of this association. Eight of the churches are located in Pickens County.

Lebanon District serves most of the African American Baptist Churches in the central part of Pickens County. It dates from 1872 or 1874. In 1895 Dr. Boothe noted that the association's churches had about 2,000 members. I do not know the history of all of the churches, and I am not certain that this is a complete and accurate list.

Mt Calvary, Carrollton
Spring Hill, Pickensville
Pine Grove, Carrollton

First Baptist, Reform
Shady Grove, Aliceville
Cedar Grove, near Old Memphis
New Canaan, Aliceville
New Salem, Olney
New Providence, Carrollton
Elbethel, Ethelsville
Mt. Hebron, Aliceville
Mt. Pleasant, Carrollton
New Light, Reform
Halbert, Ethelsville
Salem, Carrollton
Good Hope, Aliceville
New Wright, Aliceville,
Union Valley, Aliceville

In December of 2007 the Lebanon Association published a history of its churches. It was edited by Geneva Brooks. It includes First Aliceville, St. John, Bigbee and Baptist Grove, also. It offers the histories of 23 congregations. Bro. Hugh Shambry is the moderator of the Lebanon Association.

Missing from this list are several other Missionary Baptist churches in Pickens whose associational affiliation is not known to me. Several of them may be in the Northbound Bethlehem association.

First Dancy, Dancy
Antioch, Dancy
Cluster, Dancy
Mt. Nebo, Aliceville

I believe that several of the churches in these three associations have their origin in bi-racial congregations after Emancipation. I know that Crossroads claims that Mt. Pleasant came out of it. It would seem to figure that the two Springhills have a common beginning. New Salem is probably connected to old Unity. And it is generally understood that Pine Grove came out of old Big Creek. And there are probably several congregations which were planted along the way but no longer continue.

Northbound Bethlehem has for its moderator Bro. Napoleon Jones. Bro. Bobby Lee Ellis is well connected there, I understand. Boothe lists 51 congregations in that association in 1895. I recall Bro. Ellis telling me that there are that many in Sumter County today, perhaps more. That association has a few churches in Pickens but the bulk of its churches are in Greene and Sumter.

Dr. Boothe writes in his book, *Cyclopedia of the Colored Baptists of Alabama,* that there were only three Missionary Baptist African American congregations in 1865. But 30 years later he could count about 800. What outstanding growth. Consider all of the pastoral leadership that emerged. Think of the struggle of getting meeting places and organizing churches. He quotes one of the founders of Bethlehem Association as saying that none of the founders were literate. The tradition of Canaan is similar. Certainly this was a "God thing".

Boothe lists the churches in Bethlehem Association by Post Office. New Providence is listed as being served by the Vienna Post Office. This may well be the African American congregation which came out of Providence in Warsaw following the Civil War. And it may be the source of First Baptist of Dancy. A second Post Office which would have served South Pickens County was at Sherman. Boothe lists Galilee, Antioch, Little Zion and Mt. Tabor. Warsaw served Mt. Pleasant and Union Grove. I have included in this material both the list of Boothe for Greene and Sumter as well as the lists of Bigbee and Union associations, wondering if there are some clues as to origins of African American churches in those counties as well.

It appears that currently there are 34 African American Missionary Baptist Churches located in Pickens County, Alabama. They are doing good work and having inspiring worship.

There are many good stories of mission endeavor as beginning with no congregations in 1865 to having grown to34 congregations presently. I wish that we could capture some of this story. Boothe provides some clues and some direction. Perhaps there are other bits of information which we might gather to expand the story. The new history of Lebanon is a good beginning.

Galilee Baptist Church, Panola, Alabama

Evangelism of the Slaves and Freedmen
Union Baptist Association 1835 to 1875
Gary Farley

Job was a slave, born in Africa and brought to America in 1806. He was sold to the Evans family. He learned to read and write, became a Christian in 1812 and then a minister of the Gospel. He moved with his owners to Alabama in the early 1820s and to Pickens County in 1833. He united with the Pilgrims Rest Baptist Church near Pickensville. He died in 1835. His wife died two years later. Elder Hosea Holcombe wrote that Job was greatly loved and highly regarded as a minister of the Gospel, well received in white, mixed and slave congregations.

Job is not mentioned in the minutes of the Union Baptist Association, probably because it was founded in the year of his death. Certainly in part due to his efforts there were slave members of the churches of this association from the earliest days of their existence. Beginning in 1845 one finds a series of resolutions adopted at the annual meetings of the Union association calling for the evangelization of the slaves, their instruction in the teachings of the Gospel and their inclusion in worship services of the churches. The following year the churches of the association begin to list in their statistical reports the number of slave (colored) members in their congregations. By 1855 25 of the 27 churches in the association reported slaves among their membership. In many of the churches half or more of the members were slaves. Grants Creek reported 105 of 212; Unity, 87 of 171; and Enon, 77 of 154. The numbers reported in the annual minutes of the Union Association are as following:

Date–Slave Members/ or Freedmen Members

1846	118	1847	363	1848	398	1849	510	1850	323*	1851	323
1852	377	1853	432	1854	441	1855	569	1856	636	1857	659
1858	631	1859	635	1860	603	1861	627	1862	640*	1863	681
1864	735	1865	783*	1866	682	1867	602	1868	329	1869	371
1870	298	1871	289	1872	189	1873	72	1874	54	1875	44

*The drop in membership in 1850 reflects the loss of four churches in Greene County to a newly formed Baptist association, Bigbee.
*The 1862 membership reflects the beginning of the Civil War. Note that the slave membership grew rapidly for the first decade and then leveled off. This may reflect the movement of planters and their slaves on west into Arkansas and Texas. It grew again during the war. This may reflect a spiritual concern related to the uncertainty of the period.
*In 1865 which marked the end of the war and the beginning of freedom, the numbers of African Americans in the churches of the Union (now Pickens) Baptist Association peaked. The white membership in that year was 1803. It also had grown. The Freedmen began to form churches of their own; some moved away; and the number of the Freedmen the churches of the Union Baptist Association dropped dramatically over the next decade.

During the period from 1835 to 1875 the annual meetings of the Union Association were much like a camp meeting. Great crowds of persons came, white and black. They began on Saturday with preaching and some associational business, Sunday was given to evangelistic preaching, worship, and upon the invitation of the host church the celebration of the Lord's Supper. Repeatedly in the reports found in the minutes of the association one finds that services would be held in the meeting house for the slaves and the white congregation met in an arbor outside. I do not know the reason for this, but I imagine it was because the meeting house might best accommodate the number of slave participants. Often the speaker of the hour for the gathering of the slaves was Elder Redmon Jones. After freedom came, a note found in the 1867 recommends to the emerging Black congregations Elder Jones as a minister and a counselor in maters related to church life. I imagine that he, like Job, was a respected African American preachers.

Any student of the Reconstruction period that followed the conclusion of the Civil War is aware of the tensions that were experienced in communities, in counties and in the state government of the states that had formed the Confederacy. One finds some glimpses of this in the minutes of the Union Association from 1866 to 1870. Resolutions speak of distrust between the races, of Yankee agitators, and of hard times. Initially, encouragement is offered for the churches to divide into white and black congregations, sharing a minister and a building. Apparently, this happened in the Big Creek Church. Its near neighbor, Pine Grove Baptist Church, dates its founding from 1868. The fact that Big Creek reported 33 Freedmen members in 1866 and only in 1868 seems to support this. Mt Zion went from 86 to 10 in the same period. Enon (now Aliceville First, but then in the Garden Community) went from 129 Freedmen in its membership to none. Providence went from 25 to 4. At Unity the 86 Freedman members have departed by 1872. In may instances churches led by Freedmen pastors were developed, which were separate from the old mother church. In some cases members of neighboring white and black churches have a continuing memory of their former relationship.

It would be an interesting study to learn as much as possible the historic connection between the white and the black Baptist churches in Pickens county from their old church records. Further, is would be a good study to look at the five or more communities where the church that existed in 1865 has died or moved and a Black Baptist Church remains. Today there are 30 to 40 African American Baptist Churches. Most of them are connected either to the Lebanon or the Canaan-Pickensville Association.

Interestingly, after 1870 the focus of the Union Association shifted to promoting Sunday Schools, in churches and in communities without churches. Undoubtedly, in specific communities the black and white Baptist churches continued to have relationships, but this was no longer a topic at the annual meetings of the Union Association.

In the 1970s and 1980s the successor of the Union Association, Pickens, returned to an interest in developing relationships with the African American Churches of the county. Associational Missionary, Oel Hendrix, worked cooperatively with the Black associations in the area for a major evangelistic crusade in 1976. Howard Extension courses were offered here to strengthen the leadership, pastoral and lay in the African American churches. This was a passion of Brother James Parnell of Stansel. And the men of the Pickens Association assisted those of the Lebanon Association in the construction of a District building near Carrollton.

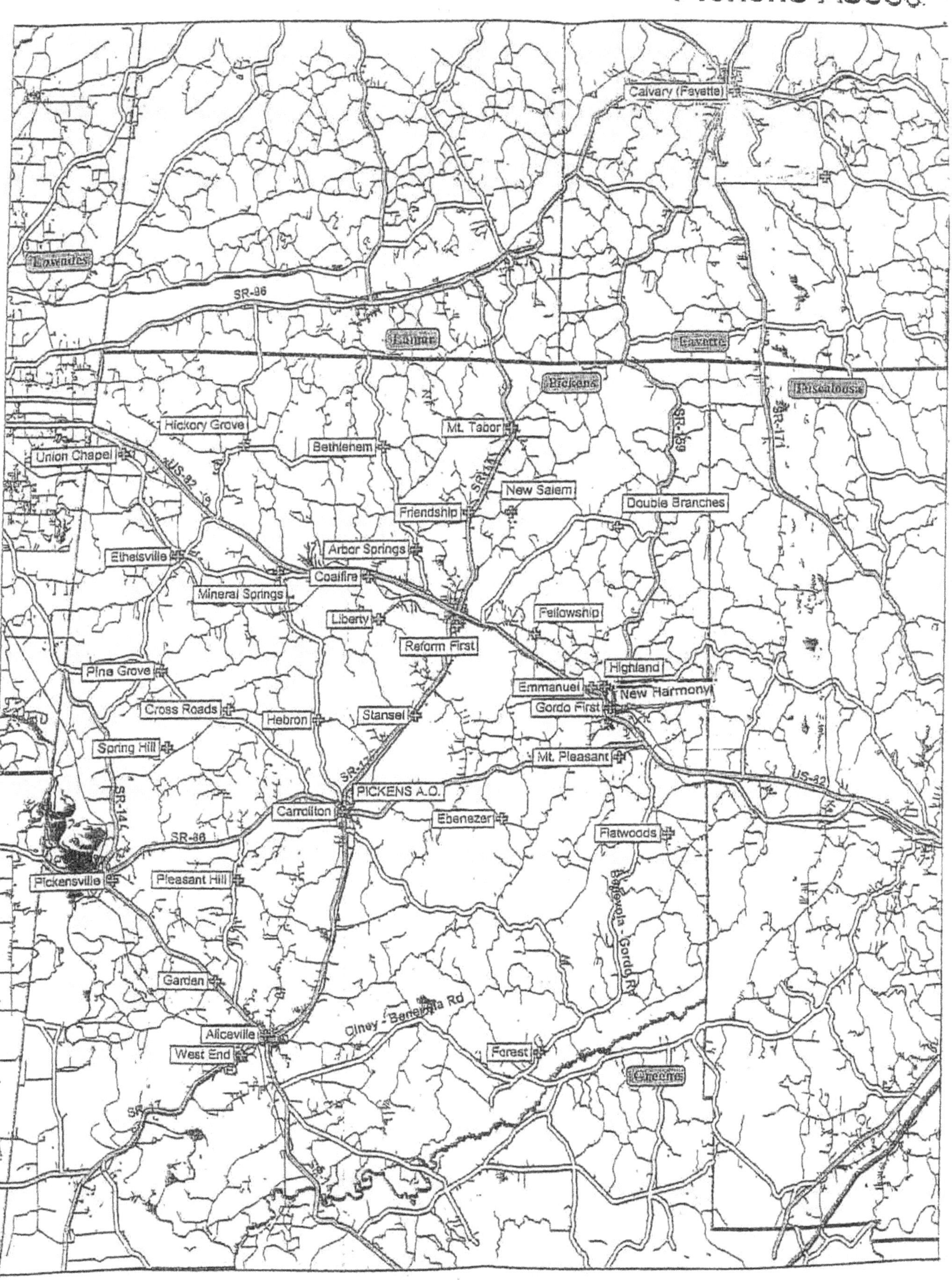

Calvary (Fayette)
Lowndes
SR-96
Lamar
Fayette
Pickens
Tuscaloosa
SR-159
SR-171
Hickory Grove
Mt. Tabor
Bethlehem
Union Chapel
US-82
New Salem
Double Branches
Friendship
Arbor Springs
Ethelsville
Coalfire
Mineral Springs
Fellowship
Liberty
Reform First
Highland
Pine Grove
Emmanuel
New Harmony
Gordo First
Cross Roads
Hebron
Stansel
Spring Hill
Mt. Pleasant
US-82
SR-14
PICKENS A.O.
Carrollton
Ebenezer
SR-86
Flatwoods
Pickensville
Pleasant Hill
Garden
Aliceville
West End
Forest
Greene

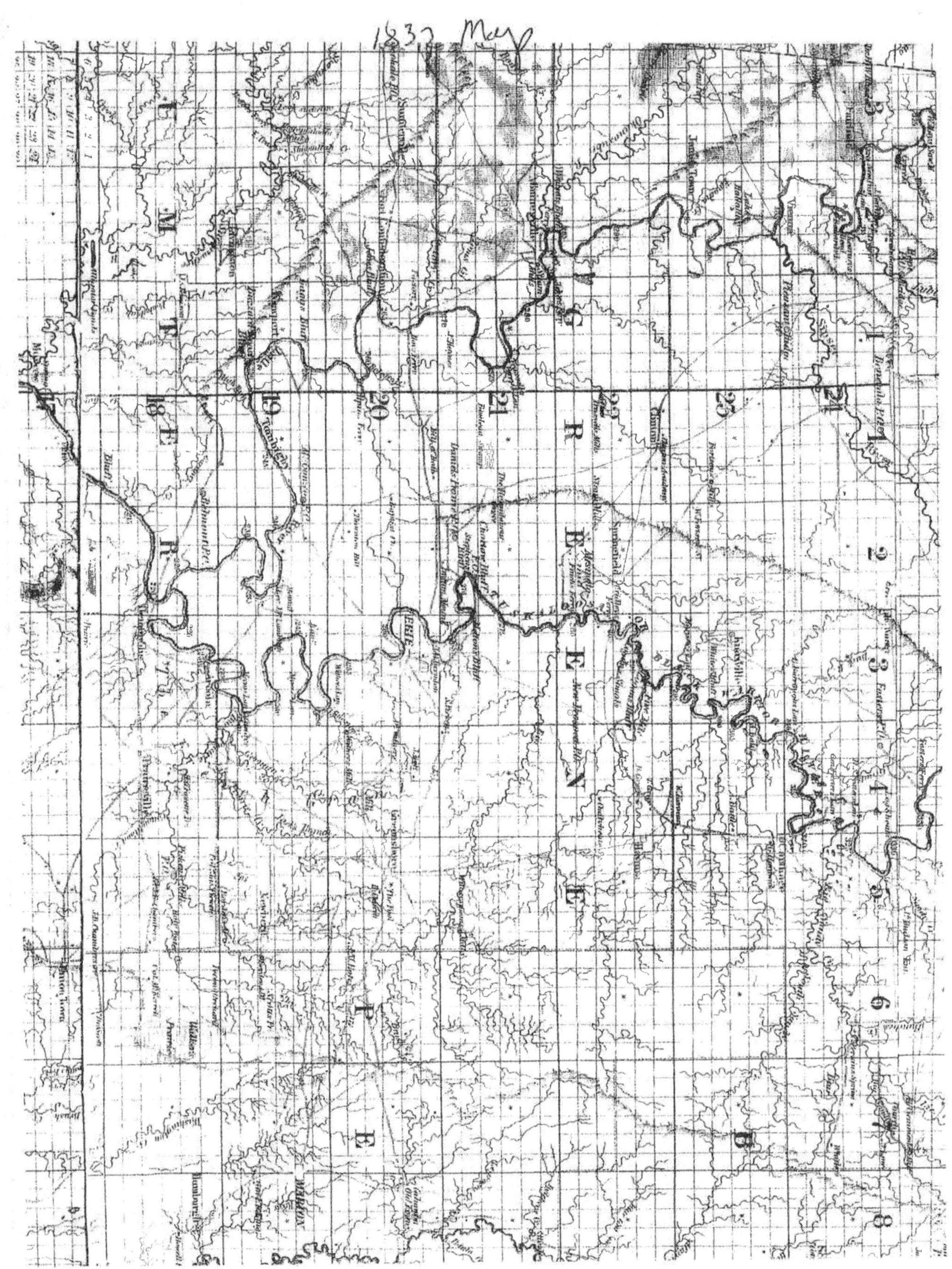

1837 Area Map

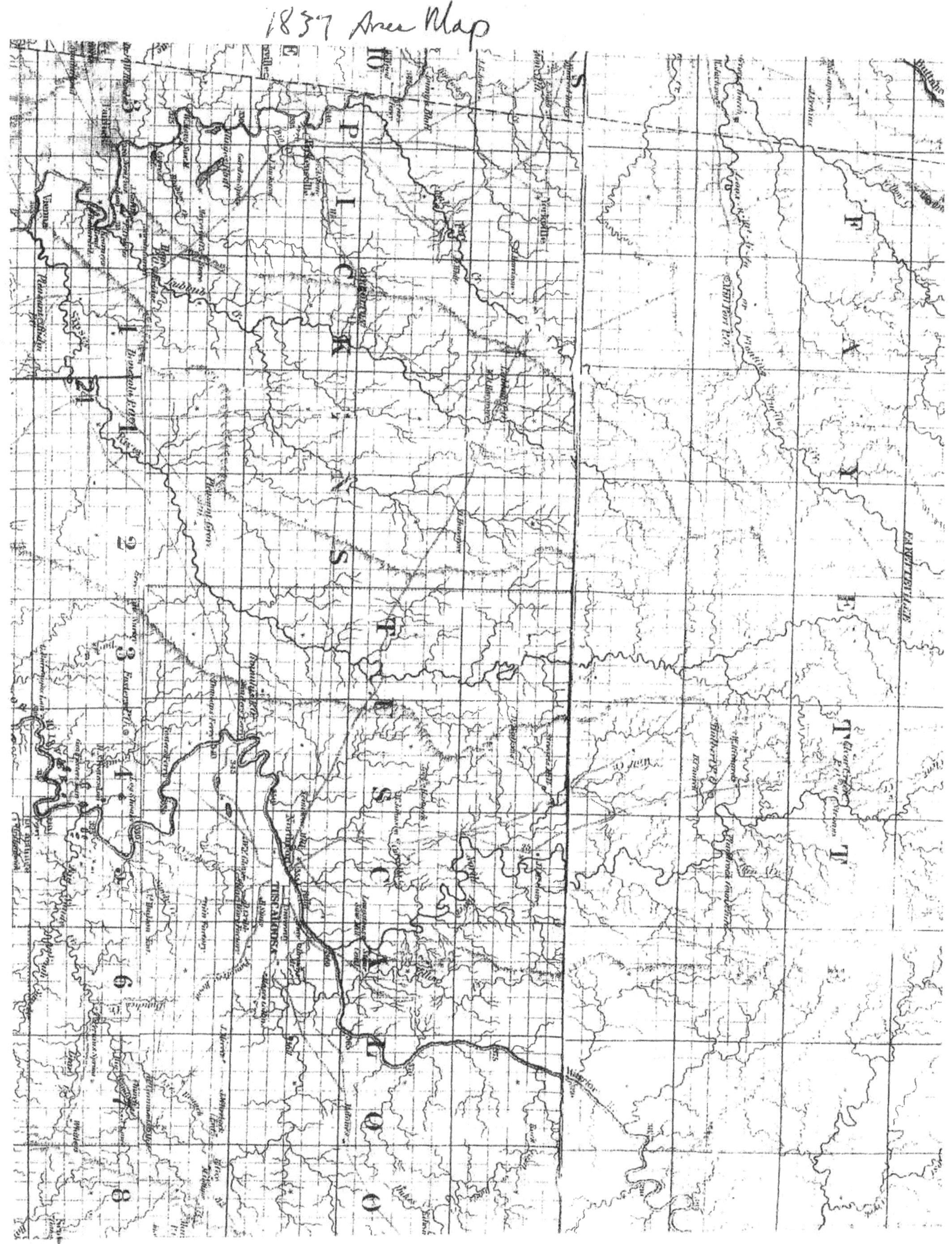

Gleanings from the Annual Minutes
Union Baptist Association. 1841-1875

Gary Farley

Here is Pickens County we are blessed with a complete set of minutes dating from 1835. In this article I will be picking up beginning in 1841 and taking note of the events reported in the associational minutes that seem to me to be of great local and historical significance on through 1875. (See annual of 2008 for material on events from 1834 to 1840.)

1841. South Carolina, now Ethelsville, joins from the Columbus Association. This church was constituted in 1824, and this is the second oldest in the asssociation.

1842. Grant's Creek, Tuscaloosa, joins from the Cahaba Association. This church continued for about 80 years in the association. Its pastor, Elder J.C. Foster was moderator of Union Association for 24 years. The missionary heritage of the association is closely tied to this man and this church. I wonder if Grant's Creek's decision to unite with Union was not an intentional effort by the pro-missionary forces in the state to solidify mission support in the Union Association. The Foster family also provided leadership at First Baptist of Tuscaloosa and in the Tuscaloosa Association.

Apparently, the Pilgrim's Rest Church that was pro-missions changes its name to Spring Hill in this year and relocates from the old Pilgrim Rest Building at mile marker 7 on route 14 to the Springhill Academy building, near its present location. Thomas Williams continues as a leader, there and in the association. He was a legislator and planter. This church continues as a member. (When the Primitive Baptists separated from Union Association about 1838, the pastor of Pilgrim's Rest, near Pickensville, was a leader of the anti-mission board sentiment. His church seems to have splintered into three, perhaps four, congregation. Initially, there seems to have been a Primitive and a Missionary Baptist Pilgrim's Rest Church. There was an Oak Ridge Missionary Baptist about four miles north and a little west of Pickensville. It was led by the Nash family. And in 1847 the Missionary Baptist started a church back in Pickensville.)

The first of many resolutions related to the support and usefulness of Sunday Schools is adopted. Education was a passion of the Fosters and the Grant's Creek church.

1843. Mt. Pleasant, a new congregation made up of mostly folk from South Carolina, is formed near Gordo and unites with the association. It continues as a member to the present. This calls for a shifting of district alignments. From almost its beginning the association had four districts which clustered the church in the north, south, east and west portions of the association which then included churches in Tuscaloosa and Greene, as well as Pickens Counties. (Later there were churches in Lamar, sand today in Fayette, and Sumter too.) This organizational structure continued for many years. Each district met in the summer, prior to the annual meeting. It was a meeting for Deacons and Pastors, primarily. It involved some training. (Note: apparently, the Lebanon Missionary Baptist Association continues this heritage with 5th Sunday Pastor and Deacon Union Meetings.)

A process is initiated this year that brings the association into active affiliation with the Alabama State Convention. It had moved slowly to do this due to some continuing "anti-boards" sensitment in some of the congregations. Soon, the association is sending messengers to it, as well as corresponding with neighboring associations–Columbus and Tuscaloosa on a regular basis. These three associations were the strong missionary oriented ones in this area. Ministers moved back and forth among them. This relationship continues to the present. (Recently, the Pickens Association assisted in the planting of the Eastwood church in Tuscaloosa County and worked with the Golden Triangle Association to provide a ministry for Hispanics in Aliceville and in Columbus. Calvary served as the mother church for Grace in Columbus.) Later the association will also send messengers to the Southern Baptist Convention

1844. Zion transfers from the Tuscaloosa Association. It was formed in 1838, perhaps as a result of the missions controversy.. Its address was Pleasant Grove. (In 1864 Mt. Pleasant, Zion and Corinth form a circuit with Elder A. A. Spiller as pastor of all three and the missionary for the association.) This church served the Zion community north of Gordo. It died about the time of World War II.

1845. Mt Moriah church joins from the Columbus Association. The pastor is Ellis Gore. It was near the modern-day village of McShan.

A resolution calling for the oral instruction in the Christian faith of the slaves is adopted.

Another resolution approves of the formation of the Southern Baptist Convention which had occurred earlier that year in Augusta, Georgia.

1846. Carrollton joins as a new church.

Again a resolution calls for active evangelization of the slaves.

1847. Three new churches join–Pickensville, Bridgeville and Salem. The locations of the first two continue to be known. My guess is that Salem may be the old church north of the current New Salem. Its messengers are named Yeatman, Drake, and Smiley. The pastor is a Perry. The post office address is Yorkville. Later Gore will be pastor.

1848. Arbor Springs joins. The messengers are T. S. Thomas, a pastor, a Trailer, and T. Deloach who will become a pastor, I believe. I think that this congregation is the predecessor the current Arbor Springs church. It dies about 1868 and then is revived in 1872, as New Arbor Springs. There is controversy about election and free will related to the North River Association, in Walker County involving Columbus and Tuscaloosa Associations. Union does not join in.

Salem becomes New Salem. It has 22 members. Gore is pastor.

1849. Providence church joins from Columbus Association. This church was near where Hickory Grove now is, about two miles west of the former village of Liberty. An African American Baptist Church named Providence still serves this area. It may well be the continuation of this church. Providence in the old Union Association closed in the 1890s.

Bethlehem which was formed in 1835 joins from the Tuscaloosa Association. It continues as a member of the association down to the present. (It and Forest will celebrate its 175th anniversary in 2010.)

Four Greene County churches, Friendship, Clinton, Eutaw and Pleasant Ridge left the association to help form a new association, Bigbee.

New Salem also withdraws from the association, probably because it has adopted the Free Will, or Arminian theology. Matthew Lyon, a printer, editor and lawyer, is ordained at Carrollton. He has a fruitful ministry in Alabama and Mississippi. His biography appears in the

1850. Ellis Gore has converted to the Free Will Baptist position. Mt. Moriah which he founded a few years earlier, pulls out of the association along with New Salem. This is the beginning of the Free Will movement in West Central Alabama. Mt. Moriah had 72 members and New Salem 25. The language referring to the division seems to be congenial. The Union Association leadership speaks of personal good will, although there are theological differences. The Free Will Baptist Association that serves our county is still called Mt. Moriah. And this church is seen as the "mother" church of the Free Will Baptist movement in this area.

1851. South Carolina (Ethelsville) excludes 37 members. This seems to be related to the Free Will doctrinal issue. Some charges regarding his theological perspective are brought concerning their pastor, Dabney Duncan, but he is successful in convincing the Union Association that he continues to be Calvinistic and a missionary Baptist. He is retained in the fellowship and provides good leadership for many years thereafter. Martha Crawford of Grant's Creek is appointed as a missionary to China. She will be the first of 21 as of 2010.

1852. The first of several statements supporting abstinence from alcohol is adopted. A lament is raised about the spiritual lukewarmness the churches and the hardness of the work.

1853. Memphis church asks to join Union but is told that it must first withdraw from its present membership in the Choctaw Association. This is accomplished in 1855.

Memorials for M. C. Curry and for T. Williams are printed.

1854. An offering for Martha Foster Crawford, missionary to China, is passed through the association from Grant's Creek to the Foreign Mission Board of the Southern Baptist Convention.

During these years well-known Baptist leaders such as Basil Manly, Sr. and Jr., Charles Manly, Daniel Bestor, George Washington Banes, and Russell Holman attend and speak at the annual meetings of the association.

1855. Mineral Springs church joins. This church was comprised of the Calvinistic members of the Mt. Moriah church. Also, $31 is collected to help finance the training of Charles Bain of the Buck Creek (later Bethel) church in Tuscaloosa County. He is attending Howard College. There is also mention of a gift of jewelry to be sold to support missions from students at the Spring Hill Academy. (I understand that it was located where the Spring Hill community center is now located. It was a two story building.)

1856. C. Bain returns from college to be hired as the missionary of the association. By now the association has an Executive Committee which hires and supervises a missionary who works within the association to plant new churches and to help needy churches as supply.

A book depository for the association is noted. A.M. Hanks of the Unity church manages it for the association. It sells religious books to ministers and others.

Note is take on the death of Elder Charles Stewart. He was one of the pioneer ministers and helped keep the association missionary during the controversy some 20 years before. He lived in the Big Creek community and pastored that church, as well as others. His home was the two story frame home still standing on route 86 to the west of the road to the site of Big Creek.

1857. Dr. D. O. Baird M.D. comes to the annual meeting as a fraternal messenger from the Columbus Association. For more than 50 years he will be one of the outstanding leaders of our association. By 1860 he has become pastor of Bethlehem. (He donates the land on which the present churchhouse stands.) He completes his ministry after 1901 as the founding pastor of Gordo First. He continues there until 1908 and dies the following year. Some years he would pastor six churches. He was also a physician.

Shiloh church in Greene County joins the association. It is now a member of the Tuscaloosa association. And Pleasant Ridge which had been a member, then joined Bigbee a couple of years before, and then returned to Union, now goes on back to Bigbee.

Only six of the churches report Sunday School work.

Money to assist the widow of Elder Richard Wilkins, another of the founding ministers, was raised. She was destitute. The Wilkins are buried at Hebron. When she died a year later, the association bought her tombstone.

Money is also given to help Elder J. N. Ackers replace his horse which had just died. Apparently, he had worn it out in his ministry.

A resolution asking for the churches to help Carrollton church pay the debt it had incurred in the building of its new church, is adopted.

Note is taken that the annual meeting is being held in the new meeting house of the Spring Hill church. This may help us date when the current building was constructed, ca. 1857. It along with Pickensville Methodist and Soule's Chapel Methodists is one of the oldest church buildings in Pickens County.

Memphis church disappears from the list. It may have joined another association, or it may have died. This is the only church that I am aware of south and west of the Tombigbee that was ever a member of the association, until the coming of Galilee in Panola.

Interestingly, there is a resolution favoring the publications of J. R. Graves. Graves had just launched the Landmark movement in Southern Baptist life. In subsequent years there will be resolutions supporting the publications of A. C. Dayton, a colleague of Graves, as well. At this point; however, I do not know of the Landmark issue becoming a divisive one in this association, however. (Landmarkism, among other things, was opposed to cooperation by Baptists with other Christians.)

Through out the 1850s missions offerings are taken at the annual meetings. They seem meager. Offerings for Domestic and Foreign Missions brought from the churches are also meager. Interestingly, the churches gave much better financial support to associational missions.

1858. The annual Circular Letter to the churches is a defense of the practice of slavery. Given its presuppositions about truth and how to interpret scripture, it is a well reasoned piece. A. M. Hanks was the principal author. Since 1838 the association has had one of its ministers write a letter dealing with some point of doctrine almost every year. This document was read to the association. If approved, it was printed in the minutes and sent to the churches with the hope that it would be read in each of them as well. (There is an article on this subject in the 2008 annual.)

Note that at this time the total membership in the churches of the Union Association is comparable to that of Tuscaloosa and Columbus Associations. Union had 26 churches and 2,058 members.

The association recommends G. M. Lyles as a potential missionary to the Indians. This did not happen. For many years he was a leading pastor in the association. The minutes seem to indicate that there was a strong interest in missions with the Indians in the association. Bigbee had its own missionary to the Indians.

1859. Apparently inspired by the efforts to assist Nancy Wilkins the association formed a Ministerial Aid Society. Money is raised to help retired ministers and their families.

1860. The state of religion report, which focuses on the association, again complains about the spiritual lukewarmness of the populous.

1861. Note is taken of the need and opportunity for evangelism within the Confederate Army.

1863. Elder W. H. Robinson, is commended to the domestic board as a potential missionary to the army. I do not think that this happened, but he continued for many years to be an effective pastor in Union and in Columbus associations.

1864. Corinth, a new church in Tuscaloosa County, now just across the line and off of US 82, joins. It along with Zion and Mt. Pleasant form a field of church with A. A. Spiller as pastor. Today this church is in the Tuscaloosa Association.

Memorial for Elder James Toole is published.

1865. Springhill, I think the one in Lamar, joins, although the minutes say Fayette. Very little mention is made in the minutes about the Civil War. But the church minutes often mention those who have died in the war and those who professed faith in Jesus while serving in the army. But in a recent publication *The Cruel War,* one finds the letter exchanged by Grant and Melinda Taylor members of Forest. Their everyday life struggles, prayers, and faith in God in a difficult time prove to be inspiring.

1866. Pleasant Grove, the one in Lamar, near the modern town of Millport, joins.

A resolution addresses tension between the white and former slave members in many of the churches. This is a recurring theme for the next several sessions of the association.

1867. Recommendation is made that the churches encourage the Freedmen members to form separate, but related congregations. Redmon Jones is recommended to the churches to assist in this and as pastor for these new congregations. It seems that the whites wanted to maintain as much control as they could of these new churches, however.

1869. Again discussion is held concerning the need to help the Freedmen create churches of their own. There seems to be some movement toward recognizing and encouraging their independency from the church of which they were formerly members.

Quarterly meetings of the Sunday School leaders is called for. This is initiated the following year at the Carrollton church. Sunday School becomes the passion of the association for the next several years. This is true across the country.

1870. Memorial for J. W. Taylor. He is a second generation pastor, and the author of several of the recent circular letters of the association.

1871. Money is provided for J. L. West to study for the ministry at Howard College. A few years later he offers to repay what the association had given to him, apparently because he felt led not to return to the association to do ministry. The association released him to go elsewhere and would not accept repayment.

1872. This is the first correspondence with the New River and the Yellow River Associations to the north. They served mostly Fayette and Lamar Counties. Also correspondence is renewed with the Choctaw Association which had churches in Sumter and Choctaw Counties as well as in Mississippi.

It is recommended to the churches of the association that they begin weekly prayer meetings. Someone has suggested that one of the fruits of the Civil War was in institution of prayer meetings in the churches.

1873. Very few of the Freedmen continue membership in the churches of the association. The association begins to send messengers to the Lebanon District Association which was comprised of the new Freedmen congregations. Richard T. Hanks is pastor at Pickensville. He will become pastor of FBC Dallas, Texas and editor of the Baptist Standard of Texas. New Arbor Springs church comes into the association. This appears to be a restart.

1874. Sunday schools are reported at Carrollton, Pickensville, Corinth, Zion, Forest, Ebenezer, Forest, Grant's Creek, and Hall's School (near Gordo). This number will grow over the next decade.

1875. Chalcedony church joins. It is in Tuscaloosa County. It had a difficult life. I believe that it may continue but as a Independent Baptist church.

Note is taken of the death of John L. Foster, deacon at Grant's Creek and the father of Martha Foster Crawford, missionary to China. The 30 churches of the association reported 1,538 members. Forty-four of these were Freedmen.

This concludes a summary of the minutes of the first 40 years of the Union Baptist Association. Its territory had changed, somewhat. Most of the churches in Greene County were gone. Several churches north of Coldfire Creek had joined it from Columbus and Tuscaloosa Associations. A couple of the churches were located in what is now south Lamar, and six were in Tuscaloosa. It had weathered three losses of churches to what became other segments of the Baptist movement--Primitive, Free Will, and African American. It had planted new congregations in the areas where they had lost churches and where population had grown. At this point only the churches in Carrollton and Pickensville might be considered town churches. The others were in the open country, or nearby a hamlet. It is obvious that the churches were small, averaging only about 50 active members each. Many pastors served multiple congregations. Most of the member churches met only one weekend per month. They would meet on a set Saturday afternoon to conduct church business. Often a major concern would be the resolution of problems that separated the church members. There would be a worship service that evening. They again on Sunday there would be another worship service. The meeting houses at Spring Hill and Ebenezer are arranged much like those of this period were. The next fifty years will see many additional changes.

Gleanings from the Annual Minutes
Union (Pickens) Baptist Assocition
1876-1925

In the first 40 years of the association, as you have read in the companion articles, the association was formed, went through several times of crisis and adjustment—missions controversy, freewill defection, loss of the freedmen, the Civil War and Reconstruction--prospered and grew stronger and more effective. In this article we will glean from the minutes for the next 50 years and the point where the association changes its name and adjusts its boundaries, to comply with the wishes of denominational leadership.

As we look at the minutes we will see that Sunday School became a major focus of the association following the Civil War on through the end of the century. Just before the end of the 19th Century railroads began to build through the association. This resulted in the formation of several new towns. Consequently, church planting became a major focus of the association. Leadership in the association was provided by a set of pastors and laypersons who proved to be good leaders. The association appears to have been cooperative with the state and national conventions. Often the association would elect delegates to the Southern Baptist and the Alabama Baptist Conventions. And for the most part it experienced good relationships with neighboring associations.

During much of this period the association met over a weekend in the Fall with business on a Saturday, worship on Sunday, and more business on Monday.

1877. Prairie, now West Greene, came into the association. Among the charter members were Grant and Melinda Taylor whose letters to one another during the Civil War were recently published as *The Cruel War*. The publications of J. R. Graves are commended by the documents committee. However, I did not see any indication that Landmarkism, a movement with which Graves is identified, ever had a following in the association.

1878. Received the Antioch church from Pickens. It is called a new church. It's clerk was a Bridges and the address Carrollton. Perhaps it was in the Union Chapel community south of Carrollton.. (There had been a congregation called Antioch in the 1830s, but it was never a member of the association and seems to have faded from the scene. And there is a continuing Antioch community northwest of Reform.) The new Antioch which joined in 1879 was dropped from the association in 1887. So, it did not prosper.

1879. Interestingly, the association resolves to assist Elder J. G. Thornton in getting his education either at Howard College, or at Southern Seminary. Note is taken of the death of Elder Dabney Duncan. He had pastored in the association for about 30 years. He is buried at Cross Roads. E. T. Winkler, president of the Home Mission Board of the SBC, as was often the case, had come from Marion to attend the annual meeting.

1880. Funds are raised to help with the education of V. W. Barnett and of J. J. Taylor at Howard College. Barnett, the minutes of 1883 note, died quite young. Taylor served for more than 30 years as a missionary in Brazil. Through the years the association provided those called into the ministry with funds for college and for books. Taylor made a great contribution to missions in Brazil. He served as writer and editor of Sunday School materials. He also translated books which were used to train the native men for preaching. He was the son of Grant and

Melina Taylor.

Temple Hill church of Temple Post Office was added to the association this year. It was dropped in 1887. This may have been near Flatwoods, perhaps a logging town. The association continued to send representatives to the Lebanon Association which included many of the new Freedmen congregations in the area. L. M. Stone, Jr., noted educator and college president in the area, as well as pastor, continued to participate in the annual meetings. (See the historical monument at his home in Carrollton.)

1881. Relationships with the Bigbee association were restored. There had been an earlier controversy over a church there receiving into membership a person who had been excommunicated by one of the Union churches. The McBee Creek church became a member of the association. The church at Providence is dropped. This was near today's Hickory Grove. A Missionary Baptist Church continues to thrive at Providence.

1882. In the Sabbath Schools report a call for each congregation to worship every Sunday was issued. It would be many decades before this goal would be approached.

1883. Flatwoods moves into membership with the association. MP Smith, a pioneer pastor in Greene County died. Temperance seems to be rising as a major concern along with the promoting of Sunday Schools.

1885. The fiftieth annual session was held at Hebron. Sardine Hildreth served as moderator. He replaces long-time moderator J.C. Foster of Grant's Creek. Hix Chappelle served as clerk. All three of these men served the churches and the association for many years. The Kennedy Baptist Church petitioned the association for membership. This is a church that G. M. Lyles, in cooperation with the association and the state convention, had played a role in forming. Kennedy was a new town on a new railroad line across south Lamar County. Interestingly, the report of the Foreign Mission Board lists for the Tungchow station in China as missionaries T. P. Crawford, Martha Crawford, Mrs. S. J. Holmes, Miss Lottie Moon, the Joiners and the Devaults. Martha Crawford was from the association, and a cousin of retiring moderator, J. C. Foster. (Note Lottie Moon was mentored in mission work by our Martha Foster Crawford. Read Wayne Flynt's *They Carried the Gospel to China.*)

1886. Added the Nazareth church in Tuscaloosa County. Apparently, it did not prosper and closed in a few years.

1887. The new church at Millport becomes a member. Note is taken of the death of G. M. Lyles another of the 2nd generation of pastors in the association. He is buried at Mineral Springs. The report of the Sunday School convention noted that there were 34 schools operating with more than 1,500 enrolled. There were several of these schools which were not in constituted churches. My guess is that they were meeting in public school building and community centers. Also I noted that some of these later became churches; eg, Pleasant Hill and Coalfire. There was also a branch SS in Jena down by Fosters. In the 80s and the 90s several outreach Sunday Schools appear on the annual lists. Then, and now, outreach Bible study is a strategy for evangelism and church planting.

1888. I believe that this is the first time when a female was seated among the messengers from the churches, Miss Lillie Hildreth. She was from Pickensville. The moderator of the association, Elder Sardine Hildreth, was from the same church and probably a near relative.. This was the year that the WMU Auxiliary to the SBC was formed. Bethlehem was the host of the meeting in this year.

New Salem petitioned to become a member of the association. It was located north of

Reform in the building which had housed Salem in 1850, a congregation which then became Free Will. Ole Hendrix thought that this was a restart of the Salem church which dated from 1847 . And Mike Hall tells me that some of the old Salem building was moved to Friendship to be used in its building there. At that point the name was changed.

The list of Sunday Schools for this year reports five which are not attached to one of the member churches,Vandever, Oak Grove, Sylvan, Pleasant Hill, and Coalfire. Note that in years to come the latter two would grow into churches.

1890. The association voted to ask the churches to take up a special offering in December to benefit "our Foreign Missionary, Miss Mary J. Thornton." Ms Thornton was from the Bethel Church in Tuscaloosa County. She had been appointed two years earlier to the China mission. In 2011 we plan to do an appendix which will feature the tales of the foreign missionaries from our association.

Corinth and Flatwoods asked to be allowed to join the newly forming association of Sipsey. This was approved. Flatwoods returned to the association in 1896. The list of Sunday Schools included Pine Grove. In 1908 a new church would come out of this effort. Schools were also at Olney and at Port Oak.

1891. A letter from Martha Foster Crawford and Mary Jane Thornton, Baptist missionaries from the association to China, was read at the meeting. They chide Baptists for not sending more missionaries. And they ask "adopt and support some family already on the field or one that will be forth-coming: if not a family, then a single missionary. Can not the 2166 Baptists of your Association do this? Let this question be put to the various churches composing your body for action next year, the centennial of modern Baptist missions. We come not asking for money to build church-houses, support schools, employ native preachers and Bible women, all of which we consider to be the work of the people when converted, but we come asking you to send us more men and women to go from house to house, village to village, city to city preaching Christ to lost and dying men. Shall we not heed our Savior's command and give the gospel to every creature? May God's richest blessings rest and abide with you."

The association responded positively and set up a support fund named for Mary Jane Thornton. They called for $600. At the date of the publication of the minutes only $42.40 had been received. This is not addressed the following year. But in 1892 the Crawfords, Ms. Thornton and others resigned from the FMB/SBC and formed the Gospel Mission group. It was informed by Landmark theology. It contended that missionaries ought to dress and live like the natives; they ought to be supported directly by churches and/or associations, and that native workers should not be paid by a mission board, but rather raise their own support. The famous Lottie Moon agreed with some of their points, particularly those related to dress and living arrangements, but did not reject the concept of support being raised by national mission boards.

1892. The Pleasant Grove church from near Gordo petitioned the association for membership. It is now the New Harmony church in Gordo. The deaths of two of the former moderators and associational leaders, John C. Foster of Grant's Creek and Sardine Hildreth of Pickensville were noted in the minutes.

1893. G. W. Kerr, who would serve many of the churches for decades to come, begins receiving some financial assistance so that he can attend Kennedy High School. Later he is helped to attend Howard College. His home was at Fellowship.

1894. The association continues to send and receive fraternal messengers to Lebanon Association. Consideration was given to starting a local preparatory school. But in 1896 the association decides, that given the financial situation in the country, this is not a good time to attempt it.

1895. Hickory Grove petitions for membership. It seems to be replacing the church at Providence which had closed a few years earlier. Flat Woods which had moved to the Sipsey Association when it was formed, asks to return. This is accomplished the following year.

1896. The association votes to seat two Duncan ladies as messengers from the McBee church. Cornelius Chapel becomes affiliated with the association. It continues near Buhl and is in the Tuscaloosa Association. Money was raised to assist W L. White, a local pastor, to attend seminary and for J. D. Ray to continue his education. Temperance seems to be a growing concern.

1897. Among the contributions was one from Bethel for the Sister Bostick Education Fund. Mary Jane Thornton who had gone to China as a missionary nine years earlier. She had married widowed missionary G. P. Bostick in 1893. Like many of the missionaries of that era she died on the field in 1903. Bethel was her home church. It continues in the Tuscaloosa Association. Union Center which becomes Stansel church becomes a part of the association. We are exploring the possibility that George Bostick was kin to General Bostick of Pickens, a founding member of Carrollton Baptist Church.

1898. Note is made of the building of a railroad line across the county which would link Columbus and Tuscaloosa. Called upon the state convention for assistance in planting new congregations. Note is made of the death of M.G. Lofton, age 57, one of the pastors.

1899. New churches at Reform and Ethelsville are listed. The old South Carolina church had moved to the new town of Ethelsville on the railroad line. J. W. Caldwell planted the church at Reform and G.W. Kerr revived and moved the South Carolina church to Ethelsville. The Executive Committee asked that a new congregation be formed in the new town of Gordo. Interestingly, the fact that the Methodists and the Presbyterians were seeking to plant churches in Gordo was seen as a motivation for the Baptist to move on this opportunity. D. O. Baird preached the missionary sermon that year. And soon he became the planter of the new congregation in Gordo.

A letter from Martha Crawford and Mary Thornton Bostic, missionaries to China, was read and replied to by the association. And the Baptist Young People's Union is noted by a reference to one being started in the Masonic Hall in Sylvan, Alabama for the Grant's Creek and Bethel churches. I find it interesting that neighboring congregations were cooperating in this way. Note is made of the death of pastor J. B. Small. He had come to the area in 1890. An investigation reports that it appeared that the Oak Ridge and the McBee Creek churches had disbanded. Also in this year reports from the WMU are begun at the annual meetings, although in the early years the reports are read by one of the pastors, women not being invited to speak to the meeting. The WMU in the association was headed by Mrs. S. A. Robertson, wife of the moderator, who in turn was the driving force behind the Sunday School movement for many decades.

1900. The 20th Century opened with 34 active churches and 2 inactive with a total of 2338 members in our churches. Four of the churches were in Lamar County, three in Greene and five in Tuscaloosa. At this point Union is similar in size and membership to Tuscaloosa and Columbus Associations. And while we continue to grow well in the next century our population remains at about the same level. The other associations grow much more, but this is triggered by growing population. In fact, a higher percent of the people in the bounds of our association are now members of our churches than in 1900. This is not true for our neighboring associations.

1901. New churches at Gordo and Union Chapel are accepted into the association.

1902. Note is taken of the death of pastor J. H. Curry. (A stained glass window which honors him from the Northport church can be found today at our Hebron church .). His son, M. B. Curry became an attorney and was moderator of the association for many years and its historian. Pastors Calvin Upchurch and J. W. Caldwell are also memorialized. Caldwell had served as a missionary in the association.

1903. Union Center changes its name to Stansel. The association helps J. M. Mills with his education. He will become a leader in the association for many years.

1904. The association is asked to help with the cost of constructing a church house in the new town of Aliceville. The Enon congregation will relocate there. (Note: the decision by our forefathers to relocate two churches and start two new ones in the emerging railroad service towns in Pickens County made a great difference in the life of the Baptist movement here. I am thankful that these men had a mission vision.)

1905. Fort Springs church, Fernbank, was accepted into the association. (This church was located about two miles north of Fernbank. It has long since died and was probably replaced by the current Fernbank church. Back in these days the association appointed messengers to the SBC and the State Convention. Often it was Dr. Baird, or M. B. Curry, or W.G. Robertson. I do not know from the minutes how often they were able to attend. Memorialized this year was Hix Chappell. He was clerk of the association for more than 20 years and a pastor of several of the churches.

1906. It seems that the practice of having a Sunday School convention has fallen away. But the meetings by districts (4) of the churches prior to the annual meeting continued.

1907. Friendship is added to the association. It replaces the New Salem church which in turn replaced the Salem church north of Reform. In the report on foreign missions note is made of the fact that Martha Foster Crawford from the Grant Creek Church had served in China for 55 years. And although she was no longer connected with the FMB of the SBC, the association was proud of her. The report was made by L. S. Foster, her kinsperson. Interestingly, Ms. Addie Cox first appears in this same set of minutes. She has replaced Mrs. Robertson as the WMU leader for the association. She was only 22. In 1918 she was appointed as a missionary to China. (Martha Foster Crawford had died there in 1909.) Addie served there for more than 30 years, until the Communists drove her out. Then she served on in Formosa.

1908. No newsworthy components.

1909. The association honored their long-time moderator, W. G. Robertson with a silver loving cup. Pine Grove is accepted into the association. It is represented by Ms. Cora Moore, who is seated. She is the first women messenger for several years.

1910. Continue to stress the importance of Sunday School. M. B. Curry suggests that someone in the association be given the title of Sunday School Secretary and promote its extension and expansion. Four persons are presented to the body---two young women as missions volunteers, Zeda Barrett and Hilda Upchurch, and two young men for ministry, H. T. Mills and R. Marler. (I only know about Marler's ministry. Indeed he did pastor for many years here and in Tuscaloosa.) Decides to follow the lead of the SBC and consider being involved with the Layman League. There is an appendix to this annual with a history of the first 75 years of the association. It is prepared by M. B. Curry, an attorney, who was active in the association and who would be the moderator for many years. D. O. Baird who had pastored for about 50 years was memorialized. (Also there is a report of the annual meeting of the WMU in Carrollton with Ms. Kathleen Mallory as speaker. She was a well known leader. Ms. Addie Cox seems to be providing good leadership.) There were 39 churches with 3159 members at this point. Note the great growth in this decade.

1911. M. B. Curry is elected moderator after Robertson declares that he can no longer serve. Two additional young men ask for assistance with ministerial education--R. D. Smith and Jesse McAllister. Mills, who had applied for aid the previous year is employed with a David Bryan to serve as a revival team in the association for a part of the year. For the first time in quite a long time, with a moderator who is a lawyer, the constitution and rules of decorum are printed in the minutes. McAllister becomes pastor at Cornelius Chapel.

1912. G. W. Kerr presented a resolution asking for all the young preachers who desired help with getting educated to express this to the moderator during the meeting. I found this to be of interest because Kerr had been helped earlier by the association, and because of our current efforts to provide seminary extension classes here in the association. From this point the reports of SBC and ALSBOM agencies are more fully reported in the minutes.

1913. A M. Forbes, the ALSBOM fieldworker for Sunday School and WMU, spoke to the annual meeting. The churches reported 34 Sunday Schools with 1,220 enrolled. Special praise was offered to the church at Kennedy which had 202 enrolled, but only 98 members in the church. The Executive Board had offered a position to Ms. Addie Cox to work with children and women. She declined to take it on fully, but offered to do as much in these areas as her time allowed. However, she moves to Birmingham and becomes a "pastor's assistant".

1914. For the first time the WMU report is made by a woman, Mrs. B. G. Killingsworth. It was decided to resurrect the Sunday School Conventions in the Association.

1915. All day singings were criticized in the meeting. This criticism were repeated in subsequent years. But they seem to have survived in various forms down to the present.

1916. Implemented a plan for holding district 5th Sunday meetings. Recall that most of the churches held worship only one Sunday per month. The new Pleasant Hill church petitioned for membership. In time it will replace the old Big Creek church. Asked Huda Barrett, who had surrendered for missions several years earlier, to do mission work in the association during the coming year. Also, provision was made for a newly licensed minister, A M. Perrigin, to be tutored by J. C. Vandiver of Stansel. Pastors were encouraged to share some books with Bro. Perrigin. One of the older ministers, J. L. Ray, volunteers to do evangelism and coalportage during the year without pay. A coalporter sells religious books.

1917. Instituted a practice of having each church to make a brief report on its health. This practice was reinstituted a few years back by the association. Nothing new under the sun. The state of religion in the association was very positive. One wonders if the World War had anything to do with the revival of religious interest.

1918. The first mention of collecting a railroad car load of food for the Orphans Home is entered in the minutes. It is announced, reluctantly, that the churches in Lamar County (Millport, and Kennedy) will be moving into the Lamar Association in the coming year. This reflected an effort by the SBC to encourage the boundaries of associations to be redrawn along county lines. In that Kennedy had the largest Sunday School, this was a major loss. There was rejoicing concerning the acceptance of the Prohibition Amendment A call for enforcement was sounded. The Executive Board announced that six of the churches were forming a "field" which would allow for a pastor to work with all of them and live in Ethelsville on the field. These were

Ethelsville, Union Chapel, Hickory Grove, Pine Grove, Mineral Springs and Spring Hill. Over the next several years this arrangement, with some modifications continued. The first pastor was H. H. Buzbee, Jr. Some of the funding came from the State Board of missions.

1919. Esther Curry was elected clerk and treasurer. This is the first woman to serve as an officer of the association. M.B. Curry continued as moderator. Lamar churches, Fort Springs and Springhill, continue with the Union Association. The War has resulted in increased denominational income which is reflected in expanded programs and activities. Also the organizations are expanded. And programs for financial advance were developed and launched. Specifically, the 75 million program was promoted. Q. D. Haney had become pastor of the Ethelsville field. For many years the the death of pastors and deacons had been reported and commented on. For the first time a women, neither a pastor nor a deacon but a WMU leader, Mrs. T. H. Sanders of Aliceville, was among those whose death was noted.

1920. Positive feelings about the future of the work locally and across the denomination are expressed.

1921. Fort Springs in Lamar disappears. Pleasant Grove in Lamar is back in. H. G. Carpenter is a new minister and is aided with getting an education. C. H. Morgan is now the pastor of the Ethelsville field.

1922. The BYPU work is praised. Not mentioned, but of great importance, was its effectiveness in forming Baptist couples and preparing them for marriage. Note that the associational meeting continues to be a three day one and that often there was preaching both in the building and on the outside in a grove or brush arbor. Bethel and New Hope move to the Tuscaloosa Association, and Springhill in Lamar to Lamar. This seems to have been an amiable departure. But it is interesting that the next annual meeting was to be held in Beulah in Greene. The first report from the Baptist Hospital is found in these meeting. It is evident that the focus on the meetings has become the work of the denomination and its institutions and programs beyond the area association. Three more new ministers are identified and help for them is requested--.A. Bryant, Roy Lee Bonner, and Edward Bonner.

1923. Appeal to continue to help the young ministers get an education. Changed to a two day meeting.

1924. With the loss of churches to Tuscaloosa and Lamar Associations, the UBA is down to 32 congregations with 2928 members. The name of the association is changed to Pickens, although there are still four churches in other counties. W. S. Curzan is now the pastor of the Ethelsville field. By this time the four town churches--Aliceville, Carrollton, Gordo and Reform--are the largest and the best supporters of the association. Shiloah announces that it plans to leave for Tuscaloosa County Association.

1925. This was an important year for the SBC. The Cooperative Program was adopted for funding the work. The association adopts the assessment of $6,000 as its plan for gifts to the CP. The CP will become a major feature of the denominational work down to the present. For the first time all of those church members who had died were listed in the minutes. Grant's Creek is not listed as a member church. It had been an important member for about 80 years. It continues in Tuscaloosa Association and is pastored by Mike Griffin, our friend and former pastor at West End.

Gleanings from the Minutes of the
Pickens Baptist Association—1926—2010

1926. Ms. Addie Cox attended the meeting from her mission post in Kaifeng, China. Noted that Hickory Grove was planning to relocate closer to the Liberty School and help was asked for from the state convention and from the associated churches.
1927 Given the recent discussions concerning the Cooperative Program, it is worth noting that the association was asked to raise $4,000 for the CP in the following year. This was a little less than the churches had contributed in 1926. In 2008 our churches contributed $290,569 to the CP. The men's brotherhood movement was launched in the association at this meeting. Professor L. J. Howell was the initial leader.
1928 The association agreed to help fund the college education of Jim Swedenberg, a young minister. (What benefits came to the association, Alabama, and the Kingdom of God from this unselfish act. He pastored many of our churches. He led in building programs and many of these churches. He headed up what became ALCAP, and he was a teacher in our public schools. One son and one daughter became missionaries under the FMB. Noted that the association received $8.00 from the sale of the Hopewell church property. I believe that this was in the Speed's Mill community.
1929 This was the occasion of the association adopting the "study course" program of the Sunday School Board. In our library at the association we have a good collection of books used in the program which was very popular for the next 50 years. It played a key role in the effectiveness of the denomination and its programs. At its peak there were many study courses offered by the churches each year. Some had to do with methods of doing Sunday School, Discipleship Training, Music, and Mission work. Others dealt with study of books of the Bible and doctrine. (Gary Farley wrote the 1977 Doctrinal Study Book, *The Doctrine of God.*) While study course work continues to this day, it draws far fewer participants, something that it seems has weakened the Baptist movement An effort was made to start a church in the Bostic community. Apparently, it was not successful. And there was a call to have a school for preachers in our association in cooperation with the Sipsey Association.
1930 Mt. Tabor joins the association from Sipsey. This church dates from 1839, but like several churches in the northeast part of Pickens County had been connected with first Tuscaloosa and then Sipsey Associations. The association agreed to help fund the education of two pastors, James Pate and C. O. Bryant. For many years Brother Bryant faithfully served churches in our association.
1931 The associational WMU reports collecting $60 for Ms. Addie Cox of employ "Bible Women" to help her in her work in China. The 28 churches in the association reported 3,139 members, with no report from Flatwoods.
1932 Note is made of the passing of long-time leader W. G. Robertson. He was a layman and merchant in Carrollton. He was a great supporter of Sunday Schools. He served for many years as the moderator of the association. (Note: for more than a century memorials have been printed in the annual minutes of our association. Persons interested in their family history are invited to make use of the minutes in our office.)

alcohol sales. Alas, Satan keeps working. Note is made of plans to, in conjunction with neighboring associations to gather up a railroad car of food for the Baptist orphanage in Troy. This was a major mission of the association for many years until changes in federal law brought it to an end.

1934 The church buildings at Pine Grove and Ethelsville had burned during the year. In spite of being in the midst of the Great Depression, the churches were asked to raise funds to help these churches build back. They did, and these churches continue to be places of worship and witness.

1935 The Pleasant Grove Church (Bump) asked to come into the association. It dates from 1900 and had previously been in the Sipsey Association. It later left and then returned to us and is now known as New Harmony in Gordo. Note is made of a bequest to the Orphanage by the late Edgar L. Smith of Carrollton.

This year marked the 100th anniversary of the formation of the association. Moderator and lawyer M. B. Curry presented a history of the association which is found in the minutes of that year. It is interesting that our current moderator is also a lawyer and a former member of the same law firm that M. B: Curry was a member of. A pageant was written and directed by Mrs. J. B. Killingsworth of Aliceville to commemorate this anniversary.

1936 A concern during this time was to help with the financial woes of a Baptist academy in Eldridge, Alabama. Also, the financial plights of the mission boards were a continuing concern. The missionary forces were cut back due to the lack of funds. The Home Mission Board seems to have been focused on reaching various ethnic groups in the U.S. The FMB was working in only 15 countries back then. Today it is more than 125.

1937 God calls into ministry Ulman Moss and Don Strickland. Both are aided by the association to attend Howard College. Ulman will go on to serve with the FMB in Venezuela, Columbia and Mexico. In 1938 these young men are deployed by the association to help the struggling congregation at Ethelsville, to start a work at the Mt. Vernon school (?), and the Smith school (?).

1938 The project of loading a car of food for the orphan's home continues to be a major activity. Pleasant Grove returns to Sipsey Association.

1939 The desire to have a worker to focus on developing the Sunday Schools surfaces again as a concern in the association. Laymen, Dr. L. Alexander and J. T. McShan are becoming leaders, roles that they will play for many years.

1940 The new Coalfire Church comes into the association. This is the first new congregation in Pickens County for many years. The Cooperative Program continues to be funded via an apportionment strategy.

1941 Two more new churches, Aliceville Second (Westend) and New Salem come into the association. Note is made of the WMU hosting Rhussus Perry, a woman of color, to work with African American women, I assume in the Lebanon Association, to promote the organization of WMU work.

1942 Interest in planting new churches in Bostick and at Smith school are mentioned.. Interestingly, no mention is made concerning the World War and its impact. This comes in the next year. The American Bible Society makes a report for the first time. This will be a feature for many years.

1943 Hubert Ray, another ministerial student from the association at Howard, is aided by the association. The first of what we call today the On Missions Celebration was

conducted. References to the war appear including from the orphan's home a note about their former residents now serving, some of whom are captured
1944 The Garden Church comes into the association. Note is made the HMB developing programs for city missions and for rural churches. These will be significant new directions in the work of that Board for the next several decades. Gary Farley would become the last director of the rural church program for the HMB. This move seems to have been a refocusing to work with associations, as contrasted with doing direct mission work. The recent discussions related to GCR in the denomination appears to involve a return to direct mission work. Based on the report from the state convention of this year, it seems to me that there is evidence of a shift in relations between the convention and association, a move toward greater support and cooperation. Much of this can be explained as the result of increased funds due to greater employment driven by the war.
1945 M.B. Curry announced that after 35 years, he would no longer serve as moderator. With the war ending, there seems to be great excitement about the work of the mission boards. There is talk of starting a new church in the Dancy area. Funds from the sale of the land where the old Big Creek Church had been were used to put up a monument and provide for the upkeep of the cemetery. The later soon passed into the hands of the Pine Grove Missionary Baptist Church. (No mention is made in the minutes of the demise of this church and of Zion about this time.) VBS now comes to the fore. A decade earlier mention was made of the fact that three of the churches had held VBS. Also during 1945 the first of regular simultaneous revival meetings by Southern Baptists across the nation was launched. Surely, the end of the war brought a new day for us. Yet another young minister, James W. Bouchillon, is helped by the association to attend Howard.
1946 The Second World War is over. Men and women are returning home. Visiting at the annual meeting is Addie Cox our missionary to China and her friend Ellen Carver who is not otherwise identified in the minutes. Layman and dentist in Gordo, L. Alexander, becomes the new moderator. Note is made of this being the centennial year of the Southern Baptist Convention. Note is made of James Swedenberg becoming the director of ALCAP. The association provided support for Emma Burgin who was then a student at Southwestern Seminary. At this time only Aliceville, Reform and Gordo held worship every Sunday. Others were either once a month or twice a month. Several of the pastors served four churches each month. The practice of taking an offering for the Orphanage at the annual meeting was reaffirmed. It is interesting to note that Hebron is being pastored by a student at Southern Seminary in Louisville, Ky. Some commute.
1947 The association raised money to buy an automobile for Ulman Moss, a son of the association who was going to Columbia, South America as a missionary. One gets from the reports on Southern and Alabama institutions and programs that the focus upon promoting the work of the denomination was growing. And there were good things happening. The Zion church above Gordo was re-instated in the association. But it did not prosper. The minutes suggest that Dr. J. R. Stuckey, pastor at Aliceville First, was the primary leader of the association and pastor of its largest church. Visitors included Ulman Moss.
1948 Ms. Emma Burgin reports on associational promotion work. At this meeting arrangements are made to hire her as the associational missionary. Her task was to help the churches move toward having the base programs—Sunday School, Training Union, Missions Education and music. She also urged the churches to move toward having

worship every Sunday. She and her peers brought about great church in the work of Baptist Churches. It this time the state convention began a practice which continues to the present of helping with the salary of the DoAM and with health insurance for the DoAM. Tom Collins of Carrollton promoted the idea of having an associational camp during the summer. Only 46 attended. It was held at the Lubbub Lodge.

1949 Mention is made of the death of long-time moderator, M. B. Curry. The camp at Lubbub Lodge drew 80 children this summer. The idea of planting a church across the Tombigbee River was again presented. (In God's timing, this happened in 2008 when Galilee came into our fellowship.) Also the idea was advanced that the association develop a camp site of its own. (The old site of Mt. Tabor was, I understand, proposed by Tom Collins).

1950 A motion was made that the annual meeting be held in two churches each fall, rather than in only one. Tom Burgess of Carrollton and associational SS director made a strong plea for the churches to develop an active program of Bible Study. This year our churches conducted 23 VBSs with 900 enrolled.

1951 A new church named Mars Hill asked to come into the association. J. W. Caldwell had become the new associational missionary. Attention is given to the need for an additional congregation in Gordo. The association began a radio ministry. This included our local preachers. But FBC Aliceville and Forest sponsored the local broadcast of The Baptist Hour.

1952 M Night attendance for the previous year had been 215. Bro. Joe Ray is assisted by the association in his educational efforts at Howard College. He had a long and fruitful ministry across Alabama. (I would like to have information about all of our sons and daughters in ministry mentioned in these historical summaries.)

1953 Among the new pastors in the association was Cecil Eugene Junkin. Preparation was made for a Sunday School growth campaign called "A Million More in 54". The Hollywood (now Highland) Church in Gordo came into the association. The Zion church, north of Gordo, is dropped since it was no longer active. A visual aids committee was formed.

1954 H-day, now Samford Day was promoted, apparently for the first time, at this meeting. Also, the Baptist Student Union was highlighted with the hope that college students from our churches would become involved in this ministry. The association continued its tradition of opposing the use of alcohol as a beverage. Jim Swedenberg, from the association, was the state leader in this field. As a followup of the Million More emphasis, the theme for 1955, Magnify Church Membership, was presented. And the basic church programs—Sunday School, WMU, Training Union, Brotherhood and the like were strongly stressed at this and similar meetings during this era.

1955 More than 2,700 were enrolled in Sunday School in the 33 churches of the association. This was up more than 150. Several young people in the association are listed as volunteering for missions and for ministry. Included is Ellis Tate who continued until recently to pastor in a neighboring association.

1956 Addie Cox is recognized among the visitors. She had only recently retired at age 70 from the Foreign Mission Board. The Executive Board is expanded to include all pastors, the officers of the association, and one person from each of the 32 churches. Unity Church near Aliceville is noted to have disbanded. The churches sent over 25,000 pounds of produce to the Children's Home from the association. All of the churches with the exception of West Greene were in Pickens County.

1957 Familiar names, David Barrentine, Bob Causey, and Chester Free appear in the minutes. Several pastors who went on to serve in larger places for many years also appear in our minutes during this era—James Auchmuny, Dudley Wilson, and Mel Deason. Joseph Dean becomes the missionary for the association. Both former missionaries of the association continued to live in and serve the association in various ways. Emma Burgin was treasurer for many years. Addie Cox spoke to the association about her work in China.

1958 Work was begun on providing a home for the missionary. Tom Burgess provided a lot. The association became incorporated.

1959 Note is made of Bobby Ellis who died this year in Gordo after many years as pastor of New Home Missionary Baptist. Bro. Ellis was serving in 1958, while a student at Selma University, as chaplain in a prison camp in Heflin, Al. At this point some 50 years ago the association had 30 congregations with a combined membership of 4,226. Of these about 3,000 lived in our area. The Sunday Schools enrolled 2,189, Training Union (now Discipleship Training) had 1,189 enrolled. In 19 of the churches. The WMU had 658 in its various groups, also in 19 of our churches. Brotherhood work was only in 7 of the churches with a membership of 184. Baptisms in the churches totaled 136 for the year, The total expenditures of the churches was $219,543.42. The churches gave $15,714.71 to the Cooperative Program during the reporting year. Please compare this with the data in the annual report for the current year.

1960 Vacation Bible school was held in 19 of the churches with an enrollment of 1,191. The founding of Mobile College was noted.

1961 The association recognized Bro. James Swedenberg as Mr. Pickens Baptist. Over the years he had pastored many of the churches and often led them in building a modern building. His daughter, Mary, served in the summer of 1963 as a VBS summer worker, appointed by the state convention.

1962 Nothing noted.

1963 Kannie Mae Alexander becomes the clerk. Emma Burgin continues as the Treasurer. Both served the association faithfully for many years. Ulman Moss is on furlow from his missionary work in Venezuela. He attends the meeting. The note on the home for the missionary stood at $6,600 and was held by Mrs. S. S. Pearson. Joe Whitt comes as pastor to FBC Aliceville and like his predecessor, Dudley Wilson becomes a leader in the association.

1964 James Swedenberg presents a biography of Ms. Addie Cox which appears in the minutes. She was among those memorialized at the next annual meeting. Added a carport to the missionary home. Mt. Tabor is aided by the state convention in its building program. Pleasant Grove (Bump) returns to the association.,

1965 Ms Addie Cox is memorialized. A resolution honor James Swedenberg .is adopted. Names like Gaylord Brownlee, Marvin Spiller, James Gentry Pauline and James Hall, Mrs. R. K. Wilson, Ward Richardson and other good folk who have done much for the association dot the minutes. Neil Nichols becomes pastor at Mt. Pleasant.

1966 John Faulkner and James Purnell come to the association. John was at Reform First and later goes to Africa as a missionary. James serves Stansel on two occasions and during the second played a key role in establishing the Baptist Center ministry. The association launched an Extension Center in cooperation with Howard College. Kannie Mae Alexander conducted three VBS clinics, two for PBA churches and one for the African American Churches here. Cheryl Fullerton of Stansel went to the state as Bible Drill winner. An associational Carol sing was held, appropriately, at Carrollton. Brother Dean attended the national rural church conference at Pass Christian, Ms.

1967 Hershel Owen appears as the preacher of the a message on state missions. He continues to serve among us. Faye Hunnicutt is on the music committee. During this era the association, like most others, served as a kind of conduit for the programs and institutions of the state and national conventions. Very little is noted in the minutes of initiatives taken directly by the association during this era. Rather it is a kind of "jobber" for the products and programs of the conventions.

1968 Fred Findley organized an associational youth choir of 65 members who presented the musical, *Good News*. James Mobes appears in the minutes at Pleasant Hill. He is now pastor at Mountain Brook in Birmingham. He and his church in recent years has contributed mightily to the rebuilding of First Baptist Church of Dancy. The association honored L. M. Perrigin. Many years earlier the association had assisted him in getting an education. Apparently, this was a good investment.

1969 Hickory Grove builds a new building. Aliceville has a branch SS in McCrory village. Brannon Pinion comes to Reform for the first time. James Cunningham is also welcomed as a new pastor. VBS was conducted in 24 of the churches. Note is make of the absence of Charlie Spiller. He had attended the previous 50 annual meetings.

1970 Vernon Blackburn, then a faculty member at the University of Alabama, comes to Pleasant Hill and later becomes pastor of Forest. He is still serving and much loved by those in both congregations

1971 Nothing of note reported.

1972 Missionary Dean dies. Ole Hendrix comes to serve the association. Jimmy Ray comes to Ethelsville as pastor and stays for 30 years.

1973 Henry Earl Trull enters the ministry as pastor at Garden. Larry Potts comes to Hebron. Ralph Windle, Jr. is at Arbor Springs. H day, now Samford day becomes a regular event in the life of the association.

1974 Tommy Hughes is ordained to the ministry.

1975 Joe Whitt makes the Christian Life report, and it is noted that he serves on the national board of the SBC Christian Life Commission. Joe also served for many years on the Samford Board. However, I believe that this is the only occasion when someone from our association has served on the board of an SBC agency. The association buys some additional land behind the parsonage for the construction of an office building, now the Lydia House. The Mission Develop Council is created, and it makes it first report.

1976 The passing of Bro. Tom Collins, evangelist and former pastor at Carrollton is noted. Many of the churches have special events to mark the national bicentennial. Wallace Russell is at Carrollton and its has significant growth. Mike Hall is at New Salem.

1977 Melvin Mordecai comes to Coldfire and a period of revival follows. Began Seminary Extension classes in cooperation with the Lebanon District Missionary Association. James Purnell was the driving force for this. I noted the significant work being done even then by Jean Powell, Emily Kirk, and Glenda Ryan.

1978 Note is made of the passing for former missionary to the association, J. W. Caldwell. On the calendar note is made of practice times for the Pickens Baptist Singing Men.
1979 Jack House and Billy Little join the list of pastors.
1980 The Fred Findley Jrs. are appointed as missionaries of the FMB to Uganda.
1981 Joe Whitt leaves Aliceville and moves to Hamilton. He had served well in the association and had led his church to be a strong supporter of missions—associations, state, national and foreign. He will return in retirement and continue to be a strong supporter of the work.
1982 The churches submitted histories of their churches which were then bound. This has proven to be a valuable resource. This project was updated in 1998.
1983 The association becomes involved in building projects in New England and in Wyoming, projects which extend for several years. J.T. Simpson, a contractor, and his wife Margaret provide leadership. One accomplishment was the repair and improvement of the old home place of Luther Rice, the man who really pulled together the Baptist of the United States beginning in 1814 to support world missions. Several persons from the association helped build a church in Shirley Basin, Wyoming. John Thomas, music minister at Reform, becomes a mission service corp staff person for this small convention of Baptists and this connection encourages our involvement there for several years. Stansel ane West End provided leadership for this work. This seems to mark a shift in the mentality of the association toward being a "full-partner" in the mission enterprise. It is a shift from the position of being a kind of funnel for the conventions. This, incidentally, is why we should never speak of "levels" in Baptist life. We are more like circles out from the local church. Associations and conventions on the same level. The difference is in the area addressed.
1984 The mission work related to construction is expanded to include a church in New York. Ole Hendrix goes to Nigeria as part of a team from Alabama to do mission work. The Thomas' are helped by the association as they join the staff of the Wyoming convention. Also the brotherhood men helped in the construction of the Lebanon District Missionary Baptist building out from Carrollton. (It seems that God impressed many in the association at about this time to be directly involved in mission projects here and elsewhere. More and more of the churches and individuals become involved in construction, evangelism and ministry projects elsewhere.)
1985 The list of newly ordained ministers for this year include Eddie Rogers, Larry Rogers, Paul Shaw, and Ray Aldridge. (As has been often the case there were others whom I do not know and wonder about what became of them (For example, a Venessa Junkin is licensed for ministry by Aliceville First.) The association celebrated 150 years. Bro. Hendrix authored a pamphlet about our history. Also the wall mural which now hangs in the offices which had been crafted by women from our churches, was presented. And also, professionally done pictures of all of the churches were presented. These now hang in the office. The process for relocating the office at its present location is begun. Carrollton sends the first of many mission groups to Brazil.
1986 Began work on preparing the new site for the offices. Held an On Mission Celebration.
1987 Dr. Lon Alexander was honored for his 99th birthday. WestEnd had a fire. Began the volunteer chaplaincy program at the hospital. Had to combat the forces who wanted

to turn Pickens County wet. (After several more failed attempts, the wet forces get legislation that allowed a small town in a dry county to vote itself wet. In 2010 we saw the consequences of this strategy in Aliceville and Fayette.)

1988 The Hendrix retire after 16 years. They move to Boaz. Vonceil Duckworth serves as office secretary while the association is without a missionary. West End dedicates its new building which replaces the one burned. Continue to help support the Thomases in Wyoming. The WMU created a quilt from pieces provided from each church. It is on display in the Hendricks Conference room.

1989 Ernie Carroll comes as missionary. His wife Renay serves as secretary. Bethlehem church is burned. It is helped by the state convention in its effort to rebuild. Soon this church will experience phenomenal growth with Ronnie Elmore as pastor. Mike Shell completes 15 years as treasurer and is replaced by Diane Elliott. Jim Cooley is pastor in Aliceville.

1990 Emmanuel Church is formed in Gordo and will seek membership in the association. The WMU choir is formed. Work is nearing completion on the new associational building. The Executive Board held its August meeting in it. The Baptist Center ministry has been launched. So, it is marking its 20st anniversary in 2010. James Purnell, pastor at Stansel served as coordinator. Clayton Grammer becomes active in leading the Brotherhood work.

1991 Prayer was a major emphasis in the association. Henry Blackabey came to Gordo First and spoke on this subject. The state convention provided mobile chapels to help the churches at Pickensville, Bethlehem, and Emmanuel. The new office building was dedicated. The practice of having a snack supper with the Executive Board meeting was established. Note was made of the death of former foreign missionary Ulman Moss. Emmanuel comes into the association. Mrs. Peggy Mullins became the Treasurer of the association. She continued in that role for 16 years. Along with her husband, Gene, they provided great service for the association.

1992 Note is taken of the fact that the Mars Hill congregation has become inactive. Steps are taken to turn the old associational office building into the Lydia Guest House.

1993 Mike Bonner and Mike Owen are ordained.

1994 Kannie Mae Alexander retired after 31 years of service as the clerk of the association. She was replaced by Vonceil Duckworth. Mrs. Alexander died recently. Carolyn Eatman becomes the office secretary.

1995 Note was taken of the passing of Bro. Ole Hendricks long-time DoAM. (Son Randy is now doing youth ministry in the Birmingham area.) The conference room at the associational office building was named in honor of Ole Hendricks. Mary Swedenberg, on leave from her post as our missionary in Japan, visited in the churches of the association. Our jail ministry was launched. Today we involve ministers from other denominations. Gordon McGlown is the leader of the ministry today.

1996 Note is taken of the death of Miss Emma Burgin, the first associational missionary in the modern period. Also Bro. James Purnell is honored for his work in the association. He is moving to the Birmingham area.

1997 A Disaster Relief trailer is purchased and equipped. Ernie Carroll resigns and moved to the Friendship Association in Blount County. Gary Farley is called as DoAM. He comes from the old HMB. He will work in a part-time capacity. A weekly pastors' prayer breakfast is established with Sid Lanier as chief cook. This continues to be a key ingredient in the life of the association.

1998 The debt on the building is retired. This frees up money for more mission work. We help former Gordo pastor Scott McQueen to plant a church in Tuscaloosa. American Family Radio opens a Christian radio station in Carrollton. Held an associational mission fair featuring the work being done by the churches and their members in mission projects here and around the world. Aliceville First celebrated its 175th anniversary. The annual pastors retreat was inaugurated at Mike Hall's North Pickens Christian Conference Center.

1999 Participated in the Franklin Graham crusade in Tuscaloosa. Mass Choirs presented an Easter Cantata at Reform and Aliceville. Well attended. Nell Jones completes a decade as WMU director. Linda Cobb takes on this role. Mrs. Jones and her husband Glenn, launch our senior adult ministry. The WMU earlier had created a cookbook to raise funds for foster children. This year it held a barbeque for this purpose. Rickie Jackson is ordained to the ministry. Ethelsville celebrated its 175th anniversary. An Addie Cox Missions heritage day is held. Our association is featured in the Commission magazine of the International Mission Board for our great mission heritage. We established a contingency fund which has grown to $50,000. The interest from this fund helps provide scholarships to members of our churches going on to college and professional schools. It also can be drawn upon to fund emergency needs of the association. Began a series of annual school prayer walks in the late summer. The association responded to the revolution in electronic communication by putting up a web page and by using e-mail as a major means of communication with pastors and church leaders.)

2000 Double Branches (Old Corrs) petitions to join the association. It dates from 1864. It has been in the Sipsey Association. A new church in Fayette, now Calvary, petitions to join the association. Our first Senior Adult Revival was held at Stansel. This has become a fixture of the life of the association. A patriotic musical event was held at the stadium in Carrollton. Hired Kevin Drewry as a summer youth worker. He continued in this role for three summers. We began adding display cabinets to the Ole Hendrix conference room to honor our foreign missionaries. So far these include Addie Cox, the Ulman Mosses, Mary Swedenberg, the John Faulkners, and the Glen Davises. (Currently, we are working on a cabinet to commemorate the associational sponsored mission trips since 2004.)

2001 Pleasant Grove of Gordo, now New Harmony, petition to join the association. It is a new congregation, a remnant of the old Bump church. On Mission Celebration, something that the association has done every five years since World War II, was held. Bethlehem introduced us to a block party event. Since 2005 this has become a staple of the work of the association, here and elsewhere. We began an Hispanic ministry, coming out of the OMC. It is now a congregation in Aliceville. Rural Mail carriers began making major contributions of food to the Baptist Center. It becomes the defacto food back for the county. Brannon Pinion returns to FBC Reform. The Pinewood Derby for RAs becomes an important ministry of the association. It has found a continuing home at Pickensville First.

2002 Holly Homan becomes the associational secretary. Gene Dawkins becomes pastor at Pine Grove. Tim Meherg becomes pastor at Union Chapel. An "in the association" mission trip is held with FBC of Dancy. More than 200 of us were involved in mission trips outside of the association. DoAM Gary Farley spent a month working with small churches in Australia. We began our yearly deacons appreciation banquet.

2003 Susie Turner becomes the office secretary. Carrollton Baptist Church donated the Ammons house to the association. It is now the studio for WALN and WCSO, AFR stations in our county. Began broadcasting the Sunday School lessons weekly on the local cable. Our pastors' group served as the model for a new program for pastors in rural churches which was sponsored by the Resource Center for Pastoral Excellence of Samford University. Amy Williams went from FBC Aliceville to China to teach English in China. By doing so our connection with China was re-established. She spent two years there and this past summer taught in Hong Kong.

2004 Melvin Mordecai becomes pastor at Union Chapel. Calvary sponsored a new church in Columbus, Ms. Dr. Robert Smith, preaching professor at Beeson, came to FBC Reform to preach and provide a seminar on preaching. Charlie Wilson, Jack House, and Randy Gray came to minister among us. Marcus Jimenez became pastor of our Hispanic congregation. We were honored by a visit from a mission team from Venezuela. Ulman Moss from our association was the first SBC missionary to that country. Dr. and Mrs David Tuten went as missionaries to Africa. Mary Swedenberg returned from Japan and began working with Japanese at the new Honda. Plant. The association mission team went to work with a church in Vermont. Janet Estis came to work as our summer youth worker. She continues to the present as a volunteer worker for the association, focusing on our missions and Bible teaching work. She is a graduate of Southwestern Seminary. We are blessed to have her working with the association. . The weekly Sunday School lessons moved to the radio. Sid Lanier was the facilitator of these lessons. They continue. Hershel Owen is now the facilitator. Mt. Pleasant took on the Christmas Shoebox ministry for the area. It has added a Celebrate Recovery ministry which has branched out to Stansel.

2005 Workers from our churches rehabbed 3 homes with funds coming from the income of the Baptist Center. Gary Farley, DoAM, was recognized at the state convention as Rural DoAM of the year. Initiated annual wild game suppers. Associational Mission Team to Moline, Ill. Dr. Farley began to serve on the Alabama Baptist Historical Commission. Most of our churches have cooperated by having their old records microfilmed. The association responded to the needs from Katrina by loading a 48ft trailer with materials and donating rehab funds to persons that Bro. Jack House knew near Gulfport.

2006 With the arson of four rural churches in our area the association became deeply involved in helping these churches recover. Westend hosted work crews and fed them. Workers from many of our churches helped with rebuilding Dancy and Galilee. The sign at Dancy spoke to the world. "Forgive them for they know not what they do." When asked why would help these churches, our DoAM replied that we are Great Commandment Christians—we love God and we love our neighbors. The mission team went to Beaver Creek, Ohio. We purchased and outfitted a Block Party trailer which has become a major thing in our ministry. We had an OMC. Several of the missionaries had roots in our association. We interviewed them and prepared DVDs to share with the churches. It was announced that a Federal Prison will be built in Aliceville. It will open in 2011. We have been working to prepare for this by launching the 100 Godly Women movement.

2007 Started a monthly Diabetic Support Group meeting at the PBA office. Started a Beeson Divinity School Extension program. Both have proven to be very successful. Constructed a storage room on the back of the PBA building. Charles Ashcraft who has lead construction teams from the association for many years oversaw the work. The Kirks led a team to the Ukraine. And the mission team also went to Wolfe County, Kentucky.
2008 The mission trips were to Brazil and to Niles Michigan. Our connection with Baptist work in Brazil dates back to the beginnings about 1885. James Taylor from Forest worked there for more than 30 years. Fellowship and Ebenezer celebrated their 175th anniversaries. The builders team worked on the facilities of Global Outreach in Tupelo. Shawn McDaniel was ordained. Galilee Missionary Baptist Church of Panola came under the watchcare of the association. Dr. Thrath Curry, after 24 years of service, retired from the memorials committee. Her reports have been a highlight of the annual meetings. We hosted Team Impact. Nearly 100 persons prayed to receive Christ.
2009 The association sponsored a team to Brazil. The North American mission team worked several block parties and VBSs in and around the association. Parker Windle became a Journeyman with the IMB in Europe. A new church, Covenant of Peace was begun by Bro. Lonnie Hinton. It is locating near our Union Chapel church, just off US 82 near the Mississippi line. Buddy and Emily Kirk were recognized by the state convention as Volunteer Missionaries of the year .Liberty celebrated its 175th anniversary. Brannon Pinion retired from Reform First.
2010 The Mission team returned to Brazil. They connected with Landon Williams who had recently gone from Aliceville to serve as a Journeyman for the IMB there. And we sent a team to work with Street Reach in Memphis. Both were successful. We celebrated the 175th anniversary of the association. In the coming year we will be beginning to do ministry at the new Federal Prison in Aliceville. The association combated the effort to vote to allow the sale of Alcohol in Aliceville. We were not successful. Bethlehem and Forest celebrated their 175th anniversaries. The Disaster Relief team went to Sand Mountain. During the coming year we plan to celebrate our mission hereitage. We prepared a DVD of the life and ministry of Addie Cox which will have its premier showing at Carrollton Baptist Church, October 24, at 2:30pm. This is the anniversary of the birth of Ms. Cox.

HISTORICAL TABLE

Table showing where the Union (Pickens) Baptist Association held its meeting from 1835 to 2010, inclusive and the moderator and clerk:

YEAR	DATE	PLACE	MODERATOR	CLERK	INTRODUCTORY PREACHER
1835		Bethany	Richard Wilkins	W. R. Stansel	
1836		Rehoboth	Henry Petty	Henry Harrison	
1837		Big Creek	H. Petty & R. Wilkins	J. H. Taylor	
1838		Unity	Richard Wilkins	J. H. Taylor	
1839		Beulah	Charles Stewart	J. H. Taylor	
1840		Clinton	William Manning	J. H. Taylor	
1841		Pilgrim's Rest	William Manning	J. H. Taylor	
1842		Enon	William Manning	J. H. Taylor	
1843		New Hope	W. R. Stansel	J. H. Taylor	
1844		Pleasant Ridge	W. R. Stansel	J. H. Taylor	
1845		Fellowship	J. H. Taylor	A. M. Hanks	
1846		Unity	J. H. Taylor	A. M. Hanks	
1847		Beulah	J. H. Taylor	A. M. Hanks	
1848		Friendship	J. H. Taylor	A. M. Hanks	
1849		Mt. Moriah	M. P. Smith	A. M. Hanks	
1850		Enon	Charles Stewart	A. M. Hanks	
1851		Grant's Creek	Jno. C. Foster	A. M. Hanks	

1852		Fellowship	Charles Stewart	A. M. Hanks	
1853		Big Creek	Charles Stewart	A. M. Hanks	
1854		Unity	Dabney Duncan	A. M. Hanks	
1855		Grant's Creek	J. A. Hodges	A. M. Hanks	
1856		Fellowship	Jno. C. Foster	A. M. Hanks	
1857		Spring Hill	Jno. C. Foster	A. M. Hanks	
1858		Enon	J. C. Foster	A. M. Hanks	
1859		Bethel	J. C. Foster	A. M. Hanks	
1860		Carrollton	J. C. Foster	A. M. Hanks	
1861		Providence	W. F. Spraggins	A. M. Hanks	
1862		Pickensville	W. F. Spraggins	A. M. Hanks	
1863		Beulah	George M. Lyles	A. M. Hanks	
1864		Fellowship	G. M. Lyles	A. M. Hanks	
1865		South Carolina	William Ashcraft	A. M. Hanks	
1866		Mt. Zion	J. C. Foster	J. W. Taylor	
1867		Grant's Creek	J. C. Foster	J. W. Taylor	
1868		Pleasant Grove	J. C. Foster	J. W. Taylor	
1869		Oak Ridge	J. C. Foster	J. W. Taylor	
1870		Unity	J. C. Foster	H. B. Chappell	
1871		Beulah	J. C. Foster	H. B. Chappell	

1872		Fellowship	J. C. Foster	H. B. Chappell	
1873		Mineral Springs	J. C. Foster	H. B. Chappell	
1874		Enon	J. C. Foster	H. B. Chappell	
1875		Forest	J. C. Foster	H. B. Chappell	
1876		Corinth	J. C. Foster	H. B. Chappell	
1877		Big Creek	J. C. Foster	H. B. Chappell	
1878		Carrollton	J. C. Foster	H. B. Chappell	
1879		Bethel	J. C. Foster	H. B. Chappell	
1880		Spring Hill (L)	J. C. Foster	H. B. Chappell	
1881		Spring Hill (P)	J. C. Foster	H. B. Chappell	
1882		Pickensville	J. C. Foster	H. B. Chappell	
1883		Grant's Creed	J. C. Foster	H. B. Chappell	
1884		Pleasant Grove	S. Hildreth	H. B. Chappell	
1885		Hebron	S. Hildreth	H. B. Chappell	
1886		Unity	S. Hildreth	H. B. Chappell	
1887		Beulah	S. Hildreth	H. B. Chappell	
1888		Bethlehem	S. Hildreth	H. B. Chappell	
1889		Big Creek	S. Hildreth	H. B. Chappell	
1890		Prairie	S. Hildreth	H. B. Chappell	
1891		Bethel	W. G. Robertson	H. B. Chappell	

1892		Spring Hill (L)	W. G. Robertson	M. G. Lofton	
1893		Arbor Springs	J. P Lee	M. G. Lofton	
1894		Enon	J. P. Lee	M. G. Lofton	
1895		Forest	J. P. Lee	M. G. Lofton	
1896		Kennedy	W. G. Robertson	M. G. Lofton	
1897		Spring Hill (P)	W. G. Robertson	M. G. Lofton	
1898		Carrollton	W. G. Robertson	W. L. White	
1899		Shiloh	W. G. Robertson	W. L. While	
1900		Millport	W. G. Robertson	W. L. White	
1901		Cross Roads	W. G. Robertson	J. L. Harper	
1902		Unity	W. G. Robertson	J. W. Caldwell	
1903		Beulah	W. G. Robertson	H. B. Chappell	
1904		Reform	W. G. Robertson	J. B. Hodo	
1905		Stansel	W. G. Robertson	J. B. Hodo	
1906		Aliceville	W. G. Robertson	A. T. Ezell	
1907		Grant's Creek	W. G. Robertson	A. T. Ezell	
1908		Bethlehem	W. G. Robertson	A. T. Ezell	
1909		Gordo	W. G. Robertson	A. T. Ezell	
1910		Big Creek	W. G. Robertson	J. M. Mills	
1911		Bethel	M. B. Curry	J. F. Hodge	

1912		Mineral Springs	M. B. Curry	J. F. Hodge	
1913		Knnedy	M. B. Curry	J. F. Hodge	
1914		Hebron	M. B. Curry	J. F. Hodge	
1915		Forest	M. B. Curry	J. F. Hodge	
1916		Liberty	M. B. Curry	J. F. Hodge	
1917		Friendship	M. B. Curry	A. T. Ezelle	
1918		Liberty	M. B. Curry	J. E. Hendley	
1919		New Hope	M. B. Curry	J. E. Hendley	
1920		Ethelsville	M. B. Curry	W. F. Barnard	
1921		Ebenezer	M. B. Curry	W. F. Barnard	
1922		Cross Roads	M. B. Curry	J. M. Mills	
1923		Beulah	M. B. Curry	J. M. Mills	
1924	Sept. 10-11	Pine Grove	M. B. Curry	J. M. Mills	F. M. Barnes
1925	Sept. 9-10	Gordo	M. B. Curry	J. M. Mills	W. A. McCain
1926	Sept. 8-9	Carrollton	M. B. Curry	J. M. Mills	H. C. Todd
1927	Sept. 7-8	Unity	M. B. Curry	J. M. Mills	J. O. Colley
1928	Sept. 5-6	Bethlehem	M. B. Curry	J. M. Mills	E. E. Johnson
1929	Sept. 17-18	Arbor Springs	M. B. Curry	J. M. Mills	J. Y. Brooks
1930	Sept. 23-24	Spring Hill	M. B. Curry	J. M. Mills	E. O. Jackson
1931	Sept. 9-10	Mt. Pleasant	M. B. Curry	J. M. Mills	H. G. Johnson

1932	Sept. 6-7	Reform	M. B. Curry	J. M. Mills	J. O. Colley
1933	Sept. 7-8	Fellowship	M. B. Curry	J. M. Mills	L. E. Barnes
1934	Sept. 4-5	West Green	M. B. Curry	J. M. Mills	L. E. Barton
1935	Sept. 3-4	Aliceville	M. B. Curry	J. M. Mills	F. M. Barnes
1936	Sept. 8-9	Pine Grove	M. B. Curry	J. M. Mills	C. F. Moffitt
1937	Sept.	Stansel	M. B. Curry	J. M. Mills	O. C. Weaver
1938	Sept. 6-7	Forest	M. B. Curry	J. M. Mills	J. R. Swedenburg
1939	Sept.	Mineral Springs	M. B. Curry	J. M. Mills	J. B. Johnson
1940	Sept. 3-4	Ebenezer	M. B. Curry	J. M. Mills	L. B. Wages
1941	Sept. 9-10	Pleasant Hill	M. B. Curry	J. M. Mills	J. R. Swedenburg
1942	Sept. 8-9	Union Chapel	M. B. Curry	J. M. Mills	E. L. Edens
1943	Sept. 7-8	Mt. Tabor	M. B. Curry	J. M. Mills	A. M. Nix
1944	Sept. 5-6	Pickensville	M. B. Curry	J. M. Mills	L. Q. Porch
1945	Sept. 4-5	Hickory Grove	M. B. Curry	J. M. Mills	Lester R. Stokes
1946	Sept. 3-4	Liberty	L. Alexander	J. M. Mills	J. R. Swedenburg
1947	Sept. 9-10	Aliceville 2nd	L. Alexander	I. C. Kuykendall	B. A. Wilson
1948	Sept. 7-8	Hebron	L. Alexander	I. C. Kuykendall	Ulman Moss
1949	Sept. 6-7	Gordo	L. Alexander	R. W. Brandon	J. R. Stuckey
1950	Sept. 5-6	Reform	L. Alexander	R. W. Brandon	J. R. Swedenburg
1951	Sept. 4-5	Aliceville Arbor Springs	L. Alexander	R. W. Brandon	L. B. Marion

1952	Sept. 9-10	Forest Ethelsville	L. Alexander	R. W. Brandon	O. M. Fox
1953	Sept. 8-9	Cross Roads Bethlehem	L. Alexander	R. W. Brandon	W. S. Scott
1954	Sept. 7-8	Stansel Flatwoods	O. M. Fox	R. W. Brandon	J. R. Swedenburg
1955	Sept. 6-7	Pleasant Hill Friendship	O. M. Fox	R. W. Brandon	Gardner Walker
1956	Sept. 4-5	Hebron Fellowship	A. L. Bray	T. W. Buford	T. W. Buford
1957	Sept. 3-4	Spring Hill Liberty	A. L. Bray	Marvin Spiller	David Renaker
1958	Sept. 9-10	Stansel Pine Grove	E. Byron Davis	Marvin Spiller	Gaylord Brownlee
1959	Sept.8-9	Mineral Springs Mt. Pleasant	F. O. Cork	Marvin Spiller	Dudley Wilson
1960	Sept. 6-7	Gordo Pleasant Hill	F. O. Cork	Marvin Spiller	George Bagley
1961	Sept. 12-13	West End Bethlehem	F. O. Cork	Marvin Spiller	Chester Free
1962	Sept. 11-12	Reform Friendship	L. D. Wilson	Emma Burgin	F. O. Cork, Jr.
1963	Sept. 10-11	Ethelsville Forest	J. R. Swedenburg	Kannie M. Alexander	Jack Mason

1964	Oct. 6-7	Pickensville Carrollton	Mel Deason	Kannie M. Alexander	G. A. Pratt
1965	Oct. 5-6	Fellowship Aliceville	Jack Mason	Kannie M. Alexander	Jerry Riley
1966	Oct. 4-5	Gordo Bethlehem	P. Joe Whitt	Kannie M. Alexander	J. L. Mouchett
1967	Oct. 3-4	Reform Stansel	P. Joe Whitt	Kannie M. Alexander	J. H. Faulkner
1968	Oct. 8-9	Cross Roads Flatwoods	P. Joe Whitt	Kannie M. Alexander	Herchel R. Owen
1969	Oct. 7-8	Carrollton Pleasant Hill	J. H. Faulkner (2 Mo) James Purnell (10 Mo)	Kannie M. Alexander	Earl Surber
1970	Oct. 6-7	Mt. Pleasant Aliceville First	James Purnell (8 Mo) Chester Free (4 Mo)	Kannie M. Alexander	Jack Brown
1971	Oct. 12-13	Gordo First Reform	P. Joe Whitt	Kannie M. Alexander	Chester Free
1972	Oct. 10-11	Stansel Hebron	Brannon Pinion	Kannie M. Alexander	P. Joe Whitt
1973	Oct. 8-9	Highland Flatwoods	Brannon Pinion	Kannie M. Alexander	A. G. Smith & Oel Hendrix
1974	Oct. 14-15	Pickensville Mt. Pleasant	Brannon Pinion	Kannie M. Alexander	Ralph Windle, Jr.
1975	Oct. 13-14	Cross Roads Arbor Springs	Ron Jackson (8 Mo) Richard Mason (4 Mo)	Kannie M. Alexander	Ron Jackson

1976	Oct. 11-12	West End Friendship	Richard Mason	Kannie M. Alexander	Tommy Hughes
1977	Oct. 10-11	Gordo First Pleasant Hill	Richard Mason (9 Mo) Wallace Russell (3 Mo)	Kannie M. Alexander	Max Davis
1978	Oct. 9-10	Aliceville First Reform First	Wallace Russell	Kannie M. Alexander	J. L. Mouchette
1979	Oct. 8-9	Mt. Pleasant Stansel	Bill Jones (9 Mo) Buddy Kirk (3 Mo)	Kannie M. Alexander	Bill Jones
1980	Oct. 13-14	Cross Roads Carrollton First	W. O. (Buddy) Kirk	Kannie M. Alexander	Larry Weeks
1981	Oct. 12-13	West End Mineral Springs	James Jordan	Kannie M. Alexander	Neil Nichols
1982	Oct. 11-12	Ethelsville Gordo First	James Jordan	Kannie M. Alexander	Jack D. House
1983	Oct. 17-18	Aliceville First Reform First	Willie Crawford	Kannie M. Alexander	Neil Nichols
1984	Oct. 15-16	Arbor Springs Pleasant Hill	Willie Crawford	Kannie M. Alexander	John Kitchens
1985	Oct. 14	Cross Roads	Neil Nichols	Kannie M. Alexander	Dr. Earl Potts
1986	Oct. 13-14	Mt. Pleasant Friendship	Neil Nichols	Kannie M. Alexander	Terry Hawkins
1987	Oct. 19-20	Gordo First Carrollton First	Daniel Gandy (11 Mo) Dr. Earl Potts (1 Mo)	Kannie M. Alexander	Clyde Strickland
1988	Oct. 17-18	West End Reform	Larry Potts	Kannie M. Alexander	Paul Osborn

1989	Oct. 16-17	Cross Roads Arbor Springs	Clyde Strickland	Kannie M. Alexander	Frank Sims
1990	Oct. 15-16	Highland Aliceville First	Clyde Strickland	Kannie M. Alexander	Gary Smith
1991	Oct. 14-15	West End Flatwoods	Clyde Strickland	Kannie M. Alexander	Scott McQueen
1992	Oct. 12-13	Bethlehem Stansel	Tom Woodard	Kannie M. Alexander	Clyde Strickland
1993	Oct. 11-12	Gordo First Ethelsville	Tom Woodard	Kannie M. Alexander	Dawson Morrison
1994	Oct. 11-12	Mt. Pleasant Friendship	James Purnell	Vonceil Duckworth	Eugene Junkin
1995	Oct. 9-10	Cross Roads Arbor Springs	Sid Lanier	Vonceil Duckworth	Todd Burkhalter
1996	Oct. 14-15	Pickensville Reform First	Sid Lanier	Vonceil Duckworth	Herchel Owen
1997	Oct. 13-14	Flatwoods Mineral Springs	Sid Lanier	Vonceil Duckworth	Lee Wheat
1998	Oct. 12-13	Carrollton Aliceville First	Marc Howard	Vonceil Duckworth	Steve Thomas
1999	Oct. 11-12	Gordo First Ethelsville	Marc Howard	Vonceil Duckworth	Sid Lanier
2000	Oct. 9-10	West End Emmanuel	James Cooley	Vonceil Duckworth	Mike Hall

2001	Oct. 8-9	Cross Roads Reform First	James Cooley	Vonceil Duckworth	Rev. Tim Jones
2002	Oct. 7-8	Pickensville First Friendship	Rickey Jackson	Vonceil Duckworth	Lee Wheat
2003	Oct. 13-14	Bethlehem Stansel	Rickey Jackson	Voneil Duckworth	Michael Trull
2004	Oct. 9-10	Mt. Pleasant Arbor Springs	Mike Hall	Vonceil Duckworth	Glen Standifer
2005	Oct. 10-11	Calvary Mineral Springs	Mike Hall	Vonceil Duckworth	Hershel Owen
2006	Oct. 9-10	Aliceville First Carrollton First	Pat Powell	Vonceil Duckworth	David Falgout
2007	Oct. 8-9	Springhill Friendship	Charlie Wilson	Vonceil Duckworth	Charlie Wilson
2008	Oct. 13-14	Bethlehem Stansel	Charlie Wilson	Vonceil Duckworth	Rickey Jackson
2009	Oct. 12-13	Cross Roads Flatwoods	Buddy Kirk	Vonceil Duckworth	Brannon Pinion
2010	Oct. 11-12	New Salem Aliceville First	Buddy Kirk	Vonceil Duckworth	Mike Hall

2011	Oct. 10-11	Gordo First Ethelsville	Jack House	Vonceil Duckworth	Glenn Sandifer
2012	Oct. 15-16	Emmanuel West End	Jack House	Vonceil Duckworth	Herchel Owen
2013	Oct. 14-15	Highland Pickensville	Leonard Hill	Vonceil Duckworth	Shawn McDaniel
2014	Oct. 14-15	Arbor Springs Hebron	Leonard Hill	Vonceil Duckworth	Glen Kennedy
2015	Oct. 12-13	Calvary, Fayette Galilee, Panola	Sam Wiggins	Vonceil Duckworth	Tim Meherg
2016	Oct. 10-13	Flatwoods Mineral Springs	Glenn Sandifer	Vonceil Duckworth	Jordan Lollar
2017	Oct. 15-16	Reform Mt. Pleasant	Glenn Sandifer	Vonceil Duckworth	Charlie Wilson
2018	Oct. 15-16	Carrollton New Salem	Glenn Sandifer	Vonceil Duckworth	Shawn McDaniel

1Pioneer Pastors
Pickens Baptist Association
1835–1890

Formerly Union

List of pastors and the churches they severed (Note: in some instances a church was not being served by a pastor at the time when the annual church letter was submitted to the association. In those years the name of the church will not appear. In a companion list the names of the churches affiliated with the association each year will be listed. And the third document will present biographical information about some of these early ministers. Note these churches met one week-end per month. This made it possible for many of the ministers to serve four congregations.)

Your help is solicited in gathering biographical information, place of burial, and pictures of these pastors.

1835

Charles Stewart -Big Creek (four miles west of Carrollton off of State 86 a short distance.)
Henry Petty -Pilgrim Rest (North of Pickensville), Bethlehem of Greene Co., Rehobeth of Greene Co.
J. H. Taylor --Enon (In Garden community, now FBC of Aliceville), Unity (Northeast of Aliceville about four miles) Forest
E. Wilbanks --Bethel of Greene
Jere Pearcell --Canaan (Later Clinton) and Five Mile in Greene
J.P. Taylor --Serepta (Near Flatwoods)
R. Marsh --Springfield (later Eutaw in Greene Co).
Robert Wilkins --Ebenezer, Fellowship, Liberty
W. Nash --Bethany
M.P. Smith --Buck Creek in Tuscaloosa Co.
Tom Willingham --Friendship in Greene. At Forkland, now at Boligee.

1836

Charles Stewart --Big Creek
Henry Petty --Bethlehem, Pilgrim Rest, Rehobeth
J. H. Taylor --Enon, Unity and Forest
E. Wilbanks --Bethel
J. P. Taylor --Serepta
R. Marsh --Springfield
R. Wilkins --Ebenezer, Liberty, Fellowship
M. P. Smith --Bulah in Tuscaloosa Co.
Jere Pearcell --Canaan, Five Mile
W. Nash --Bethany
Tom Willingham --Friendship

1837

The year the association divided over the topic of support for mission boards. List reflects the letters or reports of the affiliated church of that year.

C. Stewart --Big Creek
H. Petty --Pilgrim Rest
W. Cook --Enon
M.P. Smith --Bethel, Bulah, and Buck Creek
J. H. Taylor --Unity, Forest
T. Willingham --Springfield, Friendship.
R. Wilkins --Ebenezer, Fellowship, Liberty
T. S. Thomas --Salem, Bethany

(Several of the churches did not have pastors at the time of the annual meeting.)

(Note: Petty, W. Cook, Jere Percell, and J.P. Taylor were the leaders of the Primitives and departed from the association, forming the Pilgrim Rest Baptist Association.)

1838

C. Stewart --Big Creek, Liberty

William Manning --Pleasant Ridge of Greene Co., Pilgrim Rest, (a pro-missions congregation meeting in the old meeting house north of Pickensville) and Concord (this becomes Clinton)

WW. Nash --Enon, Oak Ridge(located just west of State 14 just before getting to Mississippi, near Pine Grove.)

J. H. Taylor --Unity, Forest and Antioch of Perry Co.

M. P. Smith --Springfield, Bulah, Buck Creek

T. Willingham - Friendship (Note this is the first year after the split. Some churches did not have pastors.)

1839

C. **Stewart** --Big Creek, Liberty

W. Manning --Pleasant Ridge, Pilgrim Rest, Concord

J. H. Taylor --Enon, Unity, Forest

R. Wilkins --Ebenezer

M. P. Smith --Bulah, Buck Creek in Tuscaloosa County

T. S. Thomas --Fellowship

T. Willingham --Friendship in Greene

W.W. Nash --Oak Ridge

J. R. Smith --New Hope in Tuscaloosa

W. Stansel --Pleasant Ridge

1840

C. Stewart --Big Creek, Liberty

W. Manning --Pleasant Ridge, Pilgrim Rest, Concord

J. H. Taylor --Enon, Unity, Forest, Hopewell (In the Speed=s Mill Community)

M. M. Wallace --Springfield

R. Wilkins --Ebenezer

M. P. Smith -- Bulah, Buck Creek

T. S. Thomas --Fellowship

T. Willingham --Friendship

W.W. Nash --Oak Ridge

J. H. Smith --New Hope of Tuscaloosa Co.

W. **Stansel** --Mt. Zion (Came out of Bethany. In the latter Bethany community.)

1841

T. S. Thomas --Fellowship

W. **Manning** --Pleasant Ridge, Concord, Mt. Zion

C. Stewart --Big Creek, Fellowship, Liberty, South Carolina (now Ethelsville)

A. Elledge --Hebron, Hopewell

W.W. Nash --Oak Ridge

S. McGowen --Pilgrim Rest

J. H. Taylor --Enon, Unity

R. Wilkins --Ebenezer

M. P. Smith --Bulah, Buck Creek, Forest

W. Hood --New Hope

1842

W. F. Barrett --Friendship

W. Manning --Pleasant Ridge, Concord, Mt. Zion

C. Stewart --Big Creek, Fellowship, Liberty, South Carolina

A. Elledge --Hebron

W.W. Nash--BOak Ridge, Spring Hill(formerly Pilgrim's Rest)

J. H. Taylor --Enon, Unity

R. Wilkins--BEbenezer

D. D. Peterson --Hopewell

M. P. Smith --Bulah, Forest, Buck Creek

W. Hood --New Hope

J. A. Hodges --Grant's Creek (Came from the Cahaba Association. The church leadership was strong advocates of Sunday School work and missions.)

1843
M. B. Clement --Friendship
W. Manning --Pleasant Ridge, Concord, Eutaw, Spring Hill
T. S. Thomas --Mt. Zion, Ebenezer
C. Stewart --Big Creek, Fellowship, Liberty, South Carolina
A. Elledge --Hebron
W. W. Nash --Oak Ridge
J. H. Taylor --Enon, Unity
R. Wilkins --Ebenezer, Mt. Pleasant
Patterson --Hopewell
M. P. Smith --Forest, Buck Creek
W. Hood --New Hope
J. A. Hodge --Grant's Creek, Beulah

1844
T. Willingham -Friendship
W. Manning --Pleas. Ridge, Eutaw, Spring Hill
S. S. Lattimore --Concord (Becomes a leader of Mississippi Baptists)
T. S. Thomas --Mt. Zion, Hebron
C. Stewart --Big Creek, Liberty, South Carolina
W. W. Nash --Oak Ridge
R. Wilkins --Fellowship, Ebenezer, Mt. Pleasant, Zion
J. H. Taylor--Enon, Hopewell, Liberty
M. P. Smith --Bulah, Forest, Buck Creek
W. Hood --New Hope
E. B. Teague BGrant=s Creek

1845
(This is the year that the Southern Baptist Convention was formed.)
M. B. Clement --Friendship
J. Morris --Clinton, Pleasant Ridge
E. B. Teague --Eutaw (Leader among Alabama Baptists, educator.)
A. M. Hank --Mt. Zion
C. Stewart --Big Creek, Liberty, South Carolina (now Ethelsville)
J. H. Taylor --Spring Hill, Enon, Unity, Hopewell
C. B. Sanders --Hebron
W.W. Nash --Oak Ridge
R. Wilkins --Fellowship, Ebenezer, Mt. Pleasant, Zion
M. P. Smith --Bulah, Buck Creek
H. R. Morgan --Forest
W. Hood --New Hope
J.C. Foster --Grant's Creek (Becomes long-term moderator of the association)

1847
M. B. Clement -- Friendship
S.S. Lattimore --Clinton
J. H. Taylor --Pleasant Ridge, Spring Hill, Unity
E. B. Teague --Eutaw
A. M. Hanks --Mt. Zion, Hopewell (Merchant and long-time clerk of the assn)
C. Stewart --Big Creek, Liberty (planter, state representative and county officer)
C. B. Sanders --Hebron
W.W. Nash --Oak Ridge
T. S. Thomas --South Carolina (county judge)
R. Wilkins --Fellowship, Ebenezer, Mt. Pleasant
E. Gore --Mt. Moriah (mother church of Free Wills. Came from Columbus Assn. Near Mineral Springs).
W. Stansel --Enon
I. Parker --Zion
M. P. Smith --Bulah, Forest
J. C. Foster --New Hope, Grant=s Creek

1848
M. B. Clement --Friendship
E. B. Teague --Clinton, Eutaw
J. H. Taylor --Pleasant Ridge, Spring Hill,

1848 cont.
Fellowship, Unity
C. Stewart --Big Creek, Liberty
C. B. Sanders --Hebron
A. M. Hanks --Mt. Zion, Hopewell
W. R. Nash --Oak Ridge
D. Duncan --South Carolina, Bridgeville (three miles southeast of current Aliceville)
E. Gore --Mt. Moriah
W. Stansel --Carrollton, Enon
E. Smith --Pickensville
J. M. Perry --Salem (perhaps, above today=s New Salem)
R. Wilkins --Ebenezer, Mt. Pleasant
I. Parker --Zion
M. P. Smith --Bulah, Buck Creek, Forest
J. C. Foster --New Hope, Grant=s Creek

1849
M. B. Clement --Friendship
E. B. Teague --Clinton, Eutaw
J. H. Taylor --Pleasant Ridge, Spring Hill, Pickensville, Unity
A. M. Hanks BMt. Zion
C. Stewart BBig Creek
C. B. Sanders BHebron, Mt. Pleasant
R. Wilkins BLiberty, Ebenezer
D. Duncan BOak Ridge, South Carolina
T. S. Thomas BFellowship
E. Gore BMt. Moriah, New Salem
M. C. Curry BCarrollton, Hopewell, Pickensville
W. H. Robinson BArbor Springs (predecessor of the our current church by that name.)
W. Stansel BEnon
R. Wilkins BEbenezer
I. Parker BZion
M. P. Smith BBulah, Forest, Buck Creek
J. C. Foster BNew Hope, Grant=s Creek

1850
M. B. Clement BFriendship
E. B. Teague BClinton, Eutaw
a missionary to China by SBC
J. H. Taylor BPleasant Ridge, Bridgeville
Jesse Thomas BBethlehem of Pickens. Comes in from Columbus Assn. Son of T.S. Thomas.
A M. Hanks BMt. Zion
C. Stewart BBig Creek
C. B. Sanders BLiberty, Oak Ridge, Fellowship, Mt. Pleasant
D. Duncan BSouth Carolina, Providence. Comes in from Columbus Assn.
E. Gore BMt. Moriah, New Salem
M. C. Curry BCrrollton, Enon, Bridgeport
W. H. Roberson BArbor Springs
M. Lyon BEbenezer. Editor of a newspaper and in Carrollton Church.
H. R. Morgan BZion
M. P. Smith BBulah, Forest, Buck Creek
J. C. Foster BNew Hope, Grant=s Creek. (Note: Ellis Gore becomes Free Will Baptist and takes Mt. Moriah and New Salem out of the association. Also most of the Greene County churches unite with the Sumter County churches to form the Bigbee Association.)

1851
Jesse Thomas BBethlehem
W. H. Roberson BArbor Springs, Mt. Pleasant, Ebenezer, Hopewell
C. B. Sanders BLiberty, Fellowship, Oak Ridge, Hebron
1851 (continued)
M. C. Curry BCarrollton, Enon, Bridgeville
D. Duncan BProvidence Buried at Crossroads.
J. H. Taylor BSpring Hill, Pickensville
C. Stewart BBig Creek, Cross Roads (An

Aarm@ out of Big Creek)
A. M. Hanks BMt. Zion
M. P. Smith BBulah, Buck Creek, Forest
J. C. Foster -- Grant=s Creek, New Hope
H. R. Morgan --Zion
(Martha Crawford who grew up in Grant's Creek and was attending Clinton to study with E. B. Teague. Married T. H. Crawford and was appointed as a missionary to China by the FMB of the SBC.)

1852
J. Deloach --Arbor Springs, Liberty
C. B. Sanders --Fellowship, Oak Ridge, Hebron
M. C. Curry --Carrollton, Enon, Bridgeville
M. Lyon --South Carolina
J. H. Taylor --Spring Hill, Pickensville
C. Stewart --Big Creek, Cross Roads
A. M. Hanks --Mt. Zion, Unity
I Parker --Hopewell
M. P. Smith --Bulah, Buck Creek, Forest
J. C. Foster --Grant's Creek
H. R. Morgan – New Hope, Zion

1853
D. Duncan --Ebenezer, South Carolina, Bethlehem
J. Deloach --Arbor Springs, Liberty, Mt. Pleasant
C. B. Sanders --Fellowship, Oak Ridge
M. Lyon --Carrollton, Spring Hill
Strawn --Providence
C. Stewart --Big Creek, Cross Roads
M. C. Curry --Pickensville, Enon
T. S. Thomas --Bridgeville
A.M. Hanks --Mt. Zion, Unity
M. P. Smith--Forest, Bulah, Buck Creek
J. C. Foster --Grant's Creek

1854
D. Duncan --Bethlehem, South Carolina
J. Deloach --Arbor Springs, Liberty
I. Parker --Mt. Pleasant
C. B. Sanders --Fellowship, Oak Ridge
M. Lyon --Providence, Spring Hill, Pickensville
C. Stewart --Big Creek, Cross Roads, Enon (some missing)
1855
G. M. Lyles --Bethlehem
J. Deloach --Arbor Springs, Liberty
C. Stewart--Fellowship, Big Creek, Cross Road
D. Duncan --Carrollton, Mineral Springs, South Carolina. (Mineral Springs was composed of those in Mt. Moriah who had not accepted the Free Will position of E. Gore.)
C. B. Sanders --Ebenezer
L. Compere --Providence (Famous early missionary to Creek Indians. Alabama and Miss.)
W. Spragins --Oak Ridge, Enon, Pickensville
J. N. Acker --Hebron
W. C. Boyd –Memphis (in the river town, only briefly in the assn.
A. M. Hanks --Unity, Mt. Zion, Pleasant Ridge
M. P. Smith --Forest, Bulah, Buck Creek, New Hope
J. A. Hodge --Zion
J. C. Foster --Grant's Creek

1856
G.M. Lyles --Bethlehem, Providence, Oak Ridge. (Buried at Mineral Springs.)
J. N. Acker --Arbor Springs, Hebron, Cross Roads
J Deloach --Liberty, Mineral Springs
J. Thomas --Fellowship
D. Duncan --Carrollton, South Carolina

W. R. Scott --Ebenezer
W. Burns --Spring Hill
C.B. Sanders--BBig Creek. (Charles Steward who had organized the church in 1828 died in 1856.)
W. F. Spragins --Pickensville, Enon
A. M. Hanks --Unity, Mt. Zion
M. P. Smith --Forest, Bulah, Bethel (new name for Buck Creek), New Hope
J. A. Hodge –Zion

1857
G. M. Lyles --Bethlehem, Providence, Mineral Springs, Oak Ridge
J. N. Acker --Arbor Springs, Hebron
J. Deloach --Liberty, Cross Roads
W. R. Scott --Mt. Pleasant, Ebenezer (From deacon and clerk at Ebenezer)
J. Thomas --Fellowship
A. M. Hanks-- Carrollton, Pickensville, Unity, Mt. Zion
D. Duncan --South Carolina
W. Burns --Spring Hill
C. B. Sanders --Big Creek
W. F. Spragins --Enon
W. Ashcraft – Pleasant Ridge
M. P. Smith –Forest, Bulah, Bethel, New Hope
J. A. Hodges --Zion
J. C. Foster --Grant's Creek

1858
G. M. Lyles --Bethlehem, Providence, Mineral Springs, Oak Ridge
J. N. Acker --Arbor Springs, Hebron
J. Deloach --Liberty, Cross Road
W. R. Scott --Mt. Pleasant
W. Burns –Fellowship
A. M. Hanks --Carrollton, Unity, Spring Hill
R. Wilkins --Ebenezer. Son of first moderator.
W. F. Spragins --South Carolina, Pickensville, Enon
C. B. Sanders --Big Creek
C. Bain --Mt. Zion, Bethel, Shiloah
M. P. Smith --Forest, Bulah, New Hope
J. A. Hodges --Zion
J. C. Foster --Grant's Creek

1859
G. M. Lyles --Bethlehem, Providence, Mineral Springs, Oak Ridge
J.N. Acker --Arbor Springs, Hebron
J. Deloach --Liberty, Cross Road
W. Scott --Mt. Pleasant, Ebenezer
J. Thomas --Fellowship
W. F. Spragins --South Carolina
A. M. Hanks --Spring Hill
C. B. Sanders --Big Creek
R. M. Humphreys --Carrollton
W. Ashcraft --Enon
C. Bain --Mt. Zion, Shiloh, Bethel (Helped by association to get educated)
M. P. Smith --Forest, Bulah, New Hope
I Parker --Zion
J.C. Foster --Grant's Creek

1860
D. O. Baird --Bethlehem (also a MD)He will be a key leader for the next 50 years.)
J. N. Acker --Arbor Springs
J. Deloach --Liberty, Cross Road
W. Scott -- Mt. Pleasant, Ebenezer
J Thomas --Fellowship
G. M. Lyles --Providence, Mineral Springs, Oak Ridge, Spring Hill
W. F. Spragins --South Carolina, Big Creek, Enon
D. Duncan --Hebron
J. G. Nash --Pickensville, Carrollton
A. M. Hanks --Unity
C. Bain --Mt. Zion, Shiloh, Bethel
M. P. Smith --Forest, Bulah, New Hope

I. Parker --Zion
J. C. Foster --Grant=s Creek

1861
D. Baird --Bethlehem
J. Acker --Arbor Springs
J. Deloach --Liberty, Cross Roads
W. Scott --Mt. Pleasant, Ebenezer
J. Thomas --Fellowship
Wooten --Providence
Spragins --South Carolina, Big Creek
G. Lyles --Mineral Springs, Oak Ridge, Spring Hill
D. Duncan --Hebron
J.G. Nash --Pickensville, Carrollton
A. M. Hanks --Enon, Unity
L. B. Roberson B--t. Zion
J. C. Foster - - Forest, Grant's Creek
M.P. Smith --Shiloh, Bulah, New Home
Redmon Jones --Bethel (He seems to have been particularly effective with Freedmen.)
A. M. Bryant --Zion

1863
J. Acker --Arbor Springs
R. B. Wilkins----Liberty, Mt. Pleasant, Ebenezer
W. Ashcraft --Fellowship, Mt. Zion, Forest
Wooten --Providence
W. Spragins --South Carolina, Big Creek
1863 cont.
G. Lyles --Mineral Springs, Oak Ridge, Spring Hill
D. Duncan --Hebron
J W..Taylor --Pickensville, Carrollton
A. M. Hanks --Enon, Unity
M. P. Smith --Shiloh, Bulah
Redmon Jones --Bethel
J.C. Foster --Grant's Creek

1865
G. Lyles --Bethlehem, Mineral Springs, Oak Ridge, Spring Hill
J. Acker --Arbor Springs, Ebenezer
A. Spiller --Mt. Pleasant, Corinth, Zion
R. B. Wilkins --Liberty
W. Ashcraft --Fellowship, Mt. Zion, Forest
Wooten --Spring Hill of Lamar, Providence, Hebron
Spragins --South Carolina, Big Creek
D. Duncan --Cross Roads
J. W. Taylor --Pickensville, Carrollton, Enon
A. M. Hanks --Unity
M. P. Smith --Bulah, Shiloh
R. Jones --Bethel
J. C. Foster --New Hope, Grant's Creek

1866
R. Wilkins -Arbor Springs
I. Hollingsworth --Mt. Pleasant
W. Ashcraft --Fellowship, Carrollton, Mt. Zion, Forest
J. Acker --Ebenezer
A. Spiller –Corinth (on US 82 at county line)
M. W. Regan --South Carolina
G..W. Lyles --Mineral Springs, Spring Hill, Big Creek
W. Roberson --Oak Ridge
DeLoach --Hebron
J. W. Taylor --Pickensville, Enon
A. M. Hanks --Unity
D. Duncan --Cross Roads
M. P. Smith --Shiloh, Bulah, New Hope
Redmon Jones – Bethel
I. Parker – Zion
M.M. Blaylock BBethlehem, Spring Hill (Lamar)
J.C. Foster --Grant Creek

1867
R. Wilkins - Liberty
I. Hollingworth - Mt. Pleasant, Arbor Springs, Zion, from Ebenezer.
W. Ashcraft - Mt. Zion, Forest
A. Spiller - Corinth, Enon
Lyles - Oak Ridge, Spring Hill, Big Creek
Deloach - Mineral Springs
Smith - Bulah, New Hope
Jones - Bethel
Foster - Grant Creek
Blaylock – BBethlehem, Spring Hill (Lamar)
J. W. Watson \ – BPleasant Grove (Lamar)
J. H. Cason \ – BProvidence, Carrollton, Unity

1868
Blaylock - Bethlehem, Spring Hill (Lamar)
Spiller - Liberty, Corinth
Hollingsworth - Mt. Pleasant
Wooten - Pine Grove (Lamar)
Cason - Providence, Pickensville
Lyle - South Carolina, Oak Ridge, Spring Hill, Big Creek
J. M. Land - Mineral Springs, Hebron. He was from Springhill.
Duncan - Cross Road
Ashcraft - Enon, Unity, Mt. Zion, Forest
Smith - Shiloah, Bulah, Zion
Jones - Bethel
Foster - Grant Creek

1869
Blaylock - Bethlehem, Spring Hill (Lamar)
Spiller - Liberty, Corinth
Hollingsworth - Mt. Pleasant
Hildreth - Fellowship Buried in the Upper cemetery at Pickensville.
Wooten - Pleasant Grove (Lamar)
Lyle - Spring Hill, Big Creek, Pickensville, Carrollton
Duncan --Cross Road
Ashcraft - Unity, Mt. Zion, Forest
Smith -- Shiloh, Bulah. New Hope
Foster - Grant Creek, Bethel
Wilkins - Ebenezer
J. P. Lee - Providence, Oak Ridge, Enon
W. H. Robertson - South Carolina
Deloach - Mineral Springs, Hebron
H. Roberts - Zion

1870
Blaylock - Spring Hill (lamar)
Hollingsworth-- Mt. Pleasant
Hildreth - Fellowship, Corinth
Wooten - Pleasant Grove (Lamar)
Lyle - South Carolina, Spring Hill, Big Creek, Pickensville
Duncan - Cross Road
Ashcraft - Forest, Unity, Mt. Zion
Smith --Shiloh, Bulah, New Hope
Foster - Grant Creek, Bethel
Wilkins - Liberty
Lee - Providence, Oak Ridge
Deloach - Mineral Spring, Hebron
B. C. Howell - Bethlehem
P. F. Terrell - Ebenezer, Carrollton, Enon Teacher at Springhill Acad. Grad. Of William Jewell College, Liberty, Mo.)
J. H. Morris --Zion

1871
J. M. Carpenter --Liberty
I. **Hollingsworth** --Mt. Pleasant
Hildreth - Fellowship, Corinth
Wooten - Spring Hill (Lamar), Pleasant Grove (Lamar)
Ashcraft - Providence, Unity, Mt. Zion, Forest
J. H. Guyton - South Carolina
Lyles - Mineral Springs, Spring Hill, Big Creek
Lee - Oak Ridge

Duncan --Cross Roads
L. M. Stone, Jr -- Pickensville Famous educator. From Springhill.
Terrell - Carrollton, Ebenezer, Enon
Smith --Shiloh, Bulah, New Hope, Zion
Foster - Bethel, New Hope, Grant Creek

1872
Carpenter - Liberty, Ebenezer
Hildreth - Fellowship, Corinth
Wooten - Spring Hill (Lamar), Pleasant Grove (Lamar)
Ashcraft - Providence, Unity, Forest
Guyton - Bethlehem
Lyles - Mineral Springs, Big Creek
Lee - South Carolina, Oak Ridge, Spring Hill
Duncan - Cross Roads
Stone - Pickensville
Smith - Shiloh, Bulh, Zion
Foster - Grant Creek, New Hope
Jones - Mt. Pleasant, Bethel
Deloach - Hebron
R. Keith --Carrollton, Enon, Mt. Zion

1873
E. Howell --Bethlehem
Carpenter --Liberty, Ebenezer
Jones -- Mt. Pleasant, Bethel
Hildreth --Fellowship, Corinth
Wooten --Spring Hill (Lamar), Pleasant Grove (Lamar)
Ashcraft --Providence, Unity, Forest
Lyles --Arbor Springs, Mineral Springs, Spring Hill, Big Creek
Lee --South Carolina
J. H. Curry --Mt. Zion, Hebron
R. T. Hanks - Pickensville He moved to Texas. Pastor of Dallas FBC, Abilene FBC, and El Paso FBC, and editor of Baptist Standard.
R. Keith - Carrollton, Enon
Smith - Shiloh, Bulah, Zion
Foster - New Hope, Grant Creek

1874
Carpenter --Hebron
Jones --Bethel
Hildreth B--ellowship, Corinth
Wooten --Bethlehem, Spring Hill (Lamar)
Ashcraft - Providence, Unity, Forest
Lyles - Arbor Springs, Mineral Springs, Spring Hill, Big Creek
Lee - South Carolina, Enon
Curry --Hebron, Pickensville, Mt. Zion
Smith - Shiloh, Bulah
Foster - Grant Creek, New Hope
Wilkins - Liberty
J. A. Mitchell - Mt. Pleasant

1875
Hildreth - Fellowship, Corinth
Wooten - Pleasant Grove (Lamar)
Ashcraft --Carrollton, Unity, Forest
Lyles - Mineral Springs, Big Creek
Curry - Mt. Zion, Hebron, Spring Hill, Pickensville
Smith - Bulah, Bethel
Foster - Grant Creek, New Hope
Mitchell - Mt. Pleasant, New Hope
Wilkens - Liberty
W. C. Smith - South Carolina
Hollingsworth - Ebenezer
J. Anders -Chalcedonia

1876
Hollingsworth - Liberty
Mitchell - Mt. Pleasant, Zion
Hildreth - Fellowship, Corinth
Wooten - Spring Hill (Lamar), Pleasant Grove (L)
Lee - Providence, Oak Ridge, Enon
W. C. Smith --South Carolina
Lyles - Mineral Spring, Big Creek,

Ebenezer
Curry - Spring Hill, Hebron, Pickensville, Mt. Zion
Robertson - Cross Roads
Ashcraft Carrolton, Unity, Forest
Anders - Chaledonia
M. P. Smith - Bulah
A. M. Smith – BBethel
Foster - New Hope, Grant Creek

1877
Mitchell - Mt.Pleasant, Liberty, Zion
Hildreth - Fellowship, Corinth
Wooten - Bethlehem, Spring Hill (L), Pleasant Grove (L)
Lee - South Carolina, Oak Ridge
Lyles - Mineral Springs, Spring Hill, Big Creek, Ebenezer
Curry - Mt Zion, Hebron, Pickensville, Carrollton, Enon
Robertson - Cross Road
Ashcraft - Unity, Forest
R. A. Massey - Prairie (now West Greene)
J. L. Ray - Shiloh. Helped by Assn. To get an education.

1878
Hollingsworth - Antioch (Carrollton, PO)
Mitchell - Liberty, Mineral Spring
Hildreth - Mt.Pleasant
Wooten - Pleasant Grove (L)
Lee -Providence, South Carolina, Oak Ridge
Lyles - Spring Hill, Hebron, Ebenezer, Big Creek
Curry - Pickensville, Carrollton, Enon
Robertson - Cross Road
Anders - Chal.
Smith - Bulah
Foster - Grant Creek, New Hope
Massey - Prairie, Bethel, Unity, Mt. Zion
Ray - Shiloh, Zion
J. M. Chism - Fellowship
J. G. Thornton - Forest

1879
Mitchell --Liberty, Corinth, Mineral Spring, Fellowship
Wooten - Spring Hill (L)
Lyles - Pleasant Grove (L), Big Creek
Lee -- South Carolina, Oak Ridge
Land - Spring Hill, Cross Road
H. B. Chappelle - Hebron
Curry - Pickensville, Carrollton, Enon
Hollingsworth - Antioch
Massey - Unity, Mt. Zion, Bethel
J. E. White - Prairie
Thorton - Forest
Ray - Shiloh, Zion
Anders - Chal.
Smith --Bulah
Foster - Grant Creek, New Hope
Hilburn - Mt. Pleasant

1880
Mitchell - Liberty, Corinth, Mineral Spring
Hildreth -Arbor Springs, Ebenezer, Temple Hill (Carrollton PO)
Wooten - Spring Hill (L), Pleasant Grove (L)
Lee - South Carolina, Mineral Spring, Hebron
Land - Spring Hill, Cross Road, Oak Ridge
Chappelle - Big Creek, Hebron
Curry - Pickensville, Carrollton, Enon
Hollingsworth - Antioch
Massey - Unity, Mt. Zion, Bethel
White - Prairie
Thornton - Forest
Ray - Shiloh, Zion
Anders - Chal.
Smith - Bulah
Foster - Grant Creek, New Hope
M. Keenum - Bethlehem

Hilburn - Mt. Pleasant

1880
Keenum - Bethlehem
Mitchell - Liberty, Corinth, Mineral Spring
Hilburn - Mt. Pleasant
Chism - Fellowship
Wooten - Spring Hill (L), Pleasant Grove (L)
Hildreth - Arbor Spring, Ebenezer
Lee - South Carolina, Oak Ridge, Spring Hill
Chappelle - Hebron, Big Creek
Land-- - Cross Road
Curry - Pickensville, Carrollton, Enon
Hollingsworth - Temple Hill
Massey - Unity, Mt. Zion, Bethel
White - Prairie
Thornton - Forest
Ray -Shiloh
Anders - Chal., Zion
Smith - Bulah
Foster - Grant Creek, New Hope

1881
Mitchell - Liberty, Mt. Pleasant, Corinth, Mineral Spring
Wooten - Pleasant Grove (L)
Lee - Oak Ridge, Spring Hill
Chappelle - Hebron, Big Creek
Land - Cross Road
Curry - Pickensville, Carrollton, Enon
Massey - Bethel
White - Prairie
Thornton - Mt. Zion, Forest
Ray - Shiloh, Zion
Anders - Chal.
Smith - Bulah
Foster - New Hope, Grant Creek
Lyles - Fellowship, South Carolina, Ebenezer
M. G. Lofton - Unity. Out of Springhill.

1882
Mitchell - Liberty, Mt. Pleasant, Corinth
Wooten - Spring Hill (L), Pleasant Grove (L)
Lee - Oak Ridge, Spring Hill
Chappelle - Big Creek, Antioch
Land - South Carolina, Cross Road
Curry - Pickensville, Carrollton, Enon
Massey - Bethel
White - Prairie, Bulah
Thornton-- BMt. Zion, Forest
Ray - Shiloh, Zion
Foster - New Hope, Grant Creek
Lyles - Fellowship, Arbor Springs, Hebron, Ebenezer
Lofton - Unity

1883
D. O. Baird - Bethlehem. Buried on his farm near Bethlehem.
Mitchell --Liberty, Mt. Pleasant, Corinth, Forest
Lyles - Fellowship, Arbor Springs, Hebron, Ebenezer
J. S. Shirley - Flatwood
Wooten --Spring Hill (L)
Lee - Mineral Spring, Spring Hill
Lofton - Oak Ridge, Unity, Mt. Zion
Chapelle - Big Creek, Antioch
Land - Cross Road
Curry-- BPickensville, Carrollton, Enon
White - Prairie, Bulah
Ray - Shiloh
Anders-- BChal., Zion
W. A. Bishop - Bethel
Foster - New Hope, Grant Creek

1884
Mitchell - Liberty, Mt. Pleasant, Fellowship, Forest
Lyles - Arbor Spring, Ebenezer, Hebron

Shirley - Flatwood
Wooten - Spring Hill (L)
Lee -Bethlehem, Mineral Spring
Lofton - Unity, Mt. Zion, Oak Ridge, Spring Hill
Chappelle-- Big Creek, Antioch
Land - Cross Road
Curry - Pickensville, Carrollton, Enon
White - Prairie, Bulah, Zion
Ray - Shiloh
Anders - Chal., Zion
Bishop - Bethel
Foster - New Hope, Grant Creek
W. H. Robinson - Pleasant Grove (L)

1885
Mitchell - Bethlehem, Liberty, Mt. Pleasant
Lyles - Mineral Spring, Hebron, Big Creek
Shirley - Flatwood, Ebenezer
Lee - Mineral Springs
Lofton - Oak Ridge, Spring Hill, Mt. Zion
Chappelle - Antioch
Curry - Pickensville, Carrollton, Enon
White - Prairie, Bulah, Zion
Anders --Chal
Foster - Grant Creek, New Hope
Wood - Corinth
L.G. Williams BForest

1886
Baird --Bethlehem
W. J. Beaty - Liberty, Fellowship,
Shirley --Mt. Pleasant, Flatwoods, Ebenezer,
S.E. Hodge - Corinth, Nazareth
S.J. Wooten --Springhill (L),
J.W. Cox - Kennedy,
G.M. Lyles - Arbor Springs, Hebron,
H.B. Chappelle - Oak Ridge,
M.G. Lofton - Springhill (P), Big Creek, Mt. Zion,
J. H. Curry - Pickensville, Carrollton, Unity, Enon
J.G. Thornton - Prairie
M.M.Wood - Forest, Buelah, Bethel
J.L. Ray - Shiloh
J.W. Hosmer - Chaldony
H.H.M. Anders - Zion
J.C. Foster - New Hope, Grant's Creek

1887
Baird - Bethlehem
Beaty - Liberty, Fellowship
Shirley - Mt. Pleasant, Flatwoods, Ebenezer
Hodge --Corinth
Wooten - Springhill (L)
Cox --Kennedy
Kolb - McBee Ck
Estes - Arbor Springs
Lee - Mineral Springs.
Chappelle - Oak Ridge
Lofton - Springhill, Mt. Zion, Forest, Big Creek
Curry - Enon, Big Creek, Carrollton, Pickensville
Thornton – Unity, Prairie
Ray --Shiloah
Hamner - Chal;
Wood --Nazareth
Foster - Grant Ck, New Hope
Anders - Zion

1888
Baird --Bethlehem
Beaty - Liberty, Fellowship
Shirley - Mt. Pleasant
Hodge --Corinth
Anders --Flatwoods
J. W. Dunaway - Millport, Kennedy, Springhill (L), McBee, Mineral Springs.
Estes - Arbor Springs, New Salem
Chappelle - Oak Ridge
Lofton - Springhill, Big Creek, Mt. Zion,

Forest
Curry - Hebron, Enon, Pickensville, Carrollton
Lee --Crossroads
Thornton - Ebenezer, Prairie
Hildreth --Unity
Hamner - Shiloah, Zion
Miller - Chal.
Wood - Buelah, Bethel
Foster -- New Hope, Grant's Ck.

1889
Baird - Bethlehem, Arbor Springs, minerql Springs
Beaty - Liberty, Springhill (L), McBee, Fellowship
Hodge - Mt. Pleasant, Corinth
Anders --Flatwood
Johnson - Kennedy, Carrollton
Estes - New Salem
Chappelle - Oak Ridge
Lofton - Springhill, Big Creek, Mt. Zion, Forest
Lee --Crossroads
Curry - Hebron, Pickensville, Enon, Unity
Thornton - Ebenexzer, Prairie
Ray --Shiloah
Hamner - Chal. , Zion
Foster Grant's Ck, New Hope

1890
Ashcraft -Bethlehem, Kennedy, Arbor Springs,
Beaty -Liberty
Hodge - Mt. Pleasant, Corinth,
Dunaway - Fellowship, SpringHill, Millport, McBee Creek, Mineral Springs,
·**Anders** - Flatwoods
Estes - New Salem
Lofton -Springhill, Hebron, Big Creek
Lee - CrossRoads,
Thornton -Ebenezer, Prairie
Johnson -Unity, Forest
Curry - Enon
Ray -Shiloh,
Hamner- Chalcedony, Zion
Apsey - Bethel, Beulah
Foster -New Hope, Grant=s Creek

Pastors of Our Association from 1895 to 1945

The minutes of the association do not list pastors of the churches from 1891 thru 1894. So, we will resume our lists with 1895

1895
G.W. Kerr - Bethlehem
J.A. Estes – Liberty, Spring Hill (L),
D.O. Baird – Fellowship, Millport, Kennedy, New Salem, Arbor Springs,
S.E. Hodge – Mt. Pleasant, Ebenezer, Chalcedony
J.B. Small – Mineral Springs, Pickensville, Carrollton,
J.P. Lee – Oak Ridge, Spring Hill (P), Crossroads,
O.E. Wooten – Hickory Grove
M.G. Lofton – Unity, Enon
J.G. Thornton – Mt. Zion, Prairie, Forest, Beulah
J.D. Hamner – Shiloh,
J.H. Curry – Beulah, Grants Creek,
J.T. Bealle – New Hope
J.L. Ray – Zion

1896
D.O. Baird – Bethlehem, Liberty, Fellowship, Millport, Kennedy, Arbor Springs,
S.E. Hodge – Mt. Pleasant,
J.A. Estes – Spring Hill (L), New Salem
O.E. Wooten – Pleasant Grove, Hickory Grove
J.W. Caldwell – McBee,
J.B. Small – Mineral Springs, Pickensville, Carrollton, Enon
J.P. Lee – Oak Ridge, Spring Hill (P), Crossroads,
J.M. Anders – Ebenezer, Flatwoods
M.G. Lofton – Hebron, Big Creek, Forest
J.G. Thornton – Mt. Zion,
J.D. Cook – Prairie, Beulah
J.D. Hamner – Shiloh,
J.H. Curry – Bethel, Grants Creek
J.T. Bealle – New Hope

1896 (continued)
J.D. Ray – Zion

1897 (No List of Pastors)

1898
D.O. Baird – Arbor Springs, Bethlehem, Kennedy, Liberty, Millport
J.H. Curry – Bethel, Grants Creek
J.D. Cook – Beulah, Prairie
W.L. White – Big Creek, Carrollton, Enon, Pickensville,
T.K. Harrison – Chalcedony, Zion,
G.W. Kerr – Crossroads, New Hope, Union Center,
S.E. Hodge – Ebenezer,
J.H.M Anders - Cornelius Chapel, Flatwoods, Mt. Pleasant
J.B. Small – Fellowship,
J.W. Caldwell – Forest, Unity, Spring Hill (P)
H.B. Chappell – Hebron,
O.E. Wooten – Hickory Grove,
J.A. Estes – Mineral Springs, Spring Hill (L),
W.P. Peden – Mt. Zion,
W.J. Beaty – New Salem
J.D. Hamner – Shiloh,

1899
D.O. Baird – Arbor Springs, Bethlehem, Kennedy, Liberty, Millport,
W.L. White – Big Creek, Carrollton, Enon Pickensville
J.D. Cook – Beulah, Prairie,
J.H. Curry – Bethel, Grants Creek,
G.W. Kerr – Crossroads, Ethelsville, Union Center
J.H.M. Anders – Cornelius Chapel, Flatwoods,
S.E. Hodge – Ebenezer
W.J. Beaty – Fellowship, New Salem,
H.B. Chappell – Hebron
O.E. Wooten – Pleasant Grove, Spring Hill(L)
J.W. Caldwell – Forest, Reform, Spring

1899 (continued)
Hill(P)
J.D. Hamner - Zion

1900
.D.O. Baird – Arbor Springs, Bethlehem, Kennedy, Liberty, Millport
W.L. White – Big Creek, Carrollton, Enon, Pickensville, Reform
J.H. Curry – Bethel,
J.H.M. Anders – Cornelius, Flatwoods,
G.W. Kerr – Crossroads, Mineral Springs, South Carolina, Union Center
S.E. Hodge – Ebenezer
W.J. Beaty – New Salem, Fellowship
J.W. Caldwell – Forest, Hebron, Spring Hill(P), Unity,
C.E. Wooten – Hickory Grove, Pleasant Grove,
B.J., O'Briant – Mt. Pleasant, Zion,
J.D. RayB – New Hope
J.D. Herring – Prairie
J.D. Hamner – Shiloh

1901
D.O. Baird – Arbor Springs, Bethlehem, Kennedy, Liberty, McBee, Millport, Gordo
H.B. Chappell – Big Creek, Hebron, Spring Hill(P)
W.L. White – Bethel, Chalcedony, New Hope,
J.H. Curry – Beulah, Grants Creek,
C.C. Winters – Carrollton, Enon, Forest, Pickensville
J.H.M. Anders – Cornelius Chapel, Flatwoods
C.E. Wooten – Hickory Grove, Pleasant Grove,
B.J. O'Briant – Mt. Pleasant, Zion
W.J. Beaty – Fellowship, New Salem
J.E. Herring – Prairie,
J.D. Hamner – Shiloh,
J.A. Estes – Spring Hill(L), Union Chapel
G.W. Kerr – Mineral Springs, South Carolina.
S.E. Hodge – Union Center, Ebenezer,

1902

D.O.Baird- Arbor Springs, Bethlehem, Gordo, Kennedy, Millport, Reform,
J.W. Dickinson - Bethel, Beulah, New Hope, Grants Creek
H.B. Chappell - Big Creek, Spring Hill(P),
C.C. Winters - Carrollton, Enon, Forest, Pickensville,
J.M.M. Anders - Cornelius Chapel
G.W. Kerr- Crossroads, Mineral Springs, Shiloh, South Carolina
L.M. Stone - Fellowship, Union Center,
J. W. Caldwell - Ebenezer, Hebron,
J.A. Estes - Hickory Grove, Spring Hill (L), Union Chapel
O'Briant - Mt. Pleasant, Zion
W. J. Beaty - New Salem (soon to become Friendship)
J. E. Herring- Prairie

1903
Baird- Arbor Springs, Gordo, Kennedy, Millport, Reform, Mt. Pleasant
J.M. Cox - Bethlehem, Pleasant Grove, Spring Hill (L)
J.W. Dickinson - Bethel, Beulah, New Hope, Grants Creek
H.B. Chappell - Big Creek, Spring Hill(P)
H.M. Long - Carrollton, Enon, Pickensville,
J.M.M. Anders - Cornelius Chapel
G.W. Kerr- Crossroads, Mineral Springs, Shiloh, Unity, Stansel
J.M. Chism - Ebenezer
W.P. Peden - Fellowship
J.A. Estes - Liberty, New Salem, Union Chapel
O'Briant - Zion
J. E. Herring- Prairie

1904
Baird- Arbor Springs, Gordo, Kennedy, Millport, Reform, Mt. Pleasant
J.M. Cox - Pleasant Grove, Spring Hill (L),

1904 (continued)
Hickory Grove, Spring Hill (P), Ethelsville
O.P. Godfrey - Bethlehem
J.W. Dickinson - Beulah, Forrest, New Hope, Grants Creek
J.R. Magill - Bethel
H.B. Chappell - Big Creek
H.M. Long - Carrollton, Pickensville,
J.M.M. Anders - Cornelius Chapel
G.W. Kerr- Crossroads, Mineral Springs, Shiloh, Unity, Stansel
W.P. Peden - Fellowship
J.M. Mills - Liberty, New Salem
J.L. Ray - Zion, Flatwoods
J. E. Herring- Prairie

1905
Baird- Gordo, Kennedy, Millport, Reform, Mt. Pleasant
J.P. Rogers - Arbor Springs
J.M. Cox - Spring Hill (P), Ethelsville
O.P. Godfrey - Pleasant Grove, Hickory Grove
E.P. Smith - Aliceville, Carrollton, Pickensville
J.W. Dickinson - Beulah, Forrest, New Hope, Grants Creek
J.R. Magill - Bethel, Grants Creek
G.W. Kerr- Crossroads, Ebenezer, Mineral Springs, Shiloh, Unity
W.P. Peden - Fellowship
J.M. Mills - Big Creek, Hebron, Liberty, New Salem
J.L. Ray - Flatwoods
J. E. Herring- Prairie
W.J Beatty - Bethlehem, Fort Springs
J.D. Hemner - Cornelius Chapel
J.A. Estes - Union Chapel
S.E. Hodge - Zion, Stansel

1906
J.A. Estes - Arbor Springs, Union Chapel
E.P. Smith - Aliceville, Carrollton, Pickensville
J.R. Magill - Bethel

1906 (continued)
L.S. Foster - Beulah, Forest, Grant's Creek, New Hope
J.M. Mills - Big Creek, Ethelsville, Hebron, Liberty, Stansel
1906 (continued)
S.E. Hodge - Cornelius Chapel
J.A. Andrews - Chalcedony, Zion
J.W. Kerr - Ebenezer, Mineral Springs, Shiloh, Unity, Stansel
J.P. Peden - Fellowship
S.W. Lindsey - Fort Springs, Spring Hill (L)
J.L. Ray - Flatwoods
D.O. Baird - Gordo, Kennedy, Millport, Mt. Pleasant, Reform
J.E. Herring - Prairie
J.A. Mitchell - Spring Hill (P)

1907
J.A. Estes - Arbor Springs, Bethlehem, Union Chapel
E.P. Smith - Carrollton, Aliceville, Pickensville
A.T. Camp - Bethel
A.R. Lofton - Beulah, Forest, Grants Creek, New Hope
J.M. Mills - Big Creek, Hebron, Stansel
S.E. Hodge - Cornelius Chapel, Chalcedony
J.A. Mitchell - Crossroads, Fellowship, Liberty, Spring Hill (P)
G.W. Kerr - Ebenezer, Friendship, Unity, Shiloh
J.M. Cox - Ethelsville, Hickory Grove, Spring Hill (L)
S.W. Lindsey - Fort Springs
D.O. Baird - Gordo Mt. Pleasant, Reform
A.B. Metcalf - Kennedy, Millport
J.A. Mitchell - Liberty, Mineral Springs, Spring Hill (P)
O.P Godfrey - Pleasant Grove
J.E. Herring - Prairie
J.D. Weems - Zion

1908 - No List

1909
J.A. Estes - Arbor Springs, Fort Springs
J.F. Brock - Aliceville, Carrollton, Pickensville
J.G. Lowry - Bethel
A.R. Lofton - Beulah, Forest, Grant's Creek, New Hope
J.M. Mills - Big Creek, Hebron, Liberty, Pine Grove
J.H. Gardner- Bethlehem, Flatwoods
J.D. Hemner - Cornelius Chapel
J.A. Mitchell - Crossroads, Fellowship, Friendship, Spring Hill (P)
S.E. Hodge - Calcedonia (Chalcedony)
G.W. Kerr - Ebenezer, Unity
W.J. Godfrey - Ethelsville
D.O. Baird - Gordo, Reform, Mt. Pleasant
A.B. Metcalf - Kennedy
D.W. Morgan - Millport
Foster Mills - Mineral Springs
J.E. Herring - Prairie
D.Z. Wooley - Shiloh, Stansel
J.W. Hosmer - Spring Hill (L)
A.P. Weems - Zion

1910
J.G. Lowery - Bethel, Grant's Creek
J.A. Estes - Arbor Springs, Bethlehem, Fort Springs, Spring Hill (L)
J.F. Brock - Aliceville, Carrollton, Pickensville, Spring Hill (P)
A.R. Lofton - Beulah, New Hope, Shiloh, Forest
J.M. Mills - Big Creek, Hebron, Liberty, Mt. Pleasant
J.D. Hamner - Cornelius Chapel
Jesse McAlister - Crossroads, Union Chapel
S.E. Hodge - Calcedonia
G.W. Kerr - Ebenezer, Fellowship, Unity
Foster Mills - Friendship
O.E. Wooton - Hickory Grove
D.W. Morgan - Millport, Kennedy
Foster Mills - Mineral Springs
R.S. Marler - Pine Grove

1910 (continued)
D.Z. Wooly - Reform
A.P. Weems - Zion
J.E. Herring - Prairie

1911
J.F. Brock - Aliceville, Carrollton, Pickensville, Spring Hill (P)
R.S. Marler - Arbor Springs, Flatwoods, Fort Springs, Pine Grove
J.G. Lowry - Bethel, Grant's Creek
A.R. Lofton - Beulah, New Hope, Forest
J.M. Mills - Big Creek, Hebron, Hickory Grove, Liberty
J.D. Hamner - Cornelius Chapel
G.W. Kerr - Crossroads, Shiloh, Unity
S.E. Hodge - Ebenezer, Flatwoods
Foster Mills - Friendship, Mineral Springs
D.B. Wooly - Gordo, Reform
J.M. McCord - Kennedy
R.K. Pennington - Millport
J.E. Herring -Prairie
Jesse McAllister - Union Chapel
A.P Weems - Zion

1912
J.F. Brock - Aliceville, Big Creek, Carrollton, Pickensville, Spring Hill (P)
R.S. Marler - Arbor Springs, Bethlehem, Fellowship, Fort Springs
J.A. Dickinson - Beulah, Forest, New Hope, Shiloh
Jesse McAllister - Cornelius Chapel
G.W. Kerr - Crossroads, Unity
S.E. Hodge - Ebenezer, Mt. Pleasant
J.M. Cox - Ethelsville
Foster Mills - Friendship, Mineral Springs
J.H. Newton - Gordo, Stansel
J.M. Mills - Hebron, Hickory Grove, Liberty
A.P. Weems - Zion

1913
A.B. Metcalf - Aliceville, Carrollton, Pickensville, Stansel
R.S. Marler - Arbor Springs, Bethlehem, Union Chapel, Fellowship
L.N. Brock - Bethel
A.F. Camp - Beulah, Grant's Creek
G.W. Kerr - Big Creek, Crossroads, Unity
S.E. Hodge - Ebenezer, Flatwoods, Mt Pleasant
J.H. Newton - Ethelsville, Gordo, Reform
J.A Dickinson - Forest, New Hope, Shiloh
Foster Mills - Friendship, Mineral Springs
A.T. Camp - Grant's Creek
J.M. Mills - Hebron, Hickory Grove, Liberty, Spring Hill (P)
Frank Wilson - Kennedy
J.F. Bell - Millport

1914
J.N. Vandiver - Aliceville, Carrollton
R.S. Marler - Arbor Springs, Bethlehem, Ebenezer, Mt. Pleasant
L.N. Brock - Bethel
J.A. Estes - Big Creek, Pine Grove
J.H. Newton - Ethelsville, Gordo, Reform
S.E. Hodge - Fellowship, Flatwoods
J.M. Mills - Forest, Hebron, Liberty, Spring Hill (P)
Foster Mills - Friendship, Mineral Springs
W.B. Earnest - Grant's Creek, New Hope, Shiloh
O.E. Wooten - Hickory Grove
J.C. McCollum - Kennedy
T.W. Shelton - Millport, Spring Hill (L)
H.A. Estes - Pine Grove
J.E. Herring - Prairie
G.W. Kerr - Zion
J.E. Herring - Prairie

1915
J.N. Vandiver - Aliceville, Carrollton, Stansel
R.S. Marler - Arbor Springs, Ebenezer, Flatwoods, Mt. Pleasant
L.N. Brock - Bethel, New Hope

1915 (continued)
T.W. Shelton - Bethlehem, Kennedy, Millport, Spring Hill (L)
J.D. Brock - Beulah
J.A. Estes - Big Creek, Crossroads, Pine Grove
J.M. Mills - Forest, Hebron, Spring Hill (P)
A.T. Ezell - Fellowship, Ethelsville, Union Chapel, Pine Grove
Foster Mills - Mineral Springs, Friendship
H.G. Johnson - Gordo, Reform
John W. Stewart - Grant's Creek
J.E. Herring - Prairie
G.W. Kerr - Shiloh, Unity

1916
J.N. Vandiver - Aliceville, Carrollton, Stansel
J.C. Vandiver - Arbor Springs, Bethlehem, Friendship, Liberty, Mineral Springs
L.N. Brock - Bethel, New Hope
J.D. Cook - Beulah
R.S. Marler - Ebenezer, Mr. Pleasant, Flatwoods
A.T. Ezell- Ethelsville, Fellowship, Pine Grove, Union Chapel
H.G. Johnson - Gordo,
J.W. Stewart - Grants Creek
J. H. Longerier - Kennedy, Millport,
J. M. Mills - Forest, Hebron, Pleasant Hill, Spring Hill (P)
J.E. Herring - Prairie,
G.W. Kerr -Shiloh, Unity
T.W. Shelton - Spring Hill (L)
Elisha Brown - Zion

1917
J.N. Vandiver - Aliceville, Carrollton, Stansel
J.C. Vandiver - Arbor Springs, Friendship, Liberty, Mineral Springs
O.E. Wooten - Bethlehem, Spring Hill (L)
J.D. Cook - Beulah
J.D. Hamner - Cornelius Chapel
R.S. Marler - Ebenezer, Fellowship, Mt. Pleasant

1917 (continued)
A.T. Ezell - Ethelsville, Pine Grove, Union Chapel
J.M. Mills - Forest, Hebron, Pleasant Hill, Spring Hill (P)
J.W. Shelton - Fort Springs
H.G. Johnson - Gordo,
J.M. Cox - Hickory Grove
J.H. Longerier - Kennedy, Millport
J.E. Herring - Prairie
H.D. Wilson - Reform
G.W. Kerr - Shiloh, Unity
E.N. Brown - Zion

1918
J.N.Vandiver - Aliceville, Carrollton,
R.S. Marler - Arbor Springs, Bethlehem, Ebenezer, Flatwoods, Mt. Pleasant
J.C. Vandiver - Bethel, Grants Creek, New Hope
J.D. Cook - Beulah
P.B. Chastain- Big Creek
H.H. Buzbee - Ethelsville, Hickory Grove, Mineral Springs, Pine Grove, Spring Hill (P), Union Chapel
J.M. Mills - Forest, Hebron, Pleasant Hill
J.A. Mitchell - Fellowship
J.M. Cox - Fort Springs
Foster Mills - Friendship
H.H. Hagood - Kennedy
H.G. Johnson - Gordo, Liberty, Prairie
A.H. Mahaffey - Reform
G.W. Kerr - Shiloh, Unity
J.A. Estis - Spring Hill (L)
E.N. Brown - Zion

1919
J.E. Cook, Jr. - Carrollton, Aliceville
R.S. Marler - Arbor Springs, Gordo, Mt. Pleaant
J.C. Vandiver - Bethel, Grants Creek, New Hope
J.A. Estes - Bethlehem,
J.D. Cook - Beulah
P.B. Chastain - Big Creek

1919 (continued)
O.D. Haney - Ethelsville, Mineral Springs, Pine Grove, Hickory Grove
J.A. Mitchell - Fellowship, Liberty
J.M. Mills - Forest, Hebron, Pleasant Hill
Foster Mills - Friendship

1920
J.E. Cook, Jr. - Aliceville, Carrollton
J.A. Estes - Arbor Springs, Bethlehem, Pleasant Grove
H.G. Johnson - Beulah
J.D. Hamner - Cornelius Chapel
J.A. Mitchell - Cross Roads, Fellowship, Liberty
R.S. Marler - Ebenezer, Friendship, Gordo, Mt. Pleasant
E.A. Brown - Flatwoods
J.M. Mills - Forest, Hebron, Pleasant Hill
L.M. Peragin - Spring Hill (L)
E.S. Pool - Reform
G.W. Kerr - Shiloh, Stansel, Unity

1921
J.E. Cook, Jr. - Aliceville, Carrollton
J.A. Estes - Arbor Springs, Bethlehem, Pleasant Grove
A.N. Reeves - Bethel, Grants Creek, New Hope
H.G. Johnson - Beulah
J. D. Hamner - Cornelius Chapel
J.A. Mitchell - Cross Roads, Fellowship, Liberty, Spring Hill (P)
R.S. Marler - Ebenezer, Fellowship, Gordo, Mt. Pleasant
C.H. Morgan - Ethelsville, Hickory Grove, Mineral Springs, Pine Grove, Union Chapel
J.M. Mills - Forest, Hebron, Mt. Pleasant
G.W. Kerr - Shiloh, Stansel, Unity
L.M. Perrigin - Spring Hill (L)

1922
J.E. Cook, Jr. - Aliceville, Carrollton, Prairie, Pickensville
F.M. Mathews - Arbor Springs, Reform,

1922 (continued)
Stansel
J.A. Estes - Bethlehem, Pleasant Grove
H.G. Johnson - Beulah, Grants Creek
H.G. Carpenter - Cross Roads, Flatwoods
R.S. Marler - Ebenezer, Fellowship, Friendship, Gordo, Mt. Pleasant
C.H. Morgan - Ethelsville, Hickory Grove, Pine Grove, Union Chapel, Mineral Springs
J.M. Mills - Forest, Hebron, Pleasant Hill
J.A. Mitchell - Liberty, Spring Hill (P)
G.W. Kerr - Shiloh, Unity

1923
J.E. Cook, Jr.- Carrollton, Aliceville, Pickensville, Prairie
J.A. Estes - Arbor Springs, Bethlehem,
H.G. Johnson - Beulah, Grants Creek
H.G. Carpenter - Big Creek, Cross Roads
R.S. Marler - Ebenezer, Fellowship,Flatwoods, Friendship, Gordo, Mt. Pleasant
E.N. Brown - Cornelius Chapel, Zion
J.M. Mills - Forest, Hebron, Pleasant Hill, Stansel,
C.H. Morgan - Ethelsville, Hickory Grove, Mineral Springs, Pine Grove, Spring Hill (P)
J.A. Mitchell - Liberty,
N.O. Patterson - Reform
G.W. Kerr - Shiloh, Unity
J.F. Sansing - Union Chapel

1924
W.A. McCain - Aliceville, Carrollton, Pickensville, Prairie
J.A. Estes - Arbor Springs, Bethlehem,
H.G. Johnson - Beulah, Grants Creek, Stansel
E.N. Brown - Cornelius Chapel, Zion
H.G. Carpenter - Cross Roads
R.S. Marler - Ebenezer,
W.S. Cruzan - Ethelsville, Mineral Springs, Hickory Grove, Pine Grove, Spring Hill (P)

1924 (continued)
N.O. Patterson - Fellowship, Reform
J.M. Mills - Forest, Hebron, Pleasant Hill
C.A. Bryant - Friendship, Liberty,
H.C. Todd - Gordo, Mt. Pleasant
J.F. Sansing - Union Chapel
G.W. Kerr - Unity

1925
W.A. McCain- Aliceville, Carrollton, Pickensville, Prairie
J.A. Estes - Arbor Springs, Bethlehem
H.G. Johnson - Beulah, Stansel, Unity
H.G. Carpenter - Big Creek,
E.N. Brown - Cornelius Chapel, Flatwoods
C.A. Bryant - Ebenezer, Fellowship, Friendship, Liberty, Pleasant Hill
J.M. Mills - Forest,
H.C. Todd - Gordo, Mt. Pleasant, Reform
W.S. Cruzan- Hickory Grove, Mineral Springs, Spring Hill, Ethelsville
J.F. Sansing - Union Chapel
J.W. Fore - Zion

1926
W.A. McCain - Aliceville, Carrollton, Pickensville, Prairie
J.A. Estes - Arbor Springs,
J.M. Cox - Bethlehem,
H.G. Johnson - Beulah, Stansel, Unity
C.A. Bryant - Big Creek, Ebenezer, Liberty, Pleasant Hill, Fellowship
E.N. Brown - CorneliusChapel, Flatwoods
J.F. Sansing - Cross Roads, Union Chapel
W.S. Cruzan - Ethelsville, Hickory Grove, Mineral Springs, Pine Grove, Spring Hill
J.M. Mills - Forest
H.C. Todd - Friendship, Gordo, Hebron, Mt. Pleasant, Reform
L.M. Perrigin - Zion

1927
C.E. Johnson - Aliceville
J.A. Estes- Arbor Springs, Bethlehem

1927 (continued)
H.S. Johnson - Beulah, Stansel
W.A. McCain- Carrollton, Pickensville, Prairie
E.N. Brown - Cornelius Chapel, Flatwoods
J.F. Sansing - Cross Roads,
C.A. Bryant - Ebenezer, Fellowship, Liberty, Stansel
J.M. Mills - Forest,
R.L. Bonner - Friendship
J.O. Bledsoe - Gordo, Hickory Grove, Mt. Pleasant, Pine Grove
H.C. Todd- Hebron, Reform
J.Y. Brooks - Spring Hill (P), Union Chapel
C.N. Travis - Unity
L.M. Perrigin - Zion

1928
E.E. Johnson - Aliceville
H.T. Carpenter - Arbor Springs
1928 (continued)
C.A. Bryant - Bethlehem, Cornelius Chapel, Ebenezer, Fellowship, Liberty, Pleasant Hill
H.G. Johnson - Beulah, Stansel
W.A. McCain - Carrollton, Cross Roads, Pickensville, Prairie
J.Y. Brooks - Ethelsville, Hickory Grove, Mineral Springs, Pleasant Grove, Spring Hill (P), Union Chapel
E.N. Brown - Flatwoods
J.M. Mills - Forest
J.O. Bledsoe - Friendship, Gordo, Mt. Pleasant
H.C. Todd - Hebron, Reform
C.N. Travis - Unity,
L.M. Perrigin - Zion

1929
E.E. Johnson - Aliceville, Prairie
J.Y. Brooks - Arbor Springs, Ethelsville, Hickory Grove, Mineral Springs, Pine Grove, Union Chapel
H.G. Johnson - Beulah, Stansel
E.U. Calvert - Carrollton, Cross Roads,

1929 (continued)
Pickensville, Spring Hill (P)
C.A. Bryant - Cornelius Chapel, Ebenezer, Liberty, Pleasant Hill, Bethlehem
G.W. Kerr - Fellowship,
J.M. Mills - Forest
J.R. Swedenburg - Friendship
J.O. Bledsow - Gordo, Mt. Pleasant,
H.C. Todd - Hebron, Reform,
C.N. Travis - Unity

1930
E.O. Jackson - Aliceville, Prairie, Unity
J.W. Wells - Arbor Springs,
B.B. Burks - Bethlehem, Fellowship,
E.U. Calvert - Carrollton, Cross Roads, Pickensville, Stansel
C.A. Bryant - Ebenezer, Pleasant Hill
J.Y. Brooks - Ethelsville, Hickory Grove, Mineral Springs, Pine Grove
E.N. Brown - Flatwoods,
J.M. Mills - Forest
J.R. Swedenburg - Friendship, Liberty
T.H. Farr - Gordo, Mt. Pleasant
H.C. Todd - Hebron, Reform
R.J. Shelton - Union Chapel
E.P. Channell - Zion
G.H. Vaughn - Mt. Tabor

1931
E.O. Jackson - Aliceville, Unity
J.W. Wells - Arbor Springs, Bethlehem,
J.L. Watson - Beulah
J.R. Curry - Carrollton, Cross Roads, Pickensville, Prairie, Spring Hill (P)
T.H. Farr - Ebenezer, Fellowship, Gordo, Mt. Pleasant
J.M. Mills - Ethelsville, Forest, Hickory Grove,
H.C. Todd - Hebron, Reform
J.R. Swedenburg - Liberty, Stansel, Friendship
J.Y. Brooks - Mineral Springs, Pine Grove
G.H. Vaughn - Mt. Tabor
C.A. Bryant - Pleasant Hill
R.J. Shelton - Union Chapel

1932
E.O. Jackson - Aliceville, Unity
Grady Bowles - Arbor Springs,
J.M. Mills - Bethlehem, Ethelsville, Forest, Mt. Tabor
J.L. Watson - Beulah,
J. R. Curry - Carrollton, Cross Roads, Pickensville, Prairie
S.E. Walker - Ebenezer,
T.H. Farr - Fellowship, Gordo, Mt. Pleasant
E.N. Brown - Flatwoods,
J.R. Swedenburg - Friendship, Liberty, Stansel
H.C. Todd - Hebron, Reform
J.H. Humphries - Hickory Grove
C.A. Bryant - Mineral Springs, Pleasant Hill
J.Y. Brooks - Pine Grove
H.G. Carpenter - Spring Hill (P),
R.J. Shelton - Union Chapel

1933
E.O. Jackson - Aliceville, Unity
O.C. Kidd - Arbor Springs, Fellowship, Hickory Grove
J.M. Mills - Bethlehem, Forest,
J.L. Watson - Beulah
J.R. Curry - Carrollton, Pickensville, Prairie
H.G. Carpenter - Cross Roads, Ethelsville, Pleasant Hill, Spring Hill (P)
S.E. Walker - Ebenezer, Mt. Tabor
E.N. Brown - Flatwoods
J.R. Swedenburg - Friendship, Stansel,
T.H. Farr - Gordo, Mt. Pleasant
H.C. Todd - Hebron, Reform
Grady Bowles - Liberty
C.A. Bryant - Mineral Springs
J.Y. Brooks - Pine Grove
R.J. Shelton - Union Chapel

1934
E.O. Jackson - Aliceville, Unity
G.H. Bowles - Arbor Springs, Liberty
O.C. Weaver - Bethlehem

1934 (continued)
J.L. Watson - Beulah
J.R. Curry - Carrollton, Pickensville, West Greene,
H.G. Carpenter - Cross Roads, Ethelsville, Pleasant Hill, Spring Hill (P)
S.E. Walker - Ebenezer, Mt. Tabor,
T.H. Farr - Fellowship, Gordo, Mt. Pleasant
E.N. Brown - Flatwoods
J.M. Mills - Forest
H.C. Todd - Hebron, Reform
J.W. Askew - Hickory Grove, Pine Grove
C.A. Bryant - Mineral Springs,
R.J. Shelton - Union Chapel
J.L. Strickland- Zion

1935
C.F. Moffitt - Aliceville, Unity
R.S. Marler - Arbor Springs, Friendship,
O.C. Weaver - Bethlehem, Hickory Grove
E.B. Farrar - Beulah
J.R. Curry - Carrollton, Pickensville, West Greene
H.G. Carpenter - Cross Roads, Pleasant Hill, Spring Hill
J.V. Johnson - Ebenezer,
T.H. Farr - Fellowship, Gordo, Mt. Pleasant
E.N. Brown - Flatwoods
J.M. Mills - Forest
J.R. Swedenburg - Hebron
Grady Bowles - Mineral Springs
C.A. Bryant - Liberty, Stansel
J.W. Askew - Pine Grove
J.B. Wages - Union Chapel
J.L. Strickland - Zion
W.T. Roberts - Pleasant Grove

1936
C.F. Moffitt - Aliceville, Unity
O.C. Weaver - Arbor Springs, Bethlehem, Hickory Grove
E.B. Farrar - Beulah,
J.R. Curry - Carrollton, Pickensville, West Greene

1936 (continued)
H.G. Carpenter - Cross Roads, Spring Hill (P)
J.V. Johnson - Ebenezer
J.R. Swedenburg - Fellowship, Hebron, Liberty, Pleasant Hill, Pine Grove
E.N. Brown - Flatwoods
J.M. Mills - Forest
R.S. Marler - Friendship
B.B. Burks - Gordo, Mt. Pleasant, Reform
C.A. Bryant - Mineral Springs
T.W. Shelton - Mt. Tabor
C.L. Manderson - Pleasant Grove,
H.G. Carpenter - Spring Hill (P)
L.B. Wages - Union Chapel
J.L. Strickland - Zion

1937
C.F. Moffitt - Aliceville, Unity
Lester Stokes - Arbor Springs, Hickory Grove
O.C. Weaver - Bethlehem
E.B. Farrar - Beulah
J.R. Curry - Carrollton, Pickensville, West Greene
J.R. Swedenburg - Cross Roads, Hebron, Pine Grove, Pleasant Hill, Spring Hill (P)
J.V. Johnson - Ebenezer
R.S. Marler - Fellowship, Friendship
B.B. Burks - Gordo, Mt. Pleasant, Reform
S.E. Walker - Mineral Springs
1937 (continuedd)
W.O. Presson - Stansel
L.B. Wages - Union Chapel
J.L. Strickland - Zion

1938
J.B. Johnson - Aliceville, Unity
Lester Stokes - Arbor Springs, Mt. Tabor
J.R. Curry -Carrollton, Pickensville, West Greene
J.R. Swedenburg - Cross Roads, Hebron, Liberty, Pine Grove, Pleasant Hill, Spring Hill(P)
E.D. Strickland - Ebenezer, Ethelsville

1938 (continued)
R.S. Marler - Fellowship, Friendship
J.M. Mills - Forest
W.W. Izzard - Gordo, Reform, Mt. Pleasant
S.E. Walker - Mineral Springs
W.O. Presson - Stansel
L.B. Wages - Union Chapel
Edward Skelton - Zion

1939
J.H. Johnson - Aliceville, Unity
L. Stokes - Arbor Springs, Bethlehem, Mt. Tabor
J.L. Watson - Beulah
J.R. Curry - Carrollton, Pickensville, West Greene
J.R. Swedenburg - CrossRoads, Hebron, Pine Grove, Pleasant Hill, Spring Hill (P)
E.D. Strickland - Ebenezer, Ethelsville,
R.S. Marler - Fellowship, Friendship,
E.N. Brown - Flatwoods
J.M. Mills - Forest
W.W. Izaard - Gordo, Reform
S.E. Walker - Hickory, Liberty, Mineral Springs
L.B. Wages - Union Chapel
J.L. Strickland - Zion

1940
J.B. Johnson - Aliceville, Unity
L.R. Stokes - Arbor Springs, Bethlehem, Friendship, Mt. Tabor
J.L. Watson - Beulah
J.R. Curry - Carrollton, Pickensville, West Greene
J.R. Swedenburg - Cross Roads, Hebron, Mt. Pleasant, Spring Hill (P), Pleasant Hill
E.D. Strickland - Ebenezer, Ethelsville, Pine Grove
J.U. Moss - Fellowship, Stansel
E.N. Brown - Flatwoods,
J.M. Mills - Forest
B.B. Burks - Gordo, Reform
S.E. Walker - Hickory Grove, Liberty, Mineral Springs

1940 (continued)
L.B. Wages - Union Chapel
J.L. Strickland - Zion
J.A. Chastain - Coal Fire

1941
E.L. Edens - Aliceville, Unity
J.R. Swedenburg - Aliceville II(West End), Cross Roads, Hebron, Mt. Pleasant, Pleasant Hill
S.E. Walker - Arbor Springs, Spring Hill (P)
W.O. Presson - Bethlehem
J.L. Watson - Beulah
J.R. Curry - Carrollton, Pickensville, West Greene
J.A. Chastain - Coal Fire
E.D. Strickland - Ebenezer, Pine Grove
L.R. Stokes - Friendship, Mt. Tabor
H.R. Harless - Gordo,
S.E. Walker - Liberty, Mineral Springs,Spring Hill (P)
J.F. Goree - New Salem
J.R. Bancroft - Reform, Stansel
L.B. Wages - Union Chapel
J.L. Strickland - Zion

1942
E.L. Edens - Aliceville, Unity
J.R. Swedenburg - Aliceville II, Cross Roads, Hebron, Mt. Pleasant, Pleasant Hill
S.E. Walker - Arbor Springs, Spring Hill (P), Liberty, Mineral Springs, Ebenezer
J.A. Chastain - Bethlehem, Coal Fire, New Salem
J.L. Watson - Beulah
J.R. Curry - Carrollton, Pickensville, West Greene
J.B. Wages - Ethelsville, Hickory Grove
R.S. Mardre - Fellowship
L.V. Hallman - Flatwoods,
H.C. Harless - Friendship, Gordo
L.R. Stokes - Mt. Tabor, Fellowship
J.R. Bancroft - Reform, Stansel

1942 (continued)
L.B. Wages - Union Chapel

1943
E.L. Edens - Aliceville, Unity
J.R. Swedenburg - AlicevilleII, CrossRoads, Hebron, Pleasant Hill
S.E. Walker - Arbor Springs, Liberty, Mineral Springs, Ebenezer, Pine Grove
J.A. Chastain - Bethlehem, Coal Fire, New Salem, Mt. Tabor
J.L. Watson - Beulah
J.R. Curry - Carrollton, Pickensville, West Greene
William Gamble - Fellowship
L.V. Hallman - Flatwoods
E.D. Strickland - Forest, Stansel
L.R. Stokes - Friendship
Quinton Porch - Gordo,
J.B. Wages - Hickory Grove
L.B. Wages - Union Chapel

1944
J.R. Stucky - Aliceville,
James Pate - Unity, Mt. Pleasant
J.R. Swedenburg - Aliceville II, Cross Roads, Hebron, Pleasant Hill
S.E. Walker - Arbor Springs, Liberty, Mineral Springs, Spring Hill (P)
J.A. Chastain - Garden, Mt. Tabor, New Salem, Bethlehem
J.R. Curry - Carrollton, Pickensville, West Greene
H. Stickland - Coal Fire,
E.D. Strickland - Stansel, Forest
R.S. Marler - Ebenezer
J.B. Wages - Etheslville, Hickory Grove
William Gamble - Fellowship
Amon Kelly - Flatwoods
L.R. Stokes - Friendship, Pine Grove
Quinton Porch - Gordo
K.Z. Stevens - Reform
L.B. Wages - Union Chapel

1945

J.R. Stucky - Aliceville

J.R. Swedenburg - Aliceville II, Cross Roads, Hebron, Pleasant Hill

S.E. Walker - Arbor Springs, Liberty, Mineral Springs,

J.A. Chastain - Bethlehem, New Salem

J.R. Curry - Carrollton, Pickensville, West Greene

H. Strickland - Coal Fire

M.J. Ray - Ebenezer

K.Z. Stevens - Reform, Ethelsville, Unity, Spring Hill(P)

W.E. Robinson - Fellowship, Mt. Pleasant, Mt. Tabor

Amon Kelly - Flatwoods

L.R. Stokes - Friendship, Pine Grove

C.A. Bryant - Garden

Quinton Porch - Gordo

J.B. Wages - Hickory Grove,

L.B. Wages - Union Chapel

J.W. Bouchillon - Stansel

My plan is to continue this listing down to the present and share it in our next annual minutes. During the 1950's many more of our churches will no longer be yoked with other congregations and will be served by a pastor of their own.

Meanwhile, *this current listing is only a start toward recording the history of the pastoral leadership of the churches in this association.*

1. *Many of these pastors were raised here and have kinspersons still here.*
2. *Some of you know the family history of these pastors, or can find it.*
3. *Some of you will have pictures of these old pastors and can have them scanned for our records.*
4. *Some of you have good stories to share about one or more of these pastors.*
5. *Some of you know what happened to some who moved on to other fields of ministry.*
6. *Some of you know where one or more of these men is buried.*
7. *Some of you have items of theirs like a Bible which you would let us photograph.*

So, help us gather up historical data during this year when we celebrate our 175th year of mission and ministry as an association of churches.

Pastors of our Association from 1946-2010

1946
J.R. Stuckey – Aliceville
J.R. Swedenburg – West End, Cross Roads, Pleasant Hill
Amon Kelley - Arbor Springs, Ethelsville, Flatwoods, Garden
J. A. Chastain – Bethlehem
J.R. Curry – Carrollton, Pickensville, West Green
Houston Strickland – Coal Fire
M.J. Ray – Ebenezer
J.L. Watson – Fellowship
J.W. Bouchilion – Forest, Stansel
L.R. Stokes – Friendship, Pine Grove
J.L. Rowe – Gordo
J.B. Wages – Hickory Grove, Union Chapel
Wm. Fields – Liberty
S.E. Walker - Mineral Springs
W.E. Robertson – Mt. Pleasant, Mt. Tabor
Roscoe Hollimon – New Salem
K.Z. Stevens- Reform, Spring Hill, Unity

1947
J.R. Stuckey – Aliceville
J.R. Swedenburg- Aliceville II, Cross Roads, Pleasant Hill
Amon Kelley – Arbor Springs, Ethelsville, Flatwoods, Garden
J. A. Chastain – Bethlehem
Tom Collins – Carrollton
Houston Strickland – Coal Fire
M. G. Ray – Ebenezer
J.L. Watson – Fellowship
J.W. Bouchilion – Forest, Stansel
L.R. Stokes – Friendship, Pine Grove
L.G. Meadows- Gordo
O. Czarchurski – Hebron
K.Z. Stevens – Hickory Grove, Spring Hill
Bill Fields – Liberty
S.E. Walker – Mineral Springs
W.E. Robinson – Mt. Pleasant, Mt. Tabor
R.R. Holliman – New Salem
J.R. Curry – Pickensville, West Greene
B.A. Wilson – Reform, Unity
L.B. Wages – Union Chapel
J.H. Dodson – Zion

1948
J.R. Stuckey – Aliceville
J.R. Swedenburg – Aliceville II, Pleasant Hill
Amon Kelley – Arbor Springs, Ethelsville, Fellowship, Flatwoods, Garden
Houston Strickland – Bethlehem, Coal Fire
Tom Collins – Carrollton, Hebron, Unity
Vernon Bobo- Friendship
D.E. Richardson – Gordo
J.C. Thomas – Hickory Grove
L.M. Perrigin – Liberty
Clifford Johnson- Mineral Springs
W.E. Robinson – Mt. Tabor
W.S. Scott – Mt. Pleasant
R. R. Holliman – New Salem
Buford Phillips – Pickensville
Bill Fields – Pine Grove
J.R. Swedenburg – Pleasant Hill
W. S. Scott – Reform
K.Z. Stevens – Spring Hill
L. B. Wages – Union Chapel
George Abrams – West Greene
J.H. Dodson – Zion

1949
J.R. Stuckey – Aliceville
J.R. Swedenburg – West End, Cross Roads, Hebron
Hunter Strickland – Arbor Springs
Huston Strickland – Coal Fire, New Salem
David Lewis – Ebenezer

1949 continued
Foster Turner – Ethelsville, Pleasant Hill
J.W. Caldwell – Forest
W.S. Scott – Friendship, Liberty Mt. Pleasant, Reform
Bill Fields – Garden
Byron Davis – Hickory Grove, Stansel
Kirk Lucus- Gordo
Garon Hughes – Mars Hill
George Abrams – Mineral Springs, West Greene
K.Z. Stevens- Spring Hill

1950
J.R. Stuckey – Aliceville
J.R. Swedenburg – West End, Cross Roads, Hebron
Huston Strickland – Arbor Springs New Salem,
Roscoe Hallman – Bethlehem
O. M. Fox – Carrollton, Pickensville
Garon Hughes- Coal Fire,
David Lewis – Ebenezer
Harvey Pope – Ethelsville
Kirk Lucas – Fellowship, Gordo
Edwin Skelton – Flatwoods
J.W. Caldwell – Forest
W.S. Scott – Friendship, Liberty Reform, Mt. Pleasant
Bill Fields - Garden
Amon Kelley – Hickory Grove, Pine Grove
George Abrams – Mineral Springs, West Greene
Joe Baskin – Mt. Tabor
Leon Macon – Pleasant Hill
K.Z. Stevens – Springhill
Byron Davis – Stansel, Unity
John Atkins – Union Chapel

1951
J.R. Stuckey – Aliceville
J.R. Swedenburg – West End, Cross Roads, Hebron
Hunter Strickland – Arbor Springs,
Huston Strickland – Coal Fire, New Salem
David Lewis – Ebenezer
Foster Turner – Ethelsville, Pleasant Hill
J. W. Caldwell – Forest
W. S. Scott – Friendship, Liberty, Mt. Pleasant, Reform
Bill Fields – Garden
Kirk Lucas – Gordo
Byron Davis – Hickory Grove, Stansel
Garon Hughes – Mars Hill
George Abrams – Mineral Springs, West Greene
K.Z. Stevens – Spring Hill

1952
J. R. Stuckey –Aliceville
J.R. Swedenburg – West End, Cross Roads, Hebron
Huston Strickland- Arbor Springs New Salem
Roscoe Hallman – Bethlehem
O.M. Fox – Carrollton, Pickensville
Garon Hughes – Coal Fire
David Lewis – Ebenezer
Harvey Pope – Ethelsville
Kirk Lucas – Fellowship, Gordo
Edwin Skelton – Flatwoods
J.W. Caldwell – Forest
W.S. Scott – Friendship, Liberty, Mt. Pleasant, Reform
Bill Fields – Garden
(1952 continued)
Amon Kelley – Hickory Grove, Pine Grove
George Abrams – Mineral Springs, West Greene
Joe Baskin – Mt. Tabor
Leon Macon – Pleasant Hill
K.Z. Stevens – Spring Hill
Byron Davis – Stansel, Unity
John Atkins – Union Chapel

1953
Larry Bray – Aliceville
J.R. Swedenburg – West End, Cross Roads, Hebron
Amon Foster – Arbor Springs
Roscoe Holliman – Bethlehem, New Salem
O.M. Fox – Carrollton, Pickensville
Cecil Junkin – Coal Fire,
Harvey Jennings – Ebenezer
Chester Free – Ethelsville, Pine Grove
Edwin Skelton – Flatwoods,
J.W. Caldwell – Forest
W.S. Scott – Friendship, Liberty, Mt. Pleasant
Amon Kelley – Garden, Hickory Grove
E.U. Calvert – Gordo,
Woodard Adams – Mars Hill
George Abrams – Mineral Springs, West Greene
K.Z. Stevens – Springhill
Gardner Walker – Stansel
R.E. Brown – Hollywood

1954- Pastor roll not recorded

1955
Larry Bray – Aliceville
J.R. Swedenburg – West End, Cross Roads, Hebron
Amon Foster – Arbor Springs,
Roscoe Hollimon – Bethlehem,
O.M. Fox – Carrollton, Pickensville
Cecil Junkin – Coal Fire, Fellowship
C.M. Nixon – Ebenezer
Chester Free – Ethelsville, Liberty, Pine Grove
Edwin Skelton – Flatwoods
J.W. Caldwell – Forest
E.U. Calvert – Gordo
Julius Donahue – Gordo Baptist Temple
Robert Causey– Hickory Grove
Woodford Abrams – Mars Hill
George Abrams – Mineral Springs
W.S. Scott – Mt. Pleasant
Jack Crowe – New Salem
Gaylord Browlee – Springhill
T.W. Buford – Stansel

1956
Larry Bray – Aliceville
Edgar Wilmer – West End
Amon Foster – Arbor Springs
J.R. Swedenburg – Bethlehem, Cross Roads, Hebron
O.M. Fox – Carrollton, Pickensville
C.E. Junkin – Coal Fire, Fellowship
C.M. Nixon – Ebenezer
Chester Free – Ethelsville, Liberty, Pine Grove
Edwin Skelton – Flatwoods
J.W. Caldwell – Forest
Huston Croley – Friendship,
Julius Donahue – Gordo Baptist Temple
Robert Causey –Hickory Grove, Union Chapel
Woodford Adams – Mars Hill
George Abrams – Mineral Springs
Clyde Brozeal – Mt. Pleasant
C.W. Strickland – Mt. Tabor
Jack Crowe – New Salem
J.W. Stopp – Pleasant Hill
David Renaker – Reform
Gaylord Brownlee – Spring Hill
T.W. Buford – Stansel
E.P. Fendley – West Greene

1957
Dudley Wilson – Aliceville
David Barrentine – West End
Amon Foster – Arbor Springs,
J.R. Swedenburg – Bethlehem, Cross Roads, Hebron
O.M. Fox – Carrollton, Pickensville
C.W. Strickland – Coal Fire, Mt. Tabor
R. E. Brown – Ebenezer
Chester Free – Ethelsville, Liberty
Thomas Davis – Fellowship

1957 continued
Edwin Skelton – Flatwoods
J.W. Caldwell – Forest
Houston Croley – Friendship
Julius Donohue – Garden
F.O. Cork – Gordo
Noah Skelton – Gordo Baptist Temple
James M. Mosley – Hickory Grove
Amon Kelley – Mars Hill
Gaylord Brownlee – Mineral Springs
Willie Crawford – Mt. Pleasant
J.J. Crowl – New Salem
Dewey Flors – Pine Grove
Witi Butler – Pleasant Hill
David Renaker – Reform
Roy Dain – Springhill
E. Byron Davis – Stansel
George Pitts – Union Chapel
E.P. Fendley- West Green

1958
Dudley Wilson –Aliceville
David Barrentine – West End
J.R. Swedenburg – Bethlehem, Hebron
O.M. Fox – Carrollton, Pickensville
Clyde Strickland – Coal Fire
C.M. Nixon – Ebenezer
Thomas Davis – Fellowship
Edwin Skelton – Flatwoods
J.W. Caldwell – Forest
Huston Croley – Friendship
Nelson Bryant – Garden
F.O. Cork – Gordo
Noah Skelton – Gordo Baptist Temple
James Mosey – Hickory Grove
Chester Free – Liberty
Amon Kelley – Mars Hill
Gaylord Brownlee – Mineral Springs
Willie Crawford – Mt. Pleasant
Earlie Davis – New Salem
Dewey Flora – Pine Grove
W.T. Butler – Pleasant Hill
Ernest Chappell – Spring Hill
Byron Davis – Stansel
G.W. Pitts – Union Chapel
E.P. Fendley – West Greene

1959
Dudley Wilson – Aliceville
Chester Free – Arbor Springs, Liberty
J. R. Swedenburg – Bethlehem, Cross Roads, Hebron
O.M. Fox – Carrollton, Pickensville
Thomas Findley – Coal Fire
C.M. Nixon – Ebenezer
Clyde Strickland – Ethelsville, Union Chapel
Benie Hayes – Fellowship
Edwin Skelton – Flatwoods
J.W. Caldwell – Forest
Houston Croley – Friendship, Mt. Tabor
Nelson Bryant – Garden
F.O. Cork – Gordo
Noah Skelton – Gordo Baptist Temple
Byron Kornegay – Hickory Grove
Garon Hughes – Mars Hill
Gaylord Brownlee – Mineral Springs
John Springer – Mt. Pleasant
Dewey Flora – Pine Grove
W.T. Butler – Pleasant Hill
B.R. Maddox – Reform
Ernest Chappell – Spring Hill
Author Walker – Stansel
David Barrentine – West End
E.A. Findley – West Greene

1960
Dudley Wilson – Aliceville
David Barrentine – West End
Chester Free – Arbor Springs, Liberty
J.R. Swedenburg – Bethlehem, Cross Roads, Hebron
O.M. Fox – Carrollton, Pickensville
Thomas Fendley – Coal Fire
J.W. Caldwell – Ebenezer, Forest
C.W. Strickland – Ethelsville, Union Chapel
Boyce Crocker – Fellowship
Edwin Skelton –Flatwoods
Houston Lee Crowley – Friendship, Mt. Tabor

1960 continued
E.B. Carroll – Garden
F.O. Cork – Gordo
Noah Skelton – Gordo Baptist Temple
Dale McCoy- Hickory Grove
Walter Hughes – Mars Hill
Gaylord Brownlee – Mineral Springs
John Springer – Mt. Pleasant
R.R. Holliman – New Salem
Walter Jones – Pine Grove
W.T. Butler – Pleasant Hill
B.R. Maddox – Reform
Ernest Chappell – Spring Hill
W.E. Buice – Stansel

1961
Dudley Wilson – Aliceville
William Warren – West End
Chester Free – Arbor Springs, Liberty
J.R. Swedenburg – Bethlehem, Cross Roads, Hebron
O.M. Fox – Carrollton, Pickensville
Thomas Fendley – Coal Fire, Ethelsville
Elvin Champion – Ebenezer, Mars Hill
Boyce Crocker – Fellowship
Edwin Skelton – Flatwoods
Ernest Chappell – Forest
Houston Crowley – Friendship
Ferrell O. Cork – Gordo
Noah Skelton – Gordo Baptist Temple
Dale McCoy – Hickory Grove
Gaylord Brownlee – Mineral Springs
Houston Strickland – New Salem
W.T. Butler – Pleasant Hill
B.R. Maddox – Reform
George Pratt – Spring Hill
Ferrell Boone – Stansel
J.S. Clark – Union Chapel

1962
Dudley Wilson – Aliceville
James Auchmuty – West End
Chester Free – Arbor Springs, Liberty
J.R. Swedenburg – Bethlehem, Cross Roads, Hebron
O.M. Fox – Carrollton, Pickensville
Daniel Brown – Coal Fire
Elvin Champion – Ebenezer, Mars Hill
Thomas Fendley – Ethelsville
Vernon Fisher – Flatwoods
Ernest Chappelle- Forest
Houston Crowley – Friendship
Ferrell O. Cork – Gordo
Noah Skelton – Gordo Baptist Temple
Gaylord Brownlee – Mineral Springs
Cecil Junkin – Mt. Pleasant
B.L. Hobo – Mt. Tabor
Houston Strickland – New Salem
Nelson Bryant – Pine Grove
G.E. Pounders – Reform
George Pratt – Spring Hill

1963
Joe Whitt – Aliceville
W.A. Poe – Arbor Springs
J.R. Swedenburg – Bethlehem, Cross Roads, Hebron
Jack Mason – Carrollton
Dan Brown – Coal Fire
Walter Garon Hughes – Ebenezer
Thomas Fendley – Ethelsville
Neil Nichols – Fellowship
Vernon Fisher – Fellowship
Ernest Chappell – Forest, Pickensville
Houston Crowley – Friendship
Joe Stone – Garden
Billy Hogue – Gordo
Harvey Jennings – Gordo Baptist Temple
Willie Crawford – Hickory Grove
Chester Free – Liberty, Mt. Tabor
Elvin Champion – Mars Hill
Gaylord Brownlee – Mineral Springs
Eugene Junkin – Mt. Pleasant
Houston Strickland – New Salem
Dewey Flora – Pine Grove
J. M. McCain – Pleasant Hill
E.G. Ponders – Reform
George Pratt – Spring Hill
Mel Deason – Stansel
B.B. Fair – Union Chapel

1964
Joe Whitt – Aliceville
Jerry Riley – West End
W.A. Poe – Arbor Springs
J.R. Swedenburg – Bethlehem
Jack Mason – Carrollton
Daniel Brown – Coal Fire
W.G. Hughes – Ebenezer
Thomas Fendley – Ethelsville
Neil Nichols – Fellowship
Ernest Chappell – Forest, Pickensville
Chester Free – Friendship, Liberty
Joe Stone – Garden
Billy Hogue – Gordo
H. L. Jennings – Gordo Baptist Temple
Willie Crawford – Hickory Grove
Elvin Champion – Mars Hill
Gaylord Brownlee – Mineral Springs
Eugene Junkin – Mt. Pleasant
B.L. Bobo – Mt. Tabor
Houston Strickland – New Salem
George Henley – Pine Grove, Spring Hill
G.A. Pratt – Pleasant Hill
E.G. Pounders – Reform
Mel Deason – Stansel
B.B. Fair – Union Chapel
Ralph Elmore – Pleasant Grove

1965
Joe Whitt – Aliceville First
Jerry Hiley – West End
Houston Crowley- Arbor Springs
J.R. Swedenburg – Bethlehem
Jack Mason – Carrollton
James B. Cunningham – Coal Fire
Chester Free – Cross Roads, Friendship, Liberty
Douglas Haynes – Ethelsville
Royce Crocker – Fellowship
J.L. Moachett – Flatwoods
Ernest Chappelle – Forest
Henry E. Trull – Garden
David N. Blackburn – Gordo
J.E. Donahue – Gordo Baptist Temple
Ellis M. Tate – Hebron
W.A. Crawford – Hickory Grove
Elvin Champion – Mars Hill
Gaylord Brownlee – Mineral Springs
Neil Nichols – Mt. Pleasant
Eugene Junkin – Mt. Tabor, Pine Grove
George Hyche – New Salem
Ernest Chapell – Pickensville
Noah Skelton – Pleasant Grove
G.A. Pratt – Pleasant Hill
E.G. Pounders – Reform
George Henley – Spring Hill
B.B. Fair – Union Chapel

1966
Joe Whitt – Aliceville First
James Jordan – West End
Houston Lee Crowley – Arbor Springs
J.R. Swedenburg – Bethlehem
Jack Mason – Carrollton
James Cunningham – Coal Fire
Chester Free – Cross Roads, Gordo Baptist Temple, Liberty
James Fletcher, Jr. – Ethelsville
Max Bobbitt – Fellowship
J.J. Mouchette – Flatwoods
Eugene Junkin – Friendship, Mt. Tabor
David Blackburn – Gordo
Ellis K. Tate – Hebron
Willie A. Crawford – Hickory Grove
Billy Ray Oden – Mars Hill
Gaylord Brownlee – Mineral Springs
Neil Nichols – Mt. Pleasant
George Hyche – Mt. Salem
Ernest Chappell – Pickensville
Dan Brown- Pine Grove
Noah Skelton – Pleasant Grove
G.A. Pratt – Pleasant Hill
John Faulkner – Reform
James Purnell – Stansel

1967
Joe Whitt – Aliceville First

1967 continue
James Jordan – West End
Houston Crowley – Arbor Springs
J.R. Swedenburg – Bethlehem
Jack Mason – Carrollton
J.R. Swedenburg – Bethlehem
Jack Mason – Carrollton
Thomas Fendley – Coal Fire
Chester Free – Cross Roads, Highland
Dan Brown – Ebenezer
James Fletcher – Ethelsville
B.W. Allen – Fellowship, Forest
J.L. Mouchette – Flatwoods
Eugene Junkin – Friendship, Mt. Tabor
Edwin Skelton – Garden
Ellis Tate – Hebron
W.A. Crawford – Hickory Grove
G.A. Pratt – Liberty
Billy R. Oden – Mars Hill
Gaylord Brownlee – Mineral Springs
Hershel Owen – Mt. Pleasant
George Hyche – New Salem
Ernest Chappell- Pickensville
Noah Skelton – Pleasant Grove
O.D. Mason – Pleasant Hill
John Faulkner – Reform
Ellis Tate – Spring Hill
James Purnell – Stansel
Earl Surber – Union Chapel

1968
Joe Whitt – Aliceville First
Houston Crowley – Arbor Springs
J.R. Swedenburg – Bethlehem
Jack Mason – Carrollton
Harold Free- Coal Fire
Chester Free – Cross Roads, Highland
Dan Brown – Ebenezer
James Fletcher – Ethelsville
B.W. Allen – Fellowship
J.L. Mouchette – Flatwoods
Eugene Junkin- Friendship, Mt. Tabor
Clifton Thomas – Garden
James Mitchell – Gordo
Ellis Tate – Hebron
W.A. Crawford – Hickory Grove
George Pratt - Liberty
Billy R. Oden – Mars Hill
Gaylord Brownlee – Mineral Springs
Hershel Owen – Mt. Pleasant
Mayo Woolbright – New Salem
Ernest Chapell – Pickensville
George Norris – Pine Grove
Thomas Fendley – Pleasant Grove
J.O. Moebes – Pleasant Hill
John Faulkner – Reform
Ellis Tate – Spring Hill
James Purnell – Stansel
Earl Surber – Union Chapel

1969
Joe Whitt – Aliceville First
Houston Crowley – Arbor Springs
J.B. Cunningham – Bethlehem
Bronnie Nichols – Carrollton
Billy R. Oden-Coal Fire
Dan Brown – Ebenezer
William Bodiford – Ethelsville
Ralph Elmore – Fellowship
J.L. Mouchette – Flatwoods
H.G. Williams- Forest
Clifton Thomas – Garden
George Pratt – Hebron, Liberty
W.A. Crawford –Hickory Grove
Chester Free – Highland
Gaylord Brownlee – Mineral Springs
Hershel Owen – Mt. Pleasant
Cecil E. Junkin – Mt. Tabor
Mayo Woolbright – New Salem
Ernest Chapell – Pickensville
George Norris – Pine Grove
T.L. Fendley – Pleasant Grove
Jim Moebes – Pleasant Hill
Brannon Pinion – Reform
Ellis Tate – Spring Hill
James Purnell – Stansel
Earl Surber – Union Chapel
J.C. Shell – West End

1970
Joe Whitt – Aliceville First
Houston Crowley – Arbor Springs

1970 Continued
J.B. Cunningham – Bethlehem
Frank Tribble, Jr. – Carrollton
Thomas Fendley – Coal Fire
George Norris – Cross Roads
William Bodiford – Ethelsville
Ralph Elmore – Fellowship
John Mouchette – Flatwoods
H.G. Williams – Forest
Clarence Wheelus – Friendship
Clifton Thomas – Garden
Jack R. Brown – Gordo
Neil Nichols – Hebron
W.A. Crawford – Hickory Grove
Chester Free – Highland
George Pratt – Liberty
C.C. Pate – Mars Hill
Gaylord Brownlee –Mineral Springs
Hershel Owen – Mt. Pleasant
Eugene Junkin – Mt. Tabor
Dan Brown – New Salem
Earnest Chappelle – Pickensville
George Adams – Pine Grove
Noah Skelton – Pleasant Grove
Vernon Blackburn – Pleasant Hill
Brannon Pinion – Reform
Ellis Tate- Spring Hill
Earl Surber – Union Chapel
J.C. Shell – West End

1971
Joe Whitt – Aliceville First
Houston Crowley – Bethlehem
F.W. Tribble, Jr. – Carrollton
Thomas Fendley – Coal Fire
P. Osburn – Cross Roads
Garon Hughes – Ebenezer
W. Perry – Fellowship
John Mouchette – Flatwoods
H.G. Williams – Forest
Clarence Wheelus – Friendship
Clifton Thomas – Garden
Jack R. Brown – Gordo
Neil Nichols – Hebron
W.A. Crawford – Hickory Grove
Chester Free – Highland
George Pratt – Liberty
C.C. Pate- Mars Hill
Gaylord Brownlee – Mineral Springs
Hershel Owen – Mt. Pleasant
J.L. Keith – New Salem
Earnest Chapell – Pickensville
G. Norris – Pine Grove
Noah Skelton – Pleasant Grove
Vernon Blackburn – Pleasant Hill
Brannon Pinnion – Reform
Ellis Tate – Spring Hill
J. Coleman – Stansel
H.H. Crisman – Union Chapel

1972
Joe Whitt – Aliceville
S.R. Windle- Arbor Springs
Huston Crowley – Bethlehem
Frank Tribble – Carrollton
Thomas Fendley – Coal Fire
Paul Osborn- Cross Roads
Grady Pearson – Ebenezer
Jimmy Ray – Ethelsville
Clifton Patterson – Fellowship
J.L. Mouchette – Flatwoods
H.G. Williams – Forest
Clarence Wheelus – Friendship
Jack Brown – Gordo
Neil Nichols – Hebron
W.A. Crawford – Hickory Grove
Chester Free – Highland
George A. Pratt – Liberty
Dan Brown- Mars Hill
Gaylord Brownlee – Mineral Springs
Hershel Owen – Mt. Pleasant
James Keith – New Salem
Ernest Chappelle – Pickensville
W.S. Phillips – Pine Grove
Noah Skelton – Pleasant Grove
James Smithson – Pleasant Hill
Brannon Pinion – Reform
Ellis Tate – Spring Hill
Jimmy Coleman – Stansel
H.H. Crisman – Union Chapel
A.G. Smith – West End

1973
Joe Whitt – Aliceville
Ralph Windle, Jr. – Arbor Springs
Huston Crowley – Bethlehem
Frank Tribble, Jr. – Carrollton
Thomas Fendley – Coal Fire
Paul Osborn – Cross Roads
Grady Pearson – Ebenezer
Jimmy Ray – Ethelsville
Ralph Elmore – Fellowship
H.G. Williams – Forest
Robert Langdon – Friendship
Henry Trull – Garden
B.E. Nichols – Gordo
Larry Potts – Hebron
W.A. Crawford – Hickory Grove
Chester Free – Highland
George Pratt – Liberty
Dan Brown – Mars Hill
Gaylord Brownlee – Mineral Springs
Hershel Owen – Mt. Pleasant
Searcy Pate – Mt. Tabor
Travis Hunnicutt- New Salem
Ernest Chappelle – Pickensville
William Burkhalter – Pine Grove
W.E. Vaughn – Pleasant Grove
James Smithson – Pleasant Hill
Jimmy Chapman – Reform
Jimmy Coleman – Stansel
Elliott Gray, Jr. – Union Chapel
A.G. Smith – West End

1974
Joe Whitt – Aliceville
S.R. Windle, Jr. – Arbor Springs
Huston Crowley – Bethlehem
Thomas Fendley – Coal Fire
Buddy Burkhalter – Cross Roads
Grady Pearson – Ebenezer
Jimmy Ray – Ethelsville
Neil Nichols – Fellowship
Horace Hall – Flatwoods
H.G. Williams – Forest
Robert Langdon – Friendship
Henry Trull – Garden
Ronald Jackson – Gordo First
Larry Potts – Hebron
W.A. Crawford – Hickory Grove
Chester Free – Highland
George Pratt – Liberty
Gaylord Brownlee – Mineral Springs
Hershel Owen – Mt. Pleasant
John Pate – Mt. Tabor
Al Sanderson – New Salem
Thomas Hughes – Pickensville
Thomas Smothers – Pine Grove, Spring Hill
W.E. Vaughn – Pleasant Grove
James Smithson – Pleasant Hill
Billy Wallace – Reform
Richard Mason – Stansel
E.P. Gray, Jr. – Union Chapel
A.G. Smith – West End

1975
Joe Whitt – Aliceville
S.R. Windle, Jr. – Arbor Springs
Huston Crowley – Bethlehem
Wallace Russell – Carrollton
Thomas Fendley – Coal Fire
Buddy Burkhalter – Cross Roads
Jimmy Ray – Ethelsville
Lee Vail – Fellowship
H.G. Williams – Forest
Robert Langdon – Friendship
Henry Trull – Garden
Ronald Jackson – Gordo
W. A. Crawford – Hickory Grove
Chester Free – Highland
George Pratt – Liberty
Gaylord Brownlee – Mineral Springs
Hershel Owen – Mt. Pleasant
Searcy Pate – Mt. Tabor
Mike Hall – New Salem
Thomas Hughes – Pickensville
Thomas Smothers – Pine Grove, Spring Hill
W.E. Vaughn – Pleasant Grove
Bronnie Nichols – Pleasant Hill
Billy R. Wallace – Reform

1975 continued
Richard Mason – Stansel
Jimmy Wilson – West End

1976
Joe Whitt – Aliceville
W.O. Burkhalter – Arbor Springs
Elliot Gray, Jr. – Bethlehem, Mars Hill
Wallace Russell – Carrollton
Thomas Fendley – Coal Fire
E.G. Pounders – Cross Roads
Jessie Pearson – Ebenezer
Jimmy Ray – Ethelsville
Eugene Junkin – Flatwoods
H.G. Williams – Forest
Robert Langdon – Friendship
Henry Trull – Garden
Max Davis – Gordo
Mike Boykin – Hebron
W.A. Crawford – Hickory Grove
Chester Free – Highland
George Pratt – Liberty
Gaylord Brownlee – Mineral Springs
Hershel Owen – Mt. Pleasant
Searcy Pate – Mt. Tabor
Mike Hall – New Salem
Thomas Hughes – Pickensville
Thomas Smothers – Pine Grove, Spring Hill
W.E. Vaughn – Pleasant Grove
Bronnie Nichols – Pleasant Hill
James Vanderford – Reform
Richard Mason – Stansel
Donald Berry – Union Chapel
Jimmy Wilson – West End

1977
Joe Whitt – Aliceville
William Burkhalter – Arbor Springs
Elliot Gray, Jr. – Bethlehem
Wallace Russell – Carrollton
Melvin Mordecai – Coal Fire
Jessie Pearson – Ebenezer
Jimmy Ray – Ethelsville
Al Sanderson – Fellowship
Eugene Junkin – Flatwoods
H.G. Williams – Forest
J.L. Mochette – Friendship
Raymond Robertson – Garden
Max Davis – Gordo
Mike Boykin – Hebron
Max Bobbit – Hickory Grove
Chester Free – Highland
Henry Trull – Liberty
Mayo Woolbright – Mars Hill
Gaylord Brownlee – Mineral Springs
Hershel Owen – Mt. Pleasant
Searcy Pate – Mt. Tabor
Mike Hall – New Salem
Thomas Hughes – Pickensville
Thomas Smothers – Pine Grove, Spring Hill
Bronnie Nichols – Pleasant Hill
James Vanderford – Reform
W.L. Sheffield – Stansel
Michael Smith – Union Chapel
Jimmy Wilson – West End

1978
Joe Whitt – Aliceville
William Burkhalter, Jr. – Arbor Springs
Wallace Russell – Carrollton
Melvin Mordecai – Coal Fire
Willie A. Crawford – Cross Roads
Jessie Pearson – Ebenezer
Jimmy Ray – Ethelsville
Lee Vail – Fellowship
Eugene Junkin – Flatwoods
H.G. Williams – Forest
J.L. Mouchette – Friendship
Raymond Robertson – Garden
Max Davis – Gordo First
Mike Boykin – Hebron
Max Bobbit- Hickory Grove
Chester Free – Highland
Henry Trull – Liberty
Mayo Woolbright – Mars Hill
Hershel Owen – Mt. Pleasant
Searcy Pate – Mt. Tabor
Mike Hall – New Salem
Thomas Smothers – Pine Grove, Spring Hill

1978 continued
William "Bill" Jones – Reform
Wiley Sheffield –Stansel
Mike Smith – Union Chapel
Jimmy Wilson – West End

1979
Joe Whitt – Aliceville
William Burkhalter, Jr. – Arbor Springs
Wallace Russell – Carrollton
Melvin Mordecai – Coal Fire
Willie Crawford – Cross Roads
Jessie Pearson – Ebenezer
Jimmy Ray – Ethelsville
Robert Langdon – Fellowship
Eugene Junkin – Flatwoods
H.G. Williams – Forest
J.L. Mouchette – Friendship
Claudie Livingston – Garden
James Jordan – Gordo
Gary Bonner – Hebron
Max Bobitt – Hickory Grove
Chester Free – Highland
Henry Trull – Liberty
O'Neil McElroy – Mineral Springs
Hershel Owen – Mt. Pleasant
Mike Hall – New Salem
A.L. Coats – Pickensville
Clyde Strickland – Pleasant Hill
William Jones – Reform
Jack House – Stansel
Billy Little – Union Chapel
Larry B. Weeks – West End

1980
Joe Whitt – Aliceville
Donald Moore –Arbor Springs
Jack Parker – Bethlehem
Wallace Russell – Carrollton
Melvin Mordecai – Coal Fire
W.A. Crawford – Cross Roads
Jessie Pearson – Ebenezer
Jimmy Ray – Ethelsville
H.G. Williams – Forest
J.L. Mouchette – Friendship
Ralph Smith – Garden
James Jordan – Gordo
Benton Goodman – Hebron
Max Bobbitt –Hickory Grove
Chester Free – Highland
Gary Shelton – Liberty
O'Neal McElroy – Mineral Springs
Hershel Owen – Mt. Pleasant
Gaylord Brownlee – Mt. Tabor
Mike Hall – New Salem
L.A. Coats- Pickensville
A.D. Hartley – Pine Grove
Clyde Strickland – Pleasant Hill
A.L. Coats – Spring Hill
C.E. Langston –Stansel
B.W. Little – Union Chapel
L.B. Weeks – West End

1981
James Goodwin – Aliceville
Donald Moore – Arbor Springs
Wallace Russell – Carrollton
Melvin Mordecai – Coal Fire
W.A. Crawford – Cross Roads
Jessie Pearson – Ebenezer
Jimmy Ray – Ethelsville
Kenneth Webb – Fellowship
Sam Jones – Flatwoods
H.G. Williams – Forest
J.I. Mouchette – Friendship
Ralph Smith – Garden
James Jordan – Gordo
Benton Goodman – Hebron
Max Bobbitt – Hickory Grove
Chester Free – Highland
Gary Shelton – Liberty
Grady Pearson – Mars Hill
Claudie Livingston – Mineral Springs
Hershel Owen – Mt. Pleasant
Gaylord Brownlee – Mt. Tabor
Mike Hall – New Salem
A.L. Coats – Pickensville, Spring Hill
A.D. Harley – Pine Grove
William Burkhalter – Pleasant Hill

1981 continued
Neil Nichols – Reform
James Loper – Stansel
Billy Little – Union Chapel
Larry Weeks – West End

1982
James Goodwin – Aliceville
Donald Moore – Arbor Springs
Erskin Stripling – Bethlehem
Melvin Mordecai – Coal Fire
W.A. Crawford – Cross Roads
Jessie Pearson – Ebenezer
Jimmy Ray – Ethelsville
Kenneth Webb – Fellowship
Vernon Blackburn – Forest
Carl Shelton – Garden
James Jordan – Gordo
Benton Goodman – Hebron
Max Bobbitt – Hickory Grove
Chester Free – Highland
Gary Shelton – Liberty
Grady Pearson – Mars Hill
Gene Livingston – Mineral Springs
Hershel Owen – Mt. Pleasant
Mike Hall – New Salem
A.T. Coats – Pickensville, Spring Hill
Charles Whitney – Pine Grove
W.O. Burkhalter – Pleasant Hill
Neil Nichols – Reform
Jack House – Stansel
Billy Little – Union Chapel

1983
James Goodwin – Aliceville
Donald Moore – Arbor Springs
Erskin Stripling – Bethlehem
Don Cotton – Carrollton
Daniel Gandy – Coal Fire
W.A. Crawford – Cross Roads
Jimmy Ray – Ethelsville
Kenneth Webb – Fellowship
Lee Hartley – Flatwoods
Vernon Blackburn – Forest
Julius Myers – Friendship
Carl Shelton – Garden
James Jordan – Gordo
Benton Goodman – Hebron
Max Bobbitt – Hickory Grove
Chester Free – Highland
Kenneth Smith – Liberty
Grady Pearson – Mars Hill
Hershel Owen – Mt. Pleasant
George Shaw – Mt. Tabor
Mike Hall – New Salem
Ralph Smith – Pickensville
Charley Whitney – Pine Grove
Jim Shanahan – Pleasant Hill
Neil Nichols – Reform
Jack House – Stansel
Billy Little – Union Chapel
R. Archibald – West End

1984
James Goodwin – Aliceville
Donald Moore – Arbor Springs
Erskin Stripling – Bethlehem
Don Cotten – Carrollton
Daniel Gandy – Coal Fire
W.A. Crawford – Cross Roads
Jimmy Ray – Ethelsville
Kenneth Webb – Fellowship
Lee Hartley – Flatwoods
Vernon Blackburn – Forest
Bob Myers – Friendship
Randy Gray – Garden
James Jordan – Gordo
Benton Goodman – Hebron
Max Bobbitt – Hickory Grove
Chester Free – Highland
Kenneth Smith – Liberty
Grady Pearson – Mars Hill
John Kitchens- Mineral Springs
Hershel Owen- Mt. Pleasant
George Shaw – Mt. Tabor
Mike Hall – New Salem
Ralph Smith – Pickensville
Jim Shanahan – Pleasant Hill
Neil Nichols – Reform
Carl Shelton – Spring Hill

1984 continued
James Purnell – Stansel
Billy Little – Union Chapel
R. Archibald – West End

1985
James Goodwin – Aliceville
Erskin Stripling – Bethlehem
Don Cotten - Carrollton
Daniel Gandy – Coal Fire
Eddie Rogers – Ebenezer
Jimmy Ray – Ethelsville
Larry Rogers – Fellowship
Vernon Blackburn – Forest
Bob Myers – Friendship
Randy Gray – Garden
James Jordan – Gordo
Leon Winters – Hebron
Max Bobbitt – Hickory Grove
Kenneth Smith – Liberty
Grady Pearson – Mars Hill
J.P. Kitchens – Mineral Springs
Hershel Owen – Mt. Pleasant
George Shaw – Mt. Tabor
Mike Hall – New Salem
Ralph Smith –Pickensville
A.D. Hartley – Pine Grove
Jim Shanahan – Pleasant Hill
Neil Nichols – Reform
Carl Shelton – Spring Hill
James Purnell – Stansel
Billy Little – Union Chapel
Terry Hawkins – West End

1986
James Goodwin – Aliceville
W.D. Dawkins – Arbor Springs
Erskin Stripling – Bethlehem
Frank Sims – Carrollton
Daniel Gandy – Coal Fire
J.L. Fletcher – Cross Roads
Eddie Rogers- Ebenezer
Jimmy Ray – Ethelsville
Larry Rogers – Fellowship
Paul Osborn – Flatwoods
Vernon Blackburn – Forest
Bob Myers – Friendship
Randy Gray – Garden
Ronnie Elmore – Hebron
Max Bobbitt – Hickory Grove
Clyde Strickland – Highland
Kenneth Smith – Liberty
Grady Pearson – Mars Hill
Hershel Owen – Mt. Pleasant
George Shaw – Mt. Tabor
Mike Hall – New Salem
Ralph Smith – Pickensville
Neil Nichols – Reform
Carl Shelton – Spring Hill
James Purnell – Stansel
Billy Little – Union Chapel
Terry Hawkins – West End

1987
James Goodwin – Aliceville
W.D. Dawkins – Arbor Springs
Kenneth Stough – Bethlehem
F.D. Sims – Carrollton
Johnny House – Ebenezer
Jimmy Ray – Ethelsville
Clyde Stevens – Fellowship
Paul Osborn – Flatwoods
Vernon Blackburn – Forest
Ralph Smith – Friendship
A.D. Hartley - Garden
Bill Schrimsher – Gordo
Ronnie Elmore – Hebron
George Shaw – Hickory Grove
Clyde Strickland – Highland
Kenneth Smith – Liberty
Hershel Owen – Mt. Pleasant
Randy Gray – Mt. Tabor
Mike Hall – New Salem
Billy Little – Pickensville
Bob Myers – Pine Grove
Jack Rickman – Pleasant Hill
Neil Nichols - Reform
Carl Shelton – Spring Hill
James Purnell – Stansel
James Fletcher – Union Chapel
Terry Hawkins – West End

1988
James Cooley – Aliceville
W.D. Dawkins – Arbor Springs
Kenneth Stough – Bethlehem
1988 continued
F.D. Sims – Carrollton
Ronnie McDaniel – Coal Fire
Arthur Cheung – Cross Roads
Johnny House – Ebenezer
Jimmy Ray – Ethelsville
Clyde Stevens – Fellowship
Paul Osborn – Flatwoods
Vernon Blackburn – Forest
Ralph Smith – Friendship
A.D. Hartley – Garden
Bill Schrimsher – Gordo
Ronnie Elmore- Hebron
George Shaw – Hickory Grove
Hershel Owen – Mt. Pleasant
Randy Gray – Mt. Tabor
Mike Hall – New Salem
Billy Little – Pickensville
Carl Shelton – Pine Grove, Spring Hill
Jack Rickman – Pleasant Hill
James Purnell – Stansel
James Fletcher – Union Chapel
Terry Hawkins – West End

1989
James Cooley – Aliceville
W.D. Dawkins – Arbor Springs
Franklin Sims – Carrollton
Ronnie McDaniel – Coal Fire
Larry Prescott – Ebenezer
Jimmy Ray – Ethelsville
Clyde Stevens – Fellowship
Paul Osborn – Flatwoods
Vernon Blackburn – Forest
Ralph Smith – Friendship
A.D. Hartley – Garden
Bill Schrimsher – Gordo
Ronnie Elmore – Hebron
George Shaw – Hickory Grove
Clyde Strickland – Highland
Kenneth Smith – Liberty
Robert Pate – Mars Hill
Hershel Owen – Mt. Pleasant
Randy Gray – Mt. Tabor
Mike Hall –New Salem
Billy Little – Pickensville
Carl Shelton – Pine Grove, Spring Hill
Jack Rickman – Pleasant Hill
Gary Smith – Reform
James Purnell – Stansel
James Fletcher – Union Chapel
Terry Hawkins- West End

1990
James Cooley – Aliceville
W.D. Dawkins – Arbor Springs
Ronny Elmore – Bethlehem
Franklin Sims – Carrollton
Ronnie McDaniel – Coal Fire
Charles Whitney – Cross Roads
Billy Jones – Ebenezer
Jimmy Ray – Ethelsville
Clyde Stevens – Fellowship
Paul Osborn – Flatwoods
Vernon Blackburn – Forest
A.D. Hartley – Garden
Scott McQueen – Gordo
Mike Trull – Hebron
George Shaw – Hickory Grove
Clyde Strickland – Highland
Kenneth Smith – Liberty
Hershel Owen – Mt. Pleasant
Randy Gray – Mt. Tabor
Mike Hall – New Salem
John Davis – Pickensville
Carl Shelton – Pine Grove, Spring Hill
Billy Little – Pleasant Hill
Gary Smith – Reform
James Purnell – Stansel
James Fletcher – Union Chapel
Jack House – West End

1991
James Cooley – Aliceville
W.D. Dawkins – Arbor Springs
Ronnie Elmore – Bethlehem
Franklin Sims – Carrollton

Ronnie McDaniel – Coal Fire
Charles Whitney – Cross Roads
Jimmy Ray – Ethelsville
Ricky Trull – Fellowship
Paul Osborn – Flatwoods
Vernon Blackburn – Forest
Randy Gray – Friendship
Scott McQueen – Gordo
Mike Trull – Hebron
George Shaw – Hickory Grove
Clyde Strickland – Highland
Kenneth Smith – Liberty
Bill Hale – Mineral Springs
Hershel Owen – Mt. Pleasant
Ray Aldredge – Mt. Tabor
Mike Hall – New Salem
Veston Woolbright – Pickensville
Billy Little – Pleasant Hill
Gary Smith – Reform
James Purnell – Stansel
E.P. Gray, Jr. – Union Chapel
Jack House – West End

1992
James Cooley – Aliceville
W.D. Dawkins – Arbor Springs
Ronnie Elmore – Bethlehem
Ronnie McDaniel – Coal Fire
Wayne Wilkins – Ebenezer
Mike Trull – Emmanuel
Jimmy Ray – Ethelsville
Vernon Blackburn – Forest
Randy Gray – Friendship
Mike Snow – Garden
Scott McQueen – Gordo
Billy Jones – Hebron
George Shaw – Hickory Grove
Dawson Morrison – Highland
Kenneth Smith – Liberty
Hershel Owen – Mt. Pleasant
Ray Aldridge – Mt. Tabor
Mike Hall – New Salem
Tim Jones – Pickensville
Charles Young – Pine Grove
Billy Little – Pleasant Hill
Gary Smith – Reform
James Purnell – Stansel
Elliot Gray, Jr. – Union Chapel
Jack House – West End

1993
James Cooley – Aliceville
W.D. Dawkins – Arbor Springs
Ronnie Elmore – Bethlehem
Benjamin Styles – Carrollton
Ronnie McDaniel – Coal Fire
Johnny House – Cross Roads
Grady Pearson – Ebenezer
Jimmy Ray – Ethelsville
Cecil Junkin – Fellowship
Todd Burkhalter – Flatwoods
Vernon Blackburn – Forest
Randy Gray – Friendship
Scott McQueen – Gordo
Billy Jones – Hebron
George Shaw – Hickory Grove
Dawson Morrison – Highland
Kenneth Smith – Liberty
Sidney Lanier – Mineral Springs
Hershel Owen – Mt. Pleasant
Ray Aldridge – Mt. Tabor
Mike Hall – New Salem
Tim Jones – Pickensville
Charles Young – Pine Grove
Billy Little – Pleasant Hill
Gary Smith – Reform
James Purnell – Stansel
Elliot Gray, Jr. – Union Chapel
Michael Griffin – West End

1994
James Cooley – Aliceville
W.D. Dawkins – Arbor Springs
Ronnie Elmore – Bethlehem
Benjamin Styles – Carrollton
Ronnie McDaniel – Coal Fire
Johnny House – Cross Roads
Grady Pearson – Ebenezer
Mike Trull – Emmanuel
Jimmy Ray – Ethelsville
Cecil Junkin – Fellowship

1994 continued
Todd Burkhalter – Flatwoods
Vernon Blackburn – Forest
Randy Gray – Friendship
Billy Flora – Garden
Billy Jones – Hebron
George Shaw – Hickory Grove
Dawson Morrison – Highland
Kenneth Smith – Liberty
Sidney Lanier – Mineral Springs
Hershel Owen – Mt. Pleasant
Ray Aldridge – Mt. Tabor
Mike Hall – New Salem
Tim Jones – Pickensville
Charles Young – Pine Grove
Billy Little – Pleasant Hill
Gary Smith – Reform
James Purnell – Stansel
Mike Smith – Union Chapel
Michael Griffin – West End

1995
James Cooley – Aliceville
Michael Owen – Arbor Springs
Ronnie Elmore – Bethlehem
Benjamin Styles – Carrollton
Ronnie McDaniel – Coal Fire
Johnny House – Cross Roads
Grady Pearson – Ebenezer
Mike Trull – Emmanuel
Jimmy Ray – Ethelsville
Cecil Junkin – Fellowship
Todd Burkhalter – Flatwoods
Vernon Blackburn – Forest
Randy Gray – Friendship
Billy Flora – Garden
Brent Causey – Gordo
Lee Wheat – Hebron
George Shaw – Hickory Grove
Dawson Morrison – Highland
Kenneth Smith – Liberty
Sidney Lanier – Mineral Springs
Hershel Owen – Mt. Pleasant
Ray Aldridge – Mt. Tabor
Mike Hall – New Salem
Tim Jones – Pickensville
Charles Young – Pine Grove
Billy Little – Pleasant Hill
Randy Pate – Reform
James Purnell – Stansel
Mike Smith – Union Chapel
Michael Griffin – West End

1996
James Cooley – Aliceville
Michael Owen – Arbor Springs
Benjamin Styles – Carrollton
Grady Pearson – Ebenezer
Mike Trull – Emmanuel
Jimmy Ray – Ethelsville
Todd Burkhalter – Flatwoods
Vernon Blackburn – Forest
Billy Flora – Garden
Lee Wheat – Hebron
George Shaw – Hickory Grove
Kenneth Smith – Liberty
Sidney Lanier – Mineral Springs
Hershel Owen – Mt. Pleasant
Ray Aldridge – Mt. Tabor
Mike Hall – New Salem
Tim Jones – Pickensville
Charles Young – Pine Grove
Billy Little - Pleasant Hill
Randy Pate – Reform
Clyde Strickland – Spring Hill
Mike Smith – Union Chapel
Michael Griffin – West End

1997
James Cooley – Aliceville
Michael Owen – Arbor Springs
Jimmy Lucas – Bethlehem
Benjamin Styles – Carrollton
Mike Bonner – Coal Fire
Paul Shaw – Cross Roads
Grady Pearson – Ebenezer
Mike Trull – Emmanuel
Jimmy Ray – Ethelsville
Lindsey Watkins – Fellowship
Mark McGee – Flatwoods
Vernon Blackburn – Forest
Lee Wheat – Friendship

1997 continued
Raymond Robinson (interim) – Garden
Mark Howard – Gordo
Johnny House – Hebron
George Shaw – Hickory Grove
Don Bennett – Highland
Kenneth Smith – Liberty
Sidney Lanier – Mineral Springs
Hershel Owen – Mt. Pleasant
Ray Aldridge – Mt. Tabor
Mike Hall – New Salem
Tim Jones – Pickensville
Charles Young – Pine Grove
Billy Little – Pleasant Hill
Randy Pate – Reform
Clyde Strickland – Spring Hill
Steve Thomas – Stansel
Mike Smith – Union Chapel
Michael Griffin – West End

1998
James Cooley – Aliceville
Michael Owen – Arbor Springs
Tommy Hughes – Bethlehem
Benjamin Styles – Carrollton
Mike Bonner – Coal Fire
Paul Shaw – Cross Roads
Grady Pearson – Ebenezer
Mike Trull – Emmanuel
Jimmy Ray – Ethelsville
Lindsey Watkins – Fellowship
Mark McGee – Flatwoods
Vernon Blackburn – Forest
Lee Wheat – Friendship
Raymond Robinson – Garden
Marc Howard – Gordo
Johnny House – Hebron
George Shaw – Hickory Grove
Charles Whitney (Interim) – Highland
Kenneth Smith – Liberty
Sidney Lanier – Mineral Springs
Hershel Owen – Mt. Pleasant
Ray Aldridge – Mt. Tabor
Mike Hall – New Salem
Tim Jones – Pickensville
Charles Young – Pine Grove
Billy Little – Pleasant Hill
Eddie Bates – Reform
Clyde Strickland – Spring Hill
Steve Thomas – Stansel
Wes Jones – Union Chapel
Michael Griffin – West End

1999
James Cooley – Aliceville
Lindsey Watkins (Interim) – Bethlehem
Benjamin Styles – Carrollton
Mike Bonner – Coal Fire
Rickey Jackson – Cross Roads
Grady Pearson – Ebenezer
Mike Trull – Emmanuel
David Westmoreland – Ethelsville
Adam Homan – Fellowship
George Stazel (Interim) – Flatwoods
Vernon Blackburn – Forest
Lee Wheat – Friendship
Raymond Robinson (Interim) – Garden
Marc Howard – Gordo
Johnny House – Hebron
George Shaw – Hickory Grove
Charles Whitney – Highland
Kenneth Smith – Liberty
Sidney Lanier – Mineral Springs
Hershel Owen – Mt. Pleasant
Ray Aldridge – Mt. Tabor
Mike Hall – New Salem
Tim Jones – Pickensville
Charles Young – Pine Grove
Billy Little – Pleasant Hill
Eddie Bates – Reform
Clyde Strickland – Spring Hill
Steve Thomas – Stansel
Wes Jones – Union Chapel
Michael Griffin – West End

2000
James Cooley – Aliceville
Geary Hewett – Arbor Springs
Lindsey Watkins – Bethlehem
Benjamin Styles – Carrollton
Mike Bonner – Coal Fire
Rickey Jackson – Cross Roads

2000 continued
Cecil Junkin – Double Branches
Grady Pearson – Ebenezer
Mike Trull – Emmanuel
David Westmoreland – Ethelsville
Adam Homan – Fellowship
Danny Powell – Flatwoods
Vernon Blackburn – Forest
Lee Wheat – Friendship
Raymond Robertson (Interim) – Garden
Marc Howard – Gordo
Johnny House – Hebron
George Shaw – Hickory Grove
Jerry Robbins – Highland
Kenneth Smith – Liberty
Sidney Lanier – Mineral Springs
Hershel Owen – Mt. Pleasant (Gordo)
David Cullison- Calvary
Ray Aldridge – Mt. Tabor
Mike Hall – New Salem
Tim Jones – Pickensville
Barry Holland – Pine Grove
Billy Little – Pleasant Hill
Brannon Pinion (interim) –Reform
Mike Ezelle- Spring Hill
Steve Thomas – Stansel
Michael Griffin – West End

2001
James Cooley – Aliceville
Barry Holland (Interim) – Arbor Springs
Lindsey Watkins – Bethlehem
Michael Trull – Carrollton
Mike Bonner – Coal Fire
Rickey Jackson – Cross Roads
Cecil Junkin – Double Branches
Grady Pearson – Ebenezer
David Westmoreland – Ethelsville
Adam Homan – Fellowship
Danny Powell – Flatwoods
Vernon Blackburn – Forest
Lee Wheat – Friendship
Raymond Robinson (Interim) – Garden
Pat Powell – Gordo
Johnny House – Hebron
George Shaw – Hickory Grove
Jerry Robbins – Highland
Kenneth Smith – Liberty
Sidney Lanier – Mineral Springs
David Cullison – Calvary
Ray Aldridge – Mt. Tabor
Mike Hall – New Salem
Tim Jones -- Pickensville
Billy Little – Pleasant Hill
Brannon Pinion – Reform
Melvin Mordecai (Interim) – Stansel
Michael Griffin – West End
Luis Oliva – Hispanic Ministry

2002
James Cooley – Aliceville
Barry Holland – Arbor Springs
Lindsey Watkins – Bethlehem
David Cullison – Calvary
Michael Trull – Carrollton
Mike Bonner – Coal Fire
Rickey Jackson – Cross Roads
Cecil Junkin – Double Branches
Grady Pearson – Ebenezer
Hershel Owen – Emmanuel
Adam Homan – Fellowship
Danny Powell – Flatwoods
Vernon Blackburn – Forest
Lee Wheat – Friendship
Raymond Robertson (Interim) – Garden
Pat Powell – Gordo
Johnny House – Hebron
Jerry Robbins – Highland
Kenneth Smith – Liberty
Sidney Lanier – Mineral Springs
Glenn Sandifer – Mt. Pleasant
Ray Aldridge – Mt. Tabor
Mike Hall – New Salem
Tim Jones – Pickensville
Gene Dawkins – Pine Grove
Billy Little – Pleasant Hill
Brannon Pinion – Reform
James Moss – Spring Hill
David Lemoine – Stansel

2002 continued
Tim Meherg – Union Chapel
Michael Griffin – West End
Luis Oliva – Hispanic Ministry

2003
Larry Potts (Interim) – Aliceville
Barry Holland – Arbor Springs
Lindsey Watkins – Bethlehem
David Cullison – Calvary
Michael Trull – Carrollton
Mike Bonner – Coal Fire
Rickey Jackson – Cross Roads
Eugene Junkin – Double Branches
Grady Pearson – Ebenezer
Hershel Owen – Emmanuel
Mel Howton – Ethelsville
Adam Homan – Fellowship
Jack House – Flatwoods
Vernon Blackburn – Forest
Lee Wheat – Friendship
Raymond Robertson (Interim) – Garden
Pat Powell – Gordo
Mike Ezelle – Hebron
George Shaw – Hickory Grove
Jerry Robbins – Highland
Kenneth Smith – Liberty
Sidney Lanier – Mineral Springs
Glenn Sandifer – Mt. Pleasant
Ray Aldridge – Mt. Tabor
Mike Hall – New Salem
Tim Jones – Pickensville
Gene Dawkins – Pine Grove
Billy Little – Pleasant Hill
Brannon Pinion –Reform
James Moss – Spring Hill
David Lemoine – Stansel
Melvin Mordecai – Union Chapel
Michael Griffin – West End
Luis Oliva – Hispanic Ministry

2004
Charlie Wilson – Aliceville
Barry Holland – Arbor Springs
Lindsey Watkins – Bethlehem
David Cullison – Calvary
Michael Trull – Carrollton
Mike Bonner – Coal Fire
Rickey Jackson – Cross Roads
Eugene Junkin – Double Branches
Grady Pearson – Ebenezer
Hershel Owen – Emmanuel
Melvin Howton – Ethelsville
Adam Homan – Fellowship
Jack House – Flatwoods
Vernon Blackburn – Forest
Lee Wheat – Friendship
Raymond Robertson (Interim) – Garden
Pat Powell – Gordo
Randy Gray – Hebron
George Shaw – Hickory Grove
Jerry Robbins – Highland
Kenneth Smith – Liberty
Glenn Sandifer – Mt. Pleasant
Ray Aldridge – Mt. Tabor
Mike Hall – New Salem
Tim Jones – Pickensville
Gene Dawkins – Pine Grove
Robert Pate – Pleasant Grove
Billy Little – Pleasant Hill
Brannon Pinion – Reform
James Moss – Spring Hill
David Lemoine – Stansel
Melvin Mordecai – Union Chapel
David Falgout – West End
Marcos Jimenez – Hispanic Ministry

2005
Charlie Wilson – Aliceville
Barry Holland – Arbor Springs
Lindsey Watkins – Bethlehem
David Cullison – Calvary
Bob Causey (Interim) – Carrollton
Mike Bonner – Coal Fire
Rickey Jackson – Cross Roads
Eugene Junkin – Double Branches
Grady Pearson – Ebenezer
Hershel Owen – Emmanuel
Melvin Howton – Ethelsville
Adam Homan – Fellowship

2005 continued
Jack House – Flatwoods
Vernon Blackburn – Forest
Lee Wheat – Friendship
Raymond Robertson (Interim) – Garden
Pat Powell – Gordo
Randy Gray – Hebron
George Shaw – Hickory Grove
Eddie Rogers – Highland
Kenneth Smith – Liberty
David Blakney – Mineral Springs
Glenn Sandifer – Mt. Pleasant
Ray Aldridge – Mt. Tabor
Mike Hall – New Salem
Tim Jones – Pickensville
Gene Dawkins – Pine Grove
Lenwood Gilliland – Pleasant Grove
Billy Little – Pleasant Hill
Brannon Pinion – Reform
James Moss – Spring Hill
David Lemoine – Stansel
Melvin Mordecai – Union Chapel
David Falgout – West End
Marcus Jiminez – Hispanic Ministry

2006
Charlie Wilson – Aliceville
Barry Holland – Arbor Springs
Lindsey Watkins – Bethlehem
David Cullison – Calvary
Larry Potts (Interim)- Carrollton
Mike Bonner – Coal Fire
Rickey Jackson – Cross Roads
Cecil Junkin – Double Branches
Grady Pearson – Ebenezer
Hershel Owen –Emmanuel
Melvin Howton – Ethelsville
Adam Homan – Fellowship
Jack House – Flatwoods
Vernon Blackburn – Forest
Lee Wheat – Friendship
Raymond Robertson (Interim) – Garden
Jim Roberts – Gordo
Randy Gray – Hebron
George Shaw – Hickory Grove
Eddie Rogers – Highland
Kenneth Smith – Liberty
David Blakney – Mineral Springs
Glenn Sandifer – Mt. Pleasant
Ray Aldridge – Mt. Tabor
Lenwood Gilliland – New Harmony
Mike Hall – New Salem
Tim Jones – Pickensville
Gene Dawkins – Pine Grove
Billy Little – Pleasant Hill
Brannon Pinion – Reform
James Moss – Spring Hill
David Lemoine – Stansel
Melvin Mordecai – Union Chapel
Marcus Jiminez – Hispanic Ministry

2007
Charlie Wilson – Aliceville
Barry Holland – Arbor Springs
Lindsey Watkins – Bethlehem
David Cullison – Calvary
Tommy Winders – Carrollton
Mike Bonner – Coal Fire
Rickey Jackson – Cross Roads
Cecil Junkin – Double Branches
Grady Pearson – Ebenezer
Hershel Owen – Emmanuel
Melvin Howton – Ethelsville
Adam Homan – Fellowship
Leonard Hill – Flatwoods
Vernon Blackburn – Forest
Lee Wheat – Friendship
Randy Gray – Hebron
George Shaw – Hickory Grove
Kenneth Smith – Liberty
David Blakney – Mineral Springs
Glenn Sandifer – Mt. Pleasant
Ray Aldridge – Mt. Tabor
Lenwood Gilliland – New Harmony
Mike Hall – New Salem
Tim Jones – Pickensville
Gene Dawkins – Pine Grove
Billy Little – Pleasant Hill
Brannon Pinnion – Reform
James Moss – Spring Hill

2007 continued
David Lemoine – Stansel
Melvin Mordecai – Union Chapel
David Falgout – West End

2008
Charlie Wilson – Aliceville
Lindsey Watkins – Bethlehem
David Cullison – Calvary
Tommy Winders – Carrollton
Mike Bonner – Coal Fire
Rickey Jackson – Cross Roads
Eugene Junkin – Double Branches
Grady Pearson – Ebenezer
Hershel Owen – Emmanuel
Melvin Howton – Ethelsville
Adam Homan – Fellowship
Leonard Hill – Flatwoods
Vernon Blackburn – Forest
David Barrentine – Garden
David Singleton – Gordo
Randy Gray – Hebron
George Shaw – Hickory Grove
Shawn McDaniel – Highland
Kenneth Smith – Liberty
Patrick Branch – Mineral Springs
Glenn Sandifer – Mt. Pleasant
Ray Aldridge – Mt. Tabor
Lenwood Gilliland – New Harmony
Mike Hall – New Salem
Tim Jones – Pickensville
Gene Dawkins – Pine Grove
Billy Little – Pleasant Hill
Brannon Pinion – Reform
Jeremy Burrage – Stansel
Melvin Mordecai – Union Chapel
Jack House – West End

2009
Charlie Wilson – Aliceville
Larry Shelton – Arbor Springs
Craig Holliman (Interim)- Bethlehem
Blake Thompson – Calvary
Tommy Winders – Carrollton
Mike Bonner – Coal Fire
Rickey Jackson – Cross Roads
Eugene Junkin – Double Branches
Grady Pearson – Ebenezer
Hershel Owen – Emmanuel
Melvin Howton – Ethelsville
Adam Homan – Fellowship
Leonard Hill – Flatwoods
Vernon Blackburn – Forest
Chris Hunnicut – Friendship
Bob Little – Galilee
David Barrentine – Garden
David Singleton – Gordo
Randy Gray – Hebron
George Shaw – Hickory Grove
Shawn McDaniel – Highland
Kenneth Smith – Liberty
Glen Sandifer – Mt. Pleasant
Ray Aldridge – Mt. Tabor
Lenwood Gilliland – New Harmony
Mike Hall – New Salem
Tim Jones – Pickensville
Gene Dawkins – Pine Grove
Billy Little – Pleasant Hill
Tim Meherg – Reform
Bert Noland – Spring Hill
Jeremy Burrage – Stansel
Melvin Mordecai – Union Chapel
Jack House – West End
Marcus Jiminez – Hispanic Ministry
Lonnie Hinton – Covenant of Peace

2010
Charlie Wilson – Aliceville
Larry Shelton – Arbor Springs
Craig Holliman – Bethlehem
Blake Thompson – Calvary
Tommy Winders - Carrollton
Mike Bonner – Coal Fire
Rickey Jackson – Cross Roads
Eugene Junkin – Double Branches
Grady Howton – Ebenezer
Hershel Owen – Emmanuel
Melvin Howton – Ethelsville
Adam Homan – Fellowship
Leonard Hill – Flatwoods
Vernon Blackburn – Forest
Chris Hunnicut – Friendship

2010 continued
Bob Little – Galilee
David Barrentine – Garden
David Singleton – Gordo
Randy Gray – Hebron
George Shaw – Hickory Grove
Shawn McDaniel – Highland
Kenneth Smith – Liberty
Charles Empey – Mineral Springs
Glenn Sandifer – Mt. Pleasant
Ray Aldridge – Mt. Tabor
Jimmy Channel – New Harmony
Mike Hall- New Salem
Tim Jones – Pickensville
Gene Dawkins – Pine Grove
Billy Little – Pleasant Hill
Bert Noland – Spring Hill
Cody Warren – Stansel
Melvin Mordecai – Union Chapel
Jack House – West End
Marcus Jiminez – Hispanic Ministry
Lonnie Hinton – Covenant of Peace

Sustainability of Rural Baptist Churches
A Case Study
Gary Farley

Looking back over the 20th Century I find that Pickens County added seven rural and village Baptist Churches affiliated with the association. (This excludes three others that were formed in the towns of Gordo and Aliceville.) During the same century Unity, Mars Hill, Zion, and Big Creek closed. So, there was a net gain of three rural churches. This occurred in spite of the fact that the rural population of the county declined about 50 %. Today the association counts 29 of its 37 churches as being in rural settings. (Two of these rural churches came into the association at the point of transitioning from one century to the other. One is an older church; the other is new. One is in another county.) Of these 29 churches, 18 have celebrated their centennial.

While I do not have all of the data to provide exact numbers, it is evident that there has been a significant decline in the number of Presbyterian and Methodist congregations in the county. (The 1971 count was 6 Presbyterian and 16 Methodist churches in the county.) The Primitive Baptist movement also suffered a significant decline during the 20th Century. What is true here seems to be repeated across the nation. Southern Baptists have sustained in the rural places well, better than most.

Why? Some might answer decisively by declaring that God has blessed Baptist because of our orthodoxy and evangelistic effort while cursing other groups for their liberalism. But, one might also want to consider the possibility of some sociological factors contributing to the sustainability of the missionary Baptist movement in this rural setting. Below I will suggest some of these factors. Please consider them and add others that come to your mind.

1. *Locally Owned and Managed.* Each of these rural churches is autonomous. Each is operated by the folk who hold membership there. They may have put up the building. They maintain it and improve it. They select the pastor. They decide what the church will do and when it will do it. Often the pastor is not a resident of the community, so the lay leadership provides much of the pastoral care of the church. If the church were to close, they would have to accept the responsibility. A church which has not added to its facilities since 1950 is most likely to have not survived. Responding to change is crucial. All of this is to say that there is some very deep emotional involvement with the church that contributes to sustainability. This is not the case with other
forms of church connectionalism.

2. *Indigenous Preachers.* In by far the majority of instances these churches are pastored by persons with little formal training for the ministry. Most experienced a call to ministry as adults, or surrendered to it as adults, and did not go to Bible College or Seminary. Their training has come through mentoring, private study, reflective experience, and local study programs. They understand the needs and concerns of the people in the rural churches and the unchurched in the community served by the church. Their style of preaching and pastoring fits the expectations of the people that they serve.

3. *Brand Recognition.* The Baptist movement has been strong in this county since the

period of settlement prior to 1840. Of course, it seems that the missionary Baptists have gained market share across the year. The Baptist theology is familiar to most people here, although sometimes in a perverted view. Certainly, many folk are sort of predisposed to be a Baptist. Becoming a Baptist Christian is reasonably acceptable. The Baptist way and the local culture seem to intermingle. It is understood that success breeds success. But it also breeds contempt. There are some persons in most rural communities dominated by the Baptists who will never become a part of the movement for this very reason.

4. *Family Chapels.* Typically, rural churches over time evolve into family chapels. Through the process of marrying in a community, often the membership of the church will develop a good many kinship ties. It is common to find four generations of a family in the church and 4 or 5 more buried in the graveyard beside the church. So, the fertility of a kinship line is often an important factor in the sustainability of a rural church.

5. *Multibonded Relationships.* Usually, the core members of an older rural church have been in the church for many years. They have experienced joy there. They have worked through conflicts and tragedies. They have worked together to hold events and to complete successfully projects of the church. This is the coinage of ownership in a rural church. These bonds make it very difficult for a person to walk away, drop out, or move their membership elsewhere.

6. *Connectionalism.* Baptists churches connect through local associations of churches. The association has no "church" power. This means that it has no authority over a local church. Rather, its role is to provide services to the local churches and to provide opportunities for cooperative efforts by several churches. There are two other areas of connectionalism, state conventions, and the national convention for our churches. The churches belong directly to these conventions. They do not go through the association to connect with them.

7. *Associational Missionary.* I hope that I am not seen as self-serving in this point, but I deeply believe that the associational system of the missionary Baptists of the south has contributed much to our sustainability in rural settings. Early in the 20th Century denominational leadership noted the decline in the number of rural churches. The denomination was poor and could not really do much about this until after World War II which brought prosperty to the South like it had not known before. Between 1945 and 1950 most associations hired a missionary to work with the churches and adopted a plan called the Long Range Rural Church Program. Within a decade most of the rural churches which had had worship only once or twice a month began to have worship every Sunday. Likewise, they added additional programs and activities to complement the Sunday School program. And they trained workers to improve the quality of the Sunday School. This was true here in Pickens. All of this was very fortunate in its timing. Hundreds of thousands of rural Baptists had a mission to improve the life and work of their church. They invested in the work of their church. The missionary promoted resources, held events, helped out in weak churches and kept a focus on the tasks of missions and evangelism. He or she served as a friend, confident, and consultant close at hand and accessible. His or her authority was relational, not structural.

8. *Evangelism.* The Baptist movement rose to prominence during the frontier revivals of the early 19th Century. Emphasis on evangelism has continued to be our hallmark. Revival,

baptisms and additions to the membership continue to be normative expectations in the life of the rural churches. While some may question the effectiveness of these efforts, it seems to me that they have had a positive impact upon the sustainability of the rural churches. There is a commitment to witness, to do outreach, to be open and inviting toward those who are unchurched. And when additions are made positive reinforcement comes from the missionary and from the association.

9. *Missions.* The support of missions through prayer, financial support and the sending of their own sons and daughters has been of great importance to rural Baptist Churches. (Pickens has sent 21 to the foreign missions fields in the past century and a half.) It seems that a focus on missions can help a church look outward with hope, rather than look inward in despair. The church is involved in something great, important and biblical.

10. *Church Extension.* Baptists seem to just keep on planting new congregations. Here some replaced older dying ones. Others were started where there was no church of our faith present. Some were born out of controversy. The creation of new congregations, regularly, seems to contribute to sustainability of the movement. Churches for all kinds of people has been our style, rather than seeking to house diverse groups in a congregation.

Many of these ten points reinforce one another in the everyday life of the churches. For example, the revival becomes an occasion when the members are inviting others to come. They act as hosts. Their sense of ownership in enhanced. The family is expanded. Other characteristics of rural churches might be noted. However, this list of characteristics seem to contribute most to explaining, from a sociological perspective the success of missionary Baptists churches in rural areas. Here you have my assessment. I welcome your comments, questions, additions and so forth.

The coming of the Gospel light---1817-1857

Tilly and York. Trade. Others came with slaves to expand cotton plantations. Initially river and creek bottoms. Christians, mostly Baptists, Methodists, and Presbyterians. The first churches were established by 1822.

Methodists. Ebenezer Hearns. Hargrove and Ebenezer. Presbyterian. Bethany and Oak Grove. Two Maps. 1837 Enon, South Carolina, Antioch.

Apparently, about 1830 Kentucky Baptists opened near Yorkville a Choctaw Indian mission called Halbert Mission. It was connected to a school in Georgetown, Kentucky run by the kin of the Indian agent in Columbus, Ms. Due to the Indian removal during that decade, it was short-lived and mostly forgotten.

1835 Union BA., Buttehatchie, South of Coldfire. 19 churches. Pickens, Greene, and Tuscaloosa. Richard Wilkins, Henry Petty, Charles Stewart, Wm Stansel jh Taylor, Job, a slave

Division in 1837. Antiboard. Assn. map. Half.

In the next decade grew dramatically. Population nearly tripled to 17k. 4 churches north of Coldfire. Missionary folk in Primitive churches. Planted churches in new communities. Zion. Basil Manley. Grant's Creek. Protracted meetings.

Initially, Big Creek was the largest. It spun off Carrollton, Pickensville, and Crossroads.

Methodists camp meetings. All three denominations practiced church discipline. Church Covenant. Order. All three actively evangelized the slaves. All three split, north and south over slavery during the 1840s.

1850 Mt. Mariah, Ellis Gore. Free Will, Salem. Mineral Springs.

1851 Martha Foster Crawford to China.

Slaves began to hold their own worship services. Slaves were ordained to preach. Duncan Salmonds.

Annual meetings. Four days. Business in the church house. Campmeeting outside. September. Missionary to plant churches and revive weak congregations. Colportage. Circular letter. Mission funding. Aid to widows of pastors. Education of men called to ministry.

Union was moderator lead with district meeting prior to the annual meeting and an ex bd. It had churches in Pickens, south Lamar, southwest Tuscaloosa, and northwest Greene.

The churches met one weekend a month. Saturday for business and discipline. We have the minutes of these on microfilm for many of our congregations. Sunday was for worship. Consequently, many pastors served two to four churches. Most were planters, some merchants, some held political office. Based on the circular letters which some penned, they were good students of the Word.

Most of the churches were rural. Aside from Carrollton and Yorkville, all of the towns were on the Tombigbee and were ports for the shipping of cotton to Mobile

During this period the Gospel Light was well planted. Becoming a Christian was serious business. It was a matter of pleading for God to forgive one's sins and send the transforming Holy Spirit into the heart. And church membership involved becoming accountable to the church.

They Carried the Gospel Light

In the PBA Office is a plaque on which the names of missionaries who have served our association and who are serving our association carried the Gospel Light to the world. We have 26 names inscribed there. This is a significant number from our association. In March of 2000 The Commission Magazine published an article about our mission heritage.

Recall. Mission agency controversy 1837. In 1845 SBC. Some of the earlier board missionaries transferred to SBC. Then in 1850, Martha Foster from Grant's Creek. Arranged marriage with Crawford. Went out in 1851. Lottie Moon served under her.

Two of the next three were Mary Jane Thorton, Bethel, China, and JJ Taylor,
Forest and West Greene, Brazil, 1880s. She died. He served on until 1927.
Addie Cox 1918. Video. Support of her was a major factor, China
Ulman Moss – Columbia and Venezuela, and then Mexico.
James Swedenburg, Jr., Taiwan, Korea
Mary Swedenburg, Japan
John and Ann Faulkner, Africa
Gerald Davis, Philippines
Ann Fox Baskin, Malaysia
J. Russell Cox, Liberia
David and Cindy Tuten, Tanzania
Virgil and Angie Cooper, Korea, Japan, and Pacific Rim

Since 1851, for more than a century and one half.

Parker Windle, France; Landon Williams, Brazil and Chile
Independents skilled like the Harrises, China, and Amy Williams, China

The sending of the light across North America is much less well documented.

GW Baines, R.T. Hanks, Henry Trull, Mike Griffin, J. F. Brock

Other names not specifically mentioned here are on the plaque showing dates and places.

It is a proud heritage.
Pray for more workers in the harvest.
Others will use their training.

And then there is the prison. I believe that it is and will in an expanding way be a mission sending agency. Meet God. Be Discipled. Get Equipped. Go Home. Connect With a Church. Testify. Teach. Live a transformed life.

Persons with Pickens County Ties who have Served through IMB

Martha F. Crawford
China
1851-1892

Emma Puthuff
Brazil
1885-1888

James J. Taylor
Brazil
1891-1924

Addie E. Cox
China, Formosa
1918-1955

James Ulman Moss
Columbia, Venezuela, Mexico
1945-1982

Martha Ann Brandon Anderson
Philippines
1964-1975, 1978-1995

Mary Swedenburg
Japan
1969-2003

John & Anne Williams Faulkner
Rhodesia/Zimbabwe 1970-1999
Director East & South Africa 1985-1997

Gerald Davis
Philippines
1976-2007

J. Russell Cox
Liberia
1978-1980

Fred & Cathy Findley
Uganda
1979-1983

Timothy Bruce Owens
Thailand
1987-

Ann Fox Baskin
Malaysia
1988-1999

Herbert L. Geer, Jr.
Israel
1997-Present

James Reece Swedenburg, Jr.
Taiwan, Korea
1970-1980

David & Cindy Tuten
Tanzania
2003-2005

Mary Jane Thorton Bostick
China
1888-1903

Virgil & Amy Cooper
Korea, Japan, Pacific Rim
1972-2010

Parker Windle
France
2008-2012 (still serving as Pastor in France)

Landon Williams
Brazil, Chile
2009-2011 2018-present

Mike Owen
Brazil
2018-present

Our Mission Heritage 2010, Newsletter of

PICKENS BAPTIST ASSOCIATION

P.O. Box 206, Carrollton, AL 35447, (205) 367-8632

Gary Farley, Missionary

pbassn@centurytel.net www.pickensbaptist.com http://picasaweb.google.com/pickensbaptist

Our Mission Heritage: Carey, Judson, and Rice

As we celebrate 175 years of ministry as an association of Baptist churches here in West Central Alabama, I want to invite you to think with me and study our missionary heritage. Since the first of 28 missionaries from our association who have served as missionaries in other countries under appointment by the SBC Foreign/International Mission Board, Martha Foster Crawford, went to China in 1851, we will also be marking during this year the fact that someone(s) from our association has been on the foreign mission field for 150 years.

She was the first person from Alabama appointed as a missionary by our denomination, I doubt that any other association can match the record. I also doubt that many, if any, rural associations has sent as many of its sons and daughters to the mission field. (We will publish an article about her next month. You can look her up on line at the Alabama Women's Hall of Fame which is located at Judson College.)

Most, if not all, of you are familiar with the story of early missions as told in the Book of the Acts of the Apostles. Many of you memorized the mission journeys of the Apostle Paul. Some of you know of Thomas who carried the Gospel to India, of Patrick who carried the Gospel to Ireland, or of Columbo who evangelized in Scotland.

But then for nearly a millennium there was very little done to carry the Gospel to foreign lands, other than efforts to defeat the Muslims in the Near East. Africa and much of Asia was neglected. Conversion by the sword replaced conversion by the Word. This did not prove to be very effective and lasting.

With the discovery of the Western Hemisphere there were efforts to evangelize the Native Americans. Roger Williams, a Baptist, was among those who saw this as mandated for Christians. Then as the British Empire extended its reach into India and beyond in the latter part of the 18th century, a renewed interest in missions was kindled.

In 1792 a bivocational Baptist cobbler and pastor, William Carey, preached to his association in England about the responsibility he felt to share the Gospel in India. (You can find out a lot about him by viewing a video on his life which is available at the PBA. The script and a companion book on Carey was written by Timothy George, Dean of Beeson Divinity School at Samford.) Carey's work in India was a struggle. He studied the native languages and translated the Bible so that the people of India could read it and understand it. He did not have a convert for his first seven years. His wife became ill and died. He lost children as well. He worked bivocationally there in India, earning much of his support by managing an industrial plant. In time he was highly honored both in England and India. Carey is widely honored as the father of modern missions in that he developed volunteer supporting groups which would help provide the funds to send and support missionaries.

Christians here in America were also inspired by his work. Among them were three young Congregationalist students in New England–Adoniram and Ann Judson and Luther Rice. In 1811 they sailed to India where they met William Carey and his colleagues.

On the trip they studied the Bible and concluded that the Baptist understanding of conversion and baptism was correct. As persons of integrity, they knew that they must resign their current support and turn to the Baptists of America for funding. Alas, Baptists had no mission board in place and had no national organization to which they might appeal. They decided to send Luther Rice home to appeal to the Baptists to begin raising support. This he did.

And since the United States and Great Brittan were about to enter into a war, the Judson's were encouraged to continue on to Burma and begin a ministry there which in many ways paralleled that of Carey–translation of the Bible to native languages, death of family members, bivocationalism, and a long wait for converts. But in time this work was also blessed. Mr. Judson spent time in prison when England and Burma were at war. Ironically, he played an important role in brokering peace between England and Burma–helping those who imprisoned him. There is a wonderful new book about the Judson's by Alabama's own Rosalie Hunt, *Bless God and Take Courage*. (Mrs. Hunt spoke to the annual meeting of our WMU three years ago.) I encourage everyone to get a copy of her book and read it.

Luther Rice, back in America, played a key role in getting Baptists in America to form a national denomination. The organization, which first met in 1814, was called the Triennial Convention. It met, as the name indicated, at three year intervals. It formed not only a Foreign Mission Society but also a Domestic Mission Society and a college in Washington DC. Interestingly, Baptists in the South have educational institutions named for each of these pioneers–Carey, Judson, and Rice. (Our own J. T. Simpson and his wife played a key role about 25 years ago in the restoration of the home place of Luther Rice. It now serves as the campus for the New England Southern Baptist Convention.)

However, interestingly, the work of forming mission societies and supporting missionaries became a point of contention which resulted in a split within the Baptist family between those who contributed to mission societies and those who did not. Here in our association the split was right down the middle. Here the primitive, or anti-board Baptists, formed their own association, Pilgrim Rest. There are similar splits in the Baptist family in many of the eastern states. Interestingly, the work of the missionary Baptists has grown while the primitive movement has declined.

Further, the Southern Baptist Convention, which was formed in 1845, has its roots in mission controversy, as well. Even those missionary Baptists who continued to support missionaries and the boards that sent them out felt that the boards discriminated against appointing missionaries who were also slave holders. They contended that this was something like wanting financial support from persons whom could not be appointed by the mission board. And while the holding of slaves has since been renounced, the principle of being asked to support an organization which discriminates against some of its supporters continues to seem right and correct and just to many.

In 1845 when the SBC was formed, it created mission boards, something a little different from a society, to send missionaries to foreign land and to send missionaries to places and groups in this land–Native Americans, Slaves, Settlers on the Western frontier, and New Orleans. (We did pretty well in 3 out of 4.)

Some of the missionaries under appointment by the old Triennial societies transferred to the boards of the SBC. Then in 1851 Martha Foster Crawford from Grant's Creek Baptist Church, then in our association, was appointed as a missionary to China. Next month we will share her exciting story.

Meanwhile back here our association in 1837 decided to allow its churches and members to support mission boards. Only in 1842 did it decide to support the Alabama Baptist Convention which had been formed back in 1823 and had struggled to survive in its early years. In 1845 our association, then known as Union, affirmed the formation of the Southern Baptist Convention.

Locally, in this formative period our association would often commission and provide some support for one of its ministers to hold revivals in communities which had no Baptist church. Often, this effort was crowned with success and a new church was formed.

In these early days funds collected in the local churches for the support of domestic and for foreign missions were brought by the "messengers" to the annual meeting of the association and then sent to the mission boards.

One should also note that during the 19th century ministers who served here often joined those who moved on to the west and the new frontiers and found opportunity to do mission work.. Among the names I have recognized in our annual minutes who did this were George Washington Banes, the great-grandfather of President L. B. Johnson, Silas Dobbs who planted the Baptist Church in Louisville, Ms. Lee Comphere; who was a missionary to the Choctaw Indians, R. T. Hanks who became pastor of the FBC of Dallas, Texas; L.S. Foster who became pastor of FBC, Columbus, Ms, and S.S. Lattimore who became a leader for Mississippi Baptists. (Help me add to this list.)

Hopefully, you see that missions are deep in the DNA of our churches and their members. This is the reason that our churches pass along 18%, on average, of their undesignated income to mission causes. This is why they give more than 4% to support the work of this association. This is why many of us do missions locally. This is why many of us have participated in short-term mission trips in North America and to other nations. This is why our sons and daughters have become career missionaries. This is why we do well in our support of the Lottie Moon, the Annie Armstrong and the Kathleen Mallory mission offerings.

Look for special editions of the newsletter of the association during the coming year. Educate yourself about missions. Involve yourself. I am proud, and so should you be, of the role that Baptists have played in recapturing the vision of being Great Commission Christians, Matthew 28:19-20.

******Mark your calendar for our On Mission Celebration February 19-23, 2011**

Special Newsletter
Our Mission Heritage: The China Connection I

At the 1891 meeting of our association a letter from two female missionaries, daughters of our association, was read to the body. Writing from the Shantung Provence of North China the ladies chided Baptists for not sending more missionaries to share the Gospel. And they asked the messengers to "adopt and support some family already on the field, or one that that will be forthcoming. If not a family, then a single missionary. Can not the 2166 Baptists of your association do this? Let the question be put to the various churches composing your body for action next year, the centennial of modern Baptist missions. ... We come asking you to send more men and women to go from house to house, village to village, city to city preaching Christ to lost and dying me. Shall we not heed our Savior's command and give the gospel to every creature? May God's richest blessing rest and abide with you."

The association responded by committing to raise $600 in the coming year to support one of the missionaries, Mary Jane Thornton. Among the messengers was her cousin, J. G. Thornton, pastor at Forest and others of our churches for two decades. He had been helped by the association to get an education at Howard College. Mary Jane, lost her father during the Civil War. She attended the Bethel Baptist Church in Tuscaloosa County. She worked her way through old Central Female College in Tuscaloosa, graduating in 1889. The following year our Foreign Mission Board sent her to work with Lottie Moon, the Crawfords, the Bosticks, and others in north China. (You can find more of her story in *Called to China* by Rebekah Adams.)

The other author of the letter quoted above, Martha Foster Crawford, was a 40 year veteran missionary in 1891. Her story is told by Wayne Flynt and Gereald W. Berkley in *Taking Christianity to China.* She was raised in the Grant's Creek Baptist Church in the Foster's community of southwestern Tuscaloosa County. Her cousin, James C. Foster, served as pastor of that church for more than 40 years and as moderator of our association for 28 years.

The story of her call and appointment as a missionary is a most interesting one. When she applied to be a missionary, she was told that the Foreign Mission Board was not appointing single missionaries. But, about the same time a single man from Kentucky. T.P. Crawford, applied also. He was told about Martha Foster, with an apparent match-making suggestion. Crawford rode through the winter from Kentucky to Clinton, Alabama where Martha was teaching school. They courted for a couple of weeks. Then they married. They attended the meeting of the Southern Baptist Convention that Spring of 1851. In the Fall they sailed to China. Both Crawfords were smart and strong willed. Their stories, personal, as a couple, and as mission strategists, are very interesting. Martha kept a Journal throughout her life in which she recorded her experiences and thoughts. The journal has provided a wonderful window into the life of a pioneer missionary to China. Carol Anne Vaughn, now on the faculty of Samford, wrote her disseration for a PhD in history at Auburn with Wayne Flynt.

When the SBC was formed in 1845 some missionaries serving in China (and in Liberia) under the old Triennial Convention board asked to be taken over by the new board. So the new convention immediately had missionaries in China to support, encourage and reinforce. Carrying the Gospel to other cultures was still a very new thing. There was much to learn about how to do this effectively. Among the issues were:

*learning to communicate in another language

*translating the Bible into native languages

*understanding the culture and values of a different race

*handling what we now term "culture shock"

*how best to select and train persons to be missionaries

*deciding whether to live as Westerners or adapting to the food, clothing, and living arrangements of the natives *finding a strategy for winning converts—street preaching, schools, hospitals, aid.

*location in the new culture and which class of people to seek to evangelize

*how to relate to the existing culture and religion of the area where the Gospel was being presented

*dealing with the leaders of the native religion whose position was threatened if people became Christians

*decoupling oneself from the imperialism and exploitation of the natives by other Westerners, business and military

*health care (Many missionaries, including Mary Jane Thornton, died young.)

*raising children (Many sent children back to the family in the USA to raise.)

*nurturing the converts spiritually

*helping the churches become self-supporting and indigenous

*handling fear and depression in difficult times (T. P. Crawford and Edmonia Moon suffered from mental problems, as did others.)

*how best to be supported on the field—from a mission board, from churches and friends, or be self-supporting

*how does one measure effectiveness or success.

A study of the lives of the Crawfords, Mary Jane Thornton, Lottie Moon and others should cause one to honor and respect these persons for the many sacrifices they made, and the price they paid to follow the calling God laid upon their lives.

Often the missionaries did not agree concerning the best answers to these issues. Conflict resulted. And for many there was development and change in their opinions about these issues over time in an ever changing context.

And while much has been learned and many good methods found, how best to do missions is still a subject of debate and conflict. (I will return to this subject in our second study of our China connection.)

For the Crawfords their first task was to learn one of the languages of China and to be assimilated to some extent into the culture. They first stayed with veteran missionaries, the Yates in Shanghai. Then after a decade they moved to Shantung Provence. Through the years they would mentor other missionaries including the Moons, Edmonia and Lottie.

In their first two decades they preached in the streets, and Martha ran a school The 1860s were very difficult for them. The Civil War made support from America uncertain. T. P. invested in real estate and prospered. Converts were won. Following a furlough in the States in the early 1880s Crawford closed the schools and shifted focus to traveling out to villages to preach the gospel and founding congregations. They concluded that their focus was not to be on Westernizing those whom they converted to Christianity. They accommodated their dress, diet and lifestyle to the culture. They drew upon the truth that Christianity and native religions shared. They sought to demonstrate what being a Christian in the local culture would look like.

Further, T.P. reacted to abuse by some supposed converts, those who claimed to be believers in order to get a job in the mission and/or to get food from the mission. He came to believe that native congregations should be self-supporting, self-governing and self-propagating. The native churches were not to Southern Baptist churches in China. Rather, they were to develop uniquely in that culture.

While this Three-self concept has come to be widely accepted by others, Mr. Crawford also felt that missionaries ought to either be supported by local churches or associations, or be themselves self-supporting. This is behind the 1891 letter to our association. And it led to the break the following year by the Crawfords, Ms. Thornton, G. P. Bostick and others in the North China mission with the Foreign Mission Board of the SBC. In Baptist mission history this has been called "The Gospel Missions Movement". After the death of Mr. Crawford in 1902, most of the Gospel Mission missionaries returned the the FMB of the SBC. Their philosophy of missions lives on, however, among many

Independent Baptists and others.

In 1892 Mary Jane Thornton married the widowed G. P. Bostick on the field in China. She gave birth to four children in this union. Then in 1903, like many other early missionaries she died. She was only 41.

Martha Foster Crawford lived on until 1909. After only a third furlough in the USA, she had returned in 1903, after the death of T. P. Crawford. She too was buried in China. Both Martha and Mary Jane lived through the dark and difficult days of the Boxer Rebellion and its reaction to Western culture and Westerners. Both shared the Gospel well and effectively.

Recently, our churches collected the annual Lottie Moon Christmas Offering for Foreign Missions. Ms. Moon began her service in China by serving a decade with the Crawfords. Catherine B. Allen in her *The New Lottie Moon Story* tells the story of their relationship. In 1873 she joined her sister Edmonia and the Crawfords in north China. She and the others found that the most effective way of introducing the Gospel was to teach about the resurrection of Christ. (Here we tend to focus on the crucifixion.) Lottie died on the way back to the United States in 1910.

Dr. Flynt notes that not only did Ms. Moon owe much to Martha Foster Crawford, but also much is owed by Southern Baptists, China and modern missiology. No one served for a longer period. She learned how to be a missionary by being one. She changed as she felt change was proper and needed. But she stayed true to the fundamentals of the Gospel.

Apparently, her marriage was not a very happy one. She had no children of her own. But she adopted some children of China and raised them well. One of the great stories of missions is that of the Shantung revival in the early 20th century. Apparently, it sprang, in part, from the work she and Lottie Moon and others did there. This reminds me of two other books I would suggest to you for reading. One is Langdon Gilkey's *Shantung Compound.* This is an account of life in an interment camp in north China run by the Japanese during World War II. The other is the history of our Foreign Mission Board by William Estep, *Whole Gospel for the Whole World.* Dr. Estep was one of my professors at Southwestern Baptist Theological Seminary.

I cannot help to wonder what Martha and Mary Jane think of Pickens Association Baptists today our numbers have more than doubled since 1891. We have four men from our association serving with our International Mission Board. In 2009 our churches reported mission gifts totally $571,000.

In the next installment of our mission heritage we will be looking at the work of Addie Cox who served in China from 1918 to 1955. Let me encourage all of our churches to get a copy of the DVD we did recently on her life and view it in some service soon. She was quite a woman. A very effective missionary.

Martha Foster Crawford *"The Bostick's*

Special Newsletter
Our Mission Heritage
China II

When Addie Cox retired in 1955 at age 70, after 37 years of service as a foreign missionary for the Southern Baptists, she received a letter from Dr. Baker James Cauthen, also a former missionary to China and then the Executive Secretary of the Foreign Mission Board. It stated in part, "*You have had one of the most remarkable missionary careers I have had the privilege of knowing about. God has worked through you in a very definite way to bring many people to know Christ as Saviour and to encourage the hearts of those who believe on Him. Your work in China will live on in the lives of people until our Lord's return. You evidenced such love for the Chinese people and willingness to help them bear their burdens that they will always love you and think God for you.*"

High praise and prophetic insight about an amazing woman, one who grew up in our association. Recently, Dr. Thrath Curry, Bonnie Windle and others prepared a video documentary telling the story of the Life and Ministry of Miss Addie Cox. It is my hope that during 2011 each of our churches will arrange for a showing of this video in a service. I will be glad to come and show it, or a church can borrow a copy from the PBA office, or copies can be purchased from the office for $10. In any case please calendar this event. Let me whet your appetite for this video by sharing highlights of her life.

In 1885 in the Providence community, now Liberty, of Pickens County Alabama, Addie was born, one of seven children in the family of Wiley and Frances Eddins Cox. Soon the family moved to Carrollton, probably to provide a good education for the children. They lived in a home located next to where Bootie Cox now lives. Addie became a Christian and a member of the Carrollton Baptist Church at age 10.

The Carrollton Church was the home of the W. G. and S. A. Robertson. Mrs. Robertson was the driving force for the Women's Missionary Society for the association ,and he was the champion of Sunday School work as well as its moderator. In 1907, at age 22, Addie Cox assumed leadership of the WMU for the association. She was a recent graduate of the Central Female College of Tuscaloosa. This school was Baptist connected and headed by a cousin of Martha Foster Crawford our first missionary to China. (Mary Jane Thornton, our second missionary to China was also a graduate.) Addie excelled in music and drama and recitations.

In the same year the WMU opened a missionary training school connected to The Southern Baptist Seminary in Louisville, Kentucky. Addie soon entered that school and graduated in 1913. Upon her return to Carrollton she was offered a position as worker for the association among women and children, but instead she took a job as the assistant to the pastor of the FBC of Birmingham. Soon she was asked to be a fieldworker for the Alabama WMU. She served well. But missions was on her mind.

Just as World War I was reaching its climax in 1918 she was appointed to be our missionary to China and sailed from San Francisco to Shanghai. There she was connected with the Bosticks, long-time missionaries, and distant cousins we believe. She proved to be an apt learner of the Mandarin Chinese language. She was next assigned to the interior mission station at Kaifeng in the Henan Province. Initally she taught in a school for girls—English, music, and art. And while she loved this and always championed both educational and medical mission work, her heart was is direct evangelism. So, soon she was traveling to villages in the hinterland, often to places where the Gospel had never been heard. As she went she would talk with her fellow travelers about the Gospel. In a town she would draw a crowd because most had never seen a Westerner. She would typically speak to women and children, because women were not allowed to speak to men in a public setting. She loved to teach the children to sing hymns and quote Scripture. As I read about her mission efforts, my mind kept recalling the missionary hymn with the line, " I love to tell this story". This was the passion of

Miss Addie for the next 30 years as she traveled many difficult and dangerous miles in the Henan Province. She truly loved to tell the story.

In 1926 she and Blanche Rose Walker, another single female missionary to China, and apparently another Bostick kinsperson but from Texas, wrote for the WMU a wonderful little book, *Glimpses of Missionary Life.* It was widely studied by WMU circles across the convention. (Interestingly, Miss Blanche, who was a much older missionary than Miss Addie begins the book by telling about how the Crawfords and Bostics had welcomed her and mentored her in doing the missionary tasks. Interesting, in that the Crawfords and the Bostics had resigned from the FMB over a dispute concerning mission strategy.) The topics discussed are the call to missions, the many false gods of the Chinese religions, the social customs, the processes of mission work, and the results.

They concluded that the Chinese people were very superstitious. While they found some good principles in the teachings of Confucius and Budda, those which mirrored biblical teachings, they noted that these religion did not really give much of value to the everyday life of the people. Misses Cox and Walker were also critical of the fact that the people worshiped their ancestors and were fearful of evil spirits and many gods competing for their favor, much like one finds in biblical times in cultures other than the Jewish and the Christian.

They were particularly critical of the treatment of women by these faiths as well as by Islam. Women were abused and exploited. Girls were seen as a burden. Some baby girls were left to die. Addie was particularly critical of the practice of binding feet.

(Since coming to Carrollton in 1998 I have wondered about what motived the placement of the statue on the courthouse square which honors women, something very rare indeed. It was set and dedicated in 1927 soon after Miss Addie's first furlough. Could it be that in her speaking across the area she had quickened in the hearts of the county leaders a deeper appreciation for women? I am willing to believe this. Listen to this line from her pen which opens chapter three. "The attitude of any religion toward womanhood tests it value to the national life, for it is true that no nation rises higher than the mothers of the nation." True. I fear that we have not yet affirmed its truth in our denominational life.)

Glimpses continues with descriptions of the everyday work of missionaries. Miss Addie recounts many stories of her travels out from Kaifeng to the towns and villages in its district. She includes accounts of how marvelously God had moved in the hearts of those to whom she spoke. The book concludes with an an appraisal of the worth of the effort and a challenge to pray, to give, and to come and help with the work.

Certainly, her stories moved the women of our churches, association and convention to sacrificially support mission work. For example, in 1931, in the depth of the depression, one finds a note in the annual minutes of our association regarding the effort of the WMU to raise and send support to Miss Addie so that she could hire local "Bible women" to assist her in her evangelistic work. Her second furlough was in 1934-35. The fact that she was returned to her post when funds were so short must be seen as a testimony to the effectiveness of her work. Her third furlough was at the end of World War II. When she returned she took with her 16 bicycles. One for herself and the others for the native evangelists with whom she worked.

Soon after her return to China in 1926, her work was impacted by the civil war between the Nationalists and the Communists. During her third term, it was impacted by the invasion of the Japanese. And after World War II the Communists gained control of the nation and she was forced to leave in 1951. She was reassigned to Formosa. There she gathered groups of Chinese believers and formed several new churches. And after her retirement and return to Carrollton, she made trips to San Francisco's Chinatown where she used her command of the Manderin language to witness to the Gospel and disciple believers.

During her 32 years in China she also ministered to people suffering from floods and famines. She took in and protected those who suffered from these natural disasters and those displaced by war. She loved her people. And like many missionaries she became like those to whom she carried the light of the Gospel.

Tucked in the annual reports of the Foreign Mission Board to the meetings of the Southern Baptist Convention are quotes from Miss Addie about her work. They tell of hundreds of baptisms, of the protective hand of God on her life in dangerous times and places, and her planting of the seeds of the Gospel. She tells of Chinese congregations growing and become self-supporting.

When the Communists expelled missionaries in 1950, and the Bamboo Curtain fell, and we lost contact with the Christians of China, Southern Baptists prayed and grieved. But God was at work in the lives of those whom Miss Addie and her colleagues had won to Christ. More than 25 years passed and then we got a peak behind the curtain and learned that the Christian movement had grown to about 50 million. Today there are more than 100 million Christians in China in spite of continuing seasons of persecution. Certainly, the seeds she spoke of planting have come to fruition.

In the video that Dr. Thraith Curry prepared on the life and work of Miss Addie there are references to the importance of Galatians 5:22 in her personal life and to the Gospel that she shared. This is the passage which sets forth "The Fruits of the Spirit". Love, joy, peace, longsuffering, gentleness, goodness, faith, meekness, and temperance. Those who remember her, particularly during her 10 years in retirement in Carrollton, testify that these fruits certainly characterized her life. The next generation of missionaries from our association, like Ann Williams Faulkner, have told us that she made a great impression on their lives and encouraged them to respond to the call upon their lives to become missionaries. And on several occasions Chinese people have come to Carrollton to visit her grave site in the city cemetery, just down the street from her home and her church. Miss Addie Cox was a small woman from a small place, but she became a giant in the mission enterprise. Indeed, such a person should be highly praised.

Today we cannot send missionaries like Miss Addie to China and many other places in the world. New forms of mission work have emerged. For example, Amy Williams from Aliceville after completing her college work at Samford University in 2003 spent two years in China as an English teacher. She was self-supporting. She made friends. She shared the Gospel as she had opportunity. Since then Amy has shorter stints in Hong Kong and the the Philippines. (Our son Matthew has spent the past 10 years in Poland and Italy teaching English, working in our Baptist Churches, and being a witness to the Gospel.) With the closing of one door, Christians are finding ways of sharing the Gospel in other lands and among other cultures. It is my hope and prayer that others of our youth will accept the call and be missionaries. Currently Parker Windle and Landon Williams are serving as Journeymen with our International Mission Board. Also, there are increasing opportunity for older folk to folks to mission work. An example from nearby is the sister and brother-in-law of Clare Rogers who are working in Africa. And many of the folk in our association have gone on mission trips for a week or two.

Soon, we will be publishing the fourth installment of this series. It will tell the story of the connection between our association and mission work in Brazil.

Special Edition Mission Heritage-Brazil Part 1 Newsletter of

PICKENS BAPTIST ASSOCIATION

P.O. Box 206, Carrollton, AL 35447, (205) 367-8632

Gary Farley, Missionary

pbassn@centurytel.net www.pickensbaptist.com http://picasaweb.google.com/pickensbaptist

PICKENS BAPTIST'S MISSION INVOLVEMENT IN AFRICA

Part I

Missionaries appointed by FMB (IMB)

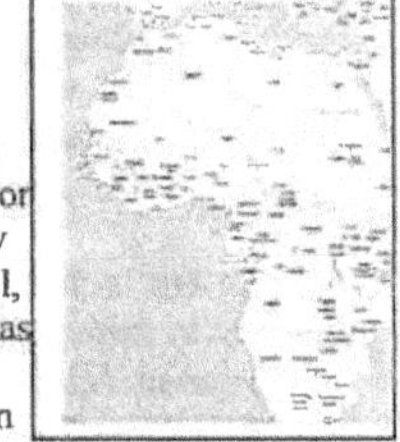

The Continent of Africa is another area where our IMB missionaries and volunteers from Pickens Baptist Association have worked over the years. Our mission heritage does not go back as many years in Africa as it does in Brazil, but the extent of the work there has been great. Included in these workers were missionaries, John Faulkner, Fred H. and Kathy Manis Findley, David and Cindy Tuten, and Russ Cox, former youth director at Carrollton Baptist Church. Volunteers have included Don Cotten, Ralph Windle, and Wallace Russell, former pastors of the association; and Bonnie Jackson Alexander, Acteens representative from the Cross Roads Baptist Church. Other fulltime missionaries and volunteers have also worked there.

John and Anne Williams Faulkner faithfully served the Lord in foreign mission services in Africa from their appointment to Rhodesia (now Zimbabwe) in July 1970 until their retirement March 1, 1999. John served as seminary teacher, camp manager, bookstore manager, in Gwelo, (now Gweru), as church developer in Que Que, (now Kwekwe), as treasurer/business manager, secretary to the Baptist Convention of Zimbabwe and church developer for the capital city of Harare. During these years from 1971 to 1984, Anne served as church and home worker in the various assignments.

In January 1985 he was appointed Associate Director of Eastern and Southern Africa and in 1987 to 1997, John served as the Area Director for Eastern and Southern Africa leading mission work in 25 countries and islands. Anne served as church and home worker, assisted John and worked among the missionary women in the area.

After reorganization of the FMB in 1997, John served in general evangelism and Anne as church and home worker in the Southern Africa region until they formally retired in March, 1999.

John, a native of Marion County, Alabama and Anne from the Springhill Community met while both were students at the University of Alabama. Anne was the youngest of twelve children born to Henry P. Williams and Johnnie Williams and was active in the Springhill Baptist Church where she made a profession of faith at an early age. Prior to appointment by FMB, John was pastor in Texas while a student at Southwestern Baptist Theological Seminary, at First Baptist Church of Reform, and at Trinity Baptist Church in Sherman, Texas, from which they answered the call to missions.

Since retirement they have made their home in St. Clair County where John pastored at the Friendship Baptist Church in Springville. Their daughter Lisa Faulkner Gallion and her husband David live in the Atlanta, Georgia area, where Lisa works mentoring junior and senior high students. Their son Mark (whose wife Belinda Bradley is a former MK also) are active in God's work and are currently serving with *To Every Tribe* Missions in Papau, New Guinea. At the present Time, John and Anne and granddaughter Clara Gallion, are visiting with them on the mission field.

Fred H. Findley, Jr., and Kathy M. Findley, are from Reform and attended the University of Alabama and Southern Seminary in Louisville, Kentucky. They began serving in Uganda in 1979 but were forced to return to the States in 1983 when an AIDS epidemic broke out there. They currently live in Little Rock, AR, where they are both involved with the ministry of Safe Places founded by Kathy in 2002. This organization provides services and advocacy to victims of sexual abuse and domestic violence. They have one son Jonathan A. Findley.

David and Cindy Tuten, members of the Carrollton Baptist Church, have served two terms in Africa, the first having been in Ogbomosho, Nigeria, at the Baptist Hospital for two months during his medical training. David worked at the hospital while Cindy did community service and worked at the seminary library.

In January 2003, they returned to the mission field being assigned to Tanzania as International Service Corp. medical missionaries. David did medical missions and Cindy again worked with home and community. During the two years of this term their daughter Paige attended Boarding School in Kenya and son Tyler was home schooled. Their daughter Amanda was a college student at Judson.

David did medical missions, remóte village missions in the bush, and weekly missions at the local leprosy colony. Transportation for these missions was by boat, helicopter, and cars. It was their practice to do evangelism work before medical missions and in the evenings after clinics to show the JESUS film which video and scenery equipment was set up by Tyler Tuten. On Wednesday evenings, David and Cindy ministered to missionaries from other denominations at a mid-week prayer time.

A most interesting mission experience that they had was in training missionaries on medical procedures at the 40/40 Mission Learning Center in tents in the wild where participants spent 40 days being acclimated to culture and climate conditions in that area. While David taught medical procedures, Cindy did home schooling for the Missionary Kids.

Amanda spent a summer with them and did VBS for the children. Also traveling with her was her friend Gee Wiggins who escorted her to Africa and came specifically for the purpose of asking the Tutens for Amanda's hand in marriage.

David and Cindy returned to the States in July 2005 and now make their home in Carrollton where he has his general medical practice at Carrollton Primary Center in the hospital's new annex building.

Russ Cox who served as Minister of Youth in the Carrollton Baptist Church from November 1975 until May 1977 while a student at the University of Alabama, was assigned as a Missionary Journeyman to Liberia, West Africa, in 1978. There he taught Bible at Ricks Institute, a school founded by Baptists in Monrovia and known to be the place of schooling for many high officials' families. Russ shares about the difficult time experienced in Liberia at the close of his term and during Janie's term while the country was in Civil War. The President of Liberia, Dr. Tolbert, who also was the President of the Liberian Baptist Convention was assassinated during a coup on the eve of the celebration of the 50th year of Baptist work in Liberia. He remembers the danger when rebels drove through the school campus for days afterwards firing off their guns. When he returned to the States, he graduated from Golden Gates Baptist Theological Seminary in California and Fuller Theological Seminary in Pasadena with a Doctorate of Divinity. He is married to Janie, another Journeyman he met and served with in Liberia.

He is now Senior Pastor at New Hope Community Church, a SBC church he helped to start in 1988. Their church is situated about 5 miles from the US/Mexico border and they have continuing ministries in Mexico. They have two grown children, Rachel and Chris.

"The lost are multitudes but these are not faceless masses. God loves them individually. His heart is broken over their lostness, for the way the power of sin and death holds them prisoner. His deepest desire is to draw them into His arms and hold them like a loving father cradles his hurting child. He wants them to know Him for who He is. He wants them to acknowledge Him as their creator, sustainer, redeemer, and judge. But the vast majority of them have never heard they even having a loving Heavenly Father, much less that He has paid a terrible price to set them free. They have never heard that God's own Son, Jesus, willingly suffered and died so they could be reconciled to God."

"That's where God's people come in. God's passion for rescuing His lost children is contagious. He calls us to give ourselves wholeheartedly to His mission; taking the good news of forgiveness and salvation to the ends of the earth. His desire becomes our desire, that one day people from every nation, tribe, and tongue would worship Him before His throne. And God is using His people in extraordinary ways." (OPERATION WORLD, IMB, Johnstone and Mandryk, 2001)

Bonnie Jackson Alexander

Our next issue will tell us about the experiences of our volunteers in Africa.

Special Edition Mission Heritage-Brazil Part 2 Newsletter of
PICKENS BAPTIST ASSOCIATION

P.O. Box 206, Carrollton, AL 35447, (205) 367-8632

Gary Farley, Missionary

pbassn@centurytel.net www.pickensbaptist.com http://picasaweb.google.com/pickensbaptist

Part II
Volunteer Work in Africa

Former pastors of our association, Don Cotten, Ralph Windle, and Wallace Russell did volunteer missions in Nigeria in 1982, 1983, and 1984 with the Alabama Baptist-Nigerian Partnership.

Don Cotten learned quickly the meaning of the missionary blessing, "May God go with you and your bags too." His bags did not reach him until three weeks after his return home. His only change of clothes was in his carry on bag and he experienced what many people from other countries know about having two suits of clothes, wearing one and washing one. He and the other 17 Alabamians were assigned to the Animo Conference Crusade in Nigeria, November 20-27, 1984. On this trip they spent Thanksgiving Day there in Africa, a day that they will never forget. It was spent with a non-traditional meal, sharing Christian fellowship with the Nigerian brothers and sisters in Christ and with the team which by now seemed like family. The team consisted of 12 preachers, four laypersons, and two singers.

They realized from this trip what even the smallest of things in life could mean such as running water, ice, sweets, air conditioning, traffic laws, and electricity. Having experienced this, they realized what our prayers mean to our missionaries on a foreign field. They recognized this as being a time of sharing with the most hospitable people on the face of the earth, in a city with more than a million population with small churches and pastors earning $37.00 per month and sharing with people hungry for the gospel.

As their plane touched down in Atlanta, the group began singing "God Bless America." Others on the plane joined in the singing and the song took on a new meaning for they realized more than ever just how God has blessing America.

Ralph Windle kept a diary of the mission to Nigeria and it helps us to see the impact made on his life. From the many army officers encountered at customs and being stopped by guards for taking pictures, one could see the effects of a country ruled at that time by the military. As with most volunteers, there was no training for preaching with an interpreter and it had to be officially "OJT (on the job training)".

After several days, Ralph indicated that he was beginning to preach with the Nigerian rhythm. It was a great joy to work with the Nigerian pastors and to spend almost two weeks there. One problem that Ralph had was in eating. Being careful not to offend his host, he explained that he would rather preach and not eat than to eat and not preach and he ate very little due to the high seasoning of food. His pastor host remarked that "he ate like a bird but preached like an elephant."

He also related the high respect given to pastors in Nigeria and said that it was the highest respect that could be given. People bowed and knelt for them and treated them as a king and queen. Pastors were called by their Christian name so Ralph had to get used to be addressed as Pastor Samuel. His time there was spent at Kaduna and in preaching in five outdoor crusades and going out in the bush to a church in the middle of the jungle on the last Sunday. They recorded 180 first time decisions and 57 rededications from crowds that numbered in the thousands each service. Sometime after Ralph's return to the States, he had a visit from a Nigerian man who told him that Rev. Bowel Beachy, one of the pastors that he had worked with was attacked by radical Muslim and macheted to death.

Also, working in Africa was Wallace Russell another former pastor of Carrollton who served there on two occasions in Lagos and Ogbomosho, Nigeria, in 1982 and in South Africa and Zimbabwe in 1994. Pastor Russell likes to share about one evening in a remote village where he preached to a crowd of 1500 to 2000 people. This service was held on a cement slab with an old pump organ playing, in very hot weather. At the end of the service between 50 and 60 people came forward. The crowd was so excited that it erupted in a holy dance raising dust that covered the people. His suit of clothing was so damp from the heat and then covered by the dust that it had to be discarded. The local church pastor shared with him later on the way back to the village that the unusual blue building at the back of the lot where the preaching was held was a Muslim mosque. The people at that mosque were threatening and trying to scare the people who wanted to come forward and hear the preaching. But God's mercy prevailed and many came to know the Lord that evening.

Bonnie Jackson Alexander from the Cross Roads Baptist Church, had the privilege to work with other Alabama Acteens and chaperones at a world conference in Swaziland and Zimbabwe during the summer of 1993. The group spent much time in training for this life changing experience and while there helped to plant a church in a refugee camp and did puppet shows at schools. Bonnie was sponsored by her church and others churches in the association.

"Years ago, a missionary sat in the dirt with some pastors in post-revolution Zimbabwe. The newly independent African nation was a dangerous place at the time. Chaos ruled in some areas. The missionary, Tom Elliff (now IMB president), had found a spiritually responsive group of people in one such place.

"Who will pastor those people?' Elliff asked the church leaders. They looked at each other. Eyes clouded. Heads shook. 'We're not going,' one pastor finally replied, speaking for the group. 'People get shot down there. Just last week, someone was shot off the top of a bus.' Another pastor reported that a missionary had been killed in the area recently.

"Well, at least we can pray,' Elliff said. So they prayed to the Lord of the harvest to send someone. The meeting dismissed. Everyone left — except one young pastor, barely out of his teens. He limped slowly over to Elliff and said, 'I'll go.'

"Wait a minute,' Elliff cautioned, stealing a glance at the pastor's thin legs. 'You heard what they said about the danger didn't you?'

"I'll go,' the young man repeated firmly. 'But you've got to promise to bring me a bicycle. I had polio and I can't walk very well. I'm about eight miles away, so walking out there is going to be tough.' Elliff promised to bring the bicycle as soon as possible. He returned a few weeks later with a two-wheeler in tow.

"Where have you been?' the pastor demanded. 'I've been walking out there and back on Wednesdays, Saturdays and Sundays. Several people are awaiting baptism.' Dumbfounded, Elliff stammered, 'What about those stories of people getting shot?'

"The young man smiled. 'Brother,' he said, 'if God could stop the mouths of the lions for Daniel, he can stop the muzzles of the guns for me.' **(Crossing the Line by Erich Bridges,** International Mission Board, 9/22/2011, copied by permission.)

Pray

Give

Go

Special Edition June 2011, Newsletter of

PICKENS BAPTIST ASSOCIATION

P.O. Box 206, Carrollton, AL 35447, (205) 367-8632

Gary Farley, Missionary

pbassn@centurytel.net www.pickensbaptist.com http://picasaweb.google.com/pickensbaptist

Our Mission Heritage V—Brazil.

As you read this newsletter these persons—Buddy and Emily Kirk, Cynthia Colvin, Billy Thomas, and Mac and Jeanne Fuqua, from our association are in Brazil on a mission trip. They are being led by Dr. Cecil Taylor, professor of Religion at the University of Mobile. Did you know that our mission heritage in Brazil dates back 126 years, very near the beginning of Baptist work there?

The story goes like this. Following the loss of the South in the Civil War several planters and their families moved to Brazil to continue their plantation lifestyle. Some were Baptists and wanted missionaries to come to Brazil and establish work. (Many of them located in the southern part of the country near San Paulo.)

At first, beginning in 1871, Southern Baptists worked with these immigrants by establishing English speaking congregations. Among the early preachers was a Jewish convert, Solomon Ginsberg. He evangelized in several of the South American countries. His biography is titled *The Wandering Jew*. Presbyterian and Methodist English speaking churches were formed during this time. And soon American Protestant missionaries were being sent to Brazil.

Brazil was a colony of Portugal and consequently Roman Catholicism was the dominant form of Christianity there. Protestantism was often persecuted. As in most of the world, religious freedom was not accepted by the government. The conflict began as missionaries began to seek to win converts from among the natives and from Portuguese speaking persons of European heritage. Since Vatican II in the early 1960s persecution has largely subsided. Since then Pentecostalism has experienced great success in Latin America. Our Baptist work has grown and the Brazil Baptist Convention is a strong one. Yet there is still much to be done. Truly, the fields there are proving to be "white unto harvest."

Accounts of Baptist work in Brazil have focused on a Texas family, William and Anne Luther Bagby and their children and descendants. The first Bagbys sailed to Brazil in 1881. They were joined by another Texan Z.C. Taylor and his wife the following year. Initially, they started work in Rio de Janeiro. A stirring account of the story of the founding of Baptist work in Brazil can be found in *The Bagbys of Brazil* by Helen Bagby Harrison.

The PBA connection began in 1885 when the Puthuffs, Emma Fox and E. A., arrived. She had been born in Pickens County but was raised in Pontotoc, Mississippi. Due to health issues, a common problem for the early missionaries, they resigned from the mission in 1890. But the following year James J. Taylor, a native of Pickens, and his wife joined the mission. They were able to serve there for more than 30 years.

James Taylor grew up in the Benevola community. The letters exchanged by his parents, Grant and Melinda Slaughter Taylor, during the Civil War, have been beautifully published by the University of Alabama under the title of *The Cruel War*. It chronicles the hardships of wives and mothers who had to maintain the home while the husband was absent in the war.

It gives insight into the early life of the Forest Baptist Church.

And it illustrates the growing disillusion with the war on the part of a struggling young family.

Taylor was educated at The Southern Baptist Seminary and taught religion at Ouachita Baptist College in Arkansas prior to his appointment as a Missionary. His wife was Ada Lumpkin, the daughter of a prominent pastor.

Initially, they served with the Bagbys in Rio, but in 1899 formed the FBC of Sao Paulo. As a former professor he was concerned with the theological training of the natives whom God was calling to ministry. And he was also concerned about the discipleship and spiritual formation of the members of the Baptist churches. He had a gift for languages which served him well as a teacher, a translator of basic texts such as Robertson's *Harmony of the Gospels*, and Sunday School lessons in the Portuguese language. So while he pastored he also taught, translated and published. (He is one those heroes with whom we can visit during the ages of eternity, one of the many joys of heaven.

In 1923 James and Ada Taylor returned to the United States. He died the following year. Dr. Cecil Taylor, who is leading the current mission, which includes our associational mission team is a kinsman of James Taylor. (There were several Taylors who have served in the association and its churches. It would be interesting to see the various connections in this family which has contributed mightily to the Kingdom work here and elsewhere.)

A century after the Puthuff's went to Brazil, and just over 60 after James Taylor retired from the Brazil mission, volunteers from our association began to go to Brazil to serve along side of our missionaries. In 25 of the 28 summers that have passed since 1985 someone from the PBA has served there. A total of 72 different persons have made 132 volunteer trips there, with some of the volunteers going year after year. Bonnie Windle from Carrollton has been the most frequent team member from the PBA churches.

And today Langdon Williams is in his second year as a full-time missionary in Brazil. He is serving under the ISC program of the International Mission Board of the SBC. Langdon served on the staff of Aliceville First Baptist. That church and Carrollton Baptist have furnished most of the volunteers.

Landon Williams in Brazil

Year after year our volunteers return with reports of great revivals and the working of God's Holy Spirit among the persons to whom they witness and to whom they present the Gospel. The volunteers have provided a variety of ministries-medical, VBS, talks in schools and jails, door to door visitation, construction of chapels and schools, street evangelism, service ministries and others.

They have worked with many fine missionaries including Bill and Barbara Mosley, Ray and Sharon Fairchild, Mrs. Thelma Bagby (note that family continues to serve in Brazil), Eugene and Freda Troop, David Henderson, Pam Kitchens, and Tony and Karen Gray. Many of these missionaries have come to minister among us, most recently the Grays were here in February as part of our On Mission Celebration. In recent years the churches and the association have provided funds to build chapels in Brazil.

Our current team will be involved with a new church plant. During the week a chapel will be constructed. The team will be reaching out in the community doing a variety of events which aim to reach our unsaved. Then at the end of the week there will be a celebrative worship and dedication of the new chapel. If it goes as it has in past years, several hundred persons will pray to receive Christ as their Savior and Lord. Please pray for the team daily.

Today the Brazil Baptist Convention has well over one million members in 6,000 congregations. Certainly it has grown through the years. But here our Alabama Convention has about as many members in 3,400 congregations. Brazil has about 200 million citizens. Alabama has about 4 million. So there is work to do there. As there is here.

Associational News

Bro. James Moss has returned to the association as pastor of Double Branches. We welcome him and Eleanor back. Bro. Eugene Junkin has retired from the pastorate. He will focus his ministry on the role of chaplain at PCMC, pastor advisor at the Baptist Center, and chaplain at Jack's of Reform.

Bro. David Blakeney has returned to the pastorate of Mineral Springs. He had previously served as youth minister at Carrollton.

Bro. Terry Billings is making himself available as an evangelist. He will be available to hold revival at churches in our association and elsewhere across the nation. Terry became a believer in 2004 and has served effectively at Mt. Pleasant and in interim roles in our churches. He is a constant witness. He has great "people skills". Please invite him to be a revival speaker at your church.

Thank you for supporting the rural mail carriers' food drive. The Baptist Center pantry is well stocked. More than 10,500 pounds were received. The donations by the different post offices were as follows: Aliceville 4,000 lbs, Carrollton 2,000 lbs, Reform 2,000 lbs, and Gordo 2,500 lbs.

The VBS season is off to a good start. The Big Apple material is well-received. Look for the July list of VBS's in the next issue of the newsletter. (Our next special edition will deal with our mission heritage in Hispanic America and will feature the work of Ulman Moss.)

Jeanne Fuqua and Bonnie Windle in Brazil

Special Edition July 2011, Newsletter of

PICKENS BAPTIST ASSOCIATION

P.O. Box 206, Carrollton, AL 35447, (205) 367-8632

Gary Farley, Missionary

pbassn@centurytel.net www.pickensbaptist.com http://picasaweb.google.com/pickensbaptist

Our Mission Heritage The Latin America Connection--VI

Ulman Moss was born in 1917 in the Flatwoods community as the seventh of nine children. His father was an owner-operator of a saw mill. The Great Depression was difficult for the family; they moved a lot in the Gordo area. Ulman and his wife Ruth, with their six children, served as Southern Baptist missionaries for 38 years in three Latin American Nations—Columbia, Venezuela, and Mexico. Their mission work extended from 1945 to 1982. Although often difficult, their efforts were blessed of God and continue to bear fruit. He tells his story in his autobiography, *Honeymoon to Retirement in Foreign Missions*. A curio cabinet and an old trunk at the Pickens Baptist Association office contain items and pictures from the long mission work of the Mosses.

Ulman was saved at Mt. Pleasant and later licensed and ordained by this church. He and his cousin, Ein Donald Strickland, attended Howard College (now Samford University) with some financial help from the association. His first pastorate was at Stansel, and later he added Fellowship. He received his theological training, his wife, and his calling to missions at Southwestern Baptist Theological Seminary in Ft. Worth, Texas. Ruth Jordan, a native of west Texas and a student at the Seminary became his bride. They shared a call to missions and accepted the invitation from the Foreign Mission Board of the SBC to work in Latin America.

During that time it was not easy to do mission work in Latin Americia. Baptist work was just beginning there. The Roman Catholic hierarchy resisted the coming of Protestant missionaries. His autobiography tells about many roadblocks that they had to face in the early years of their work. However, after Vatican II council in the early 1960s this largely subsided.

The first term of service for the Mosses was in Cali, Columbia. They focused on getting a church started there which has prospered as the FBC of Cali. They had to learn the Spanish language. At the insistence of Bro. Tom Collins, the beloved and respected pastor of Carrollton Baptist Church, the association raised funds to buy and send a 1947 Ford automobile to brother Ulman to provide transportation and greater mobility for his ministry there.

For their first furlough the Mosses accepted an invitation to teach Spanish and missions at Wayland Baptist College in West Texas. During this period a new, more conservative and church dominated government came into power in Columbia and would not allow them a visa to return to Columbia. So they were asked by our Foreign Mission Board to transfer to the just opening field of Venezuela. They went there and stayed for four terms until 1967.

This pioneer work was challenging, interesting and fruitful. While Southern Baptists were just entering this nation, there were already little congregations with Baptist learnings in place in that country. So, one of Ulman's early tasks was to make contact with these congregations to see if they and their pastors wanted to become a part of the Southern Baptist mission. Early on there were some challenges from Pentecostalism and "faith healers". Some early converts departed to other groups.

Central to his strategy was the education of both these congregations and others which had become Baptist Christians. One plank of this strategy was the opening of a bookstore where printed supplies might be accessed. A second was the formation of a "preachers school" which has since grown into a theological seminary. A third was his serving as the planter of new churches in key cities. Among these is FBC of Valencia, as pictured in this article. Fourth, he was a strong advocate of discipleship for all Christians. Ulman wanted to build a strong foundation. He did.

In 2001 Buck and Ida Smith who served with the Mosses in Venezuela were with us in our On Mission Celebration here in the association. The Smiths still had a trunk that the Mosses had given to them while in Venezuela and sent it to the association for our displays of our mission heritage. And in 2004 they arranged for a team of Venezuelan mission volunteers who had ties to the Mosses and the Valencia church, to visit in our association and help with our Hispanic work. (After their work here I took them to visit our North American Mission Board and learn about our Hispanic work in the United States. From there they went to work some more with the association in Greenville, South Carolina.) The circle had come full. We sent. They heard. They sent. We heard. God blessed. You may recall that we raised money a few years ago to help Buck purchase property for a training school for pastors to serve in the highlands area of the Amazon. This is in place and the work of evangelism and church planting in that remote area continues. It is doing well.

Through the years many volunteers from our association, particularly from FBC Aliceville, have gone on mission trips to build chapels, offer VBS, and do evangelism in Venezuela. The work of Ulman and Ruth made this possible. They opened the country. They expanded and stabilized our work. They served as mission statesmen to build and rebuild relationships between the national Baptist and the Foreign Mission Board.

Ulman was experiencing health problems attributed to the damp climate of Venezuela. So in 1968 they transferred to the mission of north central Mexico. This was much older Baptist work. There he worked with an association of churches and with the Baptist Convention of Mexico. There he focused much of his effort on promoting what we now call Discipleship Training. He saw our Baptist work as stagnated in North Mexico. He believed that for it to be revitalized the lay people needed to understand the importance of being a disciple of Jesus and what responsibilities and opportunities discipleship provides.

By training and equipping the laity of the churches there was significant revitalization of the Baptist work throughout the nation. Living along the Rio Grande, near Eagle Pass, Texas, the Mosses became involved in an innovative and effective mission program of the Baptist General Convention of Texas, The River Ministry. It works like this, churches and associations on both sides of the Rio Grande identify needs for ministry, church planting, and health issues. They present them annually at a mission fair for volunteers and groups of volunteers. Then, mostly in the summer, volunteers come and do the proposed projects. Hundreds of churches were impacted and thousands of persons have been saved as a result of this effort over the past 40 years or so. What Ulman and his Texas-side partner, Elmin Howell started very small has, like the mustard bush, become something great. It also has served as the model for similar efforts along the Mississippi River and in Appalachia. (I had a hand in this during my years at the HMB)

Ulman Moss was, like so many from our county, called by God to be a disciple of Jesus. God had great plans for him. And, as he followed, God did wonderful things through him. There is a lesson here that each of us needs to ponder.

He has many kins people still in our churches and in our county. Let us praise him and give thanks for what he accomplished for the Kingdom of God. Some years ago he went to be with God. Surely, Jesus said to him, "Well done thou good and faithful servant." What will Jesus say to you and to me?

(Note: in response to the recent article about J. Taylor and our mission work in Brazil, I received a letter and several pictures of Dr. Taylor and his family from a great-granddaughter in Texas.)

Ulman and Ruth Moss

Map of Venezuela at the PBA office

Trunk carried by Ulman Moss to Venezuela in 1945. Donated by Buck Smith, Missionary

MARY SWEDENBURG AND JAMES R. SWEDENBURG, JR.

2012 December Missionary Newsletter of
PICKENS BAPTIST ASSOCIATION
Carrollton, Alabama 35447 (205) 367-8632
Gary Farley, Missionary

MARY SWEDENBURG, MISSIONARY TO JAPAN

Mary Swedenburg was born in Reform, Pickens County, Alabama, and grew up in Hueytown, Jefferson County Alabama. Her ties have been so close and strong to Pickens Count that we have called her our own missionary.

She has warm memories of Addie Estelle Cox and the churches in Pickens County where she visited often with her father, James (Jim) R. Swedenburg, Sr., who pastored here. Mary believed that Addie Cox was the key to her Dad's love for missions and ultimately for hers. She remembers that Cross Road Baptist, one of the churches where he pastored, collected money for Addie to carry a bicycle back with her to China. This church was always active in praying for missionaries.

Mary later considered Addie Cox to be her model - her mentor. She remembered that she and her sister Martha stopped on one occasion at Addie's home in Carrollton when Addie was on furlough. Addie gave her a Chinese Gospel of John and took up so much time with them that Mary remembers even today how special it was to spend time with Miss Addie.

To understand Mary's story, it will be helpful to look back at her family and her upbringing. Her father James Swedenburg, Sr., was from the Millport area and her mother, Trannie Ola, was from Kennedy with many relatives in Pickens County. The Swedenburg family was sharecroppers in Millport and from this humble beginning went on to touch many lives over our association, the State of Alabama, and eventually over the world. Bro. Jim Swedenburg quit school to be a barber. It was then that he felt the call by God and knew that he would need to go back to school to be prepared to be a pastor. He became bi-vocational and although he had opportunities to enter the business world he knew that God had called him as a "preacher."

He pastored the churches of Hebron, Bethlehem, West End, Pleasant Hill, and Cross Roads in our association. He had a desire to see children grow in their Christian life and go on to college for an education. He did a lot of visiting and knew that if he worked with the Lord, he would have to be involved with the people, spend time with them, and encourage them. He wanted people to know Christ and the churches to grow.

Mary remembers that the family was taught that their home was built upon God; and that they were going to serve Him and serve Him she did. Mary was involved in VBS as a teenager – going to revivals – driving the car out to the get the kids – and even then could not stand that some children were not going to hear the story of Christ or have the ability to get out of their poverty.

Her Dad had a strong desire to replace wooden buildings with lasting church buildings and helped to do that at Cross Roads and Bethlehem. He knew the old way would pass away and he wanted the children to have a place to worship and grow. Many times he gave his salary back to the churches; stressed budgeting; recognized that every strong mission church had a WMU mother; wanted strong and growing churches with education and a love to serve and for the world to know Christ. He even helped with singing schools after morning worship. So, it was no surprise the his son James and his daughter Mary were called to international missions.

Mary received her education at Livingston State College, Oklahoma Baptist University and a Master of Religious Education Degree from Southwestern Baptist Theological Seminary. The she learned a very important mission concept – "Don't tell someone about Jesus unless you realize that in the next second they could be your brother or sister." She graduated from the seminary in May 1969.

Before her appointment by FMB, Mary taught school in the Hueytown High School. She was appointed by the Foreign Mission Board of the Southern Baptist Convention in June of 1969 and assigned to Japan. She received orientation from September to December. She sailed from San Francisco about January 7th and was sick for the full 2 weeks at sea. She received language study in Tokyo, and was an educational evangelist in Kitakyushu, Japan, from 1972-1980 and a religious education promoter in Shimonoseki, Japan. Mary was assigned as a church started in Tokuyama City, Japan, in 1991, and served in that position until her retirement.

Mary saw each area of her work as a blessing. At the Baptist Girls School (Seinan Jo Gakuin), she enjoyed working with the girls and learned much from them about the Japanese people. Work in Japan was slow. She felt that when she took one step forward, she went backward two steps.

When she moved to Shimonoseki, she worked in evangelism and was a church planter. She did not know anyone and had no Christian fellowship. It was an extremely lonely time but her relationship with the Lord grew greatly. This church became her fellowship. At Tokuyama she really enjoyed her ministry. It was hard work, but she and another woman began this church. Afterwards, she enjoyed the role of pastor until a Japanese pastor could be called. She enjoyed evangelism outreach, the visit in noodle shops and coffee shops to witness to people and to get to know them.

She recalls the song by Frank Sinatra, "I did it my way" but Mary knew that church planting and missions had to be done God's way. The church that she eventually planted there is still holding together after 20 years without a pastor.

She knew the church people had to grow – individually and as a church body. For her to prepare a message once a month and to take responsibility for the church to grow, she felt like Jeremiah. When home from church or work, she read Jeremiah and what God was going to do there. She wanted to think like Jeremiah, to be as forward as Jeremiah was, and to live long enough to pull together a good Japanese group. Mary would still like to go back to Japan and help the church to grow.

When asked about the success of her ministry and how God moved in it, Mary replied that thinking as she had learned to do in Japan, she could not speak of spiritual success. Rather she stated that she desired to be faithful to serve God and was only His faithful servant. He blessed what He enabled her to do. She shared that sometimes she felt His moving and sometimes she felt His silence but in all of her life, Jesus was with her to bring about His kingdom. Mary felt He was gracious to have called her and to have allowed her to be involved in His work. She rejoiced to see someone come to Christ and to follow through in baptism. She loved to meet a Christian family because they were very rare. She loved to hear how people came to Christ when it seemed impossible for someone to come to Christ from a Buddhist family. She regarded her life as very rich.

As with many things along with joy, there was sorrow, and such is the case in Mary Swedenburg's service as a missionary to Japan. Mary retired in 2004 when IMB's regulations changed and she could no longer preach as she had done for many years in church planting work. Mary was still following in the steps of her mentor Addie Cox, who said early in her term of missionary work in China, that she would rather preach than teach and was so pleased when she was allowed to go into the rural areas and preach the Gospel.

Mary has many fond memories of her days as a missionary in Japan. She is very appreciative of the curio cabinet provided by the friends at Cross Road Baptist Church to the Pickens Baptist Association to house some of her mission memorabilia.

She also remembers that in her youth in Hueytown, she did not always want to go to the church field with her father and work but wanted to stay home and be a "regular teenager." She knows those times with her parents in Pickens County were used by God to prepare her for the work He would call her to do in Japan and even now back in the States in Birmingham when she makes her home.

JAMES R. SWENDEBURG, JR., MISSIONARY TO SOUTH KOREA, TAIWAN, AND USA

James Swedenburg, oldest child of Rev. James and Mrs. Swedenburg, attended Howard College in Birmingham and later Midwestern Baptist Theological Seminary in Kansas City. He had felt the call to Gospel Ministry which was expressed in his life through pastoring, work as a chaplain, and later in mission service both nationally and internationally. After college he served in the Air Force and was stationed in Seoul, Korea. It was in Korea that he felt a strong call to do mission work there.

After leaving the military in Korea, he became a church planter with Home Mission Board and served in Charlotlaroy, PA. From Charlotlaroy, he and his wife Joyce went to Sherman, Texas, to pastor a new church start. From Sherman he went to York, PA, and from there he was appointed by the Foreign Missionary Board to the mission field in 1969. After orientation, they arrived in Seoul, South Korea, in July, 1970, and did language study there.

After leaving the military in Korea, he became a church planter with Home Mission Board and served in Charlotlaroy, PA. From Charlotlaroy, he and his wife Joyce went to Sherman, Texas, to pastor a new church start. From Sherman he went to York, PA, and from there he was appointed by the Foreign Missionary Board to the mission field in 1969. After orientation, they arrived in Seoul, South Korea, in July, 1970, and did language study there.

They felt blessed with their work with the Korean Mission Baptist Convention. The Korean Christians really believed in prayer and this made the mission work much easier. They were receptive to the Gospel and experienced growth in great ways.

The Swedenburgs, along with their three children, Michael, Steven, and Denise spent approximately six years in the country of South Korea. In Seoul the children were enrolled in Seoul Foreign School with 23 to 24 different nationalities. Later the sons attended the Korean Christian Academy and Denise went to school at the Army Base in Pusan.

During their first term in Seoul, they worked with evangelism and then later moved to Pusan, Korea, where James served as Chaplain at the (Bill) Wallace Memorial Baptist Hospital. While in Pusan, Joyce helped with the mission financial books and was mission secretary during annual meetings.

After nine years in Korea, they moved to Taipei, Taiwan, and spent three years there where James was pastor of the Calvary Baptist Church. Following this they returned to the States and after furlough, James became the Director of Missions at Greater Cleveland (Ohio) Baptist Association for three years; then as DOM to the Central Baptist Assn., Benton, AR. After retirement in 1995, they moved to Hot Springs Village, AR. His death came in January 2005 after a time of disability from a fall.

Microfilmed Records of the PBA Churches

These are available at the PBA office in Carrollton and at the Alabama Baptist Historical Collection at Samford University.

We encourage students to use these materials to write history of their churches and to do genealogical research.

We encourage those churches which have not had their records microfilmed to do so. It is free. The records will be returned. And this provides for the safety of these priceless records. Also, we encourage churches which have not had their records microfilmed for the past 10 years to do so.

Aliceville (Enon) 1823	1847 to 1961 (with 1883-1897 missing)
Ethelsville (South Carolina)1824	None. Microfilmed
Fellowship 1833	1832-2004 (with 1952-1991 missing)
Ebenezer 1833	1835-1955 (with 1836-1845 missing)
Liberty 1834	1869-2004 (with several years missing)
Forest 1835	1835-1965
Bethlehem 1835	1835-1985
Mt. Tabor 1839	1897-1967
Hebron 1841	1865-2006
Spring Hill 1842	1842-1954
Mt. Pleasant 1843	1847-1929
Carrollton 1846	1856-2004
Pickensville 1847	1931-2004
Cross Roads 1850	1877-1990 (1873-1933 missing)
Mineral Springs 1855	1855-2004
Double Branches 1864	1864-2004
Galilee 1870	None
Arbor Springs 1872	1872-1940
Flatwoods 1833	1932-2005
Hickory Grove 1894	1934-2004
Stansel 1897	1897-1962 (1929-1953 missing)
Reform 1899	1975-2004
Union Chapel 1900	1900-2000
Gordo 1901	None
Friendship 1907	1907-2004
Pine Grove 1908	None
Pleasant Hill 1916	1969-1971
New Salem 1940	
Coal Fire 1940	
West End 1940	
Garden 1944	
Highland 1951	
Emmanuel 1990	
Calvary 2000	
New Harmony	

Others	
PBA 1835	1835-2000
Big Creek 1829	1829-1917
Grants Creek 1829	1829-1959
Unity 1829	1829-1964
New Hope 1833	1833-1955
Mt Zion 1837	1837-1893. Not complete. Bethany com.
Pilgrims Rest 1828	1887-1957

We will be glad to help any of our churches take advantage of this service. We wish that all of our churches had their records microfilmed up to date.

Some Observations about the Pickens Baptist Association at Age 165

Gary Farley
Associational Missionary

In this booklet you will find some historical data about the history of your association. Let me explain the pieces to you.

1. Minutes of the founding meeting. The association was formed in 1835 by 11 churches in Pickens County, south of Coal Fire Creek, 7 in Greene, 1 in Tuscaloosa, and 1 in Perry Counties. Meeting at Bethany church (about six miles south of Aliceville on route 14 and a little bit west in the Sipsey valley) they withdrew from Buttehatchie Association. There were at this time at least three more Baptist Churches in Pickens County--South Carolina of Yorkville, now Ethelsville; Providence, near today's Hickory Grove; and Bethlehem. All three became members of the Union Association prior to the Civil War. In 1924 it changed the name to Pickens.

The 20 founding churches (1836) had 1,156 members. Given the times this was very good, I believe.

2 and 3. Lists of the Delegates (Messengers) to the 1834 Buttehatchie and the 1836 Union Association. I found it to be interesting that many of the surnames that appear on these lists are still found in the associational records of 2000. During this annual meeting we will be recognizing the descendants of the founding messengers and of our pioneer pastors. I was also interested in the fact that many of the names were of English, not Scotts-Irish, origin.

4. A map of Pickens County is marked with the location of churches that existed in 1835.

★Churches that were charter members of the association and continue to the present.

□ 1835 churches that later became a part of the association.

Other charter churches which no longer exist.①Big Creek, ②Unity, ③Bethany, ④Pilgrim's Rest, ⑤ Serepta.

In 1860, on the eve of the War, the association had grown to 26 churches with 21 in Pickens, 4 in Tuscaloosa, and l in Greene. (Several of the original churches in Greene, as well as in Pickens, had rejected the concept of mission boards and had sided with the Primitive movement in the Baptist family.) The churches reported 2074 members that year with 603 being persons of color. By 1870 most of the former slaves had left the churches of the association to form churches of their own.

Among the churches planted between 1835 and 1860 are several that continue to be members of the association. These churches are Arbor Springs, Mt. Pleasant, Mineral Springs, Spring Hill, Hebron, Cross Roads, Pickensville and Carrollton. The other 1860 churches were Oak Ridge, near the Pine Grove church, Mt. Zion near Bethany/Vienna, and Shiloh which, I am guessing, was near where Flatwoods is now.

5. Statistics from 1900. In that year the association had 37 churches. Of these 25 were in Pickens, 3 in Greene, 4 in Lamar, and 5 in Tuscaloosa.. (These were across the Sipsey mostly south of US 82 and around Fosters.) Membership in the churches stood at about 2,200 with about 1,400 of these members being in the Pickens County churches. Those whose churches date back to 1900 will want to contrast the data about their church membership with the present membership. Note that most of the churches were rural and small membership ones. Larger towns were just beginning to develop as the railroads were extended through the association and the farms and timberland of the area could join the growing national market economy by shipping their products on the railroad. (Previously, products were shipped mostly down the Tombigbee toward Mobile.) I found it interesting that the associational leaders were sensitive to the impact that the railroads would have and started new churches in Millport, Kennedy, Reform and Gordo, and revived and moved the church at Ethelsville, and moved Enon to Aliceville. This vision made it possible for the Baptist work here to respond to the changing community patterns that marked the 20th century. The work of the Kingdom, and of the Baptist part of it, has benefitted many fold from the effort expended in forming congregations in the emerging towns of the association.

6. Map of Pickens County showing the location of the member churches of the association in 1900.

Friendship was then known as New Salem. Stansel was then known as Union Center.
Churches that have been dissolved but were once members of the association. ①. McBee, ② Big Creek, ③ Oak Ridge, ④ Unity, ⑤ Zion, and ⑥ Mt. Zion.

7. Statistics from 1925. In the era when the automobile was becoming widely used and transportation routes improved, Southern Baptists encouraged associations to become more active, and so, many large associations divided and/or encouraged churches to shift their affiliation to run more along county lines, that being one bond that many of the churches might have in common. Union Association followed suite. From being an association with churches in four counties, the work was centered in one. (In more recent times, there has been some movement in the other direction, as evidenced by our neighbor, Golden Triangle, in Mississippi. It brought together three county associations into a regional association with the strength to respond to the challenges and opportunities associated with the metro area with two fine universities and a military installation.) You might note the fact that none of the churches of the association in that era worshiped every Sunday. This was true outside of the towns until the 1950s.

8. Statistics from 1990. Use this data to see some of the changes that have occurred in your church in the past decade, then compare the data with what was true of your church in 1925. Overall the Baptist work in the association has prospered. Some churches are smaller. Many are larger. There are many reasons for this. Many communities have lost population during the period. New churches have been started. Some churches may have had internal problems. Perhaps some have lost their vision and their passion for winning the lost and disciplining the saved.

Pray. Thank God. Ask God for a vision. Draw upon the power that God makes available to His churches.

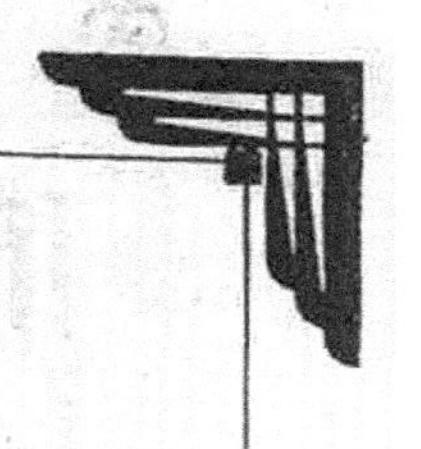

MINUTES

OF THE

CONVENTION.

BETHANY, PICKENS COUNTY, ALA. Sept. 4, 1836.

Agreeably to a resolution of the Buttehatchie Baptist Association, at her annual session, in the year 1834, proposing a division, and granting liberty to all the Churches within certain bounds, to meet by proper representation, at the time and place above mentioned, in convention, for the purpose of consulting on the propriety of said division, and of forming a new and separate associate body. The following named Churches have concurred with said resolution, and

1. The service was opened by a sermon from Elder Charles Stewart, from the 22d verse of the 118 Psalm: "The stone which the builders refused is become the head stone of the corner."

2. The Delegates then convened in the old meeting house, (giving up the new church to the congregation,) and received and read letters from the following Churches, and recorded the names of the representatives of each Church:

Big Creek.—Charles Stewart, John Milam, John George.
Pilgrim's Rest.—Henry Petty, Tho's. Williams, Curtis Williams.
Liberty.—Mathew McCrary, T. Trimune, M. Richardson.
Enon.—W. R. Stansel, L. W. Parker, S. Stone.
Bethlehem.—W. H. Cook, W. Richardson, J. Dunlap.
Bethel.—Stephen Ellis, M. Leatherwood.
Canaan.—T. West, S. Clay.
Zarepta.—John P. Taylor, E. Sullivan, S. Williams.
Unity.—John H. Taylor, John Thornton, S. Gilbert.
Rehoboth.—S. Murphy, Elisha Hunter, Isaac Brown.
Springfield.—John W. Wilson, J. McGraw, G. W. Wilkinson.
Ebenezar.—Richard Wilkins, M. Moses, S. Johnson.
Beulah.—Mathew P. Smith, M. Franklin, T. J. Drommond.
Bethany.—Green W. Wilder, Hutson Harris, Simeon Harris.
Fellowship.—L. B. Williams, John Dunn, Hesekiah Williams.
Forrest.—Berry King, Watson Shoemaker, John Carver.
Buck Creek.—Richard Levin, Francis Neal, William Neal.
Five Mile Creek.—B. Holbrook, Whitmel Travis, C. Williams.
Antioch.—Ransom Mitchell, David W. Stephens.

3. The brethren went into the choice of a Moderator and Clerk, when brother Richard Wilkins was chosen Moderator, and W. R Stansel, Clerk.

4. The Convention being now organized, it was moved by brother Isaac Brown, that we adopt the same articles of faith, abstract of principles, and rules of decorum, on which the Buttehatchie Baptist Association was constituted, for the use of our new association; and the vote was unanimous in favor of the motion.

5. Brethren Elisha Hunter and L. W. Parker, were appointed to draft a correct copy of the above mentioned Constitution, and hand it in to-morrow morning.

6. The brethren having freely consulted on the propriety of uniting and forming a new associate body, it was moved by elder H. Petty, that the Constitution be on to-morrow morning, and the motion was supported without a dissenting voice.

7. On motion of brother Brown, brethren Petty, Cook, Brown, Dunlap and Thornton, were appointed a committee of arrangement. And then adjourned until ten o'clock to-morrow morning.

SATURDAY MORNING, Sept. 5.

8. The members composing the Convention, met according to adjournment; singing and prayer by the brother Moderator, and proceeded to business.

9. On motion, read the rules of decorum and the minutes of yesterday.

10. Called on the committee of arrangement for their report; also, on the committee appointed to draft the articles of constitution, and they delivered their copies and were discharged.

11. The above mentioned articles of faith, &c., were read and compared with the original.

12. The ministers and members now agree to go forward into the constitution of the association. Elder H. Petty offered the benediction prayer, and then the brother Moderator, after a short charge, pronounced the several Churches composing this union, to be a regular constituted Baptist Association; and the brethren then gave each other the right hand of fellowship, while a song of praise was sung to the honor of him who liveth for ever and ever. It was a time of love.

13. The brethren then proposed to continue the same brethren in office as Moderator and Clerk for the association.

14. On motion, appointed the brethren Curtis, Williams, John Milam and Mathew McCrary, a committee on finance.

15. On motion, appointed William R. Stansel to be Treasurer for this association.

16. It was then resolved, that this union of Churches shall be known and distinguished by the name of the Union Baptist Association.

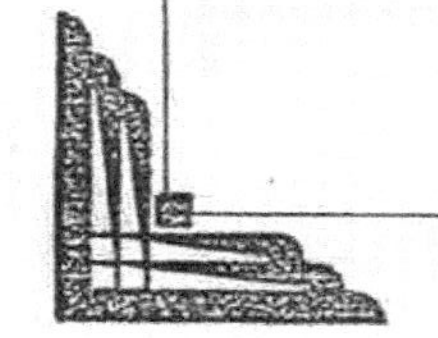

LIST OF DELEGATES FROM THE 1836 MINUTES OF UNION (PICKENS) ASSOC. ❷

Churches and Counties.	DELEGATES' NAMES. Ordained Ministers are marked in Capitols. Licenced Preachers in Italics.	Baptized,	Rec'd by letter,	Dismissed,	Excluded,	Restored,	Dead,	Total,	Monthly meetings,	For Minutes,	Association Fund,	Post Offices.	By whom supplied.
✓ Big Creek, Pickens,	CHAS. SEWART, Jas. Allen, Anthony Lathan.	13	12	11	3		3	122	2d	2 00	2 00	Corrollton	Chas. Stewart.
✓ Pilgrim's Rest, Pickens.	HENRY PETTY, Thos. Williams, Hez. Jones,	1	20		1		1	02	1st	3 00	2 00	Pickensville	Henry Petty.
✓ Enon, Pickens,	George Bald, Stephen Stone, Thomas Taylor,	1		8	2	1		62	3d	2 00	1 00	Pickensville	J. H. Taylor.
Bethlehem, Greene,	Joseph Dunlap, John Head, Jonathan Cockrell,	2	5	8	2		1	80	3d	2 00	2 00	Mesopotamia	Henry Petty.
Bethel, Greene,	William Price, Abraham Hinds, Stephen Ellis,		6	4				16	4th	1 00	75	Springfield	E. Wilbanks.
Canaan, Greene,	Thomas West, Jordan Moore, Samuel Clay,		10	9			1	62	4th	2 00	3 00	Clinton	Jere. Pearcell.
Sarepta, Pickens,	JOHN P. TAYLOR, N. Mitchell, W. Fortune,			33				47	4th	2 00	1 00	Pleasant Rid.	J. P. Taylor.
Unity, Pickens,	JOHN H. TAYLOR, John Pearson, *D. Sanders.*		13	7				38	2d	1 00	1 00	Carrollton	J. H. Taylor.
Rehoboth, Greene,	E. WILLBANKS, Simon Murphy, H. Harrison.		13	11	6		3	160	2d	3 00	3 00	Clinton	Henry Petty.
Springfield, Greene,	James McGraw, George W. Wilkinson,	8	9	7			1	68	1st	1 50	50	Springfield	Robert Marsh.
✓ Ebenezer, Pickens,	R. WILKINS, S. Johnson, John M. Petigrew,			6				24	3d	1 00	1 00	Carrollton	R. Wilkins.
Bulah, Pickens,	Thos Drummond, P. M. Brewton, M. P. SMITH.	1	6	6			1	38	3d	1 50	1 50	Foster's	M. P. Smith.
Bethany, Pickens,	*T. S. Thomas,* Green W. Wilder, David Hudson.		6	2			1	43	1st	2 00	2 00	Vienna	William Nash.
✓ Fellowship, Pickens,	L. B. Williams, Wm. Williams, Ambrose Dollar.		11					38	1st	1 00	1 50	Carrollton	R. Wilkins.
✓ Liberty, Pickens,	Fynell P. Savage, M. Richardson, T. Trimmeur,			4				12	4th	1 00	1 00	Carrollton	R. Wilkins.
Buck Creek, Tuscaloosa.	Richard Leopard, Francis Neal, Wm. S. Neal,	1	3	1	1		1	30	3d	1 00	1 00	Foster's	M. P. Smith.
Forest, Pickens.	L. B. King, Bartley Upchurch, W Shoemaker,	1	16	2	1			44	1st	3 00	3 00	King's	J. H. Taylor.
Five Mile, Greene,	Henry Williams, Chas. Williams, J. E. Stivender,	5	2	7	1		1	85	1st	2 00	2 00	Lummusville	J. Pearcell.
Antioch, Perry,	Newman Meek, D. W Stephens, B. Johnson,	3					1	31		1 50	1 00	Greensboro'	
Friendship, Greene,	T. WILLINGHAM, J. PEARCELL, R. Fleming	19	13	7	2		2	37	2d	2 00	10 00	Daniels store	T. Willingham.
		50	145	133	19	1	17	1156		35 50	40 25		

LIST OF DELEGATES TO THE 1834 BUTTEHATCHIE ASSOCIATION ❸

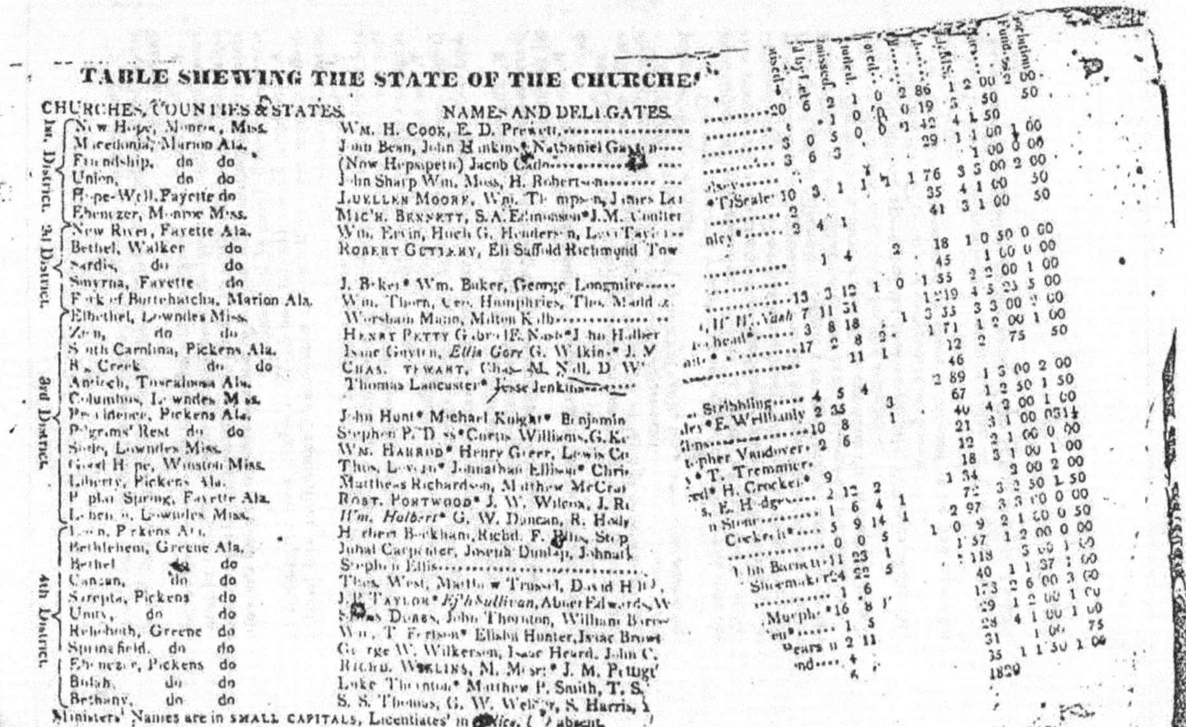

TABLE SHEWING THE STATE OF THE CHURCHES

District	CHURCHES, COUNTIES & STATES.	NAMES AND DELEGATES.
1st. District.	New Hope, Monroe, Miss.	WM. H. COOK, E. D. Prewett,
	Macedonia, Marion Ala.	John Bean, John Hankins* Nathaniel Gaston
	Friendship, do do	(New Hopspeth) Jacob Cado[illegible]
	Union, do do	John Sharp Wm. Moss, H. Robertson
	Hope-Well, Fayette do	LUELLEN MOORE, Wm. Thompson, James La[illegible]
	Ebenezer, Monroe Miss.	MIC'H. BENNETT, S. A. Edmonson* J. M. Coulter
2d District.	New River, Fayette Ala.	Wm. Ervin, Hugh G. Henderson, Levi Taylor
	Bethel, Walker do	ROBERT GUTHRY, Eli Safford Richmond Tow[illegible]
	Sardis, do do	
	Smyrna, Fayette do	J. Baker* Wm. Baker, George Longmire
	Fork of Buttehatchie, Marion Ala.	Wm. Thorn, Geo. Humphries, Thos. Maddox
3rd District.	Elbethel, Lowndes Miss.	Worsham Mann, Milton Kilb[illegible]
	Zion, do do	HENRY PETTY Gabriel E. Nash* John Halber[illegible]
	South Carolina, Pickens Ala.	Isaac Gayton, *Ellis Gore* G. Wilkins* J. V[illegible]
	Big Creek do do	CHAS. STEWART, Chas. M. Neill, D. W[illegible]
	Antioch, Tuscaloosa Ala.	Thomas Lancaster* Jesse Jenkins
	Columbus, Lowndes Miss.	
	Providence, Pickens Ala.	John Hunt* Michael Knight* Benjamin
	Pilgrims' Rest do do	Stephen P. Doss* Curtis Williams, G. K[illegible]
	Siloe, Lowndes Miss.	WM. HARROD* Henry Greer, Lewis Co[illegible]
	Good Hope, Winston Miss.	Thos. Levan* Jonathan Ellison* Chri[illegible]
	Liberty, Pickens Ala.	Matthews Richardson, Matthew McCra[illegible]
	Poplar Spring, Fayette Ala.	ROBT. PORTWOOD* J. W. Wilcox, J. R[illegible]
	Lebanon, Lowndes Miss.	*Wm. Halbert** G. W. Duncan, R. Hol[illegible]
4th District.	Enon, Pickens Ala.	Hethers Beckham, Richd. F. Bliss, Step[illegible]
	Bethlehem, Greene Ala.	Jubal Carpenter, Joseph Dunlap, Johnat[illegible]
	Bethel do do	Stephen Ellis
	Canaan, do do	Thos. West, Matthew Trussel, David H[illegible]
	Sarepta, Pickens do	J. P. TAYLOR* *Elijah Sullivan,* Abner Edwards, W[illegible]
	Unity, do do	Silas Dobbs, John Thornton, William Bir[illegible]
	Rehoboth, Greene do	Wm. T. Ferison* Elisha Hunter, Isaac Brow[illegible]
	Springfield, do do	George W. Wilkerson, Isaac Heard, John C.
	Ebenezer, Pickens do	RICHD. WILKINS, M. Moss* J. M. Pettigr[illegible]
	Bulah, do do	Luke Thornton* Matthew P. Smith, T. S.
	Bethany, do do	S. S. Thomas, G. W. Webster, S. Harris, [illegible]

Ministers' Names are in SMALL CAPITALS, Licentiates' in *Italics*, (*) absent.

Founding Churches of the Pickens (Union) Association

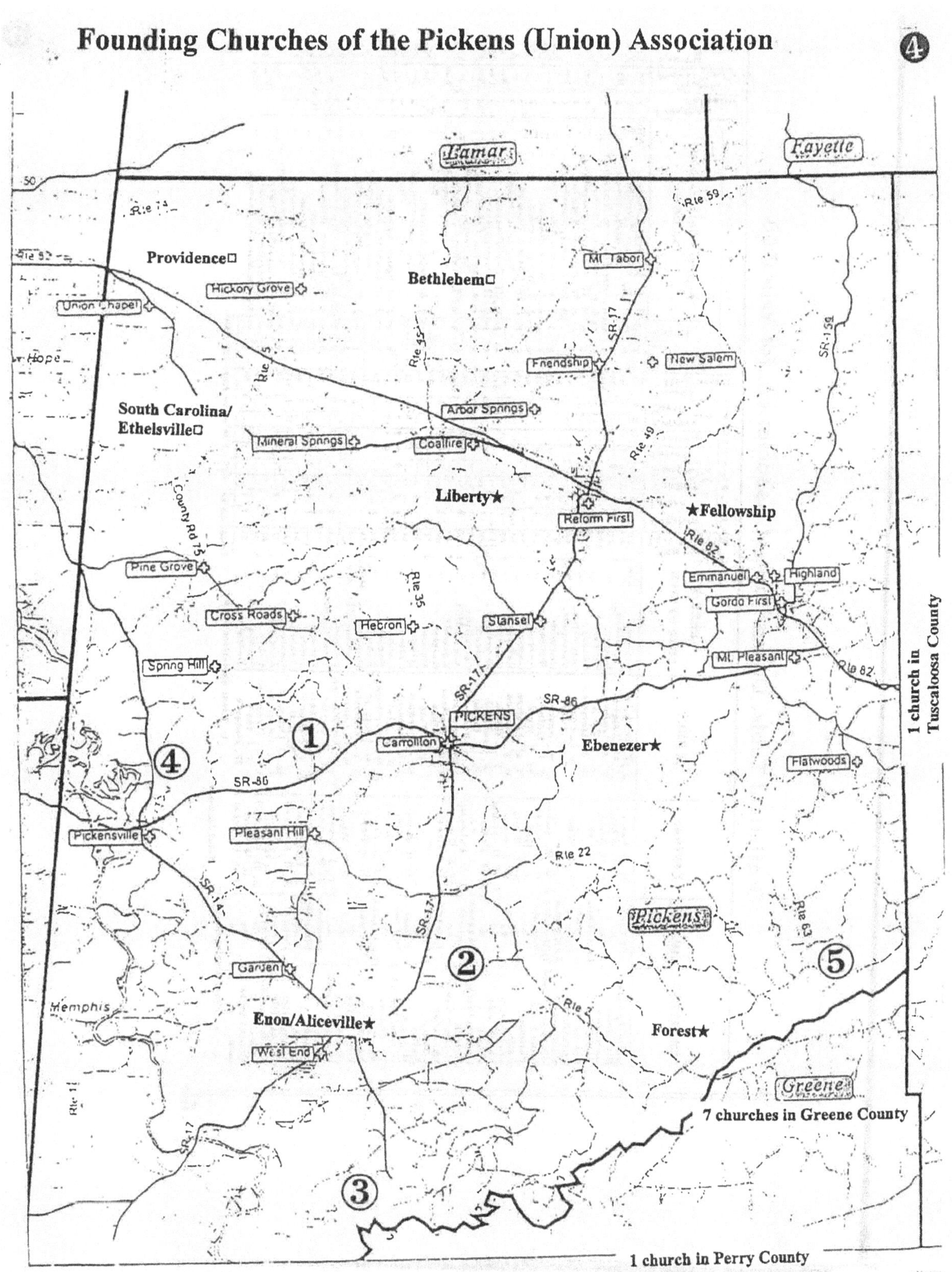

Statistical Table, Union Baptist Association, for Year 1900.

CHURCHES	COUNTY	PASTORS	CLERKS	CLERK'S POST OFFICE	Membership Last Reported	INC. BY Baptism	INC. BY Letter	INC. BY Voucher	INC. BY Restorat'n	DEC. BY Letter	DEC. BY Exclusion	DEC. BY Erasure	DEC. BY Death	Present Membership	SUNDAY SCHOOLS. Officers & Teachers	SUNDAY SCHOOLS. Pupils	SUNDAY SCHOOLS. Superintendent's Name and Post Office.	Preaching Sabbaths	Reports Prayer Meet'g	Reports Revival
Arbor Springs	Pickens	D. O. Baird	J. K. Wilkins	Reform, Ala.	72	6	5	..	..	2	1	3	2	69	4	45	W. M. Keating, Reform, Ala.	2	No	Yes
Big Creek	do	W. L. White	I. M. Noland	Carrollton, "	72	2	1	..	..	4	..	..	3	65	4	35	W. H. Bridges, Carrollton, "	2	"	Yes
Bethlehem	do	D. O. Baird	G. A. Sanford	Vassar, "	91	2	3	..	1	4	..	..	1	92			No Sunday School	3	No	"
Bethel	Tuskaloosa	J. H. Curry	A. V. Taylor	Hickman, "	207	..	..	..	..	..	..	..	2	199	3	51	Webster Thornton, Knoxville, "	4	"	No
Beulah	Greene		W. B. Durrett	Snoddy, "	169	2	3	..	..	..	..	..	1	171	5	44	S. S. Thornton, Union, "	....	"	"
Carrollton	Pickens	W. L. White	S. L. Cox	Carrollton, "	53	2	2	..	..	..	..	..	1	56	4	62	W. G. Robertson, Carrollton, "	2	Yes	Yes
*Chalcedony	Tuskaloosa		T. M. Pate	Northport, "	32	..	..	..	..	..	..	..	..	32	3	23	D. W. Hamner, Romulus, "	2	No	No
*Cornelius Chapel	Tuskaloosa	J. H. M. Anders	D. W. Hamner	Romulus, "	57	..	2	..	..	..	..	..	1	58			D. W. Hamner, Romulus, "	4	No	"
Cross Roads	Pickens	G. W. Kerr	F. H. Oglerly	McShan, "	45	13	4	..	..	4	..	..	..	61	5	31	J. N. Mullins, Carrollton, "	2	"	Yes
Ebenezer	do	S. E. Hedge	W. T. Hardy	Noland, "	67	6	6	..	..	6	..	..	..	73	5	48	A. I. Brown, Noland, "	2	"	Yes
Enon	do	W. L. White	T. H. Sanders	Garden, "	45	..	..	..	..	..	..	..	1	44	4	30	J. T. White, Garden, "	3	"	Yes
*Fellowship	do	W. J. Beaty	R. F. Johnson	Reform, "	56	..	..	..	..	6	..	..	1	49	4	25	P. H. Howard, Reform, "	3	"	"
Flat Woods	do	J. H. M. Anders	T. J. Burks	Raleigh, "	47	..	3	..	..	2	..	1	..	42			No Sunday School.	3	"	No
Forest	do	J. W. Caldwell	J. Upchurch	Benevola, "	117	..	..	..	..	..	..	..	..	118	6	35	W. H. Teer, Benevola, "	1	No	"
Grant's Creek	Tuskaloosa		R. H. Foster	Sylvan, "	120	1	5	..	..	2	..	..	2	127	5	40	R. H. Foster, Sylvan, "	2	Yes	No
Hebron	Pickens	J. W. Caldwell	J. A. Pearson	Carrollton, "	47	2	..	..	..	6	..	8	2	35	4	34	J. A. Pearson, Carrollton, "	3	No	Yes
Hickory Grove	do	O. E. Wooten	J. N. Ashcraft	Neal's Mill, "	46	2	2	..	..	5	20	..	1	25			No Sunday School.	3	"	"
*Kennedy	Lamar	D. O. Baird	W. H. Smothers	Kennedy, "	30	..	..	..	..	..	..	..	..	30	5	51	W. T. Walker, Kennedy, "	1	"	Yes
Liberty	Pickens	do	S. P. Sloan	Reform, "	72	1	1	..	..	1	..	8	1	72			No Sunday School.	4	Yes	Yes
McBee	do		J. S. Cole	McBee, "	25	..	..	..	..	..	..	..	..	25			do do	....	....	....
Millport	Lamar	D. O. Baird	G. S. Keenum	Millport, "	35	..	1	..	..	1	..	..	..	35	7	34	J. B. Hodo, Millport, "	1	No	No
Mineral Springs	Pickens	G. W. Kerr	J. D. Manning	Carlotta, "	53	..	..	..	..	1	..	4	..	48			No Sunday School.	3	No	No
Mt. Pleasant	do	R. J. O'Briant	W. W. Hall	Gordo, "	46	2	2	..	3	4	2	3	..	42			do do	1	"	No
New Hope	Tuskaloosa	J. D. Ray	J. W. Robertson	Romulus, "	91	..	..	..	..	4	1	10	3	73	3	20	J. M. Smith, Romulus, "	4	No	No
New Salem	Pickens	W. J. Beaty	J. M. Pratt, jr.	Reform, "	34	5	..	..	..	5	..	..	..	34	8	25	J. H. Doughty, Reform, "	4	No	Yes
†Oak Ridge	do		H. L. Williams	Dunbar, Miss.	15	..	..	..	..	..	..	..	..	15			No Sunday School.	....	....	....
Pickensville	do	W. L. White	W. C. Long	Pickensville, Ala.	42	..	1	..	..	..	..	..	2	40	5	50	J. R. Long, Pickensville, "	1	"	No
Pleasant Grove	do	O. E. Wooten	W. W. McCullough	Kennedy, "	25	..	..	..	..	..	..	..	1	25	3	23	J. F. Herring, Millport, "	4	"	No
Prairie	Greene	J. E. Herring	M. B. Taylor	West Greene, "	69	9	2	..	2	1	1	..	1	79	4	31	M. B. Taylor, West Greene, "	2	"	Yes
Reform	Pickens	W. L. White	J. W. Gardner	Reform, "	15	5	2	..	..	..	..	..	..	22	3	60	J. W. Gardner, Reform, "	4	No	Yes
Shiloh	Greene	J. D. Hamner	W. C. McCrackin	Boom, "	104	6	2	..	1	2	2	..	2	107	5	38	A. P. Smith, Boom, "	1&3	Yes	Yes
Spring Hill	Pickens	J. W. Caldwell	J. M. Lofton	Archer, "	48	..	..	..	..	3	..	..	3	42	3	25	J. H. Stinson, Archer, "	4	No	No
Spring Hill	Lamar	J. A. Estes	G. B. Coleman	Gentry, "	144	..	..	..	..	8	3	10	4	119	9	37	G. B. Coleman, Gentry, "	2	"	Yes
South Carolina	Pickens	G. W. Kerr	J. A. Stimpson	Ethelville, "	10	..	4	..	..	..	..	1	..	13	5	40	No Sunday School.	1	"	"
*Unity	do	J. W. Caldwell	W. W. Maughan	Olney, "	65	..	..	..	..	..	..	..	..	56	4	50	W. W. Maughan, Olney, "	....	Yes	No
Union Centre	do	G. W. Kerr	Z. J. Hall	Stansel, "	31	..	..	..	..	3	..	..	..	27	6	40	J. A. Shepherd, Stansel, "	1	No	"
Zion	do	R. J. O'Briant	M. Marquis	Raleigh, "	27	1	1	..	..	2	..	..	..	26	4	25	Marion Marquis, Raleigh, "			
					2326	68	52	...	7	16	26	48	34	2209	126	1066				

* From Statistics of 1899 † From Statistics of 1898

Total Increase, —

Centennial Member Churches of Pickens Baptist Association

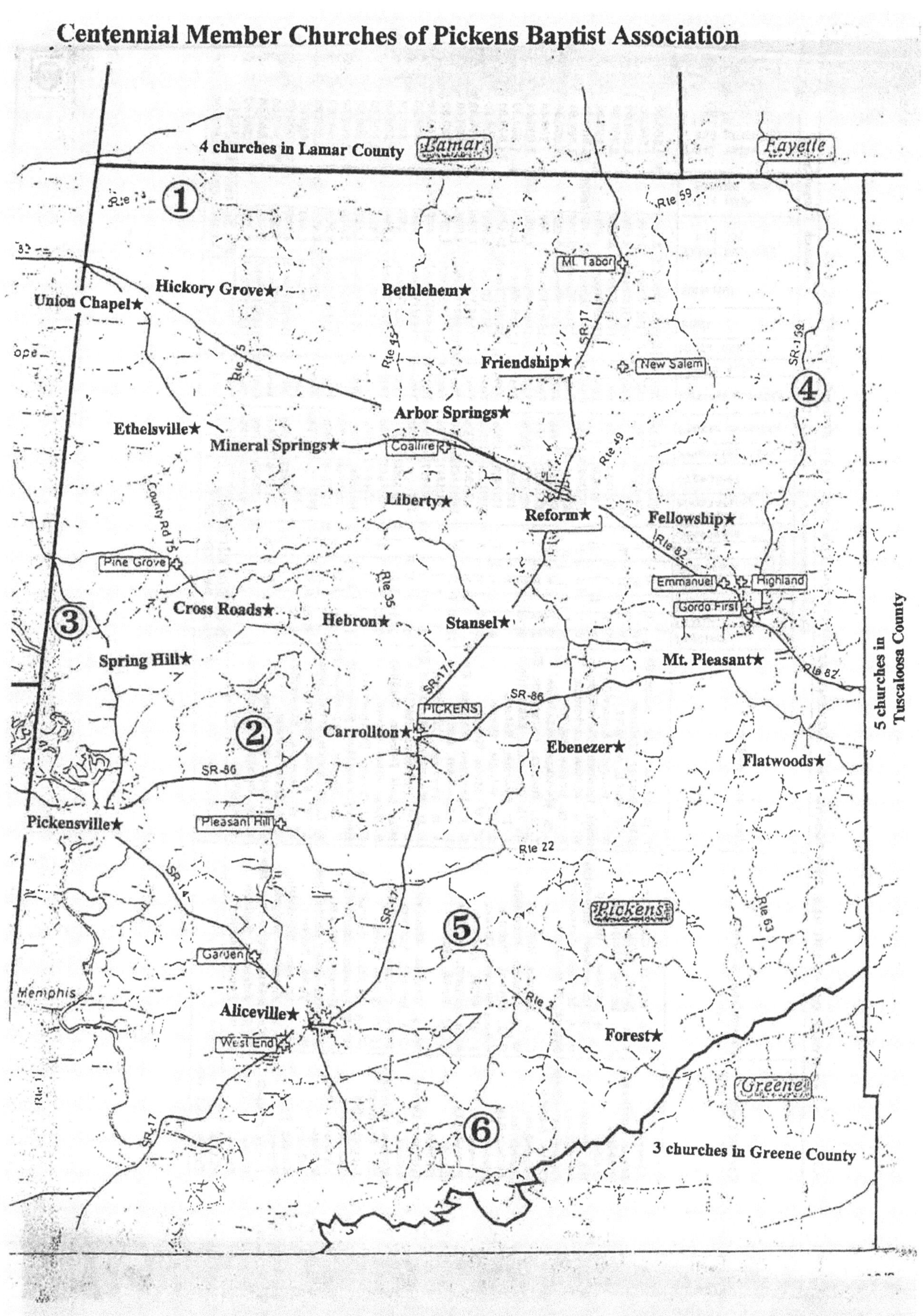

STATISTICE OF CHURCHES COMPOSING THE PICKENS ASSOCIATION, FOR THE YEAR ENDING AUGUST 31, 1925.

CHURCHES	Pastor and Address	Clerk and Address	Church Membership: Gains: Baptism	Gains: Letter	Gains: Statement	Losses: Letter	Losses: Exclusion	Losses: Death	Losses: Otherwise	Total present Membership	Church History: Organized	Preaching days	Prayer meeting	Revival meeting	Lord's supper	State paper	Built	Church Property: Material	Value building and lot	Value parsonage, etc.	Total value and property
Aliceville	W. A. McCain, Carrollton.	T. H. Sanders, Sr., Aliceville		4		1		1		151	1823	1-3	Yes	No.	4	15	1905	Wood	$ 2,500		$ 2,500.00
Arbor Springs	J. A. Estes, Millport.	Ellis Bonner, Reform	11			5		1		164	1872	2	No.	Yes	1	5	1916	Wood	1,500		1,500.00
Bethlem	J. A. Estes, Millport.	I. W. Cobb, Millport.	1			1		2		123		3		Yes	1		1914	Wood	1,000		1,000.00
Beulah	H. G. Johnson, Reform	W. B. Durrett, Knoxville.	16	4		3	1			306	1833	1	No	Yes	2		1872	Wood	2,000		2,000.00
Big Creek	H. G. Carpenter, Ethelville	Hugh Duncan, Carrollton.	3		1			1		9	1829	1		Yes			1829	Wood	500		500.00
Carrollton	W. A. McCain, Carrollton.	W. S. McGee, Carrollton	4	7		12	1	1		219	1846	2-4	Yes	Yes	4	All	1925	Brick	17,500	$2500	20,000.00
Cornelius Chapel	Brown, E N Gordo	W. G. Evans, Buhl.			1			2		58		3		Yes			1918	Wood	1,000		1,000.00
Cross Roads		J. S. Heritage, Ethelville	2	3		2		2		52	1850	1	No.	Yes	2	5	1920	Wood	1,650		1,650.00
Ebenezer	C. A. Bryant, Reform.	T. R. Sellers, Carrollton R2	2	1		6	1			188	1833	1	No	Yes	4	1	1900	Wood	700		700.00
Ethelville	W. S. Cruzan, Ethelville	W. C. Hancock, Ethelville.	2	3		6				32	1823	4	No	Yes	4	2	1900	Wood	1,000	1000	2,000.00
Fellowship	C. A. Bryant, Reform.	J. F. Pearson, Reform.				4				27	1832	3		Yes		1	1893	Wood	1,250		1,250.00
Flatwoods	Elisha Brown, Gordo.	E. H. Windle, Gordo	5			3	1	1		78	1884	3	No	Yes	1		1884	Wood	14,000		14,000.00
Forest	J. M. Mills, Reform	W. M. Moss, Gordo.	15	8		3		2		132	1834	1	No	Yes	4		1873	Wood	2,000		2,000.00
Friendship	C. A. Bryant, Reform.	S. F. Pearson, Reform, R1			2	7				97	1907	3	Yes	Yes	2		1908	Wood	1,500		1,500.00
Gordo	H. C. Todd, Gordo	L. Alexander, Gordo.	11	14	1	2		3		118	1901	2-4	Yes	No	1	All	1901	Wood	3,000		3,000.00
Hebron		S. S. Pearson, Carrollton								64	1841	3	No	Yes	4			Wood	1,250		1,250.00
Hickory Grove	W. S. Cruzan, Ethelville	J. D. Manning, Ethelville R1	2							31	1897	2	No	Yes	2	2	1898	Wood	600		600.00
Liberty	C. A. Bryant, Reform.	W. H. Robinson, Reform.	2		1	2	1			127		4	No	Yes	1		1888	Wood	800		800.00
Mineral Springs	W. S. Cruzan, Ethelville	Miss Lois Duncan, McShan.	1	1		2			9	86	1855	1	No	Yes	4		1892	Wood	800		800.00
Mt. Pleasant	H. C. Todd, Gordo	S. Tom Sims, Gordo.	3	1		4		1	1	101	1843	1	No	Yes	2	8	1844	Wood	1,500		1,500.00
Pickensville	W. A. McCain, Carrollton	M. J. Yagle, Pickensville.								23	1847	2	No				1847	Wood	1,500		1,500.00
Pine Grove	W. S. Cruzan, Ethelville	Henry Copeland, Ethelville				5	1			40	1908	3	No	No			1925	Wood	1,500		1,500.00
Pleasant Hill	C. A. Bryant, Reform.	C. O. Spiller, Carrollton R1				1		1		85	1916	2	Yes	No	4	1	1916	Wood	2,000		2,000.00
Prairie	W. A. McCain, Carrollton	E. L. Ferguson, West Greene				1		1	3	37	1876	1	No	Yes		4	1912	Wood	2,000		2,000.00
Reform	H. C. Todd, Gordo	J. W. Smith, Reform.	4	6	1	5				181		1-3	Yes	Yes				Brick	8,000	300	8,300.00
Spring Hill	W. S. Cruzan, Ethelville	N. H. Stonson, Ethelville.	5	2						38		3		Yes				Wood	1,500		1,500.00
Stansel	H. G. Johnson, Reform	Z. J. Hall, Reform.								51	1897	4	No	No			1898	Wood	1,000		1,000.00
Union Chapel	J.F.Sansing, Columbus, Miss.	J. N. Bell, Ethelville.			1	2	2	2		53	1900	2-4	No	Yes		2	1900	Wood	1,000		1,000.00
Unity	H. G. Johnson, Reform	R. E. Colvin, Aliceville.				1			3	118	1829	2	No	Yes	2	9	1855	Wood	2,500		2,500.00
Zion	J. W. Fore, Gordo.	M. Marquis, Elrod.								56	1839	3	No	No			1917	Wood	1,200		1,200.00
Totals			87	58	8	78	8	21	16	2845									$78,205	$3800	$82,005.00
Totals last year			130	65	9	98	5	24	2	2879									54,400	5005	59,405.00

DELEGATES' NAMES. Ordained Ministers are marked in Capitols. Licenced Preachers in Italics.	Baptized.	Rec'd by letter.	Dismissed.	Excluded.	Restored.	Dead.	Total.	Monthly meetings.	For Minutes.	Association Fund.	Post Offices.	By whom supplied.
HAS. SEWART, Jas. Allen, Anthony Lathan.	13	12	11	3		3	122	2d	2 00	2 00	Carrollton	Chas. St
ENRY PETTY, Thos. Williams, Hez. Jones,	1	20		1		1	92	1st	3 00	2 00	Pickensville	Henry P
eorge Bald, Stephen Stone, Thomas Taylor,	1		8	2	1		62	3d	2 00	1 00	Pickensville	J. H. Ta
oseph Dunlap, John Head, Jonathan Cockrell,	2	5	8	2		1	80	3d	2 00	2 00	Mesopotamia	Henry P
William Price, Abraham Hinds, Stephen Ellis,		6	4				16	4th	1 00	75	Springfield	E. Wilb
homas West, Jordan Moore, Samuel Clay,		10	9			1	62	4th	2 00	3 00	Clinton	Jere. Pe
OHN P. TAYLOR, N. Mitchell, W. Fortune,			33				47	4th	2 00	1 00	Pleasant Rid.	J. P. Tay
OHN H. TAYLOR, John Pearson, *D. Sanders*,		13	7				38	2d	1 00	1 00	Carrollton	J. H. Ta
. WILLBANKS, Simon Murphy, H. Harrison,		13	11	6		3	160	2d	3 00	3 00	Clinton	Henry P
mes McGraw, George W. Wilkinson,	8	9	7			1	68	1st	1 50	50	Springfield	Robert M
. WILKINS, S. Johnson, John M. Petigrew,			6				24	3d	1 00	1 00	Carrollton	R. Wilki
hos Drummond, P. M. Brewton, M. P. SMITH.	1	6	6			1	38	3d	1 50	1 50	Foster's	M. P. S
. *S. Thomas*, Green W. Wilder, David Hudson,		6	2			1	43	1st	2 00	2 00	Vienna	William
. B. Williams, Wm. Williams, Ambrose Dollar.		11					28	1st	1 00	1 50	Carrollton	R. Wilki
rnell P. Savage, M. Richardson, T. Trimmeur,			4				12	4th	1 00	1 00	Carrollton	R. Wilki
ichard Leopard, Francis Neal, Wm. S. Neal,	1	3	1	1		1	30	2d	1 00	1 00	Foster's	M. P. Sm
. B. King, Bartley Upchurch, W Shoemaker,	1	10	2	1			44	1st	3 00	3 00	King's	J. H. Ta
enry Williams, Chas. Williams, J. E. Stivender,	5	2	7	1		1	85	1st	2 00	2 00	Lummusville	J. Pearcel
ewman Meek, D. W Stephens, B. Johnson,	3					1	31		1 50	1 00	Greensboro'	
.WILLINGHAM, J.PEARCELL, R.Fleming	19	13	7	2		2	37	2d	2 00	10 00	Daniels store	T. Willing
	56	145	133	19	1	17	1156		35 50	40 25		

'ES TO THE 1834 BUTTEHATCHIE ASSOCIATION

VING THE STATE OF THE CHURCHE[illegible]

S & STATES. NAMES AND DELEGATES.

liss. Wm. H. Cook, E. D. Prewett,
John Bean, John Hankins, Nathaniel Gayton
(Now Hopsipeth) Jacob Cado
John Sharp Wm. Moss, H. Robertson
Luellen Moore, Wm. Thompson, James La
Mic'h. Bennett, S. A. Edmondson, J. M. Coulter
a. Wm. Ervin, Hugh G. Henderson, Levi Taylor
Robert Guthery, Eli Saffold Richmond Tow

J. Baker, Wm. Baker, George Longmire
arion Ala. Wm. Thorn, Geo. Humphries, Thos. Madd
Worsham Mann, Milton Kolb
Henry Petty Gabriel E. Nash, John Halber
Ala. Isaac Guyton, *Ellis Gore* G. Wilkins, J. V
do Chas. Stewart, Chas. M. Neill, D. W
Thomas Lancaster, Jesse Jenkins

John Hunt, Michael Knight, Benjamin
Stephen P. Doss, Curtis Williams, G. Ke
Wm. Harrod, Henry Greer, Lewis Co
iss. Thos. Lovejn, Johnathan Ellison, Chri
Matthews Richardson, Matthew McCra
Ala. Robt. Portwood, J. W. Wilcox, J. R
Wm. Halbert, G. W. Duncan, R. Hod
Herbert Beckham, Richd. F. Bliss, Step
Jubal Carpenter, Joseph Dunlap, Johnat
Stephen Ellis
Thos. West, Matthew Trussel, David H
J. P. Taylor, *Elijah Sullivan*, Abner Edwards, W
[illegible]

.........20 6 2 1 0 2 86 1 2 00 2 00
.........1 0 0 19 5 50 50
.... 0 0 1 42 4 1 50
.... 3 0 5 0 29 1 1 00 1 00
.... 3 6 3 1 00 0 00
.... 1 76 3 3 00 2 00
.... 3 1 1 35 4 1 00 50
T. Scale 10 3 41 3 1 00 50
.... 2
nley 2 4 1 18 1 0 50 0 00
1 4 2 45 1 00 0 00
.... 1 55 2 2 00 1 00
.........13 3 12 1 0 1 219 4 3 25 5 0
H. M. Nash 7 11 31 1 3 33 3 3 00
...... 3 8 18 1 71 1 2 00 1
head 17 2 8 2 12 2 75
.... 11 1 46
.... 2 89 1 3 00 2
4 5 4 67 1 2 50 1
Stribbling..... 2 35 3 40 4 2 00 1
E. Wellbanly 10 8 1 21 3 1 00 0
.........2 6 12 2 1 00 0
topher Vandover 18 3 1 00
T. Tremmier 1 34 2 00
H. Crocker 9 72 3 2 50
s. E. Hodges 2 12 2 2 97 3 3 00
n Stone 1 6 4 1 1 0 9 2 1 00
Cockrell 5 9 14 1 1 57 1 2 00
.... 0 0 5 118 3 00
John Barnett 11 23 1 40 1 1 37
Shoemaker 24 22 5 173 2 6 00
.... 1 6 29 1 2 00
Murphy 16 8 4 1 0

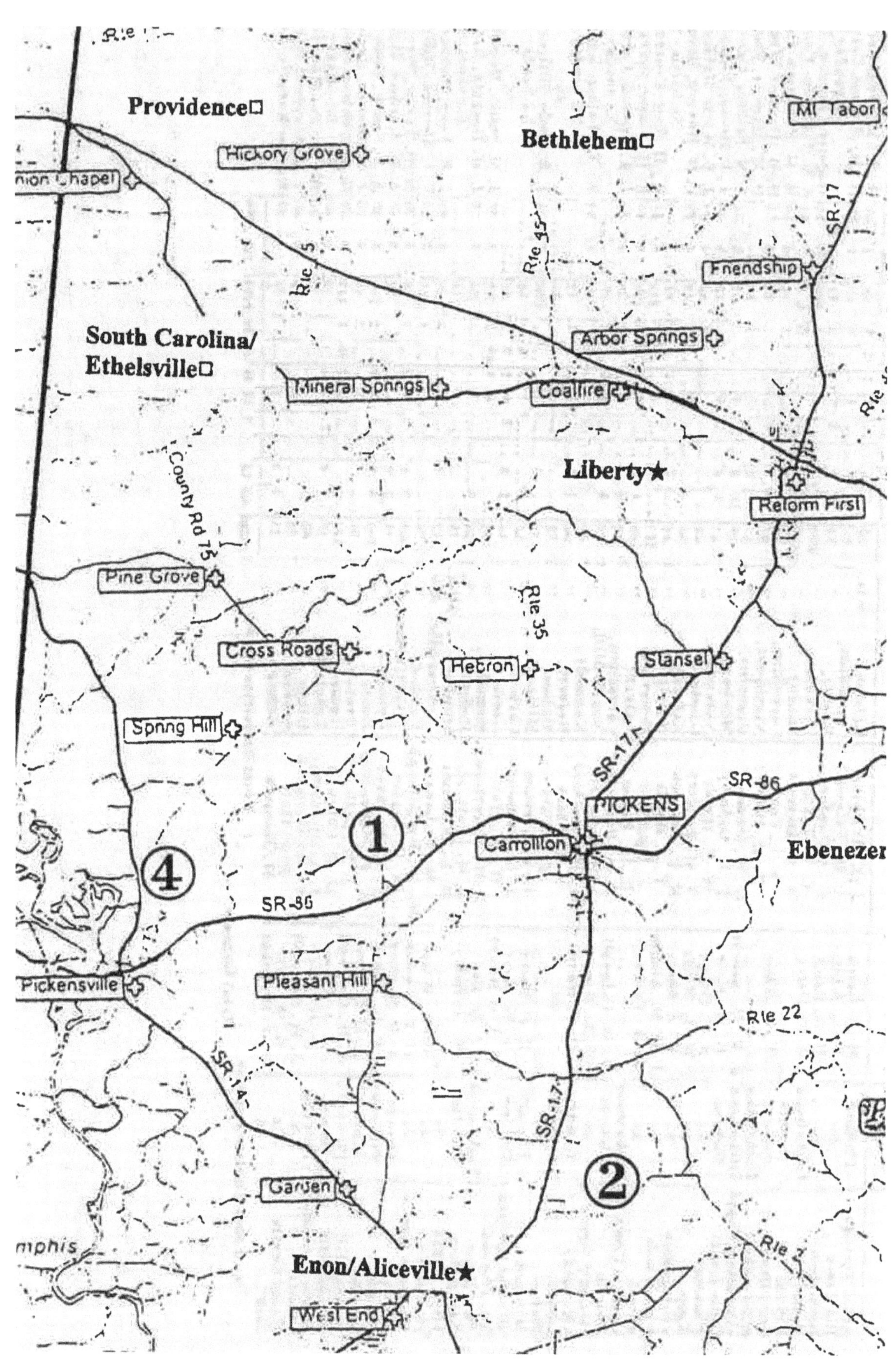
Providence□
Bethlehem□
Mt Tabor
Hickory Grove
Union Chapel
Rte 5
Rte 35
SR-17
Friendship
South Carolina/
Ethelsville□
Arbor Springs
Mineral Springs
Coalfire
Liberty★
Reform First
County Rd 75
Pine Grove
Rte 35
Cross Roads
Hebron
Stansel
Spring Hill
SR-17
SR-86
PICKENS
Carrollton
Ebenezer
1
4
SR-86
Pickensville
Pleasant Hill
Rte 22
SR-14
SR-17
2
Garden
Rte 2
Enon/Aliceville★
West End

Cooperative Ministries of the 37 Churches and Missions of the Pickens Baptist Association of West Alabama

Here is a list of some of the ministries staffed/supported by the cooperating Baptist Churches in our association. We do this so that each of the more than 4,000 resident members of our churches can be a Great Commission Christian, assisting with the extension of the Kingdom of God.

*Operate a Bible Institute connected to Beeson Divinity School for the training of newly called ministers, lay leaders, pastors and others in knowing and living the Holy Bible.

*Provide scholarships to the youth of our churches who are going on to college or trade school. Funded by interest from our contingency fund and the sale of Lifeway VBS materials.

*Recruiting and staffing a team to do evangelism at community events-S&R (Save and Rescue).

*Celebrative and Encouraging annual meetings of the association each October.

*Monthly newsletter on the back of the Alabama Baptist. Supplemented by special editions on significant matters.

*Website www.pickensbaptist.com. Features news and pictures. Also picture albums at www.picasaweb.google.com/pickensbaptist and You Tube.

*Resources for church programs and training-videos, books, speakers. Call the office.

*A voice for morality and the Baptist way in our area.

*Church Program Consultations and Church Health Reviews. Call office.

*Practical and technical advice to the churches by qualified, experienced consultants.

*Area Evangelistic Events and training.

*Baptist Center Thrift Store in Stansel. This is operated by a staff of 50 plus volunteers.

*Food, clothing and benevolence distributed through the Thrift Store.

*Lydia Guest House for visiting ministers, missionaries and evangelists.

*Support for the Cooperative Program and for the various efforts of the Alabama and the Southern Baptist Conventions in such areas as education, evangelism, child care, missions and evangelism.

*Support of an Hispanic Congregation near Aliceville.

*Support of a new church plant, Covenant of Peace, near Union Chapel.

*Senior Adult Revival each March.

*Men's Ministry Program.

*Disaster Relief Van. Equipped for chainsaw, cleanup, chaplaincy, and childcare ministries.

*Wild Game Supper in April.

* R. A. Pinewood Derby each February.

*Baptist Builders Team each summer.

*Financial support of mission teams from Baptist Center funds.

*Deacon Appreciation Banquet September

*Weekly ministry at the county jail both male and female.

*Support of the chaplaincy program at the PCMC.

*Launching the 100 godly women volunteer ministries for the coming Aliceville Federal Prison.

*School Prayer Walk in September.

*On Mission Celebration each five years. (2016)

*Contributions to new church construction from Baptist Center funds.

*Weekly pastors' Prayer Breakfast. Tuesdays at 9 am.

Signature Ministries of the Churches of the Pickens Baptist Association 2011

For many rural and small town churches it has been important for them to develop a ministry or ministries which become its signature-something that identifies it to its community and to its area. While this serves the Kingdom of God, it often serves as a way of reaching the unchurched. Here is a list of those performed by our churches, but there are probably several others.

Celebrate Recovery-Mt. Pleasant and Stansel
Anglefood-Highland
Afterschool Children's Program-Mt. Pleasant
Abortion Recovery-Ethelsville
Gathering for college and career-Mt. Pleasant
Ugly Quilts-Pleasant Hill
Ministry at Aliceville Nursing Home-Galilee and Garden
Ministry at Salem Nursing Home-Reform and Arbor Springs
Ministry at Sansing Care Home-Carrollton and Aliceville
Community Health Fairs-Galilee
Tutoring after school program-Covenant of Peace
Sermon distribution and website-Friendship and Arbor Springs
Ester Prayer Group-Carrollton
Heaven Bound Clown Ministry-Pickensville
Annual Women's Gathering-Pickensville
Worship service for the deaf-Mt. Pleasant
Praise Worship Team-Mt. Pleasant and Highland
Wednesday night gatherings for youth-Highland, Carrollton, Aliceville, Hickory Grove, and New Salem
Fourth of July Celebration-Springhill
Boy Scout troop sponsorship-Galilee
Bibles for the Aliceville Prison-Coalfire
Southern Gospel Concert-Highland and Carrollton
College and Career-Highland
Puppet Ministry-New Salem
Unity Grove Camp Meeting-New Salem
Worship Service on Cable-Aliceville
Children's Choir- Aliceville and Reform
Christmas Store at Salem Nursing Home-New Salem and others
Fire and Rescue Annual Benefit-New Salem
The Golden Girls-Pickensville
Music Training for children-Galilee
Weekly Women's Bible Study-Gordo First
Knitting group-Emmanuel
Block Parties-Carrollton, Galilee and Ethelsville

I hope that in reviewing this list some of you will identify other ministries now in place, will think of other needed ministries, and some will be inspired to provide a similar ministry through their church. Note also the list of cooperative ministries which the association sponsors in order that every person who is a member of a PBA church can be a Great Commission Christian. Note, also, that several music ministries and the Round Pen Ministry are based in churches of the associaiton.

*Annual Pastors' Retreat. January
*Fellowship of Pastor/Staff wives. Each first Tuesday evening.
*Radio Sunday School Lesson. Sunday at 8am WKBB 100.9
*Provide a facility for the offices of these American Family Radio Stations.
*Block Party Trailer.
*Associational WMU.
*Resources and Mentoring for young pastors
*Fellowship events for pastors and their families.
*Diabetes Support Group each 3rd Tuesday at noon.
*Host at PBA building many community meetings.
*Pastoral Sustenance Network 2 and 4 Thursdays 6:30 Mt. Pleasant.
*Support and send mission teams from the association nationally and internationally each summer.
*Help with mission projects in the area.
*VBS Clinics.
*Events for children and youth during the year.
*Associational Week of Prayer each May.

The associational office is at 250 Reform Street in Carrollton. For more information call 205-367-8632. We welcome your questions, suggestions and always will help you find opportunities volunteer. Pray for the work of the association.

Monument/Monuments
Big Creek Baptist Church
Gary Farley

In the weeds along side of a dirt road, across from the Pine Grove Memorial Garden, a short distance north of state highway 86, a few miles west of Carrollton is a marker celebrating the life of a pioneer church in Pickens County, Alabama. Long since closed, its building gone, this church leaves other monuments–Ebenezer, Carrollton, Cross Roads, and Pleasant Hill Baptist Churches and Pine Grove Missionary Baptist Church–five daughters. A dozen or more ministers of the Gospel were sent out from this church. And, in a sense the Pickens Baptist Association was birthed here, as well.

Big Creek Baptist Church was constituted at the beginning of 1829. Brothers Silas Dobbs and Charles Stewart formed the presbytery. Dobbs soon moved on to pastor the Baptist church in Louisville, Mississippi, and served there for many years. Stewart, a planter and politician, pastored the Big Creek Church until his death in 1856, almost 27 years later. His home still stands, a big white house, on route 86 a little to the west of the Big Creek road.

The church adopted as its Articles of Faith and its Rules of Decorum the ones subscribed to by its association, Buttehatchie. The original 14 members were:

Natty Gilmore	Nancy Jones
John Mangum	Agnes Hudspeth
Charles Nall	Rebecca Mangum
Samuel Adair	Jemima Mangum
Matthew Gilmore	Nancy Huggins
Robert McVey	Alecy Johnson
	Rebecca Adair
	Pheobe Clark

Within two months the first African American united with the church. Milly was her name. In September of 1830 Sam, an African American, joined Big Creek by letter. Within a few years about 30, or about one-third of the membership, were African American.

Natty Gilmore and Dempsey White were selected as the first deacons. In July of 1829 church clerk Robert McVey was able to write in the minutes of a church business meeting, "The church...was found to enjoy fellowship and peace." While this was the desired state for this church and others, this was not often the case. Like other Baptist churches of that age, Big Creek disciplined its members. When one was suspected of sins such as intoxication, profanity, theft, dishonest business dealings, infidelity in marriage, conflict with another church member, fighting, or even failure to attend church regularly, charges might be brought. Deacons would be assigned to talk with the person charged. They would report their findings to the church. Generally, if a person was falsely charged, or apologized, the church would "bare with them". If not, then the church would exclude them from the membership. Typically, they did not do this hastily.

As one reads the old minutes of the church, it is interesting to note that often the excluded person would come later and apologize to the church and be reinstated. Also, one notes that members who were "wild" and excluded several times in their youth would sometimes in their mature years become "pillars" of the church.

In 1833 Big Creek has some members exit to form a new congregation, Ebenezer, which is east of Carrollton. Richard Wilkins, one of the ministering elders of the Big Creek Church, became its founding and long-time pastor. This church, in the language of the time, was termed an "arm" of Big Creek prior to becoming an independent congregation. The minutes of 1835 mention the formation of another new arm at the "Cross Roads" meeting house. It will be 15 years before this arm will become the second daughter of Big Creek. (Often a community in those days would construct a meeting house for the general use of its residents. In many cases it would become the incubator for a new church.)

In 1834 Anthony Latham joins the church. He will become a deacon and leader in the church for many decades. The following year John Curry joins. The Curry family will also be leaders in the church for many, many years. The Mullins family also arrives in this time frame.

In 1837 the church licenses the first of many of its members to the Gospel Ministry. Brother Lizenby may have moved on west because he does not appear in the associational records. Then in 1839 Peter, a slave is licensed to preach. In 1843 one finds an action of the church allowing Peter to preach in the meeting house. I assume that this was to the African American members and others. In December of 1848 the church grants a letter to Peter and his wife. The letter notes that he is "a preacher of the Gospel". Note is also made of the fact that he is property of the Estate of Thomas Ivy. One might assume that he and his wife have been sold as a part of the settling of the estate. Montgomery Curry was ordained to preach in 1847. The associational minutes for 1853 lament his death, noting that he has recently moved to the Columbus, Mississippi association. Another who was ordained was Samuel Adair. He seems to have moved to Texas soon. He never pastored here.

Among the many issues in the old church minutes that the modern reader would like to know more about is the exclusion of a member in 1839 for the "killing of a negro". Was this person also punished by the civil authorities? Did he repent for his crime? The reader only knows that a few years later, he is back in the membership of the church, a member who was excluded several more times for various charges such as intoxication, profanity and fighting.

Like many rural churches Big Creek allowed their meeting house to serve other functions. In 1842 the membership allowed a school to be conducted in it. One finds a note in the 1844 minutes that called for allowing the "blacks" to hold worship services in the school house. This is representative of the general mind set in the association in the 1840s of actively seeking to evangelize the African Americans. For the first of several times the minutes reflect a motion that the deacons attend, and by implication, oversee the worship services of the African Americans. In the minutes for 1848 one finds an interesting decision to "arrange for the comfort of the blacks during worship." Does this refer to adding onto the church, building a balcony, separate toilet facilities, or just what? An action of the church in 1853 allowed the African Americans to worship in the meeting house on the 3rd Sunday of each month. It may be that the seeds of Pine Grove Missionary Baptist Church were planted at this time, and it became a kind of "shadow congregation" within Big Creek, another kind of arm." As we will note shortly, the full separation of the congregations will occur about 1866.

Several members, Bostics, Lyons and others are granted letters in 1845 for the purpose of forming a new congregation in Carrollton. Then in 1850 this happens again as Cross Roads is formed. Included were some of the Allens and some of the Mullins.

The minutes for 1843 provide an interesting historical side-light. Note is taken that Henry Petty, who had baptized a person seeking to "letter in" to Big Creek, had been excluded the previous year from "Spring Hill, formerly Pilgrim Rest." This is interesting because Petty had been a major player in a drama that unfolded in the fall of 1837 at the Big Creek meeting house. At the annual meeting of the Union Baptist Association, a division occurred between those churches which opposed working with and contributing to mission boards and those which did not. Petty was the leader of those who were opposed and the pastor of Pilgrim Rest. The opposition later formed a new association, the Pilgrim Rest Primitive Baptist Association. Petty's church was divided on the issue. In 1842 the pro-mission board and pro-Union Baptist Association portion of the church relocated to the Spring Hill community and adopted a new name, apparently reconstituting. (I am not certain of the actual location of the old Pilgrim Rest church. I think it was near Pickensville. The Pilgrim Rest Church building in the Pleasant Hill community was build in 1882 and that church relocated there at that time. It gave its old building to an African American Primitive Baptist congregation.) Pastors Stewart and Wilkins had been the leaders of the pro-mission board forces. I wonder if they were not still at odds with Petty.

In 1851 Brother Ephram, a slave, is allowed "to act in public capacity". I think that this was similar to licensing him to preach. He is later disciplined by the church. In the 1850s and 1860s several of the African American members, like the white ones, are disciplined. But for the most part, it seems that the congregation was even handed in its actions. One evidence of this is that one minister in the congregation was excluded, thus ending his ministerial career, and another was forbidden from preaching for a time. Apparently, he moved on as nothing more is heard of him..

In 1854 Charles Bain, a young man the association had aided in attending Howard College, is ordained by the church. In 1862 one of its deacons, A. A. Spiller is ordained to the ministry. He served many of the churches after that. When Brother Charles Stewart died in 1856 the church memorialized him. He was replaced as pastor by C. B. Sanders. Sanders, as was often the case in that era, was already a member of the church.

During the Civil War 9 men of this church were memorialized for dying in the service of the nation. At the end of the war the church reported 30 male white members, 68 female white members, and 30 freedmen.

In the fall of 1866 the freedmen members of the church ask to be allowed to form a separate congregation. Apparently, by this time many of the freedmen had withdrawn to form their own church, but freedmen members continued in Big Creek until the mid 1870s. In its own history Pine Grove Missionary Baptist church, the fourth arm of Big Creek, recalls that it built a building on the Mack McCully place in 1868 and that Duncan Salmond was pastor of the church.

In 1868 J. H. Curry is licensed to preach. March of 1873 women, for the first time, take a hand in the formal work of the church. Sallie Latham and Martha Jones collect $59.00 for the pastor, G. W. Lyles. In 1875 Hix Chappell begins to preach. He will serve Big Creek for many years and also be a force in the association.

Two additional entries in the minutes books relate to the Pine Grove Missionary Baptist Church. In 1878 and again in 1884 Pine Grove asks to use the meeting house for the annual meeting of the Lebanon Association. My guess is that this was because of the large crowd anticipated. Permission was granted.

In 1895 R. S. Marler unites with the church during a revival. His family had already joined. He would later pastor many churches in the Union and the Tuscaloosa Associations. Another of its pastors was M. G. Lofton. When he died in 1897 Big Creek joined with Forest,

Hebron and Unity in "raising a memorial for him."

In 1916 about 40 members of Big Creek formed the Pleasant Hill Baptist Church about three miles south. It is more convenient for these members, some of whom lived in the Union Chapel community. This was its fifth arm. The founding pastor was J. M. Mills who had formerly pastored Big Creek. The last minutes of the church date from 1917.

The church disappears by 1940. For a short time the association held deed to its property including the cemetery. This was transferred to the Pine Grove Missionary Baptist Church.

Big Creek is no more. But it has left many monuments--churches and people.

I shared this brief article with you for several reasons: (1)To show the sort of thing one can do with the old minutes of our church, many of which we now have readily available on microfilm in our office; (2)To encourage those churches which have not yet taken advantage of the opportunity to have their records microfilmed at no cost: Hebron, Coal Fire, Ethelsville, Flatwoods, Garden, Gordo, Highland, Mount Tabor, New Salem, Plesant Grove, Pleasant Hill, and West End; (3)In this article I focused some on the African American membership in order to encourage the Missionary Baptist Churches of our area to learn more about their heritage by drawing upon the resources of old church minutes; (4) To demonstrate the interconnectedness of our churches; (5) To encourage our churches to study their history: and, (6) To encourage high school and college students to look into writing brief histories about their home church.

HISTORY OF FRIENDSHIP

Churches select names for a variety of reasons. Some select an important biblical place-Mt. Tabor or New Salem. Some draw their name from an area location-Arbor Springs or Reform. Still others select a name that is descriptive of a desired state-New Harmony or Friendship.

This year Friendship is marking its centennial. As the association meets with Friendship this year, we want to join them in this celebration.

We have been welcomed here by their pastor of more than a decade, Bro. Lee Wheat. He and his family live just across the road in a parsonage recently given to the church by the Otis Davidson family. This is just the most recently example of the spirit of friendship being lived out in this congregation.

It has been my observation that this congregation lives up to and gives expression of its name-Friendship is a friendly place. It ministers well to its members, to its community and to the larger area including the association.

In 1907 a group of Baptist began meeting at the Kerr School House, just up the road. Interestingly, Bro. G. W. Kerr, a noted and effective pastor of many churches in our association for many years on either side of 1900, became the first pastor. Soon, he passed the reigns to Bro. J. A. Mitchell, who served until 1920. Mitchell was another of the great ministers of this period of the life the Baptist movement in our area.

The church began with only 11 members. The family names-Pearson, Doughty, Carpenter, McCrary, and Pratt are still present in Baptist life, here and in other congregations of our area. Today it reports 169 members. Across the century hundreds have trusted Jesus and became His followers in this place.

Like so many churches of that era, it had only the one large room. And like others this resulted in issues as Sunday Schools grew. And like many others, the initial solution was to run wires across the room and hang sheets on them to form temporary petitions. While this helped with sight issues, it did little for the sound issues.

Also like many other rural churches, the decade of the Great Depression was very difficult. More and better space was needed, but there was just no money. The faithful folk of Friendship donated old hens, planted plots of crops on "God's Acre" and even planted cotton on the property of the church. (God's heaven must have some very special rewards for the pastors who served faithful during the depression, often spending more to do ministry than they received from churches.)

In time, it was decided that one solution would be to dig a basement under the church. This was not an easy task. Those who participated still testify to its difficulty. But it was done successfully. One innovation was to place the baptistry in the new basement.

Like so many of the churches here, the location of Westinghouse in Reform made the 1950's a great era. There was money to do things that the church needed to have done. The old building was cut down and bricked. Concrete steps replaced older wooden ones. An educational wing was added. And then the fine family life center was built in the 1980's.

Through the years Friendship has been a progressive and missionary church. It has ordained six of its men to the Gospel Ministry: Bro. J. F. Goree, Robert Langdon, Mike Hall, Melvin Mordecai, Reed Shephard, and Billy Jones.

In 1941 Friendship agreed that there was an area about 3 miles to the east which needed a church of its own. A brush arbor was erected and a revival meeting conducted. Out of this effort was birthed the New Salem Baptist Church. For the past three decades plus it has been pastored by one of its sons, Bro. Mike Hall. Through the years their two churches have had a very cooperative relationship, doing many ministries together.

In recent years Johnny McCrary of Friendship has developed a ministry called Round Pin Ministries. In it he works with several horses and shares what he has learned about life from breaking and training horses. He has taken the ministry to over 50 churches across West Alabama. Check his web site: www.roundpenministry.com.

So, this church enters its next century well-housed, well-led, and well-blessed. Certainly, it is a church that lives up to its name.

Friendship Baptist Church, Organized in 1907
Lee Wheat, Pastor

Spring Hill Missionary Baptist Church

Gary Farley

For 165 years there has been a Missionary Baptist Church in Pickens County Alabama with the name Spring Hill. However, the records of the old Union Baptist Association indicate that its roots are older by 10 to 20 years. Early Baptist historian Hosea Holcombe supports this. Writing in 1840 he notes two churches near Pickensville called Pilgrim's Rest. One was "anti-mission board" (Primitive Baptist) and was pastored by Henry Petty. The other supported missions and was pastored by William Manning. My guess is that about 1838 when the missions controversy divided the association, Pilgrim's Rest Church split into two congregations. Apparently, both continued to meet in the same building, near Pickensville, for the next 4 or 5 years. This was possible because in those days most rural Baptist churches gathered to worship and to conduct its business only one weekend per month. In 1841 the Union Association meet at the Pilgrim's Rest church. The representatives of the host church included Col. Thomas Williams.

Then in 1842 the missionary congregation moved to the Spring Hill Academy building, reconstituted itself, took a new name, Spring Hill, and replaced Pilgrim's Rest Missionary in the membership of the Union Association. The new location was on the primary stage road of the area. I suspect that one factor in relocation and name change was its proximity to the Williams family home, leaders in the church. Second, the "anti-board", or Primitive Baptist churches, had formed their association and named it Pilgrim's Rest Association. (I understand that the Williams and the Pettys were related by marriage, so perhaps the desire to lessen family discords was a third factor in this decision.) The church reported 42 members in its letter to the association in 1842 with W. W. Nash as pastor. (He also pastored the neighboring church of Oak Ridge which was located near the Mississippi state line off of the current state route 14.)

There is a note in the minutes of the Union Association for 1855 about the students at Spring Hill Academy collecting jewelry to be sold with the proceeds being given for Foreign Missions.

The next time that the association met with this church was in 1857. Note is made in the associational minutes that the meeting was held in the newly constructed meeting house of the Spring Hill church. So, it appears that the building in which we meet today dates from 1857. The arrangement of the pews reflects the late 19th and early 20th century worship pattern of rural Baptist churches. In the center pews one finds marks of an early practice of separating men and women during worship by a petition. And the pictures on the bulletin board show the gender separated entrances of that era. I have been told that a storm late in the 19th century destroyed the old front of the church and that it needed to be reconstructed. And I have been told that there was once a door behind the pulpit stand through which the slave members entered. In any case this building is the oldest structure in the county where worship continues on a regular schedule, I believe.

Through the 19th century the church was pastored by men whose name appear often in the pages of the associational minutes. And the messengers from the church to the association's annual meetings are names that are still present in the church. Apparently, the church has never had a large membership. And it is likely that the Spring Hill Baptist church located about a mile down the road, an African American congregation, was begun by former members after the Civil War.

In time a village sprang up here, called Archer. It has since passed. The school has closed, but the Spring Hill church continues. In these 160 years the church has produced many fine Christians and several persons have been called from its fellowship into ministry and missions work. Namely, James M. Land, John Hardy Curry, Milton Giles Lofton, Joseph Perry Lee, Lewis M. Stone, and Anne Williams Faulkner.

On February 24, 2002, the church had the pleasure of ordaining Bro. James Moss into the Gospel ministry. In preparation to host this annual meeting extensive work was done on te old schoolhouse which stands just across the road. Messengers enjoyed a wonderful meal in this refurbished building. While still a small rural church, it continues to be faithful. May God bless it today and until our Lord returns.

Picture taken by Dr. Gary Farley,
Brother Mike Hall with camera in foreground
Springhill Church in background, October 8, 2007

The oldest church buildings in Pickens County

BY GARY FARLEY
Pickens Baptist Association

Three of the church buildings here were built prior to the War Between the States – Pickensville UMC, Soule's Chapel UMC and Springhill Baptist Church. Of the three, only Springhill continues to house an active church. The Springhill building dates from 1857.

Its origins lie in the Pilgrim's Rest Baptist Church which was constituted in 1828 and was located on the stage road to Columbus, above Pickensville. When the Baptists divided in 1837 over the issue of whether or not to support mission and benevolent societies, this church was split. For the next five years, however, the two congregations, Primitive and Missionary, continued to share the building. Then in 1842 the Missionary congregation moved about five miles to the east and began meeting in a school building in the Archer community. Two of the primary families in this congregation, Williams and Gates, lived nearby, so it was a natural move. All of the minutes of the business meetings of the Springhill church are on microfilm and available at the office of the Pickens Baptist Association.

The original church house measures about 28 by 40 feet, with a 16 foot ceiling. In more recent times an addition was added with classrooms and bathrooms. The pews are arranged in the shape of a U, the common practice of the 19th Century for rural churches. More recently, the old public schoolhouse was turned into a gathering place for the community. Nearly 200 graves can be found across the road from the church house. There are burials from before the War Between the States, from the war itself, as well as some very recently.

The second Sunday of each August nearly 125 gallons of Brunswick stew is cooked off in a stainless steel pot. Some is eaten at the Homecoming gathering. Some is sold and the income given to support the work of the Baptist Children's Home. Other important annual events are a candlelight service on Christmas Eve and a Sunrise service on Easter morning.

About 1870 the Freedmen portion of the congregation formed another congregation, Springhill Missionary Baptist Church, about two miles west. And about 1880 the Pilgrim's Rest Primitive Baptist Church relocated to the Sapps community. Its old building can still be found there.

Several persons raised in this church have served the Kingdom of God with distinction. One was Lewis M. Stone. He was ordained by the church in 1869. A graduate of Howard College, he served as principal of female colleges in Gainesville, Starkville, Shuqualak, and Meridian. He also pastored several town churches. He was well-respected in both roles. Robert Taylor Hanks was the son of a bivocational pastor who had a farm and a store near Spring Hill. Following the War, he went to Mercer College and Southern Seminary. In 1874 he pastored at Pickensville and then went to Dallas, Texas where he served as pastor of the First Baptist Church and editor of the state Baptist newspaper, *The Baptist Standard.* Ann Williams Faulkner, and her husband John, went to Rhodesia in 1970 as missionaries and retired there in 1999. One of their sons continues this mission heritage.

Historically, Springhill, like other rural churches, served the community within about a three mile radius of its building. And like many other rural churches it has seen the population of its community grow smaller and older since the 1950's. Wisely, the members of Springhill reached out beyond its traditional community and invited residents of the Rivermont community on Lake Aliceville. Several persons from there have joined and are active in the congregation. Also, Springhill has been welcoming to persons who had been wounded in other churches elsewhere in Pickens. Several are now active there. Further, Springhill is blessed with a pastor that fits the congregation. Like most of the pastors in Pickens, Bert Noland gets most of the financial support for his family from secular work. He is an engineer at Phifer Wire. Today, on a typical Sunday morning about 20 persons meet for Bible study and worship. The fellowship is warm. Each fourth Sunday the congregation stays for lunch. The members pray for and serve one another as needed.

Later this month retired graphics arts professor, Joe Harrington, from Troy will be coming to our county to photograph all of the wooden churches here and in Fayette and Lamar counties. Please call me at 367-8632 and let me know about other wooden churches. Thanks.

Three of the church buildings in Pickens County were built prior to the War Between the States – Pickensville UMC, Soule's Chapel UMC and Springhill Baptist Church. Of the three, only Springhill continues to house an active church. The Springhill building, pictured above, dates from 1857.

History of Mt. Pleasant Baptist Church
Gary Farley

About 1840 a good number of persons moved from South Carolina to Pickens and Georgia to settle in the Bear Creek area. Soon they formed a Baptist church, near a spring which served the community and provided a place to baptize those who were being saved. They named it Mt. Pleasant, the name of a church from which many of the members had come. Among the charter members were Elmores, Stricklands, Springers, and Sheltons, names one still finds in our county. The church is first listed in the minutes of the association with Richard Wilkins as pastor in 1843. In 1849 C.B. Sanders became the pastor. W. H. Roberson became pastor in 1851. In 1857 W.R. Scott, a former deacon and clerk at Ebenezer, served as pastor. On through the early years several of the well-known preachers in Pickens served as pastor of the church.

In those days rural Baptist churches normally met one weekend a month for worship and to conduct their business. Members who became worldly were disciplined. Deacons, or a committee, would seek to restore the strayed person. Typically a revival, called a protracted meeting, would be held and new members welcomed to the congregation.

Initially, the church met in a log building. In 1871 it voted to start a Sunday School and add a monthly prayer meeting. Sunday Schools proved to be transformative for this and other rural churches because the congregation now gathered weekly. By contrast the two Primitive Baptist Churches nearby have died.

The second building, a frame one, was constructed about 1904. Like many of our rural churches a graveyard was started on the church property.

Early in the twentieth century, Dr. D.O. Baird was pastor here which he also served as the founding pastor of the new church in Gordo. In the 1950s five Sunday School rooms were added. And in 1959 the church began to have worship every Sunday. In 1972 a new brick building was dedicated. Hershel Owen had become pastor in 1969. Owen served the church for the next 34 years. The church prospered, then suddenly God told him that his ministry there was done. None of us understood at the time. Shortly, he became pastor of Emmanuel in Gordo. It had just gone through a split. He has served there ever since bringing healing and significant growth.

The church called Glenn Sandifer in 2004. The church has constructed all new buildings and has shifted from being in effect a rural church to becoming an effective urban fringe church, serving the new residents of the Gordo area. With the completion of the four-lane US 82 highway this is now happening and will only expand.

Missionary Ulman Moss was raised in this church. He pioneered Southern Baptist work in Venezuela. Leon Elmore, who served many years as the pastor of Holt FBC, grew up in this church. Mike Owen who pastors at Sycamore, AL was licensed by the church. It has long been a strong supporter of the association. In recent years it has been a leader in the shoebox ministry.

History of Reform First Baptist Church
Gary Farley

The decision of the Gulf Mobile and Ohio to build a railroad line across Pickens from Columbus to Tuscaloosa changed, profoundly, life in Pickens. New towns were established with businesses, industries, and new churches. The decision to build a second line from Reform to Mobile extended this impact. Soon the new towns of Ethelsville, Reform, Gordo, Aliceville, and Cockran became centers of commerce and residence. Many rural people relocated from the farm to town.

Reform had been a crossroads community for several decades in the nineteenth century. A post office was opened there in 1842, some 24 years after the death of Lorenzo Dow. So the Methodist version of the source of the name of the town is probably not true. The Baptist version which has Hosea Holcomb as the one telling the residents to reform is more probable. He is known to have been in the county prior to his death in 1840.

The leaders of our association, having seen the impact of a railroad line in southern Lamar County, moved quickly to plant a church in the town of Reform. The mission began in 1898 with J.W. Caldwell as mission pastor. The church was given a lot on which to build. In 1902 Dr. D.O. Baird, a crippled veteran of the Civil War, a medical doctor, and popular pastor became the pastor of the new church at Reform as well as at Gordo and also at Mt. Pleasant. He stayed until his death in 1910. The next year a tornado struck and the first church building was destroyed. Tragedy struck again in 1959 when the second building was burned. The current building was dedicated in 1960.

This November the 500th anniversary of the Protestant Reformation will be celebrated. This was when Martin Luther challenged the practices of the medieval Roman Catholic Church. Ours is the only town in the United States named Reform.

Reform has been served by some excellent pastors through the years. Ones that I have known include Neil Nichols, a distant cousin of mine, John Faulkner who left to serve as a missionary in Africa, Bill Wallace, who completed his ministry as DoAM for Cahaba Association, and Brannon Pinion, who served the church three times for a total of more than 15 years. Like most of our town churches, its age of largest attendance was in the 1970s when employment in local factories swelled the population of the towns. Since then Pickens, like many rural places, has been de-industrialized. New industrial development is anticipated, along with suburbanization, as US 82 is four laned across the county. Reform and the church may blossom again.

Most towns in the South as large as Reform have a second Baptist Church. Here New Salem, about three or four miles out in the country serves that role for the town, as does Stansel. At the time of this writing the church is without a pastor.

History of Bethlehem Baptist Church
Pickens Baptist Association
Gary Farley

We meet in the 173rd annual meeting at Bethlehem, a congregation of the same age. Bethlehem did not join with our association until 1849, however. It, like Mt. Tabor and Zion, both in the northeastern part of Pickens County were initially affiliated with the Tuscaloosa Association.

Unfortunately, the early record books of Bethlehem have been lost or destroyed. However, a study of the annual reports from Bethlehem reveal something about its membership and leadership during its early years. Like most rural church of the 1840s its membership was small and has been so most of its life. In the early years this was a community of small farms and large families. Today most of the residents work public jobs in near towns. Bethlehem has often hosted the annual meetings of the association. D. O. Baird, a stalwart leader of the association and pastor of its churches, hailed from this community and practiced medicine there. Bethlehem was also the home church of Brother James Swedenburg. He had a distinguished career as pastor of many country churches, head of the predecessor of ALCAP, and a school teacher. He planted churches and led in the constructions of new church buildings across the association. Two of his four children, James and Mary, served as Baptist missionaries in Asia.

Other well-known former pastors are Erskin Stripling, Ronnie Elmore, Houston Crowley, Elliott Gray, James Cunningham, John Cox, C. A. Bryant , and J. M. Mills.

The church building was destroyed by fire in 1989. The state convention provided a mobile chapel for the church during this time. Most of this beautiful house of worship was constructed about 1990. And with a new building came a new energy and growth during the pastorate of Ronnie Elmore. Membership grew and educational rooms had to be added. Often 200 persons would come for Sunday morning worship.

Soon conflict over worship arose and many people left. Bethlehem became a small church again. Since 1999 Lindsay Watkins has served as pastor. The church works hard at witnessing to, winning, and serving its community.

Those of you who came to Bethlehem today from the south witnessed one of the most awe inspiring sites in our area. It seems that as one approaches Bethlehem it just arises form the ground on the horizon. My heart is thrilled each time that I see this

In the data about our churches for the past year you will find data about the current membership and work of Bethlehem. Be sure to thank the membership for hosting us this year.

History of Stansel Baptist Church
Pickens Baptist Association
Gary Farley

We are meeting in the newly redecorated church building of Stansel. This congregation dates from 1897 and was first named Union Center. At that time the association was named Union and this place was near the geographical center of the association. In part because of its location in continues to e a popular meeting place for the association. It has hosted the annual meeting on several occasions and has been the only home of the annual Senior Adult Revival.

Soon after the church was constituted with 18 members, the Carrollton Short-line Railroad built through the community, just a few feet behind the church building. A train station and post office were located here and named Stansel for a leading attorney in Carrollton, a leader for the railroad, and the son of a pioneer Baptist pastor. Many wonderful stories are told about startled preachers and the arrival of a train during services.

The church experienced a great season of revival in 1915 with 32 additions, 28 by baptism. Membership peaked that year at 102, only to slip back in a couple of years. Times seem to have been tough during the depression. World War II saw many sons and daughters joining the armed forces, or otherwise involved in the war effort. A good many returned with a commitment to Jesus and to the church. Stansel prospered as it worked hard at reaching and disciplining the folk in its community.

The location of a major Westinghouse plant between Stansel and Reform meant that jobs were available. So was money to pay for expanding activity by the Stansel church.

A new church building was erected in 1946 and a pastorium in 1952. In 1954 an educational wing was added to the church. Then in 1976 another pastorium was built. And in 2003 a family life center was added.

The church has long had a heart for missions. Raised in the church Fred Findley, Jr. He and his wife went in 1980 as missionaries to Uganda. And in retirement the J. T. Simpsons served as mission volunteers in Washington and in New England. They played a key role in the development of the homeplace of Luther Rice as a shrine for those interested in our Baptist History to visit. (Rice played a key role in our involvement in missions and in the formation of a national Baptist denominational organization).

The church has also had several of its sons go into the pastoral ministry–J. M. Mills, R. S. Marler and J. W. Bouchillon. Mills and Marler had long and effective ministries in this area.

More than 40 men have served as pastors of Stansel across the years. The church is currently in the process of finding a pastor. For information about the current membership and activities of the Stansel church, look in the reports about our churches in your messenger packet. And thank a member for hosting us this year.

Historical Sketch of
Cross Roads Baptist Church
Pickens County, Alabama

As good missionary Baptists the old church at Big Creek extended an "arm" into the next community in the mid-1840s. By June 1, 1850 the congregation in the Cross Roads community had attained enough strength that a decision was made to form a congregation. Bro. Charles Stewart, the long-time pastor at Big Creek took charge of the new congregation. The charter members totaled 23. Uriah Allen and Uriah Mullins became the deacons. The following Fall the church became a member of this association. The name for the church was taken from the fact that roads connecting Columbus, Demopolis, Fayette, and Eutaw junctioned in the community. The Mullins ran an inn for travelers on these roads.

The church prospered. When war came three of its young men died from wounds suffered during the Civil War--B. F. West, John Mullins, and B.F. Mullins. They were memorialized in the minutes of the church. Several freedmen left the church in 1870 to form the Mt. Pleasant Missionary Baptist Church.

Like most rural churches of that day, the first building was a logs. The subsequent frame building was destroyed by a tornado. The present building stems from the vision of Bro. James Swedenburg, a church building in our association back in 1948. It has developed across the years and sits on a five acre tract. Out front is an ample cemetery. What a beautiful place!

Many fine pastors have served this church. In the first century, most preached there one weekend each month. Included were J. N. Acker, James DeLoach, Dabney Duncan, W. H. Robertson,, J. M. Land, J. P. Lee, G. W. Kerr, J. A. Mitchell, Jesse McCallister, J. A. Estes, Henry G. Carpenter, J. S. Sansing, W. A. McCain, E. U. Calvert, Renfroe Curry, James Swedenburg, Chester Free, George Norris, Paul Osborne, W. O. Burkhalter, E. G. Pounders, Willie Crawford, James Fletcher, Arthur Cheung, Charles Whitney, Bill Webb, Jonny House,
Paul Shaw, and Rickey Jackson who has served here since May of 1999.

This church has hosted the association many times in its 159 years. It welcomes us again.
In the statistical data found in your packet you can learn more about its membership and its current work.

Historical Sketch
Flatwoods Baptist Church
Pickens County, Alabama

This church traces its history back to 1883. In that year our association met at Grant's Creek Baptist Church and Flatwoods asked to become a member. The pastor was J.S. Shirley and the clerk was J. M. Parker. The membership was 32. The following year the membership had grown to 56. In 1888 the church hosted the annual meeting of the association. From the beginning, Sunday School has been a major focus of the church. And like other rural churches of that day it conducted worship services only one weekend each month. The early minutes of the church were burned in a home fire in 1939, so many questions about the early days remain unanswered. We do know that there was a Baptist Church in the nearby sawmill town of Pioneer at an earlier time. Perhaps, the origin of Flatwoods can be found there. Further, it may well have been an "arm" of the Mt. Pleasant, or of the Corinth Church.

When the Sipsey association was formed in 1890, Flatwoods moved to that body, but in 1897 returned to our association. In 1900 the congregation voted to build a one-room building. Like many rural churches it struggled through the Great Depression and World War II, but gained members and resources after peace returned. In 1945 a second weekend of worship was added. In 1948 a cemetery was opened. The following year the timber on the church property was cut, turned into boards and used for the construction of a new house of worship.

Soon the need for Sunday School class space was addressed with the addition of rooms. And in 1965 the church became a full-time church with worship every Sunday. In 1980 the church build a parsonage. In 1999 the sanctuary was enlarged. And most recently a fellowship hall has been added. The church is serving a growing community and its future appears bright.

God has called several ministers from this congregation–J. I. Ray, J. S. Pate, Albert Cabiness, Elliot Gray, Thomas Smothers, Derrell Crimm, and Randy Gray. And the church has been served by several excellent pastors. The current pastor is Bro. Leonard Hill. More than 130 persons have been baptized into the Flatwoods church across the years. You can look up the current membership and other important information about Flatwoods in the statistics found in your packet.

Gordo FBC History
Gary Farley

When the Union Baptist Association met in the Shiloh church in Greene County in early fall of 1899, Dr. D. O. Baird listened as the Executive Committee reported about the associational mission wor of the past year and the challenges of the coming one. He heard Brother W. L. White tell of the growth c a new town, Gordo, as the railroad line was building across Pickens County. Two hundred persons were already settled there. The Methodists and the Presbyterians were actively forming congregations in Gordo. White continued that some Baptist families were issuing the Macedonian call–come and help us start a church in Gordo. He argued that this was Baptist territory and a Baptist church needed to be formed, indeed.

Brother Baird was next on the program. His task was to preach the annual missions sermon. He had been selected for this task during the previous annual associational meeting so he had a year to reflect and prepare. His selection was both a tradition and an honor. Since 1839 and the split between the missionary and the anti-missionary Baptists, some prominent and well-loved minister had spoken to the association in support of missions at each annual meeting. Baird was then already 67 years of age. He was serving as the pastor of five churches in the association–Arbor Springs, Bethlehem, Kennedy, Millport, and Liberty. For more than 40 years he has pastored rural churches in both Columbus and Union Associations. In addition he was a licensed medical doctor. I have been told that he was somewhat crippled, perhaps the result of a wound received during the Civil War. Based on the picture of him that appears with his obituary in the 1910 issue of the associational annual, he was a slender, handsome man with thinning gray hair. His obituary states that he was a popular preacher and a key leader in the life and ministry of the association. On several occasions he had been sent to represent the association at the annual meeting of the Southern Baptist Convention.

During the year of 1898–1899 Dr. Baird had ample opportunity to see mission work first hand. South of his home near Bethlehem church a railroad line was being built across the county connecting Columbus and Tuscaloosa. The association, with the assistance of the state convention, was reviving the old South Carolina church in the new town of Ethelsville and planting a new congregation in the new town of Reform. Baird conducted a revival at Ethelsville during that year. Certainly, he recognized better than most just how the railroad would impact social and economic life in a community, because two of the churches that he was then pastoring, Millport and Kennedy, were products of church planting efforts less than a decade before when another rail line was built between Columbus and Fayette. In each case the church and town were thriving.

The associational minutes tell us that when he stood to preach his text was taken from the Ezekiel 37 passage which speaks of the challenge to bring life to dried bones. Surely, he built upon this theme to stress the importance of creating a church, a vital local expression of the body of Christ in Gordo. He may well have shared his insights from experiences in Ethelsville, Reform, Millport and Kennedy. I suspect that as sometimes happened, Baird preached to himself that day even more than to the crowd. We know the results. He experienced a call to a mission task. He must go to Gordo and plant a church. This was the call of God upon him.

Certainly there were many good reasons why this should not be so. He was nearing the biblical definition of old age, 70. He was well settled. He was pastoring 5 church that needed him. He was physically impaired. But in spite of all of this he answered the call.

Initially, his friend and fellow leader of the association, W. L. White, began holding evening services one Sunday a month in Gordo. Latter Baird cultivated these efforts and in the summer of 1901 the Gordo church was constituted with Baird as pastor. In the fall the new church united with the association. Baird continued as the pastor of Gordo Baptist until 1909. Ill and in his 80th year he resigned and then died soon thereafter. He must have planted well or else we would not be here.

The church began with only 15 members. In 1911 it counted 65; 1921, 151; 1931, 175; 1941, 204; 1951, 286; 1961, 394; 1971, 496; 1981, 450; 1991, 387; and 2000, 430. Across the years it contributed members to at least two new churches in Gordo For the first 20 years or so, the church had weekly Sunday Schools and preaching services once a month. For about the next 30 years it had worship twice a month, and for the past half century it has been a full time church. A total of 33 men have served as pastors of this church. Only one served a longer tenure than Dr. Baird. This was James Jordon from 1978 to 1987. Many of these men have made and are making other significant contributions to the Kingdom of God.

When the church celebrated its centennial in 2001, Bro. Marc Howard moved to Mississippi and is now the DoAM for Lee Association. Bro. Pat Powell came as interim and then as pastor and left in 2008 to be pastor at Emmanuel in Tuscaloosa. Soon, David Singleton came as pastor. He is currently working on a master's degree from Liberty university online. Currently the church has two worship services on Sunday morning. It is planning to expand its facilities in order to reach its growing community.

Last year it reported 246 resident members and averaged 167 in worship. Gordo First hosted the annual meeting of the association in 1925, 1949, 1960, 1966, 1971, 1977, 1982, 1987, 1993, 1999, and today. We thank the church and its pastor for the hospitality we are experiencing.

Finally, while there is much to rejoice in as the past is remembered, a future of great opportunity awaits. The four-laneing of US 82 will open up Gordo to more families who will live here and commute to jobs in Tuscaloosa. There will be additional new fields that are "white unto harvest". The church has an excellent plan for expanding and improving facilities.

Please, remember that this church was born out of a mission vision. It has been nurtured by faithful and effective servants. But it cannot rest upon the past. It must comprehend and move toward an even greater future.

History of Ethelsville Baptist Church
Gary Farley

Founded in 1824 as the South Carolina Baptist Church, this is the second oldest congregation of our association. Initially, it was located near Yorkville, a crossroads town about a mile west of here. Bro. Jacob Crocker was its first pastor.

During the first decade of its life it formed two new congregations, Mt. Moriah and Providence, to serve other emerging settlements nearby. (Mt. Moriah became a Free Will Baptist Church ca 1850 and was replaced by Mineral Springs ca 1855 in our association. Providence closed ca 1890 and was replaced by Hickory Grove.)

Like other rural and village Baptist churches of that period, this church held services one weekend per month. On Saturday they met to attend to the business of the church which sometimes involved identifying and seeking to restore inactive members and those who were not living a good Christian lifestyle. The idea was for the church to be in harmony so that it could worship on the following Sunday.

And like other churches serving a community where plantation agriculture was practiced, some of the early members were slaves. For example, in 1849 the members were 79, of whom 27 were African Americans. Among the pastors of this era were many of the pioneers of our association-Charles Stewart, Tristan Thomas, Dabney Duncan, and William Spraggins. Duncan and Spraggins were licensed by this church for the ministry. In 1870 the freedmen were dismissed by letter, I assume to form what is now Mt. Olive Missionary Baptist church, or perhaps Halbert or Baptist Grove, or El Bethel.

The South Carolina church remained small and seems to have struggled in the decades surrounding the turn of the century. Some years they did not find a pastor to lead the church. Then about 1900, when the railroad line was built through the county and the towns of Ethelsville, Reform, and Gordo were formed, this church moved to Ethlesville and changed its name. Again, some of the well-known pastors of this era were J. M. Cox, G. W. Kerr, G. M. Lyles, J. M. Mills, and W. J. Godfrey.

About 1920 Ethelsville along with Mineral Springs, Hickory Grove and Pine Grove agreed to form a *field of churches*. H. H. Buzbee pastored each of these churches lending worship on alternate Sundays. A parsonage was built in Ethelsville. By this time each of the churches, however, had Sunday Schools every Sunday. He was followed in this arrangement by Q. D. Haney C. H. Morgan, and W. S. Creezan. Some growth in membership was experienced in the 1920's.

Then tragedy struck. The church burned to the ground in 1934 when a fire on the lawn got out of control. This was during the Great Depression and times were hard. A new building was not dedicated until in 1938. During the pastorate of Donald Strickland in the following years, the church had good growth. Other well-known local pastors-J. Wages, Amon Kelly, and Chester Free followed. By the late 1950's the church had, for the first time, a membership of more than 100. The church, like most others, moved to having worship every Sunday during this time. And the church decided to build a new brick building.

In 1971 Bro. Jimmy Ray came as pastor and continued in the position for nearly 30 years. His ministry was blessed and very effective. The building was expanded. Like his predecessors he served bivocationally. In 1999 he resigned and was followed by Bro. David Westmoreland. The current pastor, Mel Howton, came in 2003. The church redid and expanded its worship center. Bro. Mel is working on a master's degree from Liberty University and also drives a school bus. The church continues to grow and do well. Last year the church reported 140 resident members and 115 in weekly worship. It looks forward to celebrating its bicentennial in 2024.

This church hosted the annual meeting of our association in 1865 and again in 1952, 1963, 1982, 1993, 1999, and today. We express our thanks to the church and to its pastor for the hospitality which we have received.

History of West End Baptist Church
Aliceville, Alabama
Gary Farley
Fall 2012

When the ATN railroad was built from Reform, Alabama toward Mobile in the first decade of the Twentieth Century, the company planted a town and named it Aliceville. In the 1920s an east-west line was built through the town, and a yarn plant was placed in the town by Alabama Mills. As was the case, often, the milling company also constructed housing for families whose adults worked in the mill.

As in most small towns the First Churches tended to be populated by the business and professional people. They had little success in reaching the mill hands. In Aliceville the pastors and leaders attempted to address this by moving the abandoned Franconia Presbyterian building from a rural setting and setting it up in the mill village. This was in 1935. The building served as a community center and as the home of a union Sunday School.

In 1939 the legendary Pickens County Baptist minister, Bro. James Swedenburg, Sr., held a successful revival in the building and a few months later constituted a new congregation with 20 charter members. It took the name of West End Baptist Church. The congregation met twice a month for worship. By August of 1941 it grew to 61 members and became a member of the Pickens Baptist Association.

In its tenth year the church bought land adjoining the community building where it was meeting and erected a building of its own into which West End moved in 1951. The church began having services every Sunday and birthed the basic programs of SBC churches—Sunday School, Training Union, Brotherhood, and WMU. The initial deacon body included W. H. Wolfe, A. G. Dillard, and Lester Kizzire. E. B. Carroll soon joined them.

In 1956, after 16 years Bro. Swedenburg resigned. Soon our friend David Barrentine came as the first resident pastor. During his pastorate the membership reached 263 resident members. West End formed a mission in the apartments located at the old prisoner of war camp and called Gerald Davis, who would go on to have a distinguished missionary career in the Philippines, to pastor the mission congregation.

In the 1960s the well-known names of Ralph Windle, Jr., and James Auchimuty appear in the records. The latter had a long career at Shades Crest in Birmingham. Bro. Ralph served well in West Alabama and East Mississippi. In 1965 the church building and its parsonage were badly damaged by a tornado. Along with the repair work an educational unit was added. In 1970 the church was again damaged, this time by a hail storm.

Also in 1970 the church established a Christian School. It met in an old town school building for two years but did not prosper. During the 1970s Bro. Jimmy Wilson proved to be a very effective pastor at the church. During the summer of 1976 Bro. Michael Griffin served as the summer youth worker. That year was one of the most fruitful in the life of the church.

In 1983 and for the next 14 years the men of West End went to build a church or related building on the mission field each summer. Bro. Charles Ashcraft was the leader. In the winter of 1987 the church suffered a serious fire. The fellowship hall was destroyed and worship was moved to the Aliceville Middle School. Soon the current CLC building replaced it.

In 1990 our own Bro. Jack House came to pastor West End. Then in 1993 Mike Griffin came as pastor. He remained for 11 years. He was followed by Bro. David Falgout for three years. Then Bro. Jack House came out of retirement to resume pastoring at West End. Membership 194 in 2011.

As with similar communities throughout the South the mill at Aliceville closed. Jobs were hard to find. New families did not come to Aliceville. However, with the opening of the Federal Prison and a wood pellet plant in the community, many hope that the population of Aliceville will grow, that West End will reach many of the new people, and that it will grow and do well. That is the prayer of us all.

History of Emmanuel Baptist Church,
Gordo, Alabama
Gary Farley
Fall 2012

In the fall of 1989, sensing a need to form a different kind of Baptist Church for the Gordo community, Pastor Bill Schrimsher and Deacons Jack Fair, Jimmy Garner, John Moss, and James Moss and their families withdrew from Gordo First Baptist and launched a new congregation. Initially, it met in a former Coca Cola bottling plant. On March 18, 1990 the church was constituted as Emmanuel with 33 charter members.

The new congregation petitioned to become a member of the Pickens Baptist Association and of the Alabama Baptist Convention. After a careful study by the Credentials Committee, the new church was accepted. A year later the congregation purchased a very visible piece of land on U.S. 82 on the north side of the town. In July of 1991 a mobile chapel was loaned to the church by the state convention and placed on this piece of land.

The founding pastor resigned at this point and the church called as pastor Bro. Mike Trull. He was a young man raised in the area who had recently been called into the ministry. The church grew under Bro. Trull. In the summer of 1992 Emmanuel build an educational building, and the chapel was returned to the state convention to be used to plant another church by the end of 1992.

Emmanuel not only launched a Sunday School but the whole set of standard Southern Baptist programs—Discipleship Training, WMU, and Brotherhood. VBS drew many children to the hillside. A special memory was the first baptismal service in September of 1993, held in the swimming pool of Jerrell Holley.

During 1996 the beautiful sanctuary that we are meeting in today was built. The design was the idea of Jack Fair. I have commended him many times on the utility of this worship space. This new facility seems to have spurred grow and additional educational and fellowship space were added soon. Worship attendance swelled to about 200 on Sunday mornings.

But, Pastor Trull fell under the influence of Evangelist Phillip Kidd of Mississippi. Kidd was an Independent Baptist whose views on race relations were stuck in the 1950s. This became divisive as Pastor Trull preached these views and announced that he was going to lead the church out of the association and out of SBC life. This issue divided the congregation pretty much down the middle.

Miraculously, it seemed to me and others, Pastor Trull and his followers decided at the last moment to withdraw, buy an old funeral home about four miles north, and formed the Calvary Independent Baptist Church. This was in October of 2001. Two months earlier Bro. Hershel Owen, after a 34 year pastorate at nearby Mount Pleasant, was led by God to resign. Emmanuel turned to Bro. Owen in November 2001 and he has served as pastor since. In my view, God, of course, knew what was going to happen and was putting his plan for Emmanuel into motion.

The church was rather static for about five years, in part rebuilding its reputation in the community. But in the past few years it has regained its numerical strength. Its fellowship is vibrant. Its financial position is strong. It is now giving more than 20 percent of its undesignated offerings to mission causes. Membership was 202 in 2011.

Back when I was teaching Sociology at Oklahoma Baptist University, I did a study for the Home Mission Board on Baptist churches in towns the size of Gordo. I found that most of the towns has a second Baptist Church. A major reason was that the population was so diverse that one congregation had difficulty in embracing everyone. The second, and sometimes a third, meant that we had churches that meet the needs and preferences of different people. They often served as kind of a pressure valve making congregational peace more probable.

History of Highland Baptist Church
Gordo, Alabama
Gary Farley
Fall 2013

In writing a short of history of West End and of Emmanuel for last year's meeting, I mentioned that throughout the South as the first church in the community grew and as the town grew and became more diversified, in most every case a second Baptist Church was formed. This was true in Aliceville, and it was true in Gordo. (In Reform nearby country churches filled this role. And the same is true in Carrollton.)

Highland was the second Baptist Church for Gordo. It was organized in 1951 by a Baptist sub-denomination lead by J. Frank Norris, controversial pastor of First Baptist Church, Ft. Worth, Texas. Its focal field was the Hollywood Mobile Home Park. Its initial membership was comprised of working class folk who were different in social status and worship style from those who attended First Baptist. The willingness of Baptist to embrace churches which were not all alike is, to my mind, one of the primary reasons for our success.

After a few years, however, the church turned to Brother Eugene Brown as pastor. He was a loyal Southern Baptist and in 1955 the church petitioned the association for membership and was accepted. In 1957 it changed its name to Highland. The church struggled along until Bro. Chester Free became pastor in 1966. He stayed for 21 years. Bro. Chester is well-remembered by many of us. To my mind he is the quint-essential Baptist minister of my youth. Outgoing, loving, generous, passionate about sharing the Gospel with everyone. He knew no strangers. He married over 1,000 couples and buried more than 1,000. His baptisms topped both figures. Once I asked him what advise he gave to young ministers. "As you go visiting always carry a box and a poke (sack). People will want to give you things. Take them. If you do not need them, someone down the road will." Great advice. And it reflects the spirit of Bro. Chester.

Through the years Highland developed a niche ministry in the form of holding several Southern Gospel Concerts each year. Ricky Morris was and is the driving force of this ministry. Many of the well-known groups—the Lesters, the Lewis Family, the New Spears, the Talley Trio, and many others have been featured.

And it developed a very strong youth program. This in turned resulted in at least eight young men and two young women entering the ministry. Shawn McDaniel, the current pastor, played a key role in this, as did Joey Lucas who is now the pastor of Stansel.

In 1986 the church added classrooms and a fellowship hall. More recently in 2011 it added a much larger fellowship hall to accommodate its youth programs. This year it became the first of our churches to participate in the Fathers-in-the-Field program. Dewayne Dunn is heading this up.

Since Highland has grown too large to be led by a bivocational pastor alone, it has wisely added to the staff with other bivocationals, Bro. Brannon Pinion and Bro. James White. The resident membership stands at 565. No baptisms last year. There were 3 new members by letter.
Total undesignated receipts were $149,981.00. We are grateful to Highland for hosting the association this year.

History of Pickensville First Baptist Church
Pickensville, Alabama
Gary Farley
Fall, 2013

A town was formed here by 1820 as the first planters settled along the Tombigbee River. Goods came up the river from Mobile and cotton was shipped down the river to the port of Mobile. It was the first seat of government for Pickens County. Stores, warehouses, hotels, schools, saloons and a Methodist Church were established. Lawyers, blacksmiths, and physicians set up shop here. Slaves were brought here and sold to planters.

Baptists were slow in coming to towns in those days. Pilgrim's Rest Baptist Church was located about two miles north of the town. It numbered in its membership the famous slave preacher Job. The missionary minded members of that church left it to form Oak Ridge further north and Springhill to the northeast by 1842. Big Creek Baptist Church was located six or so miles to the east. And to the south was Enon in the Garden community. The river was a barrier to potential church outreach to the west. It was not until 1847 that the Baptists formed a church in Pickensville.

Among the founders of the Baptist church in Pickensville was Dr. A.M. Wilkins and A.P .Bush. (Pictures of his home and of the early Baptist and Methodist church buildings can be found on the Library of Congress website, dating from 1937.)

Early pastors of the church included three presidents of the Pickensville Female Institute—J. W. Taylor, L. M. Stone, Jr., and J. G. Nash. In those days most rural and village Baptist Churches held worship only once a month. So, the pastor at Pickensville also might pastor Springhill, Enon, and Carrollton. In 1873 R. T. Hanks pastored the church in Pickensville. He had been raised in the church and his father had pastored it. He had graduated from both Mercer University and the Southern Baptist Seminary. He moved on to Texas and became a leader of Baptists there serving as pastor of the First Baptist Churches in Dallas, Abilene, and El Paso. He was also editor of the Baptist Standard. Another pastor of this era was Matthew Lyons, a lawyer, editor and writer. He went on to serve churches in Mississippi and Tennessee and edited the state Baptist paper there. Buried in the Upper Cemetery is the body of Sardine Hildreth who pastored this church and several others in the association, as well as serving as moderator for 9 years. His daughter Lillie was the first female messenger to the annual meeting of the association.

With the coming of railroads, river traffic declined. Planters shipped their cotton by rail and the town plateaued. The Female and a Male Institute closed as public education developed. The seat of county government was moved to Carrollton.

During the First World War the church ceased to hold regular worship services. But, two determined women, Mrs. M. J. Yagle and Mrs. Idona Yagle, went to pastor J. M. Mills over at Pleasant Hill and enlisted him to come and get the church up and going again. He did. It did. A weekly Sunday School was formed with newly converted M. J. Yagle as Superintendent. In 1930, J. Renfroe Curry, who also pastored Carrollton, came as pastor and stayed until 1947. It was during this time that the O. A. Stapp family moved from Carrollton to Pickensville. They provided leadership for both the church and the community for many years.

In 1958 the old antebellum church building was replaced by a brick one which now serves the youth of the church as a meeting place. In 1966 the church began worshiping every Sunday. In 1989 a parsonage was built and the family of pastor Billy Little were the first occupants. In 1992 pastor Tim Jones arrived.

The nature of the community changed with the building of the Tenn-Tom waterway about 1980. With its opening in 1985 came recreation seekers to campgrounds and the development of subdivisions such as Rivermont and Pumpkin Creek. The bridge over the river opened up a field for work to the west. Pastor Tim and the church assimilated new people with the long-time residents of the community. The congregation has grown. A new educational building was added in 1993 honoring the Stapp family. Then this auditorium was added in 1995. More recently in 2012 a fellowship hall was opened.

Pastor Jones continues to serve the church bivocationally and travels a good bit some weeks. This is made possible by some strong lay leaders who do the work of the church in his absence. Typically about 150 worship here on a given Sunday.

The waterway has not generated the growth of industry in Pickensville that was envisioned when it was built. Nor has the opening of the Federal Prison nearby. Perhaps as the Baby Boomers retire more people will retire on the lake. Three African American congregations also serve the community. The United Methodist church closed more than a decade ago.

This past year the church reported the following: 301 resident members; 3 baptisms; 12 by letter; $159,260.16 in undesignated gifts.

The story of this church is one of being constituted to serve the residents of a small town during the time prior to the Civil War. In its first two decades the membership included both free and slave members. The membership was comprised of business and professional persons as well as farmers living nearby. During its first several decades the town prospered, as did the church. Then changes in the economy and how things were transported and retailed brought decline in both. The changes in time brought a different pattern of how people lived and worshiped. Today there are only a handful of businesses in the town. Many of the persons work in places other than the community. Others are retired. The church has successfully adjusted to the changes and is no longer what it was even 50 years ago. Most of the members drive into the church from more than three miles. Most of the members did not grow up in this community or in this church. Most of the children will not spend their lives here. Apparently, instead of longing for “the good old days” this church has adjusted to these new realities. And God has blessed. The church has prospered.

Personally, I attribute much of this to the personality and ability of the pastor and his family. Coupled with this is that he has stayed the course and is now in his 22nd year of ministry here. We thank this church for hosting the association this year.

History of Arbor Springs Baptist Church
Reform, Alabama
Gary Farley
Fall, 2014

Many of the churches which were born in the 19th Century can trace their origin to an arbor, a temporary structure with boughs of trees placed on a frame, mostly as a shelter from the sun. For some the arbor was connected to an annual camp meeting like today at Unity Grove. For others it was a community revival, which proved to be successful and a continuing church grew out of it.

Further, many rural churches selected as a location for their building a site near a spring. Among our affiliated congregations Arbor, Mineral, and Springhill are obvious. Liberty, Friendship, Crossroads, Hebron, and Mt. Pleasant are others. In that era a spring was a landmark, a place of refreshment, of meeting and a place where baptizing might be held. (Here the mill pond of the Rozelle's mill seems to have been the preferred location.)

Arbor Springs lists its date of founding as November 6, 1872. For many years it was known as New Arbor Springs. So, like some others of our churches it did not survive the losses related to the War Between the States—men who died, families that pulled up stakes and moved on west, and the grim economic situation of the time. In the minutes of the association one finds Arbor Springs being formed in 1848, uniting with the association, and sending messengers to the annual meeting headed by pastor T. S. Thomas along with J.M. Deloach. So, Arbor Springs like Pine Grove, Pleasant Hill, Hickory Grove, and perhaps Flatwoods, was a re-start near where an earlier church had closed.

Like many other churches of the 19th Century, Arbor Springs became the location of a cemetery. The earliest confirmed burial there is that of William Hammett who died in the Civil War. The land was acquired from Uriah Mullins, I think an ancestor of Gene Mullins and among the founders of Crossroads. He and his wife are buried here. The deed mentions an old building which was used both as a school and as a meetinghouse.

Ms. Joyce Hester transcribed the minutes of the church from 1872 in 1998 and gathered the information found in this historical sketch. As I read the minutes, I was struck by the fact that many of the family names have been here and in neighboring churches since the beginning—McDaniel, Bonner, Shelton, Keating, McCray, Richardson, Carpenter, and Wilkins. In fact the Wilkins family provided early pastors and leaders for both of the churches hosting the association this year.

The first pastor of this church was G. M. Lyles who is buried at Mineral Springs. Like most pastors of that era, he often held four pulpits. He would come to Arbor Springs one Sunday a month. On the Saturday prior to that Sunday there would be a worship service and a business meeting. Generally, this included accepting new members by letter, granting letters to those who might be moving away, appointing messengers to associational meetings, and spending money.

Sometimes charges regarding the moral conduct of members and/or notice of the failure of members to attend the church services were dealt with. Typically, a committee would be formed to go and talk with the person about the charges. Often the person would come to the next business meeting, be forgiven, and get straightened up. Other times a person refused, and they were excluded from the membership. Often these persons would attend a revival meeting, be changed and come back into the church. Cursing, intoxication, conflict with a neighbor, dancing, and failure to attend were most common, but some cases of adultery are also found in the notes. It appears that the purposes of this process were to keep members on track, to address issues that threatened the peace of the community, and guard the fellowship. (In most communities there were persons, particularly men, who did not join a church primarily because they were not willing to accept the discipline of the church.

The building we are meeting in today is the third home of this church. It was built in 1955. It replaced an earlier wooden one from 1890. The first was a log building. The fellowship hall dates from 1989.

Dr. D. O. Baird, a pioneer physician and preacher, held his membership in this church for many years and served as pastor also. He lived in the Bethlehem community. Many of you know pastors of a more recent time—Tom Collins, Chester Free, Barry Holland, Ralph Windle, Jr., William Dawkins, Don Moore, and Mike Owen. Several pastors were raised in the church including J.A. Estes, Roy Bonner, Edward Bonner, Grady Bowles, Amon Kelly, Gary Shelton, Clyde Stevens, Cleon Kyles, and the current pastor, Larry Shelton.

Like others of our churches Arbor Springs has had the basic organizations—Sunday School, Discipleship Training, WMU, and Brotherhood. The minutes tell of protracted, or revival, meetings in the early years with tens of persons professing faith and being baptized. In its letter to the association last year, they reported the following: 120 resident members; 3 baptisms; 0 new members by letter; $65,088.00 in undesignated gifts.

Arbor Springs welcomes the association, and we are grateful to them for hosting the annual meeting this year.

History of Hebron Baptist Church
Carrollton, Alabama
Gary Farley
Fall, 2014

The church was organized in 1841. The first messengers to the association were Rev. C. B. Sanders, John Pearson, and J. M. Pettigrew. The pastor was A. Elledge. The membership stood at 25. From the associational minutes, we find that early pastors included T.S. Thomas, C. B. Sanders, J. N. Acker, D. Duncan, J.M. Deloach, and J. M. Land.

Like Arbor Springs, Hebron was weakened by the War Between the States. In 1872 only 13 members could be found. However, three women, Mrs. Hudgins, Hicks, and Ammons would not let the church close. So, God sent a pastor. John H. Curry, son of Rev. Montgomery C. Curry, and his young wife moved to the community. (He became the father of M. B. Curry, who became a lawyer in Carrollton and was moderator of the association for many years.) Here in this auditorium you see a stained glass window honoring pastor Curry. It comes from the old Northport FBC. In the fall of 1873 a revival was held which resulted in the baptism of 18 people. The church was revived and experienced a time of prosperity. In 1941 when it celebrated its centennial the church had 112 resident members. The 1873 revival brought two young men who served as deacons and pillars of the church for decades, Ben Whitaker and John Pearson.

Through the years our host churches shared pastors G. M. Lyles and Hix Chappell.

Buried in the cemetery is Bro. Richard Wilkins and his wife. He was the first associational moderator. When he died several of the churches, Ebenezer, Fellowship, and Liberty purchased the tombstone. The association started a fund for the widows of pastors to help with her financial needs. And her tombstone was purchased with funds from this offering.

The first Director of Missions for the association was a daughter of Hebron, Ms. Emma Burgin. She grew up in the WMU and BYPU. When WMU was formed at Hebron in 1916, it was called the Sunday Egg Club. This was because many farm women of that era raised chickens, sold eggs and gave an offering from that income to the support of international missions. (Perhaps PECO can be traced to this.) After she finished her studies at Southwestern Baptist Theological Seminary in 1947, she took on this role. In 1949 she went to serve as pastor's assistant in Birmingham. Later she served for many years as the treasurer of the association.

From 1907 to 1963 three pastors served Hebron with few exceptions. The first was J. M. Mills. A copy of his autobiography from the Alabama Baptist is attached. Note that he moved to the Stansel community in 1892, married and had five children. When he surrendered to the ministry, the association helped him get a basic education. He served many of our churches. He founded Pleasant Hill. He was clerk of the association for many years. He was pastor at Hebron from 1907 to 1925. He was followed by H.C. Todd, who was also the pastor at Reform. In 1935 James Swedenburg came as pastor and for most of the next 28 years pastored Hebron and other churches like Crossroads and West End and served as leader of what has become ALCAP. It served as a first church for several ministers I know, Benton Goodman, Larry Potts, Neil Nichols, Ellis Tate, and Ronnie Elmore. For the past 10 years Randy Gray has served as pastor. The church has grown, added the fine fellowship hall where we will have supper, and expanded its worship auditorium. Bro. Bert Noland who pastors Springhill grew up in this church.

Both of these rural churches represent the core of Baptist life. Solid. Progressive. Committed to their communities. Serving. Supporters of the mission enterprise. Calling out the called for ministry. In an age when the attention is often given to the mega churches and the big things they do, let's not forget who we are, and whose we are.

Hebron welcomes the association to this meeting. Soon it will celebrate 175 years of faithful service to God and community. Last year it reported 60 resident members, 2 baptisms, 4 new members by letter, and $79,244.00 in undesignated gifts.

History of Calvary Baptist Church
Fayette, Alabama
Gary Farley
Fall, 2015

Calvary is the youngest congregation in our association. On the 25th of October it will celebrate its 15th anniversary. It is located in the very best place for a rural church—within sight of the Walmart store. And there is a cemetery nearby. Husbands can die with some hope that their wife will visit their grave regularly and often.

Its story began a little less than 20 years ago when about 100 persons in and around Fayette came together around the idea of having a church which was serious about what they believed and how they behaved. They wanted quality in worship, teaching, ministry, and fellowship. In the group were persons of great talent and deep commitment to the faith.

This group formed a congregation which was located out in the country at the building of the Mt. Pleasant Baptist Church. They called Bro. David Cullison as the founding pastor. At the time he was pastor at FBC Fayette.

The congregation found that the Golden Rule Building Supply property was for sale. It is a great location on about a dozen acres with a large building. Today you can see the results of a very wise and skilled development of the property. Today it is a church which is fulfilling its goals—being an authentic New Testament fellowship. Real. Godly. Great worship. Great ministry. Discipled.

When all of this was happening, the current pastor, Blake Thompson, a part of Calvary, was serving as youth pastor at West End in Aliceville. He had graduated from Southern Baptist Seminary in Louisville. And he was falling in love with Anna Katherine Griffin, the daughter of Mike and Janet Griffin, pastor at West End. He was called to Calvary as youth pastor after they married. They have two children and are in the process of adopting another from India.

In time founding pastor, David Cullison, was called back to his home in Indiana. He is pastor of First Southern Baptist in Evansville. And Calvary called Blake as their pastor. The church has been a good supporter of our association and a contributor to our ministry to the Federal Prison.

This is the second time Calvary has hosted an annual meeting of the association. We thank them for hosting us this very nice day.

They will be selling gift products in the entry area. All income goes to support our ministry in the prison.

History of Galilee Missionary Baptist Church
Panola, Alabama
Gary Farley
Fall, 2015

Historian and minister C.C. Boothe records that in 1860 there were only four Baptist Churches that were operated by African Americans in all of Alabama. When he published the *Cyclopedia of Colored Baptists in Alabama* in 1895 there were more than 950. Galilee, which dates from about 1870, was one of these amazing church planting miracles.

Its roots are to be found in Providence Baptist Church over in the river town of Warsaw. This church had more than 400 members in 1860, most of whom were slaves. Among the men who had pastored Providence was Basil Manly, Jr., son of Basil Manly the president of the University of Alabama. Charles was a graduate of Princeton University and an early professor at The Southern Baptist Theological Seminary. He authored an early hymnal.

With emancipation many of the freedmen formed new churches with pastors of their own. For example, at Enon Baptist Church, now FBC Aliceville, the freedmen formed a new church, now named New Wright, with Duncan Salmonds as pastor. It had been kind of a shadow church within Enon with pastor Salmonds preaching. (He did similarly at Unity and at Big Creek with the current Missionary Baptist congregations of New Salem and Pine Grove as the result.) So with freedom it was ready to go. In Pickens County there were more than 40 new African American congregations reported in 1895. In Sumter County there were more than 70.

Galilee, like many of these new churches, sprang up on a plantation, in this case the Oliver place, a few miles from Warsaw. Providence closed about 1865 and was reconstituted as Stonewall Baptist Church in the village of Sherman, north and west of Panola.

However, the formation of Panola awaited the building of the ATN railroad from Reform to Mobile in the early 1900s. Panola is the word for Cotton in the language of the Choctaw Indians. It prospered into the 1960s with a cotton gin, several churches, stores and a school. But with changes in how cotton was produced and processed, and changes in transportation, the town began to lose population.

Pastor Bob Little grew up here. He went away to school at Alabama State in Montgomery. Graduated and became a professional musician. But God spoke to him and called him into ministry. His mother church, Galilee, asked him to serve her. He came about 17 years ago. God gave him a vision of moving Galilee from out in the open county to Panola and revitalizing the town.

On February 7, 2006 Galilee was burned to the ground by arsonists here in the Black Belt region, one of nine in less than a week. The Pickens Baptist Association stepped forward and played a key role in the successful efforts to rebuild these churches. Bob Lee Ellis of Gordo and I met weekly for more than six months at Jacks in Aliceville with Bro. Bob and representatives of the other churches to connect resources and needs. Volunteers came to clean up and rebuild at Dancy and to construct a new building at Galilee. Funds came to build a new building at Morning Star. Today all nine are better housed and doing well. I, as many others, learned much about grace, forgiveness and love through the process. We learned how God brings good out of what is intended for evil.

But God had more for us. Pastor Bob responded to an invitation to join with us in teaching the weekly Sunday School class on the radio. The church petitioned to be a member of the association and was accepted. Then nearly three years ago when the Aliceville Federal Prison opened, Pastor Bob and I became the founding pastors of first the Camp Community Church and of the Aliceville Body of Believers. Both congregations have prospered. They, along with a Spanish language church in the FCI, while never to be constituted churches and members of the PBA, have become foci for our mission out-reach. Luke 1:74-75 was the text for the initial worship events in each of these congregations. The Messiah is coming to defeat our enemies, sin, death and Satan, so that we can serve without fear in righteousness and holiness. For Bob and me these churches have been a blessing and the ladies tell us that they too are blessed. We believe that the Kingdom of God is being expanded and will continue to be so for years to come due to the support given to this ministry through Galilee and the association and all of its churches.

We are grateful to Galilee for hosting this annual meeting of the Pickens Baptist Association.

History of Carrollton Baptist Church

Dr. Thrath Curry published a history of this congregation in 1995, A Heritage of Faith. This article draws from it. The town of Carrollton was formed to serve as the seat of county government in 1830. Sixteen years passed before a Baptist church was established there. The date was May 24, 1846. The first pastor, William Stansel was a planter from the Garden community. The clerk, Matthew Lyon, was a printer and later became a pastor here and in Tennessee and in northwest Alabama. Most of the charter members were from the Big Creek church, about four miles west toward Pickensville.Among them were the Bostic and Lyon families. Later lawyers Nabors and Gilkeys, judge Thomas, several other families, and several slaves were added to this congregation. In the early years the church meet at the courthouse, the academy and the Methodist building. In 1857 CBC built its first meetinghouse. It looked very much like the UMC building which still stands in Pickensville.

Following the war the W.G. Robinson family move to town. He was a merchant. He became a champion of the Sunday school movement. Mrs. Robinson would become the champion of the Woman a Missionary Union here and in the association. Further, he served as moderator of the assohhciation for many years.

In most rural counties the seat of government is the largest town. This was not the case here. Perhaps the most famous former member of this church and town is Miss Addie Cox. She went to China in 1918 as a missionary. She served there until 1950 when she was forced to leave by the communists. She relocated to Formosa. The association honored her memory in 2012. Dr. Curry prepared a DVD Documentary of her life. It can be borrowed from the PBA office for viewing. In. 2009 Emily and Buddy Kirk of this church were recognized as volunteer missionaries of the year by the state convention.

Through the years the church has been blessed with good pastoral leadership. Among them was Tom Collins. He grew up in the church. He was a very effective evangelist. Among many outstanding laymen across the years was lawyer M.L. Curry. He served for many years as the moderator of the association.

Recently, the church has been served by interim pastor, Wes Jones. At the last annual meeting the church reported income of $351,191, resident membership of 213 and donations to the association of $14,461. Thank you for hosting the annual meeting this year.

History of Mineral Springs Baptist Church
Gary Farley

This church was established in 1855. A good history was written in 2005 when it celebrated 150 years. We will draw from it in this account, but I want to begin with its back story. The first Baptist Church to serve this community was formed in 1840. Its name was Mt. Moriah. Its pastor was Ellis Gore. At first it joined the Columbus Association as did its neighbors South Carolina (now Ethelsville) and Providence. The church met in a building a few miles north of here. In 1846 Mt. Moriah joined the Union (now Pickens) association. In 1850 pastor Gore decided that his beliefs were more like those of Freewill Baptists, so he traveled to North Carolina to be ordained by that group. Soon both Mt. Moriah and Salem withdrew from Union and formed a Freewill Baptist Association called Mt. Moriah. It continues with 13 church in Pickens and Tuscaloosa counties. This Baptist denomination believes more like the Methodists regarding salvation (soteriology). But they practice baptist and church organization like us.

Not all of the members of Mt. Moriah adopted the beliefs of Freewills, so in 1855 some of them formed a church here. Apparently, there was a Mineral Springs community building, so the new congregation began meeting there. The organizing minister was G.M. Lyles. He is buried near the church building in the church graveyard. The land for the church building and cemetary was given by William Shippey. The first pastor was Dabney Duncan who also served South Carolina in Yorkville.

At that time there was a mill on Cold Fire Creek and in time a cotton gin and sawmill operated by the McShan family. In time a railroad line was built through the community and still later US Highway 82. A village grew up around the mill and on the railroad with a school and stores that was called McShan. The history of Mineral Springs Baptist Church is closely tied to this town and to the McShan family.

In 1955 Gaylord Brownlee was ordained as a minister. He later served 22 years as pastor of this church. Recently, he died. In 1956 the old church house was replaced by a new one. In 1982 a pastorium was added. The family life center dates from 1995. Volleyball became a ministry of the church.

Many of us have fond memories of Bro. Syd Lanier and his wife Ethel when he was pastor here. He was a true servant of God, humble and kind. Under current pastor David Blakney the church has experienced growth and many baptisms this year. You will find more about the work of this church in the Book of Reports.

HISTORY OF THE 5 FOUNDING CHURCHES WHICH CONTINUE IN OUR ASSOCIATION

Historical Sketch
Aliceville First Baptist Church
Pickens County, Alabama

On May 21, 1905 a new church building was dedicated in the new town of Aliceville. It took as its name Aliceville Baptist Church. In reality it was the old Enon Baptist Church moved to town from the Garden community a few miles north and west of Aliceville.

Church Clerk T. H. Sanders mentioned in the minutes of the church business meeting at that time (1905) that the church with but 36 members was much smaller than it once had been. He attributed this to the fact the far fewer "white people"lived in the Garden community than in the past. History has proven that the decision to relocate was a wise one. Year after year for most of the next century the membership of the church has grown to a current total of 253 resident members.

And in 1944 a new church was formed, Garden Baptist, back in the old community from which Enon moved. Garden's membership stands where Enon's was a century ago.

The Unity Baptist Church was a similar distance north and east of the new town of Aliceville back in 1905. There is no mention in its church minutes of any formal consideration of a move to Aliceville. By the 1930s it was very weak, and in the mid-1950s it closed its doors forever.

The old Enon Church was the first one of the Baptist denomination to be formed in Pickens County. The historical markers at Aliceville Baptist and at the Garden Cemetery tell some of the story. The founding date was 1823. This seems early until one recalls that the county was created by the legislature two years earlier. It had begun in a brush arbor, built on land provided by Park Ball, and a few years before the Civil War moved to the Garden. The first book of church minutes has been lost for many years. The second book records the story from 1847 to 1883. The remaining records are intact.

Enon was much like other rural Baptist churches of that era. It held services one weekend per month. On Saturday, the congregation met for worship and to conduct its business. Normally, the pastor would moderate the business session. (Enon may have been one of four congregations, which he served on successive weekends each month.) Items of business would include "opening the doors of the church" to receive persons who wished to join; granting letters of dismissal to persons who were moving away; raising money to operate the church or to support missions; and disciplining members.

On Sunday following the Saturday business session, the church would meet again for public worship. In August this meeting would be "protracted" into the next week or two and revival services would be held. Often this would result in a baptismal service in a stream or pond near the meeting house.

Charles Stewart was pastor of Enon for its first decade. Henry Petty, William Spragins, J.H. Taylor and William Stansel were also early pastors. After the Civil War, A.M. Hanks and J.H. Curry had extended ministries at Enon.

Enon, like many of the rural Baptist churches in Pickens County, was very successful in evangelizing the slaves in the decade prior to the Civil War. At the time of emancipation it counted 125 freedmen among its membership. Also, like its sister churches one can find in the minutes of the business meetings of the Enon church a story of the development of an African American congregation which would later become a separate congregation.

The time-line at Enon for this planting of a new congregation runs like this:
*June 1850, Lewis, a slave of Thomas Jones, was allowed to preach to the black members. This action was later rescinded.
*1855, Brother Charles Bains, who served as the "associational missionary" began preaching regularly to the blacks in Enon.
*May 1856, Pastor William Spraggins begins preaching to the black people at Enon. The church reported 110 black members.
*September 1857, the church voted that the black brethren could hold prayer meetings and conferences on their own, with the supervision of the pastor and deacons.
*September 1858, Pleasant, a servant of Dr. J. Spruill was licensed to preach.
*1859, Duncan, a servant of B.B. Salmonds, was baptized. He will later become a pioneer African American pastor in Pickens County.
*January 1860, several of the slaves of Dr. Spruill were granted letters of dismissal.
*July 1863, Pleasant Spruill moved his letter back from the Oak Ridge Baptist Church. (It was located off of highway 14 near the Mississippi line.)
*May 1866, the "colored" members have secured two members to keep the meetinghouse clean as a part of an agreement to allow the black members to hold separate services.
*July 1866, note is taken of some kind of disturbance in the monthly church conference by some of the freedmen.
*August 1867, licensed Duncan Salmonds to preach.
*October 1867, the African American members asked the congregation to allow them to withdraw and form a separate congregation, which will meet in the Enon meetinghouse on weekends when the white church is not using it.
*December 1867, this is accomplished. One hundred and twenty-five members are dismissed to the new congregation. The new church is first called First Baptist Church of Pickens County. Later the word African was added. Brother Pleasant Spruill was pastor. The new church was to pay $25.00 per year as rent for the building.
*1870, the rent is raised to $50.00
*1871, Enon broke this arrangement. The reason given was that the African American congregation was damaging the building.

I found no further reference to the new congregation in the church minutes. It is sad that the relationship ended in this way. I imagine that it was reflective of the racial tensions which accompanied the period of Reconstruction. I understand the new congregation became the New Wright Missionary Baptist Church which continues to thrive and minister in the old Garden community. The congregation is now working on its history. I look forward to learning more about this daughter of Enon soon.

After moving to Aliceville, the church prospered. It became the first "full-time" church in the association, ca 1940. The town grew and became both a regional farm trade center and the home of industry. During World War II it was the site of a prisoner of war camp. It has been fortunate in its selection of pastors, many of who stayed with the church for more than a decade. Since World War II the pastors have been Raymond Stuckey, Larry Bray, Dudley Wilson, Joe Whitt, Denny Goodwin, Jim Cooley, and Charlie Wilson. It has built fine buildings to service the work of the congregation.

Many of the leaders of the association have come from the membership of Aliceville First. Its commitment to missions has been outstanding. Today two if its young men, Parker Windle and Landon Williams are serving as Journeymen with the International Mission Board of the Southern Baptist Convention. Amy Williams spent a month this summer working in China.

The late Ellis Tate, as well as Jay Spiller, Leslie Spiller, Todd Burkhalter, Larry Potts, and Jonathan Harris; contemporary ministers, are products of this church.

In the 1940's the church assisted in the formation of West End Baptist Church in the mill village near the yarn factory. It too prospered.

With the opening of FCI Aliceville, it has presented many opportunities of ministry that the church has become involved with. They have "adopted" the FCI Aliceville Staff as their focus mission in this area.

Data about the current membership and activities of the church are to be found in the packet of material and statistics you received.

We are grateful to Aliceville First Baptist, our oldest continuing and constituting church, for again hosting the annual meeting of the association.

Historical Sketch of
New Salem Baptist Church
Pickens County, Alabama

Recently, the church celebrated the 35th anniversary of Bro. Mike Hall as pastor. Since the church is only 69 years old, this means that Mike has been pastor of the church for a little more than half of its life, and, incidentally, more than half of his.

Not far north and a little west of New Salem is the Salem Cemetery. Its oldest stone dates from ca 1865. It marks the place where a Salem church was established. It united with our association back in 1847. In 1850 this church, under the influence of its pastor, Bro. Ellis Gore, left the association and united with the Freewill Baptist, becoming part of the Mt. Moriah association. Apparently, this church had died out by the mid-1880s, because a New Salem Baptist Church, in that same community asked to become a part of our association in 1887. Then in 1907 this church moved down to the Friendship School community and changes its name from New Salem to Friendship. (Note: Friendship celebrated its centennial in 2007, but in a sense it was really 20 years older than that.) I have been told that the building at Salem was cut in half and moved to the new site at Friendship and became the core of the current building.

New Salem was constituted in 1941, just before World War II. The original 10 charter members had grown to 67 by 1950. Most of the members had been a part of the Friendship church. And the relationship between these two churches has been strong across the years. Bro. Hall grew up in Friendship, as did several of its current leaders. The reason given for the formation of a new church was the distance from the area served by New Salem to Friendship.

The first building for this church was kind of a shelter built with scraps from the community. Then in the 1950s a new building of cinder blocks was constructed. Later a fellowship and Sunday School wing was added. A total of 13 pastors served the church unto 1975 when Bro. Mike Hall became the pastor. Membership had grown into the 80s by 1975.

In the last seven years the church has built two new buildings, a fellowship hall with classrooms and a sanctuary. The membership is now about 200 and growing. Bro. Mike has worked in the radio industry while pastoring the church. Today he manages two regional stations for American Family Radio. We are grateful to the church for its vision, the fruits of which we are enjoying today. The church is always welcoming to the association and anxious to host large events.

In recent years the membership of New Salem has become increasingly involved in the operation of an old campground, Unity Grove, which is about 3 miles away in the palmetto community. New Salem provides several volunteers who work at the Baptist Center Thrift Store. And it has provided leadership for an annual Christmas store for Salem Nursing Home.

Fellowship Baptist Church

Fellowship Missionary Baptist Church was organized as an arm of Antioch Baptist Church with the first enrollment of members on September 8, 1832. Nineteen members were enrolled and Ambrose Dollar was elected as the first church clerk.

CHARTER MEMBERS

Mary Bennett	Sarah Gurley	James Williams
Ambrose Dollar	David Lowe	Mary Williams
Jemima Dollar	William Maham	Rose Williams
Nancy Dunn	Easter Parker	Sara Williams
John Dunn	Joseph Parker	Sealy Williams
Elizabeth Edmunds	Hardy Redden	William Williams
Sam Gurley	Hezikish Williams	

At conference on December 1, 1832, the church designated the meeting in the next April, as the time to observe the Lord's Supper and to wash feet. Rev. Richard Wilkins was called as the first pastor at this same conference.

At conference on May 4, 1833, they asked to be constituted, and petitioned Antioch Church for letters of dismissal.

The church met in conference on July 1, 1833, and petitioned Big Creek, with their Eldership to aid the church in becoming constituted. Elders Richard Wilkins and Charles Stewart were called on to ascertain the strength of the Baptist in the Hargrove Settlement. After due examination they found number sufficient and orthodox and pronounced them a church in accordance with the principles adopted by the Cahaba Association, entitled them to all the privileges of the gospel and called the name of the church-Fellowship on the 3rd day of August, 1833. Richard Wilkins, Charles Stewart and Dempsey White were members of the Presbytery, (Stewart and White were from Big Creek)

Slaves were accepted as members in the early years of the church. In 1852 there were forty slaves on the church roll.

There is no record of what the first building was made of, but it is legendary that it was made of logs, fireplace for heat, and located in the Hargrove settlement, near the Old Camp Ground site, east of Hog Branch. The church location was changed from this location to present location in 1851.

In 1889 a building committee composed of L. B. Williams, Enoch Williams, Ambrose Dollar, S.J. Matthews and John Sallis was appointed. A wood frame structure was erected at the rear of the present building near the Dollar monument. They used shutters made of wood for windows. The building was heated with a wood burning heater. Candles were used for lights at the few night services held. This building was dedicated February 12, 1894. This was a one room building and large glass windows were used. Heat was furnished at first by a wood burning heater, later a warm morning coal burning heater was used. Kerosene and gasoline lamps were used until 1940 when electricity was made available.

Present building is carpeted with Sunday School rooms, kitchen and dining area down stairs. This new building was dedicated in December 1957. We obtained concrete tables for outside use in 1979. In August, 1990, a Sunday School wing was added onto the sanctuary. In

1991, the basement Sunday School rooms and kitchen were remodeled. We have an organ and piano that are used for our worship services. In 2000, additional dining area was added downstairs with a baptistery upstairs. In 2006, a water lock system was put in the basement. In 2008, a new sound system was put I the sanctuary. At the present time our church is debt free.

The subject of missions was brought up very soon after organization. Records show contributions were sent to Missions for Indians in Alabama , as early as 1839, as well as local and foreign missions.

A Woman's Missionary Society was organized in February, 1928, with the help of the Gordo Baptist Church. We have contributed regularly to the orphans home since its beginning.

Rev. Dan McGraw was the first minister to be ordained at Fellowship, later Rev. G.W. Kerr and Rev. Jimmy Kelly. Rev. G.W. Kerr was the only member of this church ever to be sent to the Southern Baptist Convention as a delegate. He attended the convention at Ft. Worth, Texas, in May 1934. He brought back a full report of the meeting and it is recorded in the church record book.

Rev. Tim Owens, IMB missionary to Thailand, grew up in Fellowship Church.

On August 3, 1933, the church celebrated it's 100 anniversary with Rev. G.W. Kerr as Master of Ceremonies and Hon. M.B. Curry as the guest speaker.

Two confederate soldiers, R.F. Hunnicutt and F.E. Johnson were killed in action at Resacca, Georgia in May 1864, during Sherman's march to sea. Both were members of the church here.

During the early years and until the early part of the 1900's, Saturday meetings were held. Pastors came to serve the pulpit on foot or horseback and were taken care of by members. They received very little cash offerings. In the fall, a committee was appointed to see the members for "subscription" money for the pastor the following year. Tithing as a means of financing the church is mentioned as early as 1846. Tithing among the members is still a source of the income of the church.

The communion set we now have was purchased in 1911.

Sabbath School was organized in 1861. In 1932, a B.Y. P. U. was organized. This is now known as Training Union.

We have a full time pastor and have services twice on Sunday, bible study on Wednesday night, Sunday School on Sunday morning and preaching on Sunday nights.

PASTORS

1833	Richard Wiklkins	1835	M.P. Smith
1837	Charles Stewart	1846	J. W. Guyton
1850	C.B. Sanders	1852	J.H. Taylor
1854	T.S. Thomas	1856	Jessie Thomas
1857	Willis Burns	1858	Bro. Robison
1862	W.M. Ashcraft	1867	S. Hildreth
1877	J.M. Chism	1881	George M. Lyles
1883	J.A. Mitchell	1886	W.J. Beaty
1889	J.W. Dunaway	1891	J.A. Estes
1892	D.O. Baird	1905	W.P. Peden
1911	D.Z. Wolley	1912	R.S. Marler
1914	A.T. Ezell	1916	Bro. Rockett

1917	H.D. Wilson	1919	J.M. Mills
1922	N.O. Patterson	1924	C.A. Bryant
1926	L.M. Perrigin	1930	B.B. Burks
1933	O.C. Kidd	1934	T.H. Farr
1935	J.R. Swedenburg	1936	H.G. Carpenter
1940	Ullman Moss	1941	J.L. Watson
1942	E. Donald Strickland	1943	Lewis Marler
1944	Billy Gamble	1946	W.E. Robinson
1947	Gatha Davis	1948	Amon Kelly
1950	Amon Foster	1951	Kirk Lucas
1953	Edwin Skelton	1955	Cecil Junkin
1956	Robert Thomas	1957	Thomas Davis
1959	BennyHayes	1960	Boyce Crocker
1961	Boyce Crocker	1962	Boyce Crocker
1963	Neil Nichols	1964	Neil Nichols
1965	Boyce Crocker	1966	Max Bobbitt
1967	B.W. Allen	1968	B.W. Allen
1969	Ralph Elmore	1970	Ralph Elmore
1971	Wallace Perry	1972	Clifton Patterson
1973	Lee Vails	1974	Neil Nichols
1976	Al Sanderson	1977	J.L. Noland
1978	Lee Vails	1979	Robert langdon
1980	Robert Langdon	1983	Kenneth Webb
1985	Larry Rogers	1987	Clyde Stevens
1991	Ricky Trull	1992	Cecil Junkin
1996	Lindsey Watkins	1999	Adam Homan

The following figures show our church membership:

1832	19
1900-1910	25
1910-1920	27
1920-1930	39
1930-1940	85
1940-1950	100
1950-1960	112
1960-1970	115
1970-1980	102
1980-2008	123

A cemetery was started at the first location of the church in the Hargrove settlement. The tomb inside the iron fence in the present cemetery marks the remains of the Hodo's that were first buried near Hargrove and later excavated and brought to Fellowship. The monument of William Dollar, stands on the house site of Mr. Dollar and was erected there in 1920 to honor him, the only known Revolutionary soldier ever to have made his home in this community. It was through the untiring efforts of Mr. Sam Moore the monument was erected. Mr. Dollar is buried in Mississippi. For many years the cemetery was cleaned by public workings. In the early days when there were few graves, they cleaned the cemetery and decorated the graves in the same day. It was from this beginning we have our annual Memorial and Homecoming the first Sunday in May. As the years went by families moved away and were unable to attend the workings, so a grave-yard committee was appointed to have the graves cleaned. We are grateful for our beautiful cemetery, as it is one of the best kept in the country, with the brick posts at the entrance and the fence erected around the cemetery.

Located just north of the present cemetery is the area that was used as the slave cemetery.

Ebenezer Baptist Church and Her Pastors: The Early Years
Gary Farley

Ebenezer is an old congregation, founded in 1833, an original member of the Pickens Baptist Association. It meets in a building that dates from the 1890's. Inside, the pews are arranged in the classic "U' formation characteristic of rural Baptist churches of that day. Today no one lives within two miles of the meeting house. The 20 or so persons who gather there for worship arrive on purpose.

The church numbered among its early pastors T.S. Thomas and R. B. Wilkins. Both participated in the constituting of the congregation. Both served it across the years as pastor. Wilkins was the first moderator of the Union Baptist Association when it was formed in 1835. Two years later when the association was torn in tow by controversy related to the support of mission boards, Wilkins was turned to again to serve as moderator. Thomas' support of missions cost him the pastorate of the Bethany church at that time, but he continued to be a useful minister in the churches of the association. He also served a term as a judge for the county. He died in the mid 1850's.

The records of Ebenezer church have been microfilmed and can be found at the Alabama Baptist Historical library at Samford University. There one finds a break in the records after the initial founding of the church until 1845. This report gleans some information from these records for the years from 1845 to 1865.

Father Wilkins died in the fall of 1848. The following note was made in the minutes of the church on February 17, 1849. "By motion and second agreed to take up a collection by subscription for the purpose of raising money to erect a monument to the memory of old Brother Richard Wilkins, deceased, and appointed Bro. J.D. Kee and Bro. E. Harris to raise subscription." The minutes of the January meeting of that year contain these words, "On application granted a letter of dismission to Sister Nancy Wilkins, wife of old Brother Wilkins who has been the Pastor of this church from the time of its constitution till his death." (Note: in the records, others were the preacher during some of the previous 15 years, but Bro. Wilkins was recognized as the pastor.)

In the graveyard at Hebron Baptist Church, about 12 miles distant, today one finds the monument mentioned above still marking the earthly remains of Bro. Wilkins. Beside him is the grave of Nancy. She lived another decade. In the last years of her life the association raised money to provide for her needs. And the remainder of those funds, by action of the association, was used to mark her grave as well. Another six miles or so away in the cemetery of the Liberty Baptist Church one finds the monument to their preacher son, Bro. Richard Wilkins, Junior.

The next preacher who caught my attention as I read the records of Ebenezer was Bro. William Scott. Initially, he was an active layman. In 1852, the church that he has been called of God to be a preacher. He was ordained and became the pastor of the church. One of his early actions was missionary. The nearby congregation at Hopewell, near Speeds Mill, had lapsed. Ebenezer "extended an arm" there. Several of is leaders moved their membership there.

When Scott became a preacher, he gave up his clerkship. Ebenezer turned to a good layman, Sardine Hildreth, to serve in that role. Then in 1860 he experienced a call to ministry and is "released" to preach. In time he became a leading pastor in the association and its moderator. On the heels of Hildreth came Israel Hollingsworth. In 1864 he was ordained by Ebenezer. He went on to serve several churches as well as pastor.

Bro. Scott died in the spring of 1862, apparently unexpectedly. The following was written in the minutes, "In memory of our beloved pastor, we the Baptist Church of Christ at Ebenezer do hereby certify that god in His providence has seen fit to bereave us of our beloved pastor, Brother William R. Scott for which we cannot but weep and lament our loss as a church, yet we firmly believe that our loss as a church is eternal gain for him; therefore, we are necessitated to take another pastor, when we do that our beloved Sister Scott will be greatly in the affection and praise of the church."

A couple of interesting notes come form the minutes of the church during the Civil War. One, two soldiers, Phillip Noland and I.G. Burkhalter wrote asking to become members due to their conversion in the army. Another, the church sought to discipline the members. When they fell into sin, members were expected either to repent and make things right, or else they would be excluded from the membership of the church. Stress was placed on living righteous lives. I was particularly taken, however, by the many times that this line appeared in the minutes. "The church met in conference and was found to be at peace and in harmony.

It is my hope that our churches will love their pastors as Ebenezer loved Brothers Wilkins and Scott; that our churches will continue to call out new ministers of the Gospel; that today's military will turn to God; that we will encourage holy living; that the churches will be in harmony and that each church, no matter what size will see that it has an important role to play in the kingdom work.

In 1933 when the church celebrated its centennial, it was found that 1,000 persons had been members during that time. From then to 1966 another 353 were new members. Through out the years many of the ministers who served in the association pastored Ebenezer.

Liberty Missionary Baptist Church
Reform, Alabama
Gary Farley

Tuscaloosa was the state capital and the home of the state university back in 1834 when Liberty Baptist was constituted as a church. Columbus was an important trade center. Crops of cotton were shipped via the Tombigbee to Mobile and from there to factories in England and in New England. A primitive road connected Tuscaloosa and Columbus. Stage coaches and wagons could be seen on this road carrying persons and goods to and fro.

The earlier settlers came to this area around 1815. The first settlements were along the Tombigbee and up its tributaries like Coalfire Creek. Most of the settlers were from South Carolina. Many were attracted by the prospects of fresh, fertile land for raising cotton.

The Methodists formed a congregation not too far from here about 1822, Hargrove. And one of the Hargroves was soon selected as Bishop. The first Baptist church in Pickens County, Enon, was formed in the Garden community in 1823 and the South Carolina Baptist Church was constituted near Ethelsville in the following year. Perhaps the next Baptist Church was one named Antioch, perhaps about six miles north and west of here.. And a Baptist church formed at Providence in Northwest Pickens, an arm from South Carolina, Unity at Olney, Pilgrim's Rest near Pickensville, Bethany near Vienna, and another at Big Creek before the 1820s had come to an end.

In the early to mid 1830s Baptist churches were formed, and continue at Fellowship, Bethlehem, Zion, Ebenezer, and here at Liberty. Fellowship and Liberty were on the early road from Tuscaloosa to Columbus. It struck me as interesting that early travelers on the old road would pass Baptist churches with these names. Why is this striking–because persons and churches can "go to seed," or stress excessively, either liberty or fellowship. The balanced life of a believer or of a church needs both. Certainly, a church must major on fellowship, but sometimes the fellowship results in closing out those who are not a part of the current "church family." Certainly, becoming a Christian brings a sense of liberty–liberation from guilt and from enslavement to sin, but this too can be carried to the extreme and sink into a destructive individualism which does not listen to loving counsel from anyone else. Baptist churches of this period sought to balance liberty and fellowship–they were covenanted communities of believers. The members saw themselves as responsible to one another, as accountable. They sought to grow spiritually and help one another grow more like Jesus. Certainly, back in the 1830s no mortal planned for there to be Baptist churches with the names of Liberty and Fellowship serving adjoining communities. But God's Holy Spirit has a way of creating for us "aha" moments of serendipity. And then He capped it off a couple of generations later by placing between them a third Baptist church–Reform. I take this as a message from the Holy Spirit saying–if you go to the extreme on liberty or on fellowship, reform and be balanced.

But let me move on to talk about *liberty*. The Apostle Paul is often called the Apostle of Liberty. This is because prior to his conversion on the road to Damascus, he had been such a legalist. He tried to keep all of the laws of the Old Testament–hoping to earn his salvation. God taught him that salvation was by the grace of God–it is not earned by our efforts. Salvation is freedom from the law, from enslavement to sin, from bondage to the devil, from burdensome tradition, from guilt, death and fear. The saved are set at liberty. Paul discovered soon, however, that some who were liberated by grace confused liberty with license. They neglect to understand that God still demanded obedience to His commands. Paul declared that while we are free, we are still obligated to obey the commands of God–not to be saved, but because we have been saved. Gratitude becomes the motivation for obedience in the life of the Christian.

The word "liberty" was a popular one back in the 1830s. There were still persons around who had lived through the American Revolution and the War of 1812. They reveled in the fact of liberty. They rejoiced in being free politically and spiritually. One of the reasons that the Baptist movement grew in the west was our emphasis on the freedom of the local church. No bishop or king told the church what it had to do. Rather as individuals and as churches the Baptists sought the will of God for their lives directly.

In the spring of 1833 a revival meeting was held in the Liberty community at a brush arbor. It was effective, and a group of Baptist Christians began to meet monthly at the arbor, and when the weather turned colder they arranged to meet in the nearby stagecoach inn. (A similar inn is still visible at Pickensville.) The following spring, this little flock decided that they were strong enough to organize as a congregation. They asked pioneer preachers Elders Richard Wilkins and Silas Dobbs to act as the presbytery for the meeting on May 4, 1834. The Elders found the congregation to be in order. A constitution, a statement of faith and rules of decorum were adopted, and the church was birthed.

Dobbs soon moved on to Louisville, Mississippi, where he served as pastor of the Baptist church for many years. Wilkins played a key role in the formation of the Fellowship, Ebenezer, Liberty and Hebron churches. He was the first moderator of the association (1835) and when the division between the churches favoring missions and those opposing mission societies occurred two years later with the moderator leaving with the anti-mission societies group, the association again turned to Wilkins to serve as moderator. Wilkins was much loved by the Baptists of Pickens. When he died in 1848 and was buried at Hebron they raised funds for a marker to be placed on his grave. A few years later the churches agreed to contribute to a fund to support his widow, Nancy. And when she died in 1858 the association provided funds to mark her grave. (As you know their son, Richard, Jr. was also a Baptist preacher and is buried here in the Liberty Cemetery.) I am wondering if the senior Wilkins as a founder of both Fellowship and of Liberty may have thought about what I noted earlier–we need a balance of both. Certainly, he gave evidence of their balance in his godly life.

From 1840 to 1848 Charles Stewart, another important pioneering pastor served Liberty. He lived in the Big Creek community and pastored there as well. (His home, not now in good repair, still stands on state route 86 just west of the old site of Big Creek church.) In 1849 Richard Wilkins, Jr. became pastor here. C. B. Sanders and J. Deloach, also of the second generation of pastors served here until 1863 when the junior Wilkins returned again and served through 1867. A.A. Spiller came to the pulpit of Liberty in 1868 for a couple of years with Wilkins returning in 1870. For the next few years J. W. Carpenter is pastor and then in 1874 Wilkins returns to the pastorate. During much of this time Wilkins and Deloach maintained membership in Liberty and were messengers to the association from Liberty. Hollingsworth and Mitchell, well respected pastors in the association served the church on through the 1870s. Membership in 1854 was 67. In 1874 it was 64. A decade later the membership stood at 92. In 1886 Mitchell is replaced by W. J. Beaty. The first report of a Sunday School at Liberty appears in 1887 with 50 students and 6 teachers. The superintendent is John Wilkins. When J. B. Small became pastor of Liberty in 1891 the membership stood at 100. J.A. Estes becomes pastor in 1893. And when Liberty is 60 years old its membership is 104, down from its high in 1890 of 113. In 1896 the venerable Dr. D. O. Baird becomes pastor at Liberty. He lived in the Bethlehem community and served our churches for more than 50 years. He was a Medical Doctor and was crippled by a wound suffered in the Civil War. In the report for 1900 Dr. Baird continued as pastor. The membership had dropped to 80 and the Sunday School had been discontinued. Interestingly, Forest had the largest membership of any Baptist church in our association and in Pickens County at that time with 111. It seems that the 1890s had been a hard time for the Baptist movement. Several of the churches closed. Membership dropped. But in the next decade the railroads came, towns were formed and churches planted in them and things for us were on the upswing.

In 1902 J.A. Estes becomes pastor again at Liberty. Sunday school is re-established. In 1905 J. M. Mills who was raised in Stansel and provided an education with help from the association is pastor at Liberty and the church reported 12 baptisms and a total membership at 97. Then in 1907 J. A. Mitchell, after an absence of about 30 years, returns as pastor. In 1909 J. M. Mills is back as pastor. Membership is down to 64, but there are 75 in Sunday School. Five years later Mills is still pastor and the membership has grown to 120. In 1916 J. C. Vandiver is pastor and the membership stood at 126. J.A. Mitchell is again pastor of Liberty in the 1920s. In 1924 a member of Liberty, C. A. Bryant becomes pastor. On through the Great Depression Bryant serves many of the churches in our association. Stories abound of his dedication, often walking many miles to preaching appointments. On its 90th birthday the membership of the church stood at 125. In 1930 Jim Swedenberg, another well-known pastor among us, assumed the pulpit at Liberty. He was a public school teacher, a pastor and temperance leader for the state. Like Bryant he served many of the churches in our county for decades. When the church celebrated its 100th birthday the membership stood at 130. In 1939 S. E. Walker came as pastor. He served several other churches on through the 2nd World War. He lived in Belk.

Liberty held worship services on the fourth Sunday of each month, a practice that dated from the beginning. Like other rural Baptist churches in its early years it met monthly over a weekend. On Saturday the business of the church was conducted. A major emphasis was to deal with any moral issues in the membership and any conflicts among the members. Baptist churches in those day took the covenant very seriously. It was important that the church "be in union" so that the worship on Sunday would be good and effective. When some problem was surfaced it was normal for the deacons to be sent to talk with the person to ascertain if the charges were correct and if so to invite the person to come to the next meeting, confess and be restored. Often this happened. If reconciliation could not be achieved then the church would likely exclude the sinning person from the fellowship, always with the hope that later a reconciliation might be achieved.

L. M. Perringin became the pastor in 1947, after Bill Fields had been pastor the previous year. In 1950 W. S. Scott who was also the pastor at Reform First became the pastor at Liberty. He conducted services on Saturday. I assume that the Sunday School continued on the regular day. In 1955 Chester Free, a well-known and loved pastor in the association came to Liberty. In 1958 Bro. Free became "half time" at Liberty with the church worshiping on the 2nd and 4th Sundays. In 1964 the church reported 84 resident members. Sunday School averaged 55 and VBS enroled 48 students. Westinghouse was going strong and there were jobs available in Reform. In 1967 Chester Free moved to Highland and was replaced by George. Pratt who lived in Birmingham. Pratt was pastor in 1974 when Liberty became 140 years old. The church reported 65 were enrolled in the Sunday School and 61 in VBS. Resident membership stood at 108. In 1977 Henry Trull became pastor at Liberty. He is now the pastor at Dunn's Creek in Tuscaloosa. In 1978 Gary Shelton who had served as youth pastor became the pastor at Liberty. During his ministry the church funded a worship program on radio station WRAG. Then in 1983

1983 Kenneth Smith became pastor at Liberty and continues in that position down to the present. Like most of the previous pastors Kenneth served as bi-vocational until a few years ago when he retired from secular employment. In 1984, on the 160th anniversary, the membership stood at 99 with 38 enrolled in Sunday School and at the last associational meeting Liberty reported a membership of 35 resident and 54 non-resident and an average attendance in morning worship of fifteen. Liberty moved to its current location many years ago, perhaps as many as 170. The current building was completed in 1969. Two other buildings, one log and one frame, predated this beautiful place. Like so many churches from the early days, Liberty built at a site close to a spring. This provided a natural gathering place, water for services and for baptisms. Around this location across the years people have been buried. The older cemetery is on the west side of the church building and most of the graves are marked only with fieldstones. To the north side is a newer cemetery. It is there that the earthly remains of many leaders in the church across the years, including that of pastor Wilkins, Jr, are to be found.

The community served by Liberty has seen many changes since 1834. The old stage road has moved north a couple of times and become US 82 highway. A community grew up along the new road, Coalfire, and a sister church, was planted there in 1940. Earlier a Free Will Baptist church was planted in the community. And, perhaps most significantly, the town of Reform grew up on the railroad line in about 1900. The cotton fields of the early days have been replaced with pine plantations. The population in the Liberty community has dropped.

On the 175th anniversary of Liberty we must recall that more than 100 persons were saved and began their Christian life in this church. This is likely the story of several persons here today. Many more have been discipled and discipled others in this place. It is my prayer that Liberty will continue to be a place where God is worshiped, the Gospel is proclaimed and the followers of Jesus are grown until Christ comes again. May it continue to be a place not only of liberty but also of deep fellowship.

The History of Forest Baptist Church

A petition for the organization of a regular orthodox Baptist church at the Eddins Schoolhouse occurred in the Benevola community on March 14, 1835. These 22 charter members included J.P. Taylor, William R. Stancil and Richard Wilkins; Taylor became the first pastor, and Stancil became the first clerk. The church adopted 12 Articles of Faith of the Buttehatchie Association and was named Forest Baptist Church (sometimes known as the Baptist Church of Christ at Forest). R.E. Johnson was later named clerk, and two early deacons ordained that year were Watson Shoemaker and John Carver. John H. Taylor was named the second pastor in January 1836, and he served for five years.

In June of 1836, a committee was appointed to purchase two acres of property from Gabriel Eddins and Arch Taylor to locate a meeting house, and the following month, the land was bought for $26.50, with the largest donation of $5 coming from James H. Ferguson. John Carver was named treasurer.

Like most churches of that time, they met one weekend a month, denoting Saturdays as business meetings and the seeking of the "peace of the church" to resolve issues without resorting to conflict, physical abuse or lawsuits. If an accusation was brought against a member, a committee was appointed to go to the accused, cite them for what they had done and ask them to come before the church body at the next conference. If the church was not satisfied with the results of this gathering, this person could be "privately excluded" and issued a letter of dismissal. Some examples found in the old records included not attending church, immoral conduct, stating falsehoods, living in disorder, using profane language, mistreatment of a slave, communing with the Presbyterians or Methodists, frolicking and dancing, or "playing the fiddle for others to dance."

A major split in the Buttehatchie Association occurred in 1835 over the issue of supporting missionary societies, and the issue spilled over into the church in September 1837, with 12 (of about 26) members leaving the church. The issue lasted over a year; some members returned and others left. But the church survived, and in 1839 a committee collected subscription papers to build a meeting house, and the church enrollment climbed to 63 by 1840. M.P. Smith became the third pastor in March 1841, and he served 19 years. In 1853, 13 people were saved in a revival, one of the largest one-time increases in membership. Another large increase occurred when N.A. Crawford had 11 of his slaves join the church in 1856; slaves had been attending the church since its founding. J.C. Foster was named the fourth pastor in January 1861; he preached for one year and was succeeded by William Ashcraft in January 1862 who served for three years.

PICKENS BAPTIST ASSOCIATION NOW HAS 34 CHURCHES.

THE CHURCH HISTORIES WERE WRITTEN BY DR. FARLEY IN THE YEAR THAT THE CHURCH WAS HOSTING THE ANNUAL MEETING. SOME CHURCHES WERE TOO SMALL TO HOST THE MEETING AND THEREFORE DO NOT HAVE HISTORIES REPORTED HERE.

THESE CHURCHES INCLUDE: COALFIRE, DOUBLE BRANCHES, GARDEN, HICKORY GROVE, MT. TABOR, PINE GROVE, AND UNION CHAPEL.

THESE CHURCHES WERE SMALL BUT NEVERTHELESS IMPORTANT TO THE WORK OF THE LORD IN OUR ASSOCIATION AND WE WANT THEIR NAMES INCLUDED IN THE HISTORY.

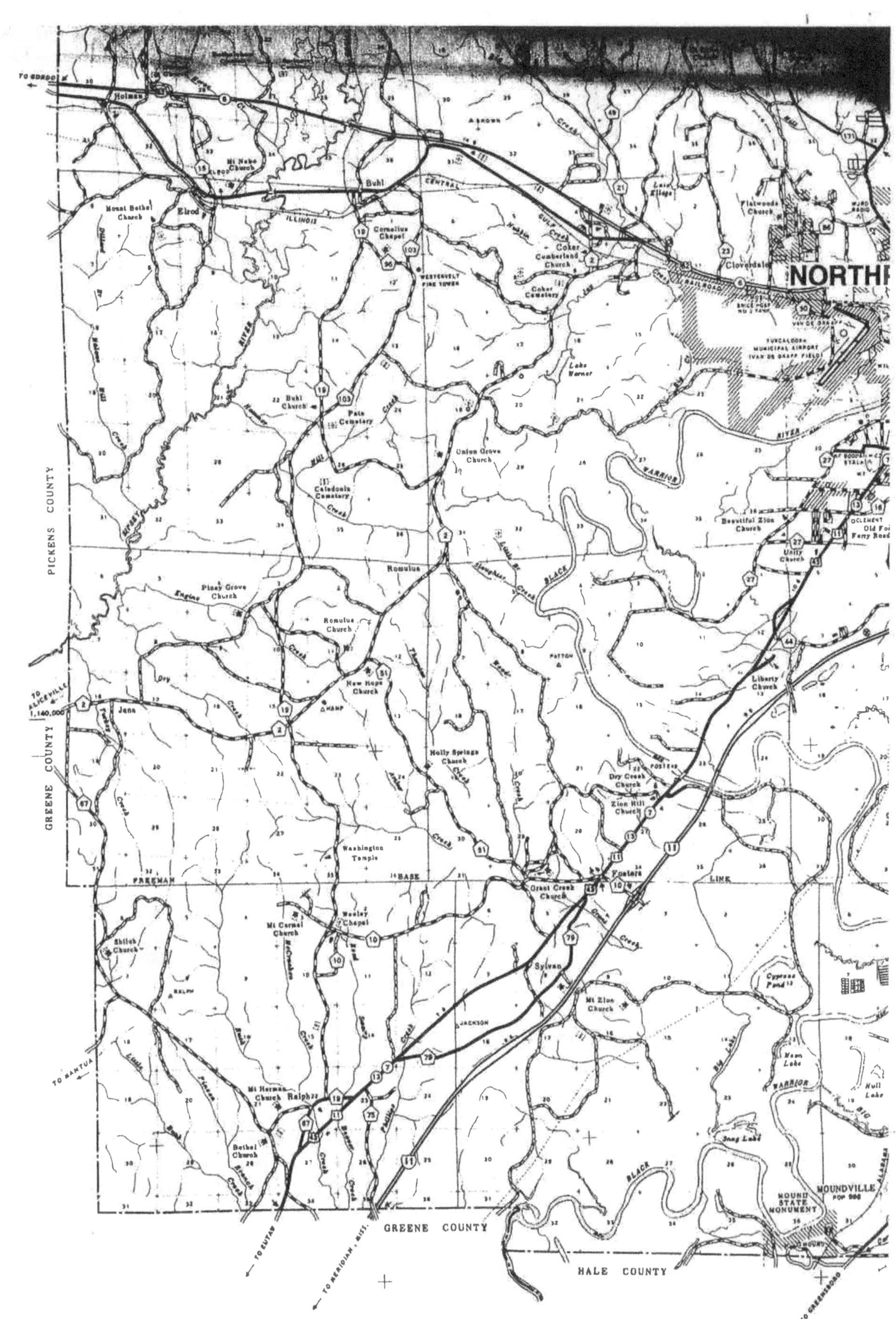

NORTHPORT
PICKENS COUNTY
GREENE COUNTY
HALE COUNTY
MOUNDVILLE

Church Membership in Pickens County During the 20th Century

Gary Farley

Recently, the Glenmary Missioners published *Religious Congregations and Membership in the United States, 2000.(RCMS)* It provides information about the number of congregations and the adherences of many religious denominations by county. Unfortunately, some denominations were not able to provide this information. For example, the report does not provide information from the Missionary Baptists and the Christian Methodist Episcopals, both of whom have many churches and adherents here in Pickens County. Neither are churches that are not connected to a denomination (independent) reported. So, it will not give us a complete picture of the religious situation in this county. In this article I will compare the data from 2000 with a similar set of data from 1906.

The 2000 Numbers

Denomination	Congregations	Adherents
Assembly of God	2	85
Catholic	1	80
Ch God (Cleve)	3	186
Ch God Prophcy	4	180
L-D Saints	1	105
Chs of Christ	5	189
Cumber Presb	1	24
Free Will Bap	9	1,321
Pent Ch God	2	110
Presb Ch (USA)	2	61
Presb Ch Amer	2	271
So Bapt Conv	34	7,512
Un Methodist	20	2,294

The total population of Pickens County in 2000 was about 21,000, with about 12,000 white. Since most of the denomination reported above are predominantly white, it appears that most of them are claimed by the some church.

Further, I have some questions about the data. I know that there are actually 38 churches in the county which are affiliated with the Southern Baptist Convention. I cannot find 20 United Methodist congregations. And I have not found anyone who knows of a Latter Date Saint congregation in the county. Conversations with Warren Lavender and David Skelton have suggested that there are actually between 140 and 150 congregations in Pickens County. So, with only 86 reported in the RCMS study, it is obvious that the totals are not complete.

The 1906 Numbers

In 1906 Pickens County had 24,402 residents. The data from that year does not report the number of congregations, but only the membership by denominations in the county. Further, some denominations were not present in Pickens County then and some which were have merged. But here are the numbers. Look at them and see what conclusion you would draw.

Denomination	Members
Baptist (Including African American)	5,644
Free Will Baptist	0
Primitive Baptist	104
Methodist Episc.	60
Methodist Prot	47
Methodist Episc., South	1,857
Africa Methodist Episc	20
Cumb. Presb	72
Colored Cumb Presb	675
Presb Church, US	287
Other Protestants	77

Questions can be raised about the figures as well. We know that there were several hundred Free Will Baptists in the county at that time. What has become of the African American Cumberland Presbyterians?

CH- List of Church Properties

1408 - 2516

Currently, the association has 34 affiliated churches, one under watchcare, and a Hispanic mission. The resident membership stands at 4,100. In addition to the five continuing founding congregations noted above these are Arbor Springs, Bethlehem, Calvary, Carrollton, Coal Fire, Cross Road, Double Branches, Ethelsville, Emmanuel, Flatwoods, Friendship, Garden, Gordo, Hebron, Hickory Grove, Highland, Mineral Springs, Mount Pleasant, Pleasant Hill, Reform, Spring Hill, Stansel, Union Chapel and West End. Galilee has applied for membership.

The association looks toward the future with hope. The four-laning of US Highway 82 across the association should help draw new residents to the area and help retain old ones. Efforts are being made to encourage people to retire to Pickens. Http://ruralretirement.us Industry is expanding both in Tuscaloosa and Columbus, MS. A branch campus for Bevell State College has opened in Carrollton. A Federal Prison will soon be built and opened in Aliceville. These developments will provide new opportunities and challenges for the churches of the Pickens Baptist Association.

Sunday Schools, the New Cause

Gary Farley

Several congregations in Pickens County have UNION in their name--Chapel, Hill, Valley. Often this is a sign that this church began in a union Sunday School. For example, on old US82 near the Mississippi line one finds Union Chapel Baptist Church. Less than a mile away is Forest UMC. And over in Mississippi one finds Bethesda Presbyterian Church, all came out of a union Sunday School.

About 1890 some Christian residents of the area put up a community building and contacted the American Sunday School Union about forming a weekly interdenominational Sunday School to meet in the community building, This was done and it prospered. Once a month the Baptists would host a worship service and on other Sundays the Methodists and the Presbyterians did likewise. In a few years the Methodists became numerous enough to start a congregation of their own. Then the Presbyterians did likewise. The Baptists were left with the old building and kept the old name. Across Pickens similar stories have occurred.

During the latter third of the 19th Century, in the established churches Sunday Schools were also formed. And in communities where there was no church like Kenny Hill and Bostick, mission Sunday Schools were established early in the 20th century which grew into churches. Since until after World War II most of the churches in Pickens had worship services only once a week, the establishment of Sunday Schools significantly changed the life of our churches. Going to church became a weekly event, rather than a monthly one. Churches began to focus on serving children. Later, Vacation Bible Schools were added to the work of many churches. This resulted in the growth of many of the churches in the county.

Through most of the Twentieth Century the American Sunday School Union selected the Bible text for lessons that were used in many Sunday Schools. Many denminational publishing houses and others like David C. Cook published quarterlies for students and teachers. A travelers across

America might attend Sunday School in a church of most any denomination and find the class studying the same Bible text that his class back home was studying.

For the Baptists the growth of Sunday Schools was closely tied to a Carrollton layman, W. G. Robinson. He was a businessman in the town. He had grown up in the Grant's Creek Baptist Church in Tuscaloosa County which was then a member of the Union, now Pickens, Association. When Robinson grew up before the war few churches conducted Sunday Schools. Apparently, seeing people go out into Eternity unprepared and seeing so many orphaned children after the war had a tremendous impact on him. He lobbied the existing churches to launch a Sunday School. He organized quarterly Sunday School Conventions where lay teachers were instructed concerning how to be effective students of the Bible and teachers of Sunday Schools.

Today, as many as 1,000 persons each week across Pickens prepare and teach Sunday School lessons in our nearly 175 churches. Others go each Sunday morning to the county jail and teach a Bible lesson. Others teach a lesson in a nursing home, and still others in the Aliceville Federal Women's Prison.

In the wake of the loss of the War between the States, Sunday Schools became for men and women like W. G. .Robinson a new cause, one that God has blessed. `

. This summer many of the churches of our county held Vacation Bible Schools, typically for one week. And some children attended three different VBS programs in three different churches. Thanks should be expressed to the several hundred volunteers who made this happen.

The Shining of the Light in changing times---1858--1946

The association was confronted by many changes during this period of nearly 90 years. First, there was a war that drew from the homes and the churches many fine young men, some of whom died and others who bore scars and disabilities all of their lives. Children lost their fathers. Second, the Freedmen formed churches of their own. New Wright, near the prison, was the first. Racial tension were real. Third. Reconstruction was difficult. Share-croping replaced slavery. Several of the churches on the 1860 map did not survive.

However, the demand for lumber to build the growing cities of the nation brought some economic relief. Several sawmill towns sprang up and churches were planted in them. However, neither the town or the church lasted long. Yet, sawmilling and pine plantations continue to be an important element in the life of the area.l

The church buildings of the nineteenth century were much like the old Pilgrim Rest building in Sapps. Many were built near a spring. With the development of public education some of the churches hosted schools and in several a school building was built adjacent to the church.

Some churches began weekly, or monthly, prayer meeting. Many added weekly Sunday School. In fact, for our Baptist forefathers, Sunday School became a passion. Quarterly Sunday School Conventions were organized. Branch Sunday Schools were opened in communities with no church. In several instances a church resulted. On other occasions such as with our Union Chapel, a union Sunday School was formed each of the three primary denominations would sponsor a monthly worship service. In this case after a few years, each denomination hived off a church of its own.

In the 1890s railroads built through the area. The first was across south Lamar. New towns were established at Millport and Kennedy. The association opened churches in these towns. A few years later the railroad built across the north of Pickens County with new towns being formed at Ethelsville, Reform, and Gordo. And yet another line was run from Reform south with the town of Aliceville coming to be. New churches were formed in Reform and Gordo with the South Carolina Church moving to Ethelsville and Enon moving to Aliceville.

The railroads made possible the industrialization of our area. Textile mill and sewing factories sprang up in five of the towns. As Gordo and Aliceville grew to more than 2,000 residents, it was obvious a second Baptist Church was needed as the population became more diverse.

For more than half of this period the moderator of the association came from Carrollton Baptist Church--W.G. Robinson and M.C. Curry. Early in the Twentieth Century the denomination encouraged associations to serve a single county. In 1924 the name of the association was changed from to Union to Pickens. As with much of the rural South our denomination had long been dominant here.

During this era most of the churches added a Woman's Missionary Union. With the appointment of one of their leaders, Addie Cox from Carrollton in 1918 as a missionary to China the passion for missions was deepened. This may have contributed to the erection of the rather unique statue on the courthouse lawn which honors womanhood. The Great Depression was hard on many of our churches. Some closed. Some survived due to the efforts of the faithful women.

The Bicentennial of the Coming of the Gospel Light to Pickens County
Gary Farley and Others

The first permanent settlers came into our area in 1817 . Among them was Josiah Tilley who settled just north of what is now Pickensville. His brother-in-law, Jonathan York, settled a little to the north near what was to be Yorkville. The goal of both was to trade with the Choctaw Indians who lived on the west side of the Tombigbee River in what was still Indian territory. So, 2017 will mark the bicentennial of the settlement of Pickens County.

While Native Americans had lived in Pickens in pre-historic times, as documented by archeologists when the Tenn-Tom Waterway was being constructed, none lived here in 1817. For, example, a significant village of the Woodland Indians was excavated near the mouth of the Lubbub Creek, south of modern Aliceville. A display of the artifacts of Native Americans can be found in the Aliceville Library.

Before 1817 the Creek Indians lived east of the Black Warrior River and the Choctaws to the west of the Tombigbee. Both tribes hunted in Pickens, which served as a kind of buffer between the tribes.

The land here became open for settlement due to the defeat of the Creek Indians at Horseshoe Bend in 1814 by General Andrew Jackson. This story is told in a book on the Creek War co-authored by a son of Pickens, Henry Sales Halbert. One can read this book by looking it up on the Google books web-page. He was born in 1837 and spent much of his life as a teacher in Choctaw Indian schools. He also prepared a dictionary of the Choctaw language, collected their tales, and captured much about their culture. His papers are available in the Alabama Archives in Montgomery.

Unlike Tilley and York, most of the persons coming to Pickens County after 1817 for a couple of decades were seeking to duplicate the cotton plantation culture and lifestyle of the old Southeast. Many brought slaves, settled on land along the Tombigbee, Sipsey, Lubbub. Big Creek, Bear, and Coldfire Creeks, cleared land and began planting cotton.

The Scots-Irish from South Carolina were among the most numerous of these resettlers. Look at a current telephone book and note the many last names beginning with Mc. As partially evidenced by some fine ante-bellum homes still found here, many were successful in this endeavor. In our local libraries you will find a book by Johnson which shows who were the first owners of lands in our county. It has current maps that will help you see who first owned the land where you live. Another source of information about the early days is a set of pictures taken of historic buildings in 1937 by a WPA photographer, Alex Bush. These are also available on line at the Library of Congress, Historic American Buildings Survey. Pickens County, Alabama.

However, in the northern part of the county there were families from parts of the Appalachian Mountains whose lifestyle was tied more to hunting and fishing and to "kitchen-garden" planting, for the family, not for commercial production. Having enough to eat and shelter, not wealth, was their goal in life. Social scientists have labeled these "being" and "becoming" lifestyles. Remnants of both are still visible here. However, history often focuses upon the affluent and neglects the "hard-scrabble" folk. Another valuable source of information about the settlement of Pickens, also found on-line, is a history written by the first editor of this newspaper, Nelson Smith.

We have a third cultural stream here in Pickens, This is the descendants of the former slaves, the freedmen. They did not elect to settle here. You might wish to read the autobiography of Wallace Turnage, a young man living near Pickensville at the time of the War Between the States. It is found in David Blight, *A Slave No More*. More than 40% of the residents of Pickens are African Americans today. Since emancipation many have opted to join the Great Migration to Northern Cities. Some have achieved much, there and here. Some have retired and returned to Pickens. Each settlement stream brought with them a set of religious, or spiritual, beliefs. So, in 2017 the bicentennial of the coming of the Gospel light to our area will be celebrated.

A fourth stream, recently introduced as temporary residents, are women incarcerated in the Aliceville Federal prison. They do not directly impact the spiritual life of Pickens, but they are impacting many of us who are doing ministry with them. They are impacting one another. And we pray that many of them will carry the Light of the Gospel to other places and nations as they leave Pickens and re-enter free society.

Many of the early settlers had been members of Baptist, Methodist, and Presbyterian Congregations back in the Carolinas, Georgia, Virginia and Tennessee. Soon after settling in Pickens, they began to form congregations. For the most part, these three denominations and their off-shoots were the basic forms of Christianity from the Appalachian Mountains to the Mississippi River and beyond during the settlement period. With the industrialization of the nation and the emergence of cities in this region, this changed. Certainly, here in Pickens, however, this was the case for more than a century.

I have identified more than a dozen topics I want to do brief articles on in the coming year. I welcome the help of those who read these articles. Corrections. Ideas for articles. Comments. Resources that will enrich this project. The next three topics will be the first Methodist, Baptist and Presbyterian congregations in Pickens--Hargrove, Enon, and Bethany.

The Future of the Gospel Light

I concluded the last article in this series on the bicentennial of the settling of Pickens County and the coming of the Gospel Light, with the observation that the future of the Gospel Light here seems bright. Most of the residents accept the truth of the Light. It is well established here. However, there are places in the world that once affirmed the Light, but are now places of darkness. Invasion, persecution, secularization and the attraction of sin have turned people away from the Gospel. So, let me conclude this series of articles by sharing the content of the Gospel. It begins with the declaration that the universe and all the creatures in it are the result of creative acts by the one true God. The purpose of the universe and of the creatures is to glorify and praise this great and good God.

Later, some of the creatures rebelled against God. Sin, disobedience toward God's will, has contaminated relationships and even nature itself. Since then the story of history is that of God, seeking through love and punishment, to redeem and restore all of creation. The Bible tells the drama of God's action toward this end. Of course, such a powerful God could have simply destroyed his enemies, he could have just simply zapped the rebel, but since his purpose is that relationships of loving service characterize humankind, this is not an option that he has taken. Rather, his son Jesus became a human like us and lived here among us. He was obedient to God. He did not rebel. So, Satan, the chief rebel, killed him. The intent of the cruel death on a cross was to save his life by rebelling against the will of God. However, even death could not turn Jesus to rebellion. And God raised him to life returning him to Heaven, and the Bible teaches that one day he will return to earth, defeat the rebellion, establish a nation where the will of God will be obeyed for a millennium, Satan and his followers will be punished and then Christians will live in the New Jerusalem with God and Jesus in love and peace, glorifying God for ever and ever.

In sum, then, the options offered to us are either to be a rebel and be punished after we die for eternity, or become a Christian, serve God until we die, and then enjoy eternal life. A rather easy choice for a prudent person, don't you agree?

Apparently, however, some folk try to fool God by joining a church, getting baptized, attending worship, contributing to the upkeep and the ministry of the church, but continue to disobey the will of God. Why do I say this? The proof is in the pudding. One time Jesus was asked about what he believed to be the greatest commandment of God. He replied, that loving, serving, glorifying and worshiping God must be the passion of a real Christian. And he continued that we should love our neighbors as well as we love ourselves. And he defined our neighbors to include our natural enemies. On still another occasion he declares Christians to be those who demonstrate love for neighbors by providing food, clothing, shelter, a cup of water, health care, and friendship to prisoners. Additionally, Jesus demanded that Christians carry and share the Gospel Light with persons and nations who had not accepted it and become obedient to the will of God. Again, and again, Jesus told his followers to seek to serve onc another.

How counter culture this is. We are taught to put our wants and needs over those of others. We are told to dominate, exploit, and even abuse others. Power and possessions are what we are to seek.

(As proof of what I am saying, please refer to and read these passages from the Bible.)

While after many years of study, there are portions of the Gospel Light that I am not fully aware of, shades that I have not fully understood, I believe that I have shared in this brief article the core points. God wills for each of us to live in love, serving one another, in a wonderful relationship. Satan fights to keep us from doing so. Our eternal destiny depends on whether or not we obey God. Golden Rule living is evidence, or visible fruit, of the fact that one is a true Christian.

Since living a life of service and sacrifice is costly, it is possible that the time might come when the Gospel Light will not burn here as brightly as it does now. So, it comes down to the current generations being faithful, and for us to pray for and teach coming generations.

In closing I want to thank editor Bo Black for letting me write and publish this series of articles. Among the mysteries that I still wonder about here are two place names with "mission" in their name, Halbert and Berry. Both are near New Hope, Ms. My guess is that each was an early mission to the Choctaw Indians. If any of the readers has some information about either or both please contact me.

To facilitate the continuing of the Gospel Light here we need pastors and lay leaders who know what the Bible teaches. Beginning on Tuesday, January 16 at 7pm a course from Samford Ministry Training Institute will begin at the Baptist Association office in Carrollton. No cost. The class will meet for 8 weeks. After completing 8 classes, a student will be awarded from Samford University.

The Era of Associational Missionaries--1948 to now

In February of 2013 the Federal Census Department announced that Pickens County was now included in the Tuscaloosa Metropolitan Statistical Area. Really! Certainly, we are as country as we have ever been. However, we have lost about 2,500 industrial jobs in recent decades and many of our residents have to work in adjoining counties. I am told that the 1960s and 1970s were the Golden Years. The towns had vibrant business districts. Saturdays were busy and folks visited with one another. But in the 1980s on to 2004, one by one the factories closed. Some families moved to nearby cities, others elected to commute. Again the residents of Pickens are making adjustments in the rhythm of their lives. From farmers and slaves, to share croppers, to loggers, to poultry producers, to factory hands, to commuters and retirees--and the churches are challenged to respond in terms of schedule, focus, and ministry.

Coming out of World War II our denomination found itself with some opportunities and challenges--three of the most significant were to become a national, as contrasted with regional church, to plant more churches in the urban areas and to encourage rural churches to expand their programs. Our focus will be on the rural.

First, some money was provided to help rural associations to hire a superintendent of missions. Here it was a daughter of the Pickens Association who had just finished getting a degree from SWBTS, Emma Burgin. One of very few women to ever hold this position. Among her accomplishments was getting VBS started here. Our association in 1948 had 31 churches with 3,716 members. Most worshiped only one Sunday each month. The total income of the churches was less than $70,000. Most of the churches met in a one room building.

Second about 1955 the denomination launched a program called The Long Range Rural Church Program. It asked for the churches to survey their field, have worship every Sunday, Add to Sunday School the other three basic programs of the denomination--BTU, WMU, and Brotherhood. Ms. Emma's successors, J.W. Caldwell and Joseph Dean, implemented this in our association. Churches continued how they could have a better church, a better community and a better world. My seminary church, Smith Fork, on the Clinton Co. Mo. prairie, went through this study. We worked on this during my time there from 1958 to 1962. When I came here in 1998, only two of the churches did not worship every week. Similar results occurred across the denomination. This brought radical change. Sunday School rooms and fellowship halls were built in most of the rural churches here. More activity. While most of the pastors here are still bivocational, they serve only one church and have become more pastor than preacher in the eyes of the churches. Jubilee, ruralchurch.us.

Ole Hendrix became DOAM in 1972. He was able to build the first office building for the association. And he led the association through the process of developing an associational strategy plan under which we still operate. The focus of this process to study the territory served by the association, discover needs for new churches and new ministries, and get them up and going. He took steps to build a larger office with room for meetings and more services.

This was completed by Ernie Carroll. And with Ernie the association started up the Baptist Center ministry in 1990, something which has made it possible for the churches to in cooperation minister not only to the poor but to also fund a variety new ministries. During his tenure weekly Bible Study at the jail and a chaplaincy program at the hospital. Also Disaster Relief.

In 1984 I joined the staff of the rural association department of the HMB. As a sociologist I was invited to help with the ASP program. When HMB became NAMB, I was looking to become a DOAM and you invited me to come. 1998I was pleased with how Ole and Ernie had used the ASP process to build a good rural association.

*Hispanic Church
*Prison ministries. Report.
*Radio SS
*Response to church burnings
*Associational Mission Trips
*More Disaster Relief. NO. 2011. 2016
*Covenant of Peace

In about a year I will be retiring. My desire is that we will use this year to restructure the association so that whomever you elect to lead the association in the years to come will a stucture that will enable this.

*impute from the churches
*look at how similar assn. Are structured.
*update job descriptions
*update constitution

As I noted in beginning.
*Different life rhythm
*social media culture
*loss of in county jobs
*prison---opportunity
*4 lane of 82
*vo-tech
*who we are

The First Continuing Congregation in Pickens

Gary Farley

Hargrove United Methodist Church was organized in 1822 and thus has the honor of being the church with the longest continuing history of a Christian congregation in Pickens. It is a couple of miles northwest of Gordo, near the Peco Hatchery. Dudley Hargrove was the driving force behind the formation of this congregation. He had moved from Tuscaloosa to Pickens a couple of years earlier. He was a local licensed preacher. But in 1819 Hargrove was rejected by the Tennessee Conference when he applied to be ordained. This was because he owned slaves. Remarkably Dudley did not break with the Methodist movement over this. Within a year (1823) he died in an accident on his farm. (Interestingly he was a grandson of Bishop McKendree at the time, and later Dudley's grandson became the bishop of the Tennessee Conference.)

John Wesley, the founder of the Methodist movement, opposed slavery and at the Christmas Conference in 1784 in Baltimore, when the American Methodist denomination was formed, it also opposed slavery. With growth, the opposition to slavery softened, so in 1841 the denomination split, north and south, over the issue. Until the 1784 conference Methodism had been a reform movement within the Church of England. The focus was on forming classes, not churches, where people would study the word of God and hold one another accountable to living righteous and holy lives. The first bishops of American Methodism were Francis Asbury and Thomas Coke. Rev. Benedict Swope, my ancestor, attended this conference and was a good friend of Asbury.

Also connected with the formation of Hargrove Methodist Church, and others in Pickens, was Ebenezer Hearn. He was the first Methodist Circuit Rider in Alabama. He was assisted by local preachers like Dudley Hargrove who served a specific congregation or class. The first church he formed in central Alabama was Ebenezer, near Montevallo, in Shelby County. The family of another ancestor, Obediah Farley, was a part of that church, and he and his wife Phoebe Hatcher Farley are buried in its cemetery.

In the Methodist system a minister like Hearn would preach often to the churches and classes in a given area. And when enough churches were formed and another circuit rider was found, and confirmed, the circuit would be divided. This happened again and again in Alabama and elsewhere. The Methodist movement grew rapidly as the nation expanded to the West.

Much of its success was tied to annual camp meetings where, after crops were laid by, crowds would come to worship, worship, hear preachers, sing, seek salvation, and take the Lord's Supper. This kind of meeting started at Cane's Ridge near Paris, Kentucky in 1803. Here in Pickens two annual camp meetings, one at Unity Grove and the other at Tabernacle, continue to the present. They date from about 1840. They are now held in July. Many families have cabins and come for a week each year. It is a wonderful experience. Hargrove hosted the Hog's Branch Campground and meeting for many years.

Here in Pickens, Methodism prospered well beyond the first century of the coming of the Gospel Light. When towns were developed, a Methodist Church was also planted in it soon. And while in recent decades some rural Methodist churches have closed, Methodism continues to be important and effective among us. Many are providing food pantries and housing

Celebrate Recovery groups for those dealing with addictions. Methodists played a key role in the planting and kindling the Gospel light here in Pickens.

Two beautiful, but now closed, Methodist Church buildings in our county are Soule's Chapel north of Benevola and Pickensville Methodist. Both buildings date from before the Civil War.

As we will see in subsequent articles, Methodism had within it three important streams which have been difficult to harmonize--hierarchical organization which called for order, a passion to see persons born again, and a focus on living a righteous and holy life. It is the ancestor of the holiness and Pentecostal movements among us.

Today Hargrove United Methodist church is a vital congregation actively sharing the Gospel light. Its future is good. It is well-housed, and like many of our early rural churches has a cemetery beside it.

The history of Methodism in Alabama tells of another early church gathered by Ebenezer Hearn here, Ebenezer Methodist, near Pickensville. It was located on a hill near the mouth of Coal Fire Creek. Named for the pioneer church planter, it probably was renamed Pickensville Methodist about 1840 when it moved to that town. It closed about 2000. Its historic building still stands in Pickensville. In 1861 the belfry of this meeting house served as the hiding place of Wallace Turnage, a run-away slave, whose autobiography appears in *A Slave No More,* by Yale history professor David Blight.

Next month I will write about the first Baptist congregation in Pickens, Enon,

HISTORY OF ALICEVILLE FIRST BAPTIST CHURCH IS INCLUDED WITH OTHER PICKENS BAPTIST ASSOCIATION CHURCHES INSTEAD OF HERE AS ONE OF THE THREE CONTINUING CONGREGATIONS.

-The First Presbyterian Church in Pickens
Gary Farley and others

On line I found an article from Alabama Historical Quarterly dated 1945 regarding the founding of Presbyterianism in Pickens. Its author was Veneta McKinney. As with the history of many early churches here, and elsewhere, it began in a community building which also housed a school. The preacher, Thomas Morrow, was sent by the Tombeckbee Presbytery, perhaps at the request of persons who had settled in the Franconia community a little north of what is now Aliceville. The charter members were mostly from South Carolina. They numbered 32 including two slaves. The first worship service was in 1836 and the church was formed in the following year. Among the members were persons who are known to be very successful planters--Hood, Summerville, Hughes and Turnipseed. The church took as its name Oak Grove. A building was erected near where Mount Hebron Missionary Baptist now stands. In 1903 with the coming of the railroad and the establishment of Aliceville, the congregation moved to the new town, as did many of the residents and businesses of old Franconia, Bridgeville, Bethany and Garden.

Like the Methodists and the Baptists, this church held its members accountable for their behavior. Living what one professed was important. Those who failed to walk in the way of Christ were subject to exclusion from the congregation. This accountability was a key factor in taming the new frontier. Often new communities were wild and wooly. But in time the Gospel and accountability to its norms brought order and stability. And this practice seems to have made life better here on the frontier.

Thomas Morrow also organized the Bethesda Presbyterian Church in 1838 in the Benevola community. He seems to have moved on and died in Morgan County. Nationally, the Presbyterians divided in the 1840s over the issue of slavery, north and south, as did the Methodists and Baptists.

Today there are Presbyterian churches in Pickens at Reform and Aliceville, a Cumberland Presbyterian church in the Antioch Community north and west of Reform and an African American CP in Pickensville and in Aliceville. This is far fewer than a century ago.

However, as I looked further, I found minutes of the Cumberland Presbyterian Synod meeting in Marion, Alabama from 1825. It lists a Bethany C. P. congregation in Pickens. Apparently, it was connected with the Bethany community south and east of Benevola. There is a large cemetery there today with some very fine monuments. No one lives near there today. I am told that most of the residents moved to Aliceville when it was opened about 1900 and its building was sold to Emory Chapel Methodist.

This small denomination had withdrawn from the larger denomination over the issue of use of revivals for evangelization in the early 1800s. The division had its roots in the Camp Meeting movement. One of the three founders of this denomination, Finis Ewing, performed the wedding ceremony of ancestors of mine out in Missouri, Larkin Dewitt and Hannah Potter Ewing.

So, while the Aliceville Presbyterian church is the oldest continuing Presbyterian congregation, it is not the first one. Both branches of Presbyterianism played an important role in bringing and establishing the Gospel light in Pickens.

About 1940 the old building of Oak Grove Presbyterian was moved to the mill village in Aliceville. A union Sunday School was started. After a time the church elected to be Baptist and is now the West End Baptist Church.

The Aliceville Presbyterian church has a great record of supporting missions in other places, notably China and South America. For many years it was pastored by Thomas Kay Sr and then Jr. More recently Jason Housewright was called as pastor.

Through the years Presbyterians have had a strong emphasis on education for ministers. When the population of the western frontier exploded in the first half of the Nineteenth Century, there were not enough Presbyterian pastors to meet the demand. Note that here, the first Presbyterian minister did not arrive until 19 years after settlement began. In the interim many who had come as Presbyterians to Pickens joined the Baptist and Methodist churches in their community.

Yet while fewer in number than the Baptists and Methodists, the Presbyterians have and continue to serve important business, professional and leadership roles in our communities.

The Nibethany Cumberland Presbyterian Church in Aliceville is likely the African American remnant of the first Presbyterian Church in our county, Bethany. The next article in this series will deal with the formation of African American congregations here.

An Early African American in Pickens County

When settlers began in 1817 to come into what became Pickens County, they settled along the Tombigbee River, some to trade with the Choctaws, but most to plant cotton. Often the planters brought with them slaves. The river provided a means of shipping cotton to the port of Mobile. And consumer goods, such as flour, sugar, coffee, tools, and cloth, could be shipped up the river. Soon a town grew up, Pickensville, which was designated the seat of government when the county, was created in 1820. Ten years later the county seat was moved about a dozen miles east to a more central location, and the town of Carrollton was established.

Little is known about the first generation of African American residents of this county. However, writing in 1840, Hosea Holcomb in his book, *The Rise of Baptists in Alabama,* tells the story of his friend, Job, a slave preacher. Job was born in Africa and brought to Charleston, South Carolina in 1806. He was sold to the Davis family. He learned to write and married. In 1812 he became a Christian and five years later he was licensed to preach in Jefferson County, Alabama. He became a much respected minister of the Gospel. The family moved on to just north of Pickensville. He became a member of Pilgrim Rest Baptist Church. He died in 1835. His wife died a couple of years later. Holcomb writes, "Few better preachers were found in Alabama in those days. Job was generally loved and respected by all who knew him. He lived a Christian and died a saint." His memory will be honored by a window in the restored Rosenwald school at Pickensville.

On Becoming Native to your Place
Albion Seeds in the Tombigbee Watershed

Pickens Church History
Gary Farley
Topics

!. The Bicentennial of the Coming of the Gospel Light
2. The First Continuing Congregation--Harcrow UMC--E. Herns
3. The First Baptist Church--FBC Aliceville-- Enon
4. The First Presbyterian Church--Bethany CP
5. New Churches for the Freedmen-- New Wright, Duncan Salmons
6. The Gospel Light Comes to Town
7. Why so Many Brands of Baptists?
8. They Carried the Gospel Light over Seas
9. The Oldest Church Buildings in Pickens County
10. Sunday Schools, the New Cause
11. How Many Churches in Pickens County?
12. The Future of the Gospel Light here, and unanswered questions

Where to from here, if anywhere?

- Shorted the newer denominations here.
- Camp meetings
- Ministries of the churches--food pantries, disaster relief, thrift store, nursing homes, mission teams, etc.
- Mystery of Berry Mission and Halbert Mission
- Pictures of the Churches
- History of schools, the role of the churches
- Religious Music, varieties in our county.
- Youtube videos of church worship in the county
- Youtube of homecomings, vbs,
- Cemeteries,and churches
- War monument--Belzoni, Ms.

The Capitals of Pickens
(Resources)

- Natural
- Social
- Cultural
- Spiritual
- Financial
- Political

- Built
- Human

Some resources for learning about the history of Pickens

- Google play. Smith's History, denominational histories in Alabama, Boothe's history of Colored Baptists in Alabama.
- Wikipedia
- WPA interviews
- Find a grave
- Library of Congress--pix
- Census records.
- Follow the drinking gourd. Underground Railroad
- Albion Seed. Boarderland, Puritans, Quakers, Aristrocacy

PBA Annual History Report
Gary Farley

As one can see from the reports in this book, it has been another full year of events, projects and programs. We have endeavored to equip our churches and the members thereof to be Great Commission doers. Evangelism, missions, service, giving, praying. Reflect on those events you participated in. Please look at the proposed calendar for the coming year. Mark those that you see yourself participating in. Celebrate the victories. Repent of failings. The windows in the PBA building were replaced.

This report will be expanded in the annual with more data from the churches regarding pastoral changes, changes in church properties and facilities, and from the churches concerning special events and projects, and other things that need to be recorded for generations to come.

Among the important purposes of our association are:

1. Undergird the programmatic work of the churches
2. To conduct area events that have evangelism at their core
3. To conduct missions and service ministries
4. To enable every member of the churches to be a great commission Christian
5. To be a full partner with ALSBOM and the SBC in the mission enterprise.
6. Uphold and witness to the moral teachings of the Scripture in our territory of service.
7. Practice the Great Commandment in our dealings with one another.

A new event was the county prayer breakfast. A diverse group attended. We were led in prayer on eight topics of community, personal and Kingdom interest. Thank Sam Wiggins for organizing this event.

The Executive Board created a personnel committee and elected the first set of members. It also voted to erect a Disaster Relief building on the property in Carrollton. The site has been cleared. Construction will begin when funds for it have been raised.

Some history of the PBA work in Aliceville Prison

In 2008 Bro. Gary learned that the prison was coming and we saw this as an opportunity to minister.

He began the 100 Godly Women organization shortly after to enlist and train for this ministry. Has now become the 100 Godly Women and Friends with over 200 signed up.

Mary Kay Beard from Birmingham and founder of Angel Tree was our guest in May 2010. She talked to prospective volunteers at the Mt. Hebron Mission Baptist Church – this group was a diverse group – including Mennonites women from across the Mississippi line.

February 2011 – as part of an On Mission Conference we invited several Chaplains to come and speak to our churches. Rebecca Lewis, Chaplain in Arkansas conducted a conference three days – twice a day – one in the morning and one in the evening - to train for prison ministry. A very good group did this.

Association Luncheon to introduce the Warden Arcola Washington-Adduci, Associate Warden, Sekoy Ma'at, Adm. Assistant and Camp Administrator, Laconya Women to the 100 Godly Women. Our speaker at this luncheon was Chaplain Charles Jones from Miss.

Annual Meeting in October 2012 – we had as guest Ken Weathersby from NAMB – Harold and Joyce Scroggs – Directors of a prison ministry in Kentucky working directly with families of inmates – and Charles Jones, Director of Prison Ministry for Mississippi Baptist Convention came by and continued his training which this time focused on members of the PBA, pastors and laymen.

At the end of 2012 residents were coming into the Camp at Aliceville – with the first group arriving on Wednesday. Three of us **BRO. GARY, PAULINE HALL AND BONNIE WINDLE,** held the first worship service there on the following Sunday, December 23rd and Rev. Bob Little led the Christmas Day service.

From this point Dr. Farley was asked to set up Protestant Worship Services at both the camp and FCI.

Dr. Farley began services in both facilities with Luke 1:74-75 – part of Zacharias's song about what the Savior would do – win a victory over Satan, disease and death and make us free to serve Him without fear in holiness and righteousness – the emphasis being that we would minister more with the residents than to them.

There has been a theme in our preaching there – That the prison experience can be like a cocoon – we pray that our ladies can return home to their families and communities as beautiful butterflies.

Somewhat surprised – that we did not anticipate that we would be expecting so many international women – INS – immigration, naturalization prisoners – a mission field and opportunity to train leaders to be missionaries – The Hispanic population there is approximately 50% with many of these ladies not speaking English or much English. A WHOLE NEW PIECE IN THE PUZZLE.

At our last Community Relations Board meeting at the prison (we have 3 people who are members of this Board which meets each quarter) the Warden announced that she had 399 Mexican citizens there – Bro. Gary says if we could reach even 20% of these – what a missionary force we could send back to Mexico. Possibly one of the largest sending body of missionaries to these countries.

AMAZING WHAT TALENT AND ABILITIES ARE THERE – Generally pretty and bright ladies.

Bro. Gary considers himself to be the pastor of the two churches that have been planted there – the **Camp Community Church at the Camp** and the **Aliceville United Body of Believers at FCI** – the main facility. The population at Camp is 300 and 1200 at FCI – Both facilities now are nearly full.

WE LEARNED THAT we didn't have to carry church in to them – CHURCH WAS ALREADY THERE – They have committed and gifted Christians – amazing every Sunday – ladies ARE ANXIOUS, EXCITED, CHEERING – THEY ARE getting a lot from the services but so are we.

We have ladies there doing prayer meetings, special events on their own – not relying on us for all the services – One special (and they all are special) put together a marvelous Christmas nativity and they are working on a Passion Play for Easter.

A lot of hard work but so rewarding for us. There are more talented people that want to do than we have schedules at this time to carry out. Pray for the development of these schedules.

A History of Pickens Baptist Association

Gary Farley

Begun in 1835

The heritage of the Pickens Association is a proud one. Founded in 1835, it weathered three crises early in its life. It decided to be missionary (not anti-missionary) and cooperative (not anti-board) and lost several churches to the Primitive or high Calvinist Baptists. It decided to be moderately Calvinistic and lost a church and some members to the Freewill Baptists. Following the War Between the States about 700 former slaves left the churches of the association to form churches of their own. Five churches from the original ones continue–Aliceville, Ebenezer, Fellowship, Forest, and Liberty–continue in the association.

Most of the congregations were desperately poor from after 1865 to the 1950s. Almost all of the pastors were bi-vocational and/or preached to several congregations. In the early years most of the congregations met only once a month to deal with business, to discipline and seek to restore members who had violated the terms of the church covenant, and to hold worship. Yet, the churches and the association kept focused on being Great Commission oriented, and God blessed.

Initially, the association was named, Union. It had churches in Pickens, Lamar, Greene, and Tuscaloosa Counties of Alabama. Today, early in the 21st century, it is a strong rural association with 35 congregations, including a Hispanic mission, in its fellowship. Collectively, the churches have about 4,000 resident members.

Early life and Missions

During the 19th Century the association was primarily an annual event which brought the people of the affiliated churches together for a three day Baptist family homecoming. Saturday and Monday focused on business. Reports or letters from the churches indicating the growth, or decline, of each would be heard. Should a church be troubled, a committee would be formed to go and seek to bring it back in order. Questions from the churches concerning doctrine or ethics might be brought to the association for deliberation and counsel. The need to plant new churches in places "Destitute of a Gospel witness might be addressed. A circular letter, actually an essay on some point of doctrine, would be read, and if accepted, sent to the churches of the association for their enlightenment.

Sunday was devoted to worship. Several messages by beloved local pastors and visiting ministers would be featured. Perhaps the highlight of the day, however, was a joint celebration of the Lord's Supper. Prayer and inspiration for the task of evangelizing and disciplining the people of the county were intertwined in the event.

By 1870 many of the churches had added weekly Sunday Schools. These were formed into an auxiliary organization that met quarterly in four districts across the association. The women formed missionary groups, and these were treated also as an auxiliary. (About 1900 women began to serve as messengers from the churches to the annual meeting.)

Missions and evangelism have been central themes of the association across the years. Martha Foster Crawford went from the association to China along with her husband in 1852. She was one of the first sent by the Southern Baptists. She severed until 1908. She mentored the famous Lottie Moon who served in the same mission station. When China was closed to missionaries (1951), another daughter of the association, Addie Cox, was among those expelled. Several others from the association have gone to South America, Africa and Asia as missionaries. Someone from the association has been under appointment by Southern Baptists for overseas missions continually since 1851. Currently, there are five. Others have served as home missionaries and pioneer church starters. We are proud of this heritage. In early times, from year to year, the association would hire one of its ministers to serve as an evangelist. But in the 1880s the State Convention began appointing area evangelists who performed this task.

The Impact of the Railroads

The coming of the railroads to the area at the dawning of the 20th century brought very significant changes in where and how people lived. Wisely, the leaders of the association recognized the need to form congregations in the emerging population centers of Gordo, Reform, Ethelsville and Aliceville. They entered into partnership with the State Board of Missions. New congregations were planted in Gordo and Reform. At Ethelsville the old South Carolina church was strengthened as a field of churches with Mineral Springs, Pine Grove, and Hickory Grove sharing a pastor. And Enon, the oldest church in Pickens, relocated in Aliceville.

Apparently, in response to this missions challenge, the association elected an executive committee and assigned to it the task of looking after the mission work and the Sunday School work of the association during the bulk of the year when the association was not meeting. Gradually, then, the association took on the added dimension of being an on-going, year around organization.

The reports and business of the association early in the 20th Century addressed issues such as temperance, world missions, ministerial education, aid for retired ministers, printed resources for study (communication), women's work, and the emerging programs of the denomination such as Baptist Young People's Union. After 1925 promotion of the Cooperative Program and the missions offerings were added.

In 1924 the association changed its name from Union to Pickens. By that time most of the churches in surrounding counties had united with an association that served its county. So, it seemed appropriate to take on the county name. Most of our neighboring associations have done the same.

A full set of minutes from the annual meetings of the association are available at the office in Carrollton and at the Alabama Baptist Historical Commission in Birmingham. Spread across its pages are the names of many pastors and laypersons who have worked in the churches and in the association. Many are memorialized in its pages. Also, the association has historical sketches of most of its churches.

Work of Associational Missionaries

The end of World War II found only four of the churches of the association worshiping every Sunday. Many of the churches were small and poor and stagnant. This was true all across the rural South. With help from the State Baptist Convention, the association hired its first year around missionary, Miss Emma. Burgin, in 1948, a product of the Hebron Church and a graduate of Southwestern Seminary. She was followed by J. W. Caldwell and by Joseph M. Dean. A layman, Mr. Dean served from 1956 to 1972. He seems to have greatly expanded the on-going promotional role of the association. In 1960 the constitution was greatly enlarged to include an expanded set of ongoing committees and job descriptions for associational officers and program leaders. The association became the distributor of programs developed by the SBC and State Convention which aided in strengthening the work of the local churches. Many of the churches moved from being part-time to full-time, at least in the sense have having worship twice each Sunday. Most became Four Star churches offering the standard programs of SBC life. The next 17 years saw the ministry of Oel Hendrix. He was gifted at building relationships and networks among people. Many of the leaders of the PBA today became involved in the work because he recognized their potential and mentored them. He further institutionalized the work of the association and focused upon promoting programs and events that would strengthen the churches. The first half century of having a regular associational missionary was rounded out by Ernie Carroll. He focused an expanding ministry activities such as the Baptist Center Thrift Store and the building of the new office with excellent facilities for associational events.

The year, 1998, opened with a new missionary, yours truly. My sense is that the program promotion role will be shifting more to the state convention. I see the association cooperating with the State in providing training which is contextualized to the needs and opportunities of our churches and their communities. We will need to partner with the state convention to help the churches be strong and effective. Each church will be encouraged to provide unique ministries and stretch out even beyond their traditional community boundaries to reach those who need that ministry or who are gifted in providing it.

Looking to the Future

I see the major on-going role of the association to be that of equipping and involving the people of the churches in doing missions in our area and around the globe. Much of this will be done in direct consultations with the leaders of individual congregations. The focus of being missionary will broaden to include being missionaries here as well as sending others and going as missionaries elsewhere. It will provide ministry and missions venues in which Christian people can serve. It will coordinate such efforts.

Increasingly, the association will become a resource center, sharing resources with the churches. Its goal will be the help each church truly be a Great Commission church. And our annual meetings will become celebrative reunions of the family where the blessings of God are identified and praise is offered to Him.

In short, the task that Ms. Burgin began in 1948 has been accomplished. In the 50 years since, Baptist work has grown and prospered here. I see God opening some new opportunities and offering some new challenges. He has gifted the people in the churches. He has provided abundant resources. There is much that we should do. There is much that we can do. Now we must cooperate and focus on efforts for new victories. The key to the work is prayer. Please pray for the expansion of God's kingdom in Pickens county.

Tombigbee and Black History Month

News Release

Tens of thousands of elementary schools will study during February about the Underground Railroad. Many will learn about a code song, "Follow the Drinking Gourd." It is set, geographically, on the Tombigbee River. Its message to the slaves was in the spring of the year that they could seek freedom by walking toward the North Star up the valley of the Tombigbee. At the headwater they will be met by an Underground Railroad conductor who will take them by water down the Tennessee and up the Ohio to Ripon, Indianna, where Rev. John Rankin would help get them started by land on the way to Canada and freedom.

The history of the Underground Railroad is an inspiring one. People, creative persons, black and white, slave and free, poor and rich, saw a need and figured out how to meet the need. No commander in chief, no committee, no funding grants, no plan, no grand design, just godly people doing what was right and good.

While it is nice to know that thousands of children across America are learning something about our place, it would be wonderful to know the story of persons here who helped with the Underground Railroad or who traveled on it. If someone among your kin was involved, please share your story with us..

In a forthcoming column the story of Wallace Turnage of Pickensville and his efforts to follow the Drinking Guard will be shared.

www.ingramcontent.com/pod-product-compliance
Lightning Source LLC
LaVergne TN
LVHW080318110826
845155LV00026B/159

* 9 7 8 1 9 5 5 2 9 5 0 6 2 *